EUROPEAN HUMAN RIGHTS CONVENTION
IN DOMESTIC LAW

EUROPEAN HUMAN RIGHTS CONVENTION IN DOMESTIC LAW

A Comparative Study

ANDREW Z. DRZEMCZEWSKI

CLARENDON PRESS · OXFORD

Oxford University Press, Walton Street, Oxford OX2 6DP
London New York Toronto
Delhi Bombay Calcutta Madras Karachi
Kuala Lumpur Singapore Hong Kong Tokyo
Nairobi Dar es Salaam Cape Town
Melbourne Auckland
and associates in
Beirut Berlin Ibadan Mexico City Nicosia

Oxford is a trade mark of Oxford University Press

Published in the United States by
Oxford University Press, New York
First published 1983
Reprinted 1985
Reprinted (new as paperback) 1985

Library of Congress Cataloging in Publication Data
Drzemczewski, Andrew Z.
European human rights convention in domestic law.
Bibliography: p.
Includes index.
1. Civil rights — Europe.   2. International
and municipal law — Europe.   I. Title.
LAW   341.4'81'094   82–14380
ISBN 0–19–825396–6
0–19–825525–X

British Library Cataloguing in Publication Data
Drzemczewski, Andrew Z.
European human rights convention in domestic law.
1. European Convention for the Protection of
Human Rights and Fundamental Freedoms
2. Civil rights (International law)
I. Title
341.4'81   K3240.4
ISBN 0–19–825396–6 ✓
0–19–825525–X

Printed in Great Britain
at the University Press, Oxford
by David Stanford
Printer to the University

Preface

This work is a revised version of a thesis which I submitted in 1980 for the degree of Doctor of Philosophy in the University of London. I wish to acknowledge the help of two persons: my original supervisor of studies Mr Cedric Thornberry, formerly a lecturer in law at the London School of Economics and Political Science and presently an official with the United Nations, for his guidance and advice, as well as Professor James Fawcett, former President of the European Commission of Human Rights, who kindly agreed to become my supervisor of studies upon the departure of Mr Thornberry from the LSE. I am especially grateful and deeply indebted to Professor Fawcett for his sympathetic guidance.

I carried out much of the background research for this book while in receipt of a University of London Postgraduate Studentship. I also received a Council of Europe Human Rights Fellowship to readapt and update the thesis for publication. I wish to express my gratitude for this financial assistance.

As a matter of presentation, I had the choice of quoting passages from the texts of constitutions, statutes, and court decisions in their original languages or alternatively to do so in respect of at least the more commonly used languages, such as French, Spanish, and German. After some hesitation, I decided to use English language translations as far as possible, with occasional reference to texts written in French. The reason for this narrow approach is twofold: my inability to appreciate the significance of certain passages reproduced *verbatim* in foreign languages, and because most of the materials which I consulted in Strasbourg were made available to me in English and French, the two official languages of the Council of Europe.

Although a person with limited linguistic abilities should not normally attempt to embark upon a comparative study of this type, the need for at least some general overview of the domestic status of the Convention in *all* the member states of the Council of Europe was felt to outweigh this consideration. As a consequence, I have made occasional reference to primary source materials which I have been unable to read myself, although their content has been checked — as far as possible — by obtaining cross-references written in other languages, or by obtaining explanations and translations of passages. The following have helped the author in this way: Mrs A.-M. Medrano-Drzemczewski, Mr S. Bein, Mrs J. Dinsdale, and Mr W. Strasser. In addition, while writing this book I received advice and help from many. I should like to thank in particular Professor C. K. Boyle, Mr H. Danelius, Mr J. Færkel, Professor J. A. Frowein, Mrs M. Gassner-Hemmerlé, Professor P.-H. Imbert, Mr O. Jacot-Guillarmod, Mr P. Lemmens, Professor H. Miehsler, Mr E. Myjer, Professor C. A. Nørgaard, Professor T. Opsahl, Mr J.-D. Pinheiro Farinha, Professor P. Van Dijk, Professor Ph. Vegleris, and Professor L. Wildhaber.

Earlier drafts of certain portions of this book appeared in the 1980 and 1981 issues of the *ICLQ* as well as in the 1977 and 1979 issues of *LIEI*.

This book is dedicated to my wife Anne-Marie, my mother, and my two sons, Peter and Alexis.

Contents

Part III: Selected Aspects of The Convention's Authority in Domestic Courts

Abbreviations

AFDI	*Annuaire français de droit international*
AJCL	*American Journal of Comparative Law*
AJIL	*American Journal of International Law*
All ER	All England Law Reports
ASDI	*Annuaire suisse de droit international*
ATF	*Recueil officiel des arrêts du Tribunal Fédéral Suisse*
Bgbl.	*Bundesgesetzblatt* (Federal Law Gazette, Austria)
Bgh.	*Entscheidungen des Bundesgerichtshofes* (Decisions of the Federal Supreme Court, FRG)
Bibliography	*Bibliography Relating to the European Convention on Human Rights* (Council of Europe, Strasbourg, Feb. 1978)
Boletín Oficial	*Boletín Oficial de las Cortes/Congreso de los Diputados* (Official Bulletin of the Spanish Parliament)
Bull. EC Suppl.	*Bulletin of the European Communities, Supplement*
Bulletin of the NJCM	*Bulletin of the Netherlands Juristen Comité voor Mensenrecht*
Bverfg.	*Entscheidungen des Bundesverfassungsgerichts* (Decisions of the Federal Constitutional Court of the FRG)
Bverwg.	*Entscheidungen des Bundesverwaltungsgerichts* (Decisions of the Federal Administrative Court of the FRG)
BYIL	*British Yearbook of International Law*
Cassin	*René Cassin, Amicorum Discipulorumque Liber* (4 vols., International Institute of Human Rights, Paris, 1969–72)
CDE	*Cahiers de Droit Européen*
CLR	Cyprus Law Reports
CMLR	Common Market Law Reports
CML Rev.	*Common Market Law Review*

Collected Texts	*European Convention on Human Rights: Collected Texts* (Strasbourg, 1981)
Collection	*Collection of Decisions of National Courts Referring to the Convention on Human Rights* (1969, Human Rights Directorate of the Council of Europe, with supplements in 1970, 1971, 1973, and 1974)
Coll. of Dec.	*Collection of Decisions of the European Commission of Human Rights*
D&R	*Decisions and Reports,* European Commission of Human Rights
ECR	European Court Reports (Reports of the Court of Justice of the European Communities, Luxembourg)
EGZ	*Europäische Grundrechte Zeitung*
EHRR	European Human Rights Reports
EL Rev.	*European Law Review*
Evans, 'Written Communication'	Sir V. Evans, 'The Practice of European Countries where Direct Effect is Given to the European Convention on Human Rights in Internal Law', Written Communication, *Proceedings of the Colloquy about the European Convention on Human Rights in Relation to Other International Instruments for the Protection of Human Rights,* Athens, 21–2 Sept. 1978 (Council of Europe, 1979)
FIDE Conference	*L'Individu et le droit européen. The Individual and European Law. Die Einzelperson und das europäische Recht.* FIDE VII (1977), (Seventh International Congress for European Law, organized by the *Fédération internationale pour le droit européen,* in Brussels, 2–4 Oct. 1975)
HRLJ	*Human Rights Law Journal*
HR Rev.	*Human Rights Review*
ICJ Reports	International Court of Justice Reports
ICLQ	*International and Comparative Law Quarterly*
ILR	International Law Reports
IR	The Irish Reports (Republic of Ireland)

IYIL	*The Italian Yearbook of International Law*
JDI	*Journal de droit international*
JORF	*Journal officiel de la République Française*
Journal of the ICJ	*Journal of the International Commission of Jurists*
JT	*Journal des Tribunaux*
Judicial Organisation	Judicial Organisation in Europe (Council of Europe, 1975)
LIEI	*Legal Issues of European Integration* (Law Review of the Europa Institute, University of Amsterdam)
LQR	*Law Quarterly Review*
MLR	*Modern Law Review*
National Reports	V. Knapp, ed., *International Encyclopaedia of Comparative Law* (1972-), vol. i, *National Reports*
NILR	*Netherlands International Law Review*
NJ	*Nederlandse Jurisprudentie*
NJW	*Neue Juristische Wochenschrift*
NYIL	*Netherlands Yearbook of International Law*
ÖJZ	*Österreichische Juristen-Zeitung*
Pas. Bel.	*Pasicrisie Belge*
Pas. Lux.	*Pasicrisie Luxembourgeoise*
PCIJ Rep.	Permanent Court of International Justice Reports
RBDI	*Revue belge de droit international*
R. des C.	*Recueil des cours de l'Académie de droit international de la Haye*
RDH/HRJ	*Revue des droits de l'homme/Human Rights Journal*
RDPSP	*Revue de droit public et de la science politique en France et à l'étranger*
RGDIP	*Revue générale de droit international public*
RHDI	*Revue hellénique de droit international*
RIDC	*Revue internationale de droit comparé*
Riv. DE	*Rivista di diritto europeo*
Riv. DI	*Rivista di diritto internazionale*
RMC	*Revue du Marché Commun*

RMT	*Rechtsgeleerd Magazijn Themis*
RTDE	*Revue trimestrielle de droit européen*
'Stocktaking'	'Stocktaking on the European Convention on Human Rights', a periodic note on the concrete results achieved under the Convention, by H. C. Krüger, Secretary to the European Commission of Human Rights (Strasbourg, 1982)
TL	*Topical Law* (Review of the Department of Law of the Polytechnic of North London)
Vfgh.	*[Sammlung der] Erkenntnisse und Beschlüsse des Verfassungsgerichtshofes* (Collection of Decisions of the Austrian Constitutional Court)
WLR	Weekly Law Reports
Yearbook	*Yearbook of the European Convention on Human Rights*
ZRV	*Zeitschrift für ausländisches öffentliches Recht und Völkerrecht*

Introductory Comments

A. The European Convention on Human Rights[1]

1. Introduction

Signed in Rome on 4 November 1950, the European Convention for the Protection of Human Rights and Fundamental Freedoms came into force on 3 September 1953. As of 1982 all twenty-one member states of the Council of Europe have ratified this instrument.[2] The First Protocol, which came into force on 18 May 1954, has been ratified by eighteen states parties,[3] while the Fourth Protocol, which came into force on 2 May 1968, has to date been ratified by thirteen member states.[4]

---

[1] For a list of books and articles on the Convention, see *Bibliography, passim*; and the select bibliography provided at the end of this book. The institutional machinery of this instrument is well known. Recent works in English on this subject include R. Beddard, *Human Rights and Europe* (1980), A. H. Robertson, *Human Rights in Europe* (1977), F. G. Jacobs, *The European Convention on Human Rights* (1975), and F. Castberg, *The European Convention on Human Rights* (1974). A valuable note on sources can be found in Robertson. Mention should also be made of the three recent international colloquies organized by the Council of Europe, in Rome (Nov. 1975), Athens (Sept. 1978) and Frankfurt (Apr. 1980). Current surveys of developments in Strasbourg are noted on a regular basis in three legal periodicals: *HRLJ, EL Rev.*, and *EGZ*.

[2] Austria, Belgium, Cyprus, Denmark, Federal Republic of Germany, France, Greece, Iceland, Ireland, Italy, Luxembourg, Malta, the Netherlands, Norway, Portugal, Spain, Sweden, Switzerland, Turkey, United Kingdom. Liechtenstein ratified the Convention on 8 Sept. 1982.

[3] i.e. all countries in n.2 above, with the exceptions of Liechtenstein, Spain and Switzerland.

[4] Austria, Belgium, Denmark, France, Federal Republic of Germany, Iceland, Ireland, Italy, Luxembourg, the Netherlands, Norway, Portugal, and Sweden. See Chart Showing Signatures and Ratifications of Council of Europe Conventions and Agreements (Strasbourg, 15 Dec. 1981). In addition, the 2nd Protocol gives the Court of Human Rights jurisdiction to give advisory opinions under certain circumstances (ratified by all contracting states); the 3rd Protocol modified the procedure used by the Commission in examining applications by eliminating the system of sub-commissions, and the 5th Protocol modified the procedure for the election of members of the Commission and judges of the Court. There is also a separate agreement — adopted in 1969 — which guarantees certain immunities and facilities to persons participating in the proceedings before the Court and the Commission. This agreement came into force on 17 Apr. 1971 and has been ratified by the following fourteen member states: Austria, Belgium, Cyprus, Federal Republic of Germany, Ireland, Italy, Luxembourg, Malta, the Netherlands, Norway, Portugal, Sweden, Switzerland,

The immediate aim of this instrument is to give practical effect to certain rights and freedoms and to provide collective international enforcement of them. They are enumerated in Articles 2 to 18 of the Convention, Articles 1 to 3 of the First Protocol and Articles 1 to 4 of the Fourth Protocol. It guarantees these rights to every individual, of whatever nationality within the jurisdiction of the contracting states (Article 1).[5] The rights in the Convention are defined with some precision, although many of them are subject to limitations on grounds such as public order (*ordre public*), national security, public safety, the prevention of disorder or crime, and the protection of rights of others. In time of war or other public emergency threatening the life of a nation, a contracting party may take measures derogating from its obligations under the Convention, although no derogation is permitted from Article 2 (right to life) except in respect of deaths resulting from lawful acts of war, from Article 3 (torture, inhuman, degrading treatment or punishment), from Article 4(1) (slavery), or from Article 7 (prohibition of retroactive criminal offences or penalties) (Article 15).[6] In addition, states are allowed to make reservations in respect of certain provisions with which domestic law does not conform, but reservations of a general character are not permitted (Article 64).[7]

Although the Convention does not contain any specific rules on how contracting parties are to implement it, Article 57 permits the Secretary General of the Council of Europe to request parties

the United Kingdom. These documents, as well as the Commission's rules of procedure (amended Dec. 1977), the Court's rules, and the Committee of Ministers' rules for the application of arts. 32 and 54 of the Convention, are reproduced in *Collected Texts*.

[5] The application of the Convention can be extended by states to the territories for whose international relations they are responsible (art. 63).

[6] For more details see R. Higgins, 'Derogation under Human Rights Treaties', 48 *BYIL* (1976/77), 281–320, esp. 288–315, J. Velu, 'Le Contrôle des organes prévus par la Convention européenne des Droits de l'Homme sur le but, le motif et l'objet des mesures d'exception dérogeant à cette Convention' in *Mélanges offerts à H. Rolin* (1964), 462–78, C. Warbrick, 'The Protection of Human Rights in National Emergencies' in F. E. Dowrick, *Human Rights. Problems, Perspectives and Texts* (1979), 69–106, and G. Trembley, 'Les situations d'urgence qui permettent en droit international de suspendre les Droits de l'Homme', 18 *CDE* (1977), 3–60.

[7] On this subject see P.-H. Imbert, 'Reservations and Human Rights Conventions', VI *HR Rev.* (1981), 28–60, S. Marcus-Helmons, 'L'Article 64 de la Convention de Rome, et les réserves à la Convention européenne des Droits de l'Homme', XLV *RIDC* (1968), 7–26, and D. Brändle, *Vorbehalte und auslegende Erklärungen zur europäischen Menschenrechtskonvention* (doctoral dissertation, University of Zürich, 1978).

to provide explanations on how their domestic law ensures effective implementation of the Convention. To date, the Secretary General has availed himself of this possibility on three occasions — in 1964, 1970, and 1975.[8]

Furthermore, Article 60 specifies that the provisions of the Convention cannot be construed as limiting or derogating from any human rights norms already ensured by existing domestic law or under any other agreement ratified by member states.[9]

2. A note on the review system

The European Convention on Human Rights is generally regarded as the most effective and advanced international system for the protection of human rights in existence today, and this is largely due to the work of its supervisory organs.[10] The three principal organs entrusted to interpret the Convention are the European Commission of Human Rights, the European Court of Human Rights, and the Committee of Ministers of the Council of Europe (Article 19).[11] Section III of the Convention, Articles 20-31, 33-7 (and also Article 48), contain provisions regarding the composition and activity of the Commission, while Section IV, Articles 38-56, regulates the composition and organization of the Court. Provisions relating to the organization and general functions of the Committee of Ministers are not as such contained in the Convention — Articles 14-21 of the Statute of the Council of Europe do so — although the Committee is provided a certain number of specific functions under the Convention,

---

[8] See Council of Europe doc. H(67)2, 10 Jan. 1967, H(72)2, 13 Mar. 1972, and H(76)15, 15 Oct. 1976.

[9] The scope and meaning of this article remain unclear: see brief reference to it in the case of *Schmidt and Dahlström*, Eur. Court HR, ser. B, vol. 19 (1977), at 108-9, and 152-3; comments by T. Opsahl, 'Substantive Rights' in *Proceedings of the Colloquy about the European Convention on Human Rights in Relation to Other International Instruments for the Protection of Human Rights*, Athens, 21-2 Sept. 1978 (Strasbourg 1979), 21-58, at 35-6; and P. J. Duffy, 'The Sunday Times Case: Freedom of Expression, Contempt of Court and the European Convention on Human Rights', V *HR Rev.* (1980), 17-53, at 25-6.

[10] For a general overview see C. Zanghi, 'Effectiveness and Efficiency of the Guarantees of Human Rights Enshrined in the European Convention' in *Proceedings of the Fourth International Colloquy about the European Convention on Human Rights*, Rome 5-8 Nov. 1975 (Strasbourg 1976), 209-55 *passim*, and also written communication of A. H. Robertson, 257-62.

[11] Art. 19 of the Convention does not mention the Committee of Ministers of the Council of Europe, for this body already existed when the Convention entered into force. See arts. 30-2, 54, and 61.

including the power of decision (Articles 31, 32, and 54).[12]

Although the special features of the review system instituted by the Convention have already provided an inexhaustible source of research, detailed examination, and appraisal by academics and practitioners alike, it is interesting to note that the Convention is a much less effective instrument than had originally been envisaged. In the words of A. H. Robertson:[13]

> ... the most important innovations which it was hoped that the Convention would contain were two: — the granting to individuals whose rights are denied, of direct access to an international organ capable of protecting them; and the institution of a juridical body on the international plane, competent to sit in judgment on the national governments. Unfortunately it was not politically possible at this juncture to obtain unanimous agreement of the acceptance of these two provisions. Each of them remains optional in the sense that it is not a necessary consequence of signature of the Convention, but depends on an express supplementary declaration by the State concerned.

As a consequence, even though the Convention mechanism is undoubtedly considered a unique precedent in international law — whereby an individual, whether he be a national or not of the state, is permitted to instigate international proceedings which may result in a judicial determination in his favour[14] — until now only seventeen states[15] have made declarations recognizing the competence of the Commission to receive such petitions lodged by 'any person, non-governmental organization or individual' claiming to be a victim of a violation of a right guaranteed in the Convention (Article 25), and nineteen states parties[16] have accepted the Court's facultative jurisdiction

---

[12] See A. H. Robertson, *Human Rights in Europe* (1977), 237-76.

[13] 'The European Convention for the Protection of Human Rights', 27 *BYIL* (1950), 145-63, at 162.

[14] For a short account of the individual's position *vis-à-vis* tribunals exercising international jurisdiction, see I. Brownlie, *Principles of Public International Law* (1979), 577-93. Further references to this subject can be found there. For more thorough studies on the role played by the individual on the international plane see A. A. Cançado Trindade, *Developments in the Rule of Exhaustion of Local Remedies in International Law, with Particular Reference to Experiments on the International Protection of Individual Rights* (doctoral dissertation, University of Cambridge, 1978), *Les dimensions internationales des Droits de l'Homme* (ed. K. Vasak, 1978), and Vasak's bibliography.

[15] Austria, Belgium, Denmark, Federal Republic of Germany, France, Iceland, Ireland, Italy, Liechtenstein, Luxembourg, the Netherlands, Norway, Portugal, Spain, Sweden, Switzerland, and the United Kingdom (including certain overseas territories).

[16] As in n. 15 above, plus Cyprus and Greece.

concerning the interpretation and application of the Convention (Article 46).[17] The individual has not been provided with access to the Court even though this suggestion was put forward at the time of the Convention's drafting. The proposal that the Commission be provided with the power to 'make recommendations to the State concerned, with a view to obtaining redress' was replaced by a more restrictive provision which relegated the function of this organ − once an application is held to be admissible − to that of trying to secure a friendly settlement on the basis of respect of human rights as defined in the Convention (Article 28(b)). When unsuccessful in so doing, the Commission is to forward a report to the Committee of Ministers expressing its *opinion* as to whether the facts disclose a breach of the Convention. Only if the Court is seised within three months from the date of transmission of the Commission's report, either by the Commission or one of the states parties which possess a vested interest in the case (Article 48), can the Court adjudicate on the given matter. Here again, this presupposes acceptance of the Court's compulsory jurisdiction by the state party or states parties in question, and this applies both to cases which originate before the Commission as interstate applications, under Article 24, as well as to those concerning individual petitions, under Article 25.

Likewise, an initial proposal to extend the powers of the Court of Human Rights − to order reparation, cancellation of an act, and the punishment of an offender − was also greatly modified.[18] The Court's decisions do not necessarily have the force of law in the legal systems of contracting states. Article 50 provides for cases in which the Court's decisions are incompatible with decisions or measures taken by domestic judicial or other authorities and where the law of a state concerned allows only partial reparation to be made for the consequences of the decision or measure in question. The Court may, in such a situation, accord just compensation to the injured party. Thus, the decisions

---

[17] Compare this instrument to the 1969 American Convention on Human Rights (in force since July 1978), esp. arts. 44, 45, and 46, OAS Official Records, OEA/Ser. K/XVI/I. 1 doc. 65 Rev. 1. Corr. 2 (7 Jan. 1970). See further Th. Buergenthal, 'The American and European Conventions on Human Rights: Similarities and Differences', 30 *The American University Law Review* (1980), 155–66; and 'The Inter-American Court of Human Rights', 76 *AJIL* (1982), 231–45.

[18] See A. H. Robertson, 'The European Court of Human Rights', 9 *AJCL* (1959), 1–28, at 5. See also published volumes of the *Collected Editions of the Travaux Préparatoires of the European Convention on Human Rights* (1975-), *passim*.

of the Court are not provided any formal precedence over final decisions of domestic courts or other authorities, nor is the Court vested with any powers under the Convention which would permit it to unify interpretations given to the Convention's provisions by domestic tribunals.[19] Nevertheless, despite these shortcomings, the decisions of the Court of Human Rights do bind the parties internationally, and the Committee of Ministers supervises the execution of the Court's judgments (Articles 53 and 54).[20] Equally, in the alternative case where the Court has not been seised in accordance with Article 48 of the Convention, states involved in proceedings are required to abide by decisions of the Committee of Ministers reached by a two-thirds majority (Article 32).

In short, although it is most certainly valid to claim that the established mechanism departs from reliance upon the traditional concepts in international law of 'nationality' and 'reciprocity' in order to protect individual rights, the facultative status of the right of individual petition, as well as of the Court's compulsory jurisdiction, unduly restricts and weakens the role played by the supervisory organs established under the Convention, and relegates this mechanism prima facie to that of a subsidiary or supplementary means of redress available to a limited number of individuals.[21]

3. *A note on the rights guaranteed*

The rather restricted catalogue of civil and political rights guaranteed by the Convention can be explained by the fact that this instrument was not really intended to create new substantive rights. It was designed primarily to place under international protection some basic or common rights presumably already

---

[19] However, the Convention may — to quote from the Court's recent judgment in the *Marckx* case — 'accelerate' the harmonious evolution of European standards: Eur. Court HR, judgment of 13 June 1979, 26, para. 58. Also see ch. 1 below, sec. B, and General Conclusions.

[20] See R. Higgins, 'The Execution of Decisions of Organs under the European Convention on Human Rights', 31 *RHDI* (1978), 1-39.

[21] See comments by the editor, VIII *RDH/HRJ* (1975), in a special issue to commemorate the Convention's 25th anniversary, 325-7 and 375-9. See further K. Vasak, 'Le Contrôle parlementaire des actes de l'exécutif concernant la ratification de la Convention et l'acceptation de ses clauses facultatives' in *La Protection internationale des Droits de l'Homme dans le cadre européen* (1961), 321-9, and A. Cocatre-Zilgien, 'Justice internationale facultative et justice internationale obligatoire', 80 *RGDIP* (1976), 691-737.

recognized by the domestic law of member states.[22] In the words of the Convention's preamble, member states of the Council of Europe had resolved 'to take the first steps for the collective enforcement of certain of the Rights in the Universal Declaration [of Human Rights]', The phrase 'certain of the Rights' was used advisedly, since this instrument is a much more modest document than the 1948 Universal Declaration and the 1966 Covenants which emerged out of the list of rights enumerated in the Universal Declaration; in fact, the rights and freedoms found in the European Convention are based upon an earlier draft of what is now the United Nations Covenant on Civil and Political Rights.[23]

The drafters of the Convention were also probably more interested in establishing a new international mechanism to permit individuals to bring proceedings against their own states — before international organs whose decisions could bind the parties — than in pressing for an elaborate catalogue of human rights. As explained by Professors Buergenthal and Sohn: '[T]he international guarantees envisaged under the Convention were at the time thought to be quite revolutionary in nature. Consequently, there was little hope that a substantial number of governments would accept them unless they could be convinced that in doing so they were not taking any serious risks.'[24]

The advocates of the Convention were also apparently prepared to accept an incomplete list of rights so that the new procedures created would not be jeopardized.[25] Thus, at the

---

[22] L. B. Sohn and Th. Buergenthal, *International Protection of Human Rights* (1973), 1149.

[23] E. Schwelb, 'Human Rights' in *Encylopaedia Britannica* (1977), 1183–9, at 1187. The texts on the UN documents can be found in *Human Rights: A Compilation of International Instruments of the United Nations* doc. ST/HR/1/Rev.1, 1978. Unlike the Universal Declaration which additionally proclaims a number of social and economic rights (now codified in the 1966 UN Covenant on Economic, Social, and Cultural Rights), the primary concern of the European Convention remains the protection of civil and political rights. And, although social and economic rights are not altogether absent from it (e.g. peaceful enjoyment of possessions, education, and the right to join trade unions), these are more fully guaranteed under the 1961 European Social Charter, in force since 26 Feb. 1965. For further details on this subject see H. Golsong, 'Implementation of International Protection of Human Rights', 110 *R. des C.* (1963) iii. 1–150, at 57–9; Council of Europe doc. H(64)3, 14 Feb. 1964; and *Bibliography of the European Social Charter* (Strasbourg, 1976), *passim*. As to recent developments, see F. G. Jacobs, 'The Extension of the European Convention on Human Rights to Include Economic, Social and Cultural Rights', **III** *HR Rev.* (1978), 166–78.

[24] Sohn and Buergenthal, n. 22 above, 1149.

[25] G. L. Weil, *The European Convention on Human Rights* (1963), 33.

time of the Convention's drafting, certain rights — such as those concerning property, education, and the guarantee of free elections — were temporarily set aside, although they were subsequently included in the First Protocol. Other rights, however, such as those for the protection of minorities, the rights to asylum, conscientious objection, protection against double jeopardy, and the protection against discrimination as a separate and self-contained right, are not guaranteed by this instrument.[26]

A summary of the legislative history of what eventually became the European Convention on Human Rights appears unnecessary since the various documents used during the Convention's drafting, reports of discussions, etc. . . . are now accessible in the published volumes of the *travaux préparatoires*.[27] It is sufficient to note for present purposes that the rights and freedoms set out in the Convention represent a compromise between two different views. Certain member states — in particular the United Kingdom and the Netherlands — favoured a precise definition of the rights to be safeguarded; others, such as France and Italy, urged a proclamation of general principles patterned on the Universal Declaration. It was finally decided that the pitfalls inherent both in too rigid a codification and in a broad statement of generalities lacking legal precision were undesirable. Instead a formula was found to make use of many of the rather loosely formulated definitions of rights already worked out by the UN Commission on Human Rights in preparing the early drafts of the 1966 Covenant, with emphasis, nevertheless, on statutory precision. This decision to establish relatively detailed definitions of the rights was probably motivated, on the one hand, by the need to provide the Convention organs with a sufficiently clear legal framework in which to work, and, on the other hand, to permit states parties to determine whether or not their domestic law conformed with the provisions set out in this instrument.[28]

---

[26] See A. H. Robertson, 'The Promotion of Human Rights by the Council of Europe', **VIII** *RDH/HRJ* (1975), 545–85, esp. 547–67, and M.-A. Eissen, 'The European Convention on Human Rights and the United Nations Covenant on Civil and Political Rights — Problems of Co-Existence', 22 *Buffalo LR* (1972), 181–216.

[27] See *Collected Editions of the Travaux Préparatoires of the European Convention on Human Rights*.

[28] K. Vasak, *La Convention européenne des Droits de l'Homme* (1964), 10–13; A. H. Robertson, *Human Rights in Europe* (1977), 5–16. Sohn and Buergenthal, n. 22 above, at 1150, express the opinion that the draftsmen of the Convention were also in part motivated by the consideration that statutory precision would enable the

B. Delimitation of the Topic of Study

1. *The Convention's basic function*

The entire idea of providing international machinery to implement the protection of human rights is based on the assumption
that certain treaty obligations in respect of domestic implementation will not be carried out, be it because of inadvertence,
lack of adequate knowledge, or due to the misuse of power for
partisan or other purposes. Where human rights are respected
and adequately enforced in domestic law, international implementation and supervision are not necessary. Professor G. I. A. D.
Draper has pointed out that:

> The general scheme of the Convention is precisely to define specific human
> rights and fundamental freedoms (the substantive law of the instrument),
> to specify the machinery for the observance of engagements undertaken
> by the High Contracting Parties and elaborate jurisdictional and procedural
> rules for its operation. The rules affect States and individuals alike. In terms
> of strict juridical analysis, it may be more accurate to say that the right of
> the individual under the Convention falls within its jurisdictional and
> procedural provisions and not within its substantive law system. The
> individual who proceeds under the Convention is not so much seeking
> the enforcement of his individual legal right as bringing to the attention
> of the competent organs under the Convention a supposed violation of the
> inter-state undertakings entered into by the High Contracting Parties in
> Article 1. An appreciation of this basic juridical position may dispel some
> current misconceptions and criticisms of the Convention. It has been
> rightly said that 'the primary purpose of the Convention is not to offer
> an international remedy for individual victims of violations of the Con-
> vention but to provide a collective, inter-State guarantee enforceable
> through Strasbourg that would benefit individuals generally by requiring
> the municipal law of the Contracting States to keep within certain bounds.'
> That would appear to be, at this moment of time, the farthest point that
> has been reached in the protection of human rights on the international
> plane.[29]

---

domestic courts of those states which distinguish between self-executing and non-self-
executing treaties to hold that the provisions of the Convention could be applied
directly without additional implementing machinery. For a response to these arguments, see Ch. 2 below.

[29] 'Implementation of the European Convention on Human Rights 1950', 2 *Israel
Yearbook on Human Rights* (1972), 99–120, at 99–100. (In this passage the author
quotes from p. 109 of D. J. Harris, 'Recent Cases on Pre-trial Detention and Delay in
Criminal Proceedings in the European Court of Human Rights', 44 *BYIL* (1970),
87–109.) Also see L. Wildhaber, 'Erfahrungen mit der Europäischen Menschenrechtskonvention', 98 *Revue de droit suisse* (1979), 230–379, at 316.

Similarly, the European Court of Human Rights has explained in confident terms that 'Unlike international treaties of the classic kind, the Convention comprises more than mere reciprocal engagements between contracting States. It creates, over and above a network of mutual, bilateral undertakings, objective obligations which, in the words of the Preamble, benefit from a "collective enforcement".'[30]

States parties to the Convention have therefore undertaken objective obligations to secure to *everyone* within their respective jurisdictions the rights and freedoms guaranteed by the Convention (Article 1). This being said, their responsibility to serve *'l'ordre public de l'Europe'* through the Convention's machinery of implementation remains — despite the rare use of Article 24 in interstate cases — purely facultative (Articles 25 and 46). Hence, the obligation to individuals is clear, although the actual protection received and 'collective enforcement' through the Convention machinery in many instances remain inadequate.

It follows that the 'Convention mechanism' was created to perform a specific, limited function, a function which it is *not* the purpose of this book to explore. Quite the contrary, it must be understood that a comparative study of the domestic status of the Convention, i.e. of the possible permeation or penetration of certain norms of this international instrument into the domestic law of contracting states, is considered by many as a study of an auxiliary development which, although very important and perhaps interesting to examine, was and remains far removed from this instrument's basic legal functioning on the international plane.[31]

2. *The specific aim of this study*

From the above comments, it transpires that this book will only focus attention upon a certain category of issues posed by the Convention's existence, although topics of related interest, such as the general problem concerning the harmonization of standards of human rights in Western Europe, will be discussed

---

[30] Eur. Court HR, *Ireland* v. *UK*, judgment of 18 Jan. 1978, ser. A, no. 25, 90–1, para. 239. (A more explicit reference to 'objective obligations to *individuals*' would have been desirable.)

[31] It is assumed, for present purposes, that there is a clear distinction between treaty obligations binding in international law and the possible reception of certain norms of such agreements into domestic law. This matter will be dealt with in Part I below.

where necessary. However, the basic aim of this study remains threefold:

(i) to determine conclusively, if possible, whether or not there exists a *legal* obligation for member states to incorporate[32] the substantive provisions of the Convention into domestic law;

(ii) to examine by means of a comparative survey the present-day 'status' of the European Convention on Human Rights in *all* the member states of the Council of Europe, i.e. its apparent reception into the legal systems of the majority of the member states, as well as its not insignificant impact upon the legal systems of other states parties; and

(iii) to concentrate attention upon three specific topics which, it is submitted, may illustrate the Convention's expanding 'authority' *vis-à-vis* domestic courts of member states. These will be (a) to observe the impact — unforeseen by most scholars a few years ago — of the Convention's application by domestic courts in relations between individuals; (b) to note the possibility of domestic courts of the ten member states of the European Community understanding some of the Convention's provisions as forming part of the corpus of European Community law; (c) to make a comparative study examining the extent to which the findings of the Convention's 'organs' actually influence domestic courts and tribunals, either in domestic court proceedings to give effect to these findings, or as guidelines which serve to clarify the extent and nature of obligations resulting from them.

The above study will, hopefully, illustrate this instrument's growing importance as an 'autonomous source' within domestic legal forums, and in particular the rather unique *sui generis* characteristics of 'Convention law'. Based upon these findings, the study will end with the suggestion that serious consideration be given yet again to the idea of instituting some form of 'preliminary ruling' procedure which could permit a more

---

[32] The word 'incorporation' is used in this study to signify the general reception of international legal norms into the domestic legal systems of states parties; this word encompasses both 'transformation' and 'adoption'. The view that 'adoption' and 'incorporation' are synonymous is therefore rejected. Cf. *Halsbury's Laws of England* (4th ed., 1977), xviii 718-19, and J. E. S. Fawcett, *The British Commonwealth in International Law* (1963), 16-18.

harmonious and uniform application of 'Convention law' by domestic courts and tribunals.

This comparative study will show, in the final analysis, that the extent to which the norms of this rather unique *international* agreement can be accommodated in the *domestic* legal systems of contracting states — as well as the position they acquire for themselves within the domestic hierarchy — depends not only upon internal constitutional considerations but also upon developments in Strasbourg. *A fundamental issue still awaits resolution*: on the one hand the European Convention on Human Rights is given the status of 'European Public Order' and is endowed with 'law-making' characteristics,[33] while simultaneously its function remains that of providing a subsidiary collective guarantee of certain rights governing relations between the individual and the national authorities.[34]

A cursory glance at developments beyond Western Europe suffices to make one aware of the derisory smallness of the rights which the Convention organs are attempting to enforce; similarly, the inadequacies of the Convention's effectiveness can be assessed by observing the limited impact of protection which this instrument, together with its supervisory bodies, actually provides to individuals in the domestic law of many countries. The Convention has been and is in certain instances interpreted juristically, cautiously, and very often in a restrictive manner; yet this instrument represents — together with the institutions of the European Community — a most vivid example of how states, possessing close cultural and other links, have been able to co-operate on a regional and functional basis. However, '[u]nderstandable as this development is, and exciting for those who participate, it could have its dangers; it may divert the attention of politicians and lawyers away from abiding and worsening problems of economic inequality, racism and the destruction of peace and the world's resources on an intercontinental or global basis'.[35] This criticism is a legitimate one

---

[33] See ch. 1 below, sec. B.

[34] Cf. Eur. Court HR: case *'relating to certain aspects of the laws on the use of languages in education in Belgium'* (merits), judgment of 23 July 1968, ser. A, no. 6, 34-5, para. 10; *Swedish Engine Drivers'* case, judgment of 6 Feb. 1976, ser. A, no. 20, 18, para. 50, *Handyside* case, judgment of 29 Apr. 1976, ser. A, no. 24, 22, para. 48; and *Ireland* v. *UK* judgment of 18 Jan. 1978, ser. A, no. 25, 90-1, para. 239.

[35] *The Times Literary Supplement*, 25 Jan. 1974, 83-4. Note, in this context, the interesting comments of C. Thornberry, in his 'memorandum' published in Minutes of Evidence taken before the Select Committee on a Bill of Rights, House of Lords,

and merits much greater attention. However, such a discussion would go beyond the ambit of the subject-matter presently under consideration.

Sessions 1976-7 and 1977-8, no. 81 (1978), 224-8, esp. at 225-6, paras. 9 and 14.

PART I

THE OBLIGATIONS
ASSUMED BY THE PARTIES
TO THE CONVENTION

General Observations

In a written communication submitted at the Third International Colloquy on the European Convention on Human Rights held in Brussels in 1970, Professor Frank C. Newman (now a Justice of the Supreme Court of California) made the following observations:

Is it true that 'among the European States, human rights and freedoms now have the force and quality of constitutional rules?' After twenty years, what really is the practical quality or force of the Convention's rules when in nine of the fifteen countries that are parties 'the Convention provisions are not, constitutionally or by legislative enactment, part of domestic law?' Internationally the Convention enjoys fame because of its focus on implementation. Yet what has become of Article 13 ('Everyone whose rights and freedoms as set forth in this Convention are violated shall have an effective remedy before a national authority . . .')? Mr Fawcett's conclusion ('Article 13 is an unsatisfactory article, difficult both to construe and to place in the Convention system') offers little encouragement.[1]

Without necessarily being able to answer in detail the question posed by Professor Newman in Part I of this study, an attempt will nevertheless be made to do so indirectly by making another perhaps more fundamental inquiry: does the Convention, directly or indirectly, impose a *legal duty* upon contracting states to implement in their respective legal systems the rights and freedoms enumerated in the Convention and in the First and Fourth Protocols? Only after this initial inquiry is completed can one try to respond to the points raised by Professor Newman.

The European Convention for the Protection of Human Rights and Fundamental Freedoms has mostly drawn attention to itself on the plane of international law, both as an international legal agreement concerning the protection of a certain category of human rights and as a possible means of bringing about eventual European unification.[2] It has for a long time been and still remains the most effective international system for the protection

---

[1] 'The Convention and World-Wide Human Rights: Some Iconoclastic Inquiries' in *Privacy and Human Rights* (ed. A. H. Robertson, 1973), 413–24, at 416–17.

[2] G. Weil, *The European Convention on Human Rights* (1963), 209. See also P. Modinos, 'Effects and Repercussions of the European Convention on Human Rights', 11 *ICLQ* (1962), 1097–108.

of human rights. Nevertheless this international machinery, as is the general case with other international forms of adjudication, tends to be cumbersome, time-consuming, and expensive, and accordingly it can be argued that its efficacy depends considerably upon the extent to which its provisions can be invoked before the courts and administrative agencies of the member states.[3] In a number of states an international treaty, once ratified, has the force of law in the domestic legal system and may be applied by the national courts. In such cases the Convention has prima facie a double value in that it provides domestic as well as international remedies for an individual alleging denial of rights; and in situations where a state has not accepted the optional provision of Article 25, the individual has perhaps an extra avenue of recourse not necessarily otherwise provided in the domestic legal system. In other states this agreement has no domestic legal force; some of these states have not even accepted the right of individual petition. This being the case, it certainly appears preferable that the rights guaranteed by the Convention be effectively secured by national courts and tribunals since an attempt at vindication through a lengthy process of an 'appeal' to the Strasbourg organs may well deprive the individual of immediate redress associated with domestic law and with it the preventive function such law is meant to perform. Hence the importance of knowing if states are *legally* obliged to incorporate this instrument's substantive provisions into their internal law.

An impression has already been created — partly justified on an examination of case-law — that the Strasbourg organs perhaps unduly sacrifice the effective protection of the individual and that they unfortunately give a rather superficial and ritualistic content to the Convention's provisions without providing the applicant adequate and immediate redress.[4] Nevertheless, the European Convention on Human Rights is the sole existing example of a relatively well-functioning and relatively sensitive international judicial or quasi-judicial machinery for the protection of an extensive category of human rights — a machinery which diverges fundamentally from the well-established but

---

[3] L. Sohn and Th. Buergenthal, *The International Protection of Human Rights* (1973), 1238.
[4] Cf. T. E. McCarthy, 'International Protection of Human Rights — Ritual and Reality', 25 *ICLQ* (1976), 261–91.

often regressive forms of protection based upon the traditional concepts of reciprocity and diplomatic activity. This regional convention has in fact established a rather specific and evolving form of '*ordre public d'Europe*' the impact of which has not as yet been sufficiently appreciated.

Chapter 1

International Treaty Obligations and the Convention

A. Established principle in traditional international law

When states ratify treaties they in effect exchange mutual undertakings to observe the terms agreed therein and this of course implies an obligation undertaken towards some other party or parties. If this instrument relates to matters which concern the domestic legal order, there exists a well-established principle or rule of international law which places contracting states under an international legal duty to ensure that their domestic law conforms to the accepted international obligations. This rule is taken for granted since otherwise the conclusion of treaties would be without effect, in that the basic tenet upon which international law is founded — *pacta sunt servanda* — would be a mere tautology. However, this is not to say that the mere existence of a measure in domestic law could *ipso facto* constitute an infringement of a treaty obligation in question; in such cases it is generally recognized that there is no infringement of an international undertaking unless and until the measure in question is actually applied and the practice violates or threatens to violate provisions guaranteed in the treaty.

This rule or principle of international law was recognized as self-evident by the Permanent Court of International Justice when it gave its advisory opinion on 21 February 1925 in the *Exchange of Greek and Turkish Populations* case. The Court stated: '. . . a principle which is self-evident, according to which a State which has contracted valid international obligations is bound to make in its legislation such modifications as may be necessary to ensure the fulfilment of the obligations undertaken.'[1]

---

[1] Advisory opinion no. 10, PCIJ (1925), ser. B, no. 10, 20. In this case the Court had been asked by the Council of the League of Nations to give an opinion on the meaning and scope which should be attributed to the word 'establishment' in a provision of an agreement regarding the exchange of Greek and Turkish populations which respectively inhabited Constantinople and Western Thrace. Similarly, in the *Free Zones* case between France and Switzerland — concerning the status of the customs-free zones of Upper Savoy — the Permanent Court said: 'it is certain that

Again, in its advisory opinion of 31 July 1930 on the *Interpretation of the Convention between Greece and Bulgaria Respecting Reciprocal Emigration*, the Permanent Court said: 'it is a generally accepted principle of international law that in relations between Powers who are contracting Parties to a treaty, the provisions of municipal law cannot prevail over those of the treaty.'[2]

This principle is applicable not only with regard to legislation in the limited sense of the term, but to domestic law in its widest connotation: a state is unable to invoke provisions of its own constitution in order to justify its non-compliance with treaty obligations. Thus, in its advisory opinion of 4 February 1932, relating to the *Treatment of Polish Nationals and other Persons of Polish Origin or Speech in the Danzig Territory*, the Permanent Court said that: 'a State cannot adduce as against another State its own Constitution with a view to evading obligations incumbent upon it under international law or treaties in force.'[3] The 1969 Vienna Convention on the Law of Treaties reiterates the principle. Article 27 stipulates: 'A party may not invoke the provisions of its internal law as justification for its failure to perform a treaty. This rule is without prejudice to Article 46.'[4] In addition Article 46 provides that:

1. A State may not invoke the fact that its consent to be bound by a treaty has been expressed in violation of a provision of its internal law regarding competence to conclude treaties as invalidating its consent unless that violation was manifest and concerned a rule of its internal law of fundamental importance.
2. A violation is manifest if it would be objectively evident to any State contracting itself in the matter in accordance with normal practice and in good faith.

Yet, although the duty to bring domestic law into line with international contractual obligations certainly exists, international law is silent with regard to the means by which this object is to be achieved. Such conformity is a matter of domestic

France cannot rely on her own legislation to limit the scope of her international obligations'. (Order of 6 Dec. 1930, PCIJ (1930), ser. A, no. 24, 12.)
[2] PCIJ, ser. B, no. 17, 32.
[3] PCIJ, ser. A/B, no. 44, 24. In this case the Court, by nine votes to four, considered that Poland was unable to invoke provisions of the Constitution of the Free City of Danzig before the High Commission of the League of Nations as conferring rights upon Polish nationals, although reference could be made by Poland to international obligations incumbent on Danzig towards Poland arising from treaty provisions in force between them or from general international law.
[4] UN doc. A/CONF.39/27. The Convention entered into force on 27 Jan. 1980.

concern, normally determined by constitutional provisions and practice of each state. It would therefore appear that one must clearly distinguish between the obligation to ensure that domestic law is compatible with actual introduction of such an instrument, *ipso jure*, into domestic law. Hence it is submitted that signatory states to the European Convention on Human Rights are considered to be free to secure the conformity of their domestic law with the international obligations under the treaty mechanism in the way which seems to them most appropriate. However, this conclusion is not shared by all international lawyers and, as will be seen later, a certain amount of disagreement has been noted in legal and academic circles. Among the reasons for this disagreement is the fact that a large number of observers have laid emphasis on the rather unique form of law that this Convention is said to have created: it is in effect an international instrument which concerns itself with a field of law traditionally reserved to constitutional law, namely the protection of the rights of individuals *vis-à-vis* the State. It is, to use the words of Lord McNair, 'a *law-making treaty* the object of which is to oblige the parties to apply certain rules of international law and, if necessary, to add or to modify their national law for this purpose.'[5]

B. The *sui generis* nature of the Convention

Unlike the 1948 Universal Declaration of Human Rights upon which it was founded, the European Convention represents more than a 'common standard of achievement'. It imposes upon the contracting states a certain body of legal principles to which they are obliged to conform. In specific cases compliance with this law is ensured by the use of the Convention's enforcement machinery. Although the Convention forms an integral part of the domestic law of many of the contracting states, it is immaterial whether or not under a national legal system the Convention's provisions are deemed to be of a greater validity *vis-à-vis* prior or subsequent domestic legislation since the system of

---

[5] 'The European Convention of 1950 for the Protection of Human Rights and Fundamental Freedoms', the first of a series of lectures published under the title *The Expansion of International Law* (81st Lionel Cohen Lecture, The Hebrew University of Jerusalem, 1962), 9–28, at 27. The 'law-making' characteristics of the Convention have also been stressed by the Strasbourg Court: see for example Eur. Court HR, *The Sunday Times* case, judgment of 26 Apr. 1979, ser. A. vol. 30, 30, para. 48.

implementation falls entirely outside the province of domestic law.[6] The basic function of this machinery — once an issue is brought before the Strasbourg organs — consists primarily of examining and determining whether domestic law as it stands complies with the provisions of the Convention. Reliance upon the traditional concepts in international law of 'nationality' or 'reciprocity' is also unnecessary. Thus, although constructed upon tenets of traditional treaty law, the Convention law transcends the traditional boundaries drawn between international and domestic law: in short, the Convention may be considered *sui generis*.

● Professor Robertson has attempted to explain this phenomenon in the following terms:[7] the law of the Convention (like European Community law) is neither domestic nor international law although it comprises elements of both. It is not simply a law applied by the Commission and Court of Human Rights since, on the one hand, the Committee of Ministers of the Council of Europe also applies it, and on the other hand, domestic tribunals also do. Robertson then adds that as the law of the Convention not only creates obligations for states but also rights which are enforceable by individuals, it establishes, in the field of civil liberties, a new legal order designed to substitute for the particular systems of individual states a common European order. Thus, although the Convention contains no provisions for a procedure to unify and harmonize the interpretation given to it by its organs, these organs nevertheless can and do manage to secure this to a limited extent.

The jurisdiction and operation of the Commission and Court are subject to rules in which the *common public interest* is overriding. For example, in cases where a 'friendly settlement' has been achieved by the parties (Articles 28 and 30) the Commission has to take into consideration possible elements of this so-called 'public interest' before deciding to terminate proceedings. To date twenty-three cases have been resolved in

---

[6] With the obvious exception relating to the rule of the exhaustion of local remedies. On this subject see numerous publications of A. A. Cançado Trindade, esp. 'Exhaustion of Local Remedies in International Law and the Role of National Courts', 17 *Archiv des Völkerrechts* (1978), 333-70, and his forthcoming book, *The Rule of the Exhaustion of Local Remedies in International Law* (Cambridge University Press, 1982).

[7] A. H. Robertson, 'The Relationship between the European Convention on Human Rights and Internal Law in General' in *European Criminal Law* (Colloques Européens, 1970), 3-13, at 12, also in his book, *Human Rights in Europe* (1977), at 231.

this manner.[8] Similarly, in the application of *Helga and Wilhelm Gericke* v. *Federal Republic of Germany*, the Commission initially refused to accept a withdrawal of the case by the applicants, observing:

that the interests served by the protection of the human rights and fundamental freedoms guaranteed by the Convention *extend beyond the individual interests of the parties concerned* . . . they have led the member
Parties to the Convention to *establish standards forming part of the public
law in Europe*; and whereas Article 19 of the Convention provides that
the Commission and Court are set up 'to ensure the observance of the
engagements undertaken by the High Contracting Parties in the present
Convention' . . . the withdrawal of an application and the respondent
Government's agreement thereto cannot deprive the Commission of the
competence to pursue its examination of the case.[9]

Consequently, the remedies available to individuals in cases where their rights have been held to be violated must be considered in the context of an interest higher than that of the aggrieved or even that of the contracting state: stress should be laid on the pre-eminence of a certain form of general interest or *ordre public*.[10] In the second interstate case brought before the

---

[8] See 'Stocktaking', 83–107, and *Annual Reviews of the European Commission of
Human Rights* (1979–81). In the case of *Karnell & Hardt* v. *Sweden*, application
4733/71 (report of Commission, 28 May 1973, 2) — which was struck off the Commission's list of cases — art. 28(b) was 'applied by analogy' since it appeared to the
Commission 'that the settlement between the parties was based on respect of human
rights' (cited in *The European Convention on Human Rights. Cases and Materials*
(ed. H. Petzold, 1981), case x, 1–11, at p. 81). (See also bibliographical note at the
end of case xi, p. 95.) The actual working of this settlement procedure is described
by the Commission's former Secretary A. B. McNulty in 'Practice of the European
Commission of Human Rights Regarding Friendly Settlement under the European
Convention on Human Rights' in *Armağan* [homage], *Professor T. B. Balta* (1974),
423–30.

[9] Application 2294/64, 8 Yearbook (1965), 315–22, at 320. (Emphasis added).
The application was eventually withdrawn and proceedings terminated by the Com-
mission in May 1966. See 'Stocktaking', 112, and 20 *Coll. of Dec.*, 86–100. The
Strasbourg Court has also — by referring to its supervisory function under art. 19 of
the Convention — had the opportunity to apply similar criteria. Cf. Eur. Court HR,
De Becker case, judgment of 27 Mar. 1962, ser. A, no. 4, esp. 24–7, paras. 10–16.

[10] See J. E. S. Fawcett, *The Application of the European Convention on Human
Rights* (1969), 264–70. The term '*ordre public de l'Europe*' must be distinguished,
for present purposes, from its inadequate English language counterpart 'public order'.
See further on this subject W. J. Ganshof van der Meersch, 'Does the Convention have
the Force of 'Ordre Public' in Municipal Law?' in *Human Rights in National and
International Law* (ed. A. H. Robertson, 1968), 97–143. (A longer version of this
article in French can be found in *Les Droits de l'Homme en droit interne et en droit
international* (1968), 155–251.) This 'concept of a general interest', as Ganshof van
der Meersch refers to it, 'comes near to the concept of *jus cogens* in international
law': see n. 29 below, p. 59. Also consult Pastor J. A. Ridruejo, 'La Convención

Commission — *Austria* v. *Italy* — the Italian Government contended that Austria should not be able to invoke provisions of the Convention relating to happenings prior to Austria's ratification of the Convention. The Commission rejected this argument. It held that:

[I]t clearly appears from these pronouncements [the Convention's preamble] that the purpose of the High Contracting Parties in concluding the Convention was *not to concede to each other reciprocal rights and obligations* in pursuance of their individual national interests but to realise the aims and ideals of the Council of Europe, as expressed in its Statute, and *to establish a common public order* of the free democracies of Europe with the object of safeguarding their common heritage of political traditions, ideals, freedom and the rule of law . . . it follows that the *obligations undertaken* by the High Contracting Parties in the Convention *are essentially of an objective character*, being designed to protect the fundamental rights of individual human beings from infringement by any of the High Contracting Parties than to create subjective and reciprocal rights for the High Contracting Parties themselves . . . [I]t follows that a High Contracting Party, when it refers an alleged breach of the Convention to the Commission under Article 24, is not to be regarded as exercising a right of action for the purpose of enforcing its own rights, but rather as bringing before the Commission an alleged violation of the *public order of Europe.*[11]

The opportunity to stress the Convention's rather special nature presented itself in the case of *Ireland* v. *UK*. The Commission's report included a separate opinion of Professor Sperduti (joined by Professor Opsahl) in which an attempt was made to show the particular importance of Article 1 of the Convention (read in conjunction with other Articles such as 50 and 57). In the opinion of the Commission's vice-president, the high contracting parties, '. . . each accepted *an obligation towards all the others together*, to guarantee respect of the Convention through their internal legal systems',[12] and this obligation necessarily encompasses 'the *ties of solidarity* which the States Parties intended to create between themselves with a view to establishing a European public order'.

In its judgment rendered on 18 January 1978, the European

Europea de los Derechos del Hombre y el 'ius cogens' internacional', in *Estudios de Derecho Internacional Homenaje al Profesor Miaja de la Muela* (1979), i, 581-90. (This subject is further dealt with in ch. 8 below.)

[11] *Austria* v. *Italy* (The *Pfunders* case), application 788/60, 4, *Yearbook* (1961), 112-82, at 138-40. (Emphasis added.)

[12] Application 5310/71, report of Commission, 25 Jan. 1976; separate opinion on the interpretation of art. 1 of the Convention, 497-9. (Original in French, emphasis original.)

Court of Human Rights appeared to reiterate — to a certain extent — the above view when it explained that 'Unlike international treaties of the classic kind, the Convention comprises more than mere reciprocal engagements between contracting States. It creates over and above a network of mutual, bilateral undertakings, objective obligations which, in the words of the preamble, benefit from a "collective enforcement".'[13]

Yet another specific characteristic of the 'Convention's law' is the fact that the Commission and Court are not necessarily tied by or confined to interpret it on the basis of what were considered by the states parties to be acceptable standards at the time of its coming into force. Often a liberal teleological or evolutive interpretation of the Convention's law is called for. Although some of the Court's earlier case-law on this subject will be cited below, this point may be illustrated by the cases of *Tyrer* v. *UK*[14] and *Marckx* v. *Belgium*,[15] decided in April 1978 and June 1979 respectively. In both these cases the Court considered that certain of the Convention's provisions had been violated even though one may hazard a guess that the Court would probably not have found any violations of the Convention some fifteen or twenty years earlier. In the case of *Tyrer* v. *UK* the Court recalled that 'the Convention is a living instrument . . . which must be interpreted in the light of present-day conditions', and that it could not 'but be influenced by the developments and commonly accepted standards in the penal policy' of the Council of Europe's member states concerning the use of judicial corporal punishment.[16] In the more recent case of *Marckx* v. *Belgium*, the Court conceded the point that 'at the time when the Convention of 4th November 1950 was drafted, it was regarded as permissible and normal in many European countries to draw a distinction . . . between the "illegitimate" and the

---

[13] Eur. Court HR, ser. A, no. 25, 90-1, para. 239. Note may also be taken of two recent judgments of the Strasbourg Court. In the case of *Marckx* v. *Belgium* (see n. 15 below, para 48) the Court equated its power to that the constitutional courts of certain member states of the Council of Europe; while in the case of *Deweer* v. *Belgium* (Eur. Court HR, judgment of 27 Feb. 1980, ser. A, no. 35, para. 49) the Court made express reference to 'the public order (*ordre public*) of the member states of the Council of Europe' when determining that art. 6 of the Convention had been breached. The obligations imposed upon states may be of a positive nature: see ch. 8 below, n. 63.

[14] Eur. Court HR, ser. A, no. 26, judgment of 25 Apr. 1978.

[15] Ibid., no. 30, judgment of 13 June 1979.

[16] As above, n. 14 (p. 15, para. 31). See also *Airey* case, judgment of 9 Oct. 1979, ser. A, no. 32, 15, para. 26.

"legitimate" family'. But, after recalling what it had said in the *Tyrer* case, the Court went on to explain that 'In the instant case, the Court cannot but be struck by the fact that the domestic law of the great majority of the member States of the Council of Europe has evolved and is continuing to evolve in company with the relevant international instruments towards full juridical recognition of the maxim *"mater semper certa est"*'.[17]

Although a subject of *obiter dicta* in both the Commission and Court, there had surprisingly for a long time existed no clearly delineated and systematic pronouncement of what could be considered a commonly acceptable and authoritative method of interpreting the provisions set out in the Convention. It was not until June 1973 that the Commission decided to accept the criteria of interpretation listed in the 1969 Vienna Convention on the Law of Treaties (Articles 31-3).[18]

---

[17] As above, n. 15 (p. 18, para. 41). The Court then went on to cite two international agreements and an official statement accompanying a bill submitted by the Belgian Government before the Senate in which reference was made to legal developments in several other member states in this field. The same could be said to apply to homosexual practices: see Eur. Court HR, *Dudgeon* case, judgment of 22 Oct. 1981, ser. A, no. 45, 23-4, para. 60. It could likewise be argued that in the case of *Kjeldsen, Busk Madsen, and Pedersen* v. *Denmark* the dissent of Judge Verdross might well have been the majority's view a number of years previously; see Eur. Court HR, judgment of 7 Dec. 1976, ser. A, no. 23, *passim*. On a previous occasion, in the case of *König* v. *FRG*, Eur. Court HR, judgment of 28 June 1978, ser. A, no. 27, 30, para. 89, it was explained that '[i]n the exercise of its supervisory functions, the Court must (also) take account of the object and purpose of the Convention *and* of the national legal systems of the other Contracting States'. (See the Commission's report in this case, 30, para. 65.) In addition consult the Commission's report of 12 July, 1977, in the case of *Brüggemann and Scheuten* v. *FRG*, application 6959/75, para. 64 and app. v, 55-90; and Eur. Court HR, case of *Engel and Others*, judgment of 8 June/23 Nov. 1976, ser. A, no. 22, 35, para. 82. Comparative law has come to play an important role on the international plane: see A. A. Cançado Trindade, 'La méthode comparative en droit international: une perspective européenne', 55 *Rev. Droit international de sciences diplomatiques et politiques* (1977), 273-87; H. Mosler, 'Nationale Gerichte als Garanten Völkerrechtlicher Verpflichtungen' in *Recht als instrument van Behoud en Verandering, Opstellen Aangeboden aan J. J. M. Van Der Van* (1972), 381-90; and W. J. Ganshof van der Meersch, 'La référence au droit interne des États contractants dans la jurisprudence de la Cour européenne des droits de l'homme', 32 *RIDC* (1980), 317-35. (An English translation is provided in 1 *HRLJ* (1980), 13-35.)

[18] Application 4451/70, *Golder* v. *UK*, report of the Commission 1 June 1973, Eur. Court HR, ser. B, no. 16, 9-16. This convention (see UN doc. A/Conf. 39/27, 289-301), came into force on 27 Jan. 1980. The following member states of the Council of Europe have ratified or acceded to this instrument: Austria, Cyprus, Denmark, Greece, Italy, Spain, Sweden, and the United Kingdom. It has also been signed by the Federal Republic of Germany and Luxembourg. The articles read as follows:

In its report in the *Golder* case the Commission observed that the rather general provisions of Articles 31 to 33 of the Vienna Convention could be viewed as an expression of customary law

'Section III — Interpretation of Treaties
Article 31
General rule of interpretation
1. A Treaty shall be interpreted in good faith in accordance with the ordinary meaning to be given to the terms of the treaty in their context and in the light of its objects and purpose.
2. The context for the purpose of the interpretation of a treaty shall comprise, in addition to the text, including its preamble and annexes:
(a) any agreement relating to the treaty which was made between all the parties in connection with the conclusion of the treaty;
(b) any instrument which was made by one or more parties in connection with the conclusion of the treaty and accepted by the other parties as an instrument related to the treaty.
3. There shall be taken into account, together with the context
(a) any subsequent agreement between the parties regarding the interpretation of the treaty or the application of its provisions;
(b) any subsequent practice in the application of the treaty which establishes the agreement of the parties regarding its interpretation;
(c) any relevant rules of international law applicable in the relations between the parties.
4. A special meaning shall be given to a term if it is established that the parties so intended.
Article 32
Supplementary means of interpretation
Recourse may be had to supplementary means of interpretation, including the preparatory work of the treaty and the circumstances of its conclusion, in order to confirm the meaning resulting from the application of article 31, or to determine the meaning when the interpretation according to article 31:
(a) leaves the meaning ambiguous or obscure; or
(b) leads to a result which is manifestly absurd or unreasonable.
Article 33
Interpretation of treaties authenticated in two or more languages
1. When a treaty has been authenticated in two or more languages, the text is equally authoritative in each language, unless the treaty provides or the parties agree that, in case of divergence, a particular text shall prevail.
2. A version of the treaty in a language other than one of those in which the text was authenticated shall be considered an authentic text only if the treaty so provides or the parties so agree.
3. The terms of the treaty are presumed to have the same meaning in each authentic text.
4. Except where a particular text prevails in accordance with paragraph 1, when a comparison of the authentic texts discloses a difference of meaning which the application of articles 31 and 32 does not remove, the object and purpose of the treaty, shall be adopted.'

It is also of importance to note that art. 5 of the Vienna Convention on the Law of Treaties stipulates that 'The present Convention applies . . . to any adopted within an international organisation *without prejudice to any relevant rules of the organisation*'. (Emphasis added.) Art. 60(5) can also be of relevance.

and general principles recognized by nations which included the contracting parties to the European Convention. The Commission made the proviso that, in interpreting this instrument, the special nature of the Convention had to be taken into account.[19] It considered that the Convention's provisions must be interpreted objectively. It cited with approval remarks made in the *Pfunders* case in support of this: 'the obligations undertaken by the High Contracting Parties in the Convention are essentially of an objective character being designed rather to protect the fundamental rights of individual human beings from infringement by any of the High Contracting Parties themselves.'[20] It added that it was wrong to interpret the Convention by reference to what may have been the understanding of one contracting state at the time of its ratification. 'Furthermore, whatever may be the case as regards an ordinary international treaty, both the Commission and the Court, whenever they have expressed an opinion on this general point, have stated that the provisions of the *Convention should not be interpreted restrictively so as to prevent its aims and objects being achieved.*'[21] The Commission then quoted passages from the Court's case-law to support this reasoning. It referred to the *Wemhoff* case in which the Court said:[22] 'Given that it [the Convention] is a law-making treaty, it is also necessary to seek the interpretation that is most appropriate in order to realise the aim and achieve the object of the treaty, not that which would restrict to the greatest possible degree the obligations undertaken by the parties.' It also cited a passage from the Court's judgment in the *Belgian Linguistic* cases, in which the Court considered 'that the general aim set for themselves by the Contracting Parties through the medium of the European Convention on Human Rights, was to provide effective protection of fundamental human rights, and this, without doubt not only because of the historical context in which the Convention was concluded, but also of the social and technical developments in

[19] Ibid., report of Commission, para. 44 at 33. The Commission added: 'For the limited guidance one may find in these provisions, it is therefore not material whether the Vienna Convention is in force for the Contracting Parties'.

[20] Ibid., at 34. Also consult Sir H. Waldock, 'The Effectiveness of the System set up by the European Convention on Human Rights', 1 *HRLJ* (1980), 1–12.

[21] Ibid., para. 44. (Emphasis added.)

[22] Eur. Court HR, *Wemhoff* case, judgment of 27 June 1968, 23, para. 8. Here the Court had to reconcile the equally authentic but not synonymous English and French versions of art. 5, para. 3 of the Convention. See also Eur. Court HR, *The Sunday Times* case, judgment of 26 Apr. 1979, ser. A, no. 30, 30, para. 48.

our age which offer to states considerable possibilities for regulating the exercise of these rights. The Convention therefore implies a just balance between the protection of the general interest of the community and the respect due to fundamental human rights while attaching particular importance to the latter'.[23] The Commission then went on to state that 'the over-riding function of this Convention is to protect the rights of the individual and not to lay down between States mutual obligations which are to be restrictively interpreted having regard to the sovereignty of these States'.[24]

In its judgment in the *Golder* case, the Court endorsed the above views of the Commission — as well as that of the British Government — and accepted to be 'guided' by Articles 31-3 of the Vienna Convention. The Court held that although the Vienna Convention had not yet entered into force, its Articles 31-3 enunciated in essence generally accepted principles of inter-national law. Consequently account must be taken of those Articles subject, where appropriate, to 'any relevant rules of the organisation' in question, i.e. the Council of Europe.[25] It then went on to hold, without even needing to resort to 'supple-mentary means of interpretation' as envisaged by Article 32 of the Vienna Convention, that Article 6(1) of the European Convention on Human Rights secures to everyone the implied right to have a claim relating to his civil rights and obligations brought before a court or tribunal, i.e. that the right of access to a court or tribunal is inherent in the right to a fair hearing guaranteed by Article 6(1).[26]

For all intents and purposes, therefore, the Strasbourg organs, when interpreting this instrument, *must* take its special nature into consideration. This is so because, as explained by the Court

[23] Eur. Court HR, case *relating to certain aspects of the laws on the use of languages in education in Belgium* (merits), judgment of 23 July 1968, p. 32. The Commission also quoted the judgment of the Court in the *Delcourt* case: see Eur. Court HR, judgment of 17 Jan. 1970, 15, para. 25.

[24] As above, n. 18, report of Commission, 40, para. 57.

[25] Eur. Court HR, *Golder* case, judgment of 21 Feb. 1975, ser. A, 18, 14, para. 29. See also n. 18 above and n. 32 below. (The observations of Mr Kellberg in the Com-mission's report in the *Trade Union 'Closed Shop'* case, 44, para. 1.2, and 47, para. 3, may be of interest in this context.)

[26] Ibid., 18, para. 36. But see the separate (partly dissenting) opinion of Judge Sir G. Fitzmaurice, esp. 52-8, para. 38-46. F. A. Mann considers that 'the Court's approach was legislative rather than teleological'. See his article 'Britain's Bill of Rights', 94 *LQR* (1978), 512-33, n. 69 at 528. At the same time at 529 he accepts that the Convention is a 'constitutional' document.

in the *Ireland* v. *UK* case, 'the Court's judgments in fact serve not only to decide those cases brought before the Court but, more generally, to elucidate, safeguard and develop the rules instituted by the Convention thereby contributing to the observance by the States of the engagements undertaken by them as Contracting Parties (Article 19)'.[27] Thus, reference to the 'interpretative provisions' of the Vienna Convention appear to both the Commission and the Court acceptable guidelines in interpreting the Convention, with the proviso that due account be taken of relevant rules of the Council of Europe.[28] The preamble to the Statute of the Council of Europe refers not only to the 'maintenance' but also to the 'further realisation' of human rights and it can therefore be assumed that the task of the Convention organs, in particular that of the Court, is to work within the 'constitutional framework' of this organization consisting of twenty-one 'European countries which are like-minded and have a common heritage of political traditions, ideals, freedom and the rule of law' (Preamble to the Convention). It is at this point also that an affinity with European Community law may be observed. As Professor Ganshof van der Meersch (Judge at the European Court of Human Rights) has observed:

The Court in Strasbourg [like its Luxembourg counterpart] uses methods of interpretation which look at the object and aim of the Convention . . . The subject of human rights is not static. It is essentially dynamic in nature and the Contracting States have been careful to say so and to recommend that attention be paid to this fact. It is all the more irreconcilable with immobility in that many of its terms refer to extremely wide and sometimes indefinite non-legal concepts which increase the role played

[27] Eur. Court HR, case of *Ireland* v. *UK*, decision of 18 Jan. 1978, ser. A, no. 25, p. 62, para. 154. Judge Sir G. Fitzmaurice called this a 'quasi-legislative operation exceeding the normal judicial function' of the Court. See his separate opinion, para. 6. Consult also his separate opinion in the *National Union of Belgian Police* case, Eur. Court. HR, judgment of 27 Oct. 1975, ser. A, no. 19, 31-4, esp. paras. 2-10. These varying methods of interpretation vividly illustrate the restrictive approach usually adopted by the 'common law' jurist on the one hand, and his 'civil law' counterpart on the other, who tends to observe a norm from a systematic and more abstract standpoint.

[28] For a recent commentary of this subject see P. J. Duffy, 'Luedicke, Belkacem and Koç: A Discussion of the Case and of Certain Questions raised by it', **IV** *HR Rev.* (1979), 98-128, at 111-18. Duffy suggests, tentatively, that the Convention organs are evolving coherent principles for interpreting the Convention, but adds that — in the light of this instrument's law-making characteristics — art. 31-3 remain of a limited value. Also see F. G. Jacobs, *The European Convention on Human Rights* (1975), 15-20; and M. Sørensen, n. 34 below, esp. 4-7.

by case-law and, therefore, of *judge-made law*, which is chiefly to be found in internal constitutional law and in the law of international organisations.[29]

This interpretation would appear to be in accordance with the view held by Lord McNair when he spoke of the duty of an international tribunal to give effect to the expressed intention of the parties, i.e. 'their intention *as expressed in the words used by them in the light of the surrounding circumstances*'.[30] And, as the late Professor D. P. O'Connell explained in his treatise *International Law* '[Article 31(1)] embodies the literal and teleological techniques of interpretation, and by failing clearly to separate them would appear to concede that whenever a problem of interpretation arises the object of the treaty must be taken into account. No precedence is allotted to the literal interpretation.'[31] Furthermore, when one adds to the above statements the 'rider' provided by Article 5 of the Vienna Convention — to the effect that its provisions apply to agreements concluded within international organizations without prejudice to any relevant rules of the organization concerned — it follows that the Convention organs should constantly strive to give a fuller effect to the basic ideas which inspired the

---

[29] 'Questions of Common Interest which may form the subject of Exchanges of Views and Information', presented at the Sept. 1977 meeting between the organs of the European Convention and the Luxembourg Court, and reproduced in *Information on the Court of Justice of the European Communities* (1977), iii. 53–82, at 65. Consult also *Judicial and Academic Conference Reports*, Luxembourg, 27–8 Sept. (1977); and N. S. Marsh, *Interpretation in a National and International Context* (International Centre of European Studies and Research, Luxembourg, 1973). In this context it is fascinating to observe the Court's use of the terms 'effectiveness' and '*l'effet utile*' (see Eur. Court HR, case of *Klass & Others*, judgment of 6 Sept. 1978, ser. A, **28**, 18, para. 34) in the light of what H. Lauterpacht has written on this subject: 'Restrictive Interpretation and the Principle of Effectiveness in the Interpretation of Treaties', 27 *BYIL* (1949), 48–85. Also see D. Simon, *L'interprétation judiciaire des traités d'organisations internationales* (1981), 674–81.

[30] *Law of Treaties* (1961) at 365. (Emphasis original.) He goes on to say, at 367, that 'while a term may be "plain" *absolutely*, what a tribunal adjudicating upon the meaning of a treaty wants to ascertain is the meaning of the term *relatively*, that is, in relation to the circumstances in which the treaty was made, and in which the language was used'. See also I. M. Sinclair, *The Vienna Convention on the Law of Treaties* (1973), esp. 69–76.

[31] *International Law* (1970), i. 255. Also see Ch. De Visscher, *Problèmes de l'interprétation judiciaire en droit international public* (1963), *passim*. For additional studies on the Convention, see R. Barsotti, 'Tendenze evolutive nell' interpretazione della Convenzione europea dei diritti dell'uomo', 59 *Riv. DI* (1976), 268–90, R. Rosolini, 'Note sulla interpretazione della convenzione', **XVIII** *Studi Parmensi* (1977), 335–9, and P. J. Duffy, n. 28 above.

establishment of this instrument, namely the protection of the individual against wrongful interference by public authorities in the contracting states.[32]

The Convention has thus created a new type of law. It is a treaty in form rather than a treaty in substance. This instrument is not a simple contract based on reciprocity; it is a treaty of a normative character which is developing an evolving notion of 'Convention law' which interpenetrates and transcends both the international and domestic legal structures. Its organs have the rather delicate and difficult task of interpreting this 'common law'. This interpretation must in turn be made in such a way as to uphold and guarantee certain established principles in broad outline and − simultaneously − its specific effect must be varied in particular cases. Furthermore, these organs can, apart from holding certain legislative, judicial, or administrative action to be in violation of the Convention's provisions, actually find that compliance with the instrument may call for positive action by the state;[33] and in so doing they − in particular the Commission and the Court − may be transforming a multinational arrangement into a novel from of common constitutional order. Additionally, the interpretative role played by the institutions introduces an emphasis on the evolutive, dynamic, and progressive elements of this set of common legal norms which must not only keep pace with social and legal advances made within the domestic legal structures of member states, but also encourage conformity and integration (and indirectly, harmonization) of legal standards. It must be understood therefore, that the Convention cannot be interpreted in the same way as other multilateral treaties of a synallagmatic character. In effect, its organs perform a similar task to that imposed upon constitutional courts which have 'the constant task of adapting rigid standards effectively and dynamically to life's ever-changing needs'.[34] For,

---

[32] For a recent study in which the 'integrating' and 'harmonizing' role of the Council of Europe is discussed, see W. Plasa, 'L'expérience d'intégration au sein du Conseil de l'Europe', 81 *RGDIP* (1977), 667–734. Also see J. Siddle, 'The Role of the Council of Europe in the Legal Field', 2 *EL Rev.* (1977), 335–47.

[33] See Eur. Court HR, *Artico* case, judgment of 13 May 1980, ser. A, no. 35, para. 36; and *Airey* case, judgment of 9 Oct. 1979, ser. A, no. 32, 14, para. 25.

[34] Statement made by Judge Ritterspach, member of the FRG's Constitutional Court: quoted by M. Sørensen, in his excellent paper, 'Do the Rights Set Forth in the European Convention on Human Rights in 1950 have the same Significance in 1975?' presented at the *4th International Colloquy About the European Convention on Human Rights*, held in Rome, 5–8 Nov. 1975 (Strasbourg, 1976), 83–109 at 89. See also *Grundsrechtsschutz in Europa* (ed. H. Mosler, R. Bernhardt, and J. Hilf,

as Professor Evrigenis has explained:

. . . l'importance de la Convention se trouverait considérablement réduit si l'on pensait que son objectif principal est l'instauration d'un système de contrôle et de sanctions internationales pour les cas particuliers d'infraction à ses dispositions. La Convention ne fut pas conçue comme un simple mécanisme de répression. Elle est surtout un instrument de *prévention générale*. Elle doit pouvoir imposer son image aux ordres juridiques nationaux en y intégrant le degré de protection des Droits de l'Homme qu'elle consacre. Cette approche de l'ensemble de la Convention paraît mieux correspondre à la volonté de ses auteurs, à son esprit général et à sa structure. Une telle interprétation 'intégrationniste' de la Convention ferait place à la conception qui voit dans cet accord international le fondement et l'instrument de création d'un *ordre public européen*, en d'autres termes la cristallisation d'un substratum juridique essentiel à la société démocratique des pays européens.[35]

1977), 212. For an analogous example from the common-law orbit see comments made by Lord Wilberforce in the recent Privy Council case of *Minister of Home Affairs (Bermuda)* v. *Fisher* [1979] 3 All ER 21, esp. at 25-6. In his article 'The Application of the European Convention on Human Rights' Professor J. E. S. Fawcett, President of the European Commission of Human Rights, wrote '. . . the application of the Convention is not then the administration of a treaty on an international plane between the Commission, as an international body, and the state parties to the treaty. Rather it is a case of a continuing interpenetration of the Convention and the internal law and practice of the Convention countries; the provisions of the Convention are a form of transnational law.' *Transnational Law in Changing Society. Essays in honour of Philip C. Jessup* (eds. W. Friedmann, L. Henkin, and O. Lissitzin, 1972), 228-41, at 237.

[35] D. J. Evrigenis, 'Le rôle de la Convention européenne des Droits de l'Homme' in *New Perspectives for a Common Law of Europe* (ed. M. Cappelletti, 1979), 341-57, at 352-3. Professor Evrigenis is a member of the European Court of Human Rights.

Chapter 2

Determination of the Exact Obligations Imposed Upon the Parties to the Convention

A. Introductory remarks

A study of the domestic effect of international agreements such as the European Convention on Human Rights gives rise to many problems. On the one hand, it needs to be determined in which respect and to what extent there is a direct relation between constitutional law and domestic procedures and treaty law. On the other hand, it needs to be determined what consequences the binding character of such an international agreement has for the judicial and other internal organs of a contracting state.

The supremacy of an international agreement over domestic legal provisions is certainly self-evident if by this it is meant that a contracting state must conform to its agreements, but what is at issue here is the problem of ascertaining the link between the two systems of law and in particular how the former is accommodated, if at all, by domestic law, taking into consideration the *sui generis* nature of the Convention. This form of enquiry necessarily touches upon the classical doctrinal controversy between the monist and dualist theories. Both these theories in effect seek to answer the question: are international law and domestic law two separate legal systems or part of the same system? The monists, such as Kelsen, Scelle, and Lauterpacht consider that international and domestic law constitute one and the same legal order and consequently the obligations imposed by an international agreement such as the European Convention are applicable domestically *per se* and need no formal reception, i.e. the adoption of international law is automatic and direct. The dualists, of whom Triepel and Anzilotti are the most eminent exponents, consider that international law and domestic law are two completely separate legal systems and that therefore international legal obligations must be transformed by the internally competent organs in order to be applicable domestically.

They argue that the State is simultaneously a subject of international law and creator of domestic law, and that consequently
no conflict between the two systems is possible.[1]

Although both schools of thought, and variants of them,
have undoubtedly fascinated generations of legal scholars and
greatly influenced the evolution of both domestic and international law, it is perhaps idle to pursue an examination of
these problems on the theoretical plane. Instead, attention
should be directed to areas considered more relevant in practice:
namely, the position of a treaty, if any, in the hierarchy of a
given domestic legal system.[2]

As will be seen in Part II, there are numerous ways in which
international treaties are incorporated into the domestic law of
the member states of the Council of Europe. Under the so-called
method of transformation, the international rules are addressed
to the contracting states who in turn use them as a basis for the
establishment of a corresponding set of rules addressed to public
authorities, individuals, or other legal entities considered to be
subjects under domestic law. Broadly speaking, it can for present
purposes be accepted that this system is used by the UK, Ireland,
and the Scandinavian countries.

Alternatively, the constitutions of some states admit the
automatic incorporation (*validité immédiate*) of a treaty into
domestic law once the treaty has been duly approved by the
legislature and subsequently concluded. France, the Netherlands,
Austria, Luxembourg, and Switzerland appear to fall into this
category. In Austria, Parliament may additionally confer on
treaties a constitutional rank, which was in fact done in the case
of the European Convention on Human Rights. The Netherlands
Constitution permits treaty provisions — subject to a special

---

[1] There are varying interpretations of these theories, and the above summary is
by no means adequate: further reference to this debate can be found in P. Guggenheim,
Traité de droit international public (1953), i. 21–44, P. Lardy, *La force obligatoire
du droit international en droit interne* (1966), 15–34, M. Virally, 'Sur un pont aux
ânes: les rapports entre droit international et droit interne' in *Mélanges H. Rolin*
(1964), 488–505, and G. Sperduti, 'Dualism and Monism: A Confrontation to be
Overcome', 3 *IYIL* (1977), 31–49. See also P. Compte, 'The Application of the
European Convention on Human Rights in Municipal Law' IV *Journal of the ICJ*
(1962), 94–133, at 96–106. The distinction between 'transformation' and 'adoption'
is not so clear-cut in countries where different methods are employed in accommodating customary international law and treaties: see D. P. O'Connell, *International
Law* (1970), 38–79.

[2] As was done by K. Holloway in her remarkable overview of state practice in
Modern Trends in Treaty Law (1967), esp. at 105–463.

approval procedure of a two-thirds Parliamentary majority — to take precedence over provisions of the Constitution itself. The French Constitution of 1958 gives treaties a greater force than laws, although they remain subordinate to the Constitution.

A third method adopted by the Federal Republic of Germany, Italy, and Turkey is similar to the preceding method in that it consists in legislative authorization to ratify a treaty, although its force in domestic law is secured by a special Act of Parliament. In such cases — generally speaking — the effect and validity of a treaty is not considered to be derived from a provision in the Constitution itself, but in respect of it.[3]

State practice, as can be seen from the above survey, certainly reveals divergencies. Yet, surprisingly, and in spite of apparent differences and diversity of constitutional techniques employed, a fairly general pattern and degree of agreement on a number of fundamental issues can be detected. This can be observed within the context of a wider study of the relationship of states' international obligations *vis-à-vis* their respective legal systems. Thus, in many instances the possibility of a conflict between domestic legal norms and a state's obligations on the international plane has led states to adapt their constitutional law and/or domestic practice either by a revision of a written constitution or, as is more often the case, through practice based on constitutional understandings, namely, tacit approval by constitutional organs in 'accommodating' international developments.[4] Developments in Austria, Belgium, and the Netherlands, and more recently in Greece, Spain, and Portugal, illustrate this point admirably. It follows that, in spite of a great diversity in the constitutional law of states, there is revealed a striking degree of uniformity both on the international plane as well as in the domestic forums of states.

Can an individual invoke the provisions of an international agreement before a domestic court? In particular, is he able to do so if it seems probable that the creation of such a right was intended by the ratifying state organ? International legal practice seems to be settled on this point. In its famous advisory opinion in 1928, the Permanent Court of International Justice confirmed what is now deemed self-evident: '. . . an international agreement,

---

[3] See Ch. Dominicé, 'La Convention européenne des Droits de l'Homme devant le juge national', 28 *ASDI* (1972), 9–40, at 12–14.

[4] Holloway, n. 2 above, at 459. Also see L. Wildhaber *Treaty-Making Power and Constitution* (1971), *passim*, and Lardy, n. 1 above.

cannot, as such create direct rights and obligations for private individuals. But it cannot be disputed that the very object of an international agreement, according to the intention of the Contracting Parties, may be the adoption by the Parties of some definite rules creating individual rights and obligations and enforceable by the national courts.'[5]

The answer to the above question is not necessarily so simple when viewed from the standpoint of constitutional law.[6] Constitutional law and domestic procedures often differ from one state to another and as a consequence no generally applicable rule exists for all states. In most countries, however, individuals may invoke treaty provisions before domestic courts when the provisions in question are deemed self-executing. Certain provisions of a treaty are considered self-executing, i.e. capable of being directly enforceable, when and if (a) the provisions are sufficiently clear and precise that they can be regarded as addressing themselves not only to the contracting states but also to the subjects of domestic law, and (b) the institutions of the contracting parties allow for the immediate application of such provisions. This double condition is usually determined by the competent domestic tribunals with reference to existing constitutional law and practice, although it should perhaps be added that the latter condition is a *sine qua non* for the determination of the former.[7] Consequently, although an international body may declare a particular provision of a treaty as self-executing it does not follow that the same provision is necessarily self-

---

[5] *Jurisdiction of the Courts of Danzig* (Pecuniary claims of Danzig railway officials who have passed into Polish service, against the Polish railway administration), advisory opinion no. 15, PCIJ (1928), ser. B, no. 15, at 17–18.

[6] These difficulties are more than adequately brought to light by M. Waelbroeck, in his book *Traités internationaux et juridictions internes dans les pays du Marché commun* (1969), *passim.* (Examples of specific problems encountered will be provided in Part II.)

[7] See M. Sørensen, 'Obligations of a State Party to a Treaty as Regards its Municipal Law' in *Human Rights in National and International Law* (ed. A. H. Robertson, 1968), 11–31, at 23–4. Note also interventions by K. Zamanek, at 43, and F. Ermacora, at 44. See also P. De Visscher, 'Les tendances internationales des constitutions modernes', 80 *R. des C.* (1952) i. 511–79, at 559. The exact meaning of the term 'self-executing' is open to varying interpretations — now further elucidated/complicated(?) by the distinction made in European Community law where certain 'directly applicable' norms may have 'direct effect' upon individuals. Thus, the above explanation is provided in simplified form and *no* attempt is made to embark upon an in-depth analysis of this complex problem. For a recent discussion on this subject see J. Verhoeven, 'La Notion d'"applicabilité directe" du droit international', *RBDI* (1980), 243–64.

executing within a given state's domestic legal system. This contradiction shows clearly that case-law has not as yet clarified this problem and, as Professor Brownlie has rightly pointed out, '[t]he whole subject resists generalization, and the practice of states reflects [in the final analysis] the characteristics of the individual constitution'.[8]

It is therefore quite clear that the direct operation and penetration of international legal norms within the domestic forum, in the vast field of international agreements, is regulated in most cases by express constitutional provisions. This state of affairs does not result from the disability of treaty provisions to be directly applicable to individuals in domestic law, but due rather to the division and separation of powers within states. In all the member states of the Council of Europe the Executive's power to negotiate, sign, and ratify treaties is conditioned upon constitutional principles which specify that the Executive is not competent to enact or modify legislation. As already noted, in some countries treaty provisions are 'transformed' by Parliament into internal law while in others 'legislative approval' to ratify is sought; the latter, when obtained, has the effect of suspending prior inconsistent legislation — and also in some cases even subsequent inconsistent statutory enactments — although *substantively* the approval is not as such law. Further complications may arise in those countries where there exists a domestic legal hierarchical structure into which international treaty norms have to be accommodated by domestic courts and tribunals, either via 'general principles of law' or by interpretations favouring 'direct application'. Consequently, the *effective* validity of treaties both on the international and domestic planes is dependent simultaneously upon their observance internationally as well as the Executive's compliance with certain constitutional limitations placed upon it internally. It follows that although it is certainly true to say that the above-described situation may signify the weakness of international law, it does not necessarily deprive it of its potentiality of direct operation within domestic law.[9] Likewise, the fact that certain provisions of international agreements possess the

---

[8] *Principles of Public International Law* (1979), at 53.

[9] Cf. H. Lauterpacht, *International Law*, in *The General Works* (ed. E. Lauterpacht, 1970), i. 286. See also A. A. Cançado Trindade, 'Exhaustion of Local Remedies in International Law and the Role of National Courts', **17** *Archiv des Völkerrechts* (1978), 333–70, at 365.

potential ingredients for domestic courts to refer to them does not necessarily mean that the said provisions may or should be used by domestic courts in their judgments.

The above discussion illustrates the problems encountered in the complex interrelationship between international treaty norms and domestic law including the difficulties in accommodating various meanings of 'direct applicability' and 'self-execution'; these no doubt have been further accentuated by the necessity of noting the specific characteristics of 'Convention law'. In effect what now has to be questioned, in the light of the information provided above, is whether Professor Teitgen's assertion that the above passage extracted from the advisory opinion of the Permanent Court in the *Danzig Railway* case[10] must apply, *mutatis mutandis*, to the Convention as '[t]his is quite certainly what was intended by those responsible for drafting the European Convention'.[11] If this were true, member states could well be *legally* bound to incorporate this instrument's substantive provisions into their respective legal systems.

B. Divergent legal opinions

Although the states parties to the Convention are under an obligation to ensure that their domestic law conforms to the provisions of the Convention, there appears to be a divergence of legal opinion as to whether or not they are free to do so in a way which is considered most appropriate to them. In other words, are the states parties under an international obligation to accord the Convention the status of domestic law?[12]

Discussion has centred on two specific articles: Article 1, which reads:

The High Contracting Parties shall secure to everyone within their jurisdiction the rights and freedoms defined in Section I of this Convention;

[10] n. 5 above.

[11] 'The European Guarantee of Human Rights: A Political Assessment' in *Proceedings of the 4th International Colloquy about the European Convention on Human Rights*, Rome, 5–8 Nov. 1975 (Strasbourg 1976), 29–45, at 39.

[12] For a virtually exhaustive list of differing views on this subject consult *Bibliography*, at 91–4. Provisions of an international agreement have domestic status, for the purposes of this study, if domestic courts can refer to them in cases brought before them, and consider them as legally binding norms. The phrase 'domestic status' therefore encompasses both situations in which the Convention is deemed directly applicable or self-executing, and those in which it has been incorporated into domestic law.

Les Hautes Parties Contractantes reconnaissent à toute personne relevant de leur juridiction des droits et libertés définis au Titre I de la présente Convention;

and Article 13, which stipulates:

Everyone whose rights and freedoms as set forth in this Convention are violated shall have an effective remedy before a national authority notwithstanding that the violation has been committed by persons acting in an official capacity;

Toute personne dont les droits et libertés reconnus dans la présente Convention ont été violés, a droit à l'octroi d'un recours effectif devant une instance nationale alors même que la violation aurait été commise par des personnes agissant dans l'exercice de leurs fonctions officielles.

When this question first came up for discussion at an International Colloquy held in Strasbourg in November 1960, Mr. Süsterhenn in his report entitled 'L'application de la Convention sur le plan du droit interne'[13] suggested that the precise and mandatory formulation of the majority of the provisions enumerated in Section I of the Convention, and their (in his opinion) clear demonstration of an intent to grant directly enforceable (self-executing) rights to individuals, left no doubt that Article 13 . . . *'contient une obligation pour tout État contractant d'incorporer les règles normatives de la Convention dans son droit interne'*.[14] He went on to explain that when the draft statute of the European Political Community was considered by an *ad hoc* Commission under the presidency of the then Minister of Foreign Affairs of the Federal Republic of Germany, there was included a formal and express provision to the effect that the Convention would form an 'integral part' of the proposed statute of the Community. Professor Pelloux was of the same opinion.[15] *'On doit . . . estimer que les dispositions relatives à la reconnaissance des libertés sont directement applicables en droit interne pour les États qui l'ont ratifiée: cette thèse peut invoquer en sa faveur le texte de l'article 1, et surtout de l'article 13, ainsi que les travaux préparatoires de la Convention.'*

[13] A. Süsterhenn, *rapport* published in *La protection internationale des Droits de l'Homme dans le cadre européen* (Council of Europe and Faculty of Law, University of Strasbourg, 1961), 303–7.
[14] Ibid., at 318.
[15] M. R. Pelloux, 'Précédents, Caractères généraux de la Convention Européenne' in *La Protection internationale des Droits de l'Homme dans le cadre européen* (1961), 59–69, at 64–5.

However, Dr Vasak, after an analysis of the arguments put forward to support the contention of an implied duty upon states to accord the Convention domestic status — and studying in particular the legal basis of Article 13 — considered that the above arguments did not appear convincing.[16] Dr Vasak agreed that, in the drawing up of the Convention the member states of the Council of Europe had intended to create rights and freedoms for the benefit of the individual, but this assurance was, above all else, to be guaranteed on the international plane. There was no doubt that the Convention provided for the individual a guarantee of enumerated rights on the international juridical plane, even though the individual himself could be barred from petitioning the European Commission of Human Rights by a state's non-acceptance of the Article 25 optional declaration. He explained that it did not follow that the Convention consequently provided necessarily to an individual rights enforceable in the domestic legal order: in effect, due to the present state of international law and the resultant 'veritable hiatus' between the two planes of law — municipal and international — the mere intentions of treaty makers — barring the express acceptance of such provisions by the contracting parties — could not in itself suffice.[17]

Conformément au droit des traités un État, qui a ratifié une convention internationale, s'il est tenu de l'exécuter peut le faire en utilisant les *moyens appropriés dont le choix est laissé à sa discrétion.* Dans le cas de la Convention de Rome, peut-on soutenir que ses auteurs ont voulu imposer aux États contractants *le* moyen précis permettant d'assurer son exécution, à savoir son incorporation dans le droit interne? Il ne le semble pas: un État, dont le droit interne assurait, déjà avant la ratification, la protection des droits énumérés dans la Convention, respecte les engagements qui résultent pour lui de la ratification tout aussi bien qu'un État dans lequel la Convention constitue une source directe du droit interne, et est appliquée comme telle par les tribunaux nationaux.

Dr Vasak then went on to conclude that the ambit of European human rights law is and remains that of 'European states' and not of 'Europeans' since the Rome Convention is not accorded the status of domestic law in all states signatories.[18]

---

[16] K. Vasak, 'L'application des Droits de l'Homme et des libertés fondamentales par les juridictions nationales (Article 13 de la Convention européenne des Droits de l'Homme)' in *Droit Communautaire et Droit National* (Semaine de Bruges, 1965), 335–50, at 339. Consult also Vasak's *Convention européenne des Droits de l'Homme* (1964), esp. 232–5.   [17] Ibid., at 339. (Emphasis original.)
[18] Ibid., at 350.

In his study of the Convention's status within the domestic
legal orders of the then fourteen contracting states, Philippe
Compte treated this problem indirectly when he posed himself
the question: do the provisions of the European Convention
form part of their municipal law? He found the answer to be
negative in the case of three states and affirmative for six.[19]
Although he considered that the provisions of the Convention
are on the whole sufficiently precise to be capable of immediate
application he disagreed with Süsterhenn that all of Section I
and Articles 1 and 2 of the First Protocol could be considered
self-executing, valid as this formula may be in German law, and
considered that this question (or rather the question of the
individual being able to avail himself of the Convention's
provisions domestically) must be considered separately for each
article and each country.[20]

Arguing on the premiss that the rights and freedoms in Section
I of the European Convention on Human Rights were so fundamental as to be capable of creating rights and duties directly
enforceable in domestic courts, Dr Golsong has reasoned that
the legislative history, or *travaux préparatoires* of the Convention
support the conclusion that the Convention was drafted, with
an aim *inter alia* of achieving for itself domestic legal status.[21]
In his Hague Academy lectures, after quoting Article 13 of the
Convention, Dr Golsong went on to say:[22]

. . . Article 13 requires an *effective* recourse without giving any indication
whether the authority called upon to decide on the recourse should be a
'court of law' or any other judicial, administrative or even parliamentary
authority. However, a recourse can only be effective if the decision reached
is binding upon all the authorities of the State concerned. If that is the
case, the decision should be based upon *existing domestic law*, as otherwise
State authorities are not legally bound to respect it. There seems to be,
therefore, a question of an international obligation being put upon *all*
Contracting States, by virtue of Article 13 of the Convention, to transform

[19] Ph. Compte, 'The Application of the European Convention on Human Rights in
Municipal Law', **IV** *Journal of the ICJ* (1962), 94–129, at 107. He could not come to
a definite conclusion with regard to the remaining five, in that precise information
relating to the solutions adopted by them was not available at the time. Today the
ratio stands at 7:14.   [20] Ibid., at 117–19.
[21] H. Golsong, *Das Rechtsschutzsystem der Europäischen Menschenrechtskonvention* (1958), at 9.
[22] Golsong, 'Implementation of International Protection of Human Rights', **110**
R. des C. (1963) ii. 101–50, at 138–9. (Emphasis original.) Compare this statement
to the author's prior, more restrained approach: 'The European Convention on Human
Rights before Domestic Courts', 38 *BYIL* (1962), 445–56, at 455–6. See also n. 27
below, esp. 64–5.

into domestic law those provisions of the Convention which grant rights and freedoms to the individual.

Although the question of the relationship between the European Convention on Human Rights and domestic law was examined at some length at the Second International Conference on the European Convention on Human Rights held in Vienna in October 1965, especially in the reports of Professors Sørensen, Verdross, and Ganshof van der Meersch,[23] it is somewhat surprising to find no general agreement with regard to the particular problem under discussion. For example, Ganshof van der Meersch and Velu, both referred to the *travaux préparatoires* to support the thesis that there exists a legally imposed duty upon the contracting parties to incorporate the Convention into domestic law.[24] Professor Sørensen, on the other hand, defended the theory which allows the contracting states to secure the conformity of their domestic law with international obligations in a way which to them appears most appropriate.[25] Verdross, in turn, argued that although in principle states are free to determine how an international treaty shall be implemented, a treaty itself may prescribe the manner in which this is to be done. He then referred to Article 13 of the European Convention and deduced from it that a right to a remedy mentioned therein presupposes that the individual provisions of the Convention have become an integral part of domestic law: 'Article 13 therefore indirectly enjoins Contracting States to incorporate the various provisions of the Convention into their municipal law in such a way that they can be applied directly by domestic courts and administrative authorities.'[26] He claimed that the

---

[23] The proceedings of the Vienna Conference were published in *Human Rights in National and International Law* (ed. A. H. Robertson, 1968). The three reports are on 11, 47, and 97.

[24] J. W. Ganshof van der Meersch, ibid., n. at 101, and J. Velu, ibid., 44-6. See also Ganshof van der Meersch's *Organisations Européennes* (1966), 362-70. This author has in fact recently taken a more pragmatic approach to this subject: 'Aspects de la mise en œuvre d'une sauvegarde collective des Droits de l'Homme en droit international – la Convention européenne' in *Mélanges F. Dehousse* (1979), I. 193-208, at 197-9.

[25] M. Sørensen, 'Obligations of a State Party to a Treaty as regards its Municipal Law' in *Human Rights in National and International Law* (ed. A. H. Robertson, 1968), 11-31. Similar views have recently been expressed by Professor D. J. Evrigenis; 'Le rôle de la Convention européenne des Droits de l'Homme' in *New Perspectives for a Common Law of Europe* (ed. M. Cappelletti, 1978), 341-57.

[26] A. Verdross, 'Status of the European Convention in the hierarchy of the rules of law', in Robertson, ibid., 47-56, at 51. See also Verdross's *Völkerrecht* (1964), 144 ff.

Convention takes precedence over municipal law of the states parties, which are obliged to make their domestic law conform to its provisions. He added that he did not consider it necessary for the Convention's provisions to be transplanted verbatim into the domestic legal structures of the contracting states and instead laid stress on the elements of compatibility of domestic legislation with the Convention's provisions.

In a relatively recent article entitled 'L'effet direct, ainsi que le rang en droit interne, des normes de la Convention européenne des droits de l'homme et des décisions prises par les organes institués par celle-ci',[27] Dr Golsong suggested that not only should the provisions of the Convention be included as an integral part of the legal systems of member states, but that this instrument apparently *requires* them to give the Convention's norms priority — on the domestic plane — over both anterior and subsequent inconsistent legislation: *'Si nous rapprochons la pratique nationale . . ., il semble que seule l'Autriche ait rempli correctement l'obligation à charge de tout État contractant de donner plein effet, en droit interne, aux dispositions convention-nelles qui sont self-executing.'*[28] This observation may, however, be read in the light of what Mr Sam Silkin, the then UK Attorney-General, said on this subject. In a lecture delivered at Queen's University, Belfast, in April 1976, he noted that 'It is arguable that by virtue of Article 13 all states party to the Convention are under a duty to provide for the complaints of violation to be determined before their existing courts or before some special human rights court or commission. It must be conceded, however, that if we [the UK] are in default under the Article, so also are many other states party to the Convention.'[29]

Even more recently, Professors Sperduti and Opsahl, both members of the European Commission, considered that there was no legal duty for states to incorporate the Convention into

[27] Published in *Les recours des individus devant les instances nationales en cas de violation du droit européen*, Colloquium organized by *l'Institut d'Études Européennes*, Brussels, 24-5 Apr. 1975 (1978), 59-83.

[28] H. Golsong, ibid., at 77, para. 13. The UK Government, in its written submissions in relation to art. 1 of the Convention, in the case of *Ireland* v. *UK* (doc. Cour (77)9 of 31 Apr. 1977, at 31), commented on this point: 'It would be bizarre indeed if the true position were, as Dr Golsong has suggested, that seventeen of the eighteen States parties were in breach of their obligation (which he derives from art. 13) effectively to implement the normative provisions of the Convention . . .'

[29] S. Silkin, 'The Rights of Man and the Rule of Law', 28 *Northern Ireland Legal Quarterly* (1977), 3-20, at 13.

domestic law;[30] although according to Opsahl, whereas there exists no express stipulation to secure the Convention's rights verbatim into internal law, there certainly does exist — under Article 13 — a duty to secure remedies to anyone who wishes to have his rights *examined*.[31] This view is supported by Jean Raymond, Deputy Secretary to the European Commission of Human Rights, who would even go further: apart from finding that Article 13 may possess a substantive 'autonomous' existence analogous to that of Article 14, he goes on to say that 'States Party are obliged by Article 13 to provide a remedy in domestic law against violations committed by private persons or by public authorities'.[32] This being said, he then refers to recent case-law of both the Commission and the Court in order to substantiate the view that Article 13 does not appear to impose a clear obligation on states to incorporate its substantive provisions into domestic law.[33]

Probably the most forceful arguments supporting the proposition that the states parties are required to give the Convention the status of domestic law have been put forward by Professor Buergenthal: 'the real significance of the Convention derives from the fact that by adhering to it the High Contracting Parties assumed two interrelated obligations. They undertook to implement the Convention within their respective jurisdictions to make it a part of their domestic law, and they pledged that an aggrieved individual "shall have an effective remedy before a national authority" to enforce the rights guaranteed in the Convention.'[34] A simplified version of his arguments can be

---

[30] G. Sperduti, 'Sur la garantie par les ordres juridiques internes des droits reconnus dans la Convention européenne des Droits de l'Homme' in *Mélanges F. Dehousse* (1979), 1. 227–30, at 227; T. Opsahl, 'Human Rights Today: International Obligations and National Implementation', 23 *Scandinavian Studies in Law* (1979), 149–76, at 159–62.

[31] Namely, the rights guaranteed by the Convention, Opsahl, ibid., at 162. As to whether an individual can be considered a 'victim' before the law which is contrary to the Convention has been applied to him, see Eur. Court HR, Case of *Klass and Others*, judgment of 6 Sept. 1978; and P. J. Duffy, 'The Case of Klass and Others: Secret Surveillance of Communications and the European Convention on Human Rights', IV *HR Rev.* (1979), 20–40, esp. at 29–33.

[32] 'A Contribution to the Interpretation of Article 13 of the European Convention on Human Rights', V *HR Rev.* (1980), 161–75, at 170. (The subject of *Drittwirkung* will be treated at length in ch. 8 below.)

[33] Ibid., at 172.

[34] T. Buergenthal, 'The Domestic Status of the European Convention on Human Rights: A Second Look', 7 *Journal of the ICJ* (1966), 55–96, at 59.

stated as follows: the Convention's provisions were intentionally drafted in clear and precise statutory language to permit its direct incorporation into domestic law because its draftsmen assumed that the 'remedy' referred to in Article 13 of the Convention can be truly effective only if it is assured promptly by domestic tribunals which must in consequence, be directly bound by its provisions. Consequently, the failure of a state to enact the Convention into domestic law is a breach of its treaty obligations.[35]

The actual wording of Article 13 does not help to clarify the above differences of opinion; in fact its exact meaning is difficult to determine with any precision. The word 'remedy' in the English version suggests reparation of redress for a breach, while the French meaning of *'recours'* tends to lay emphasis on the procedural possibility of bringing a case before a higher instance, i.e. the possibility of alleging a breach. Is it therefore sufficient to be provided a process by which the issue can be determined or must there be reparation for the breach? Although the text was originally drafted in English, the Convention organs appear to favour an interpretation more in line with the French text.[36] It also seems rather difficult to reconcile the meaning of 'violation' with that of 'alleged violation' especially within the context of breaches found by the European Court of Human Rights and the Committee of Ministers. More important still in the light of the present discussion: is it not difficult to reconcile the view — once it is accepted that 'violation' means a breach alleged by a complainant pursuing a remedy in domestic law — that the Convention may still not have to be incorporated when the said complainant claims a breach thereof?[37]

---

[35] See T. Buergenthal, 'The Effect of the European Convention on Human Rights on the Internal Law of Member States', *ICLQ* Supp. no. 11 (1965), 79–106, esp. 80–3. An excellent criticism of the views held by Buergenthal (and others) is made by R. Beddard, 'The Status of the European Convention on Human Rights in Domestic Law', 16 *ICLQ* (1967), 206–17. See also P. Mertens, *Le droit de recours effectif devant les instances nationales en cas de violation d'un droit de l'homme* (1973), esp. 142–8, and his 'Le droit à un recours effectif devant l'autorité nationale compétente dans les conventions internationales relatives à la protection des droits de l'homme' in *La protection internationale des droits de l'homme* (Institute of Sociology, Brussels University, 1977), 65–90.

[36] See, for example, the *Klass* case, and comments by Duffy, n. 31 above. Also see Raymond, n. 32 above, *passim*; and J. E. S. Fawcett, *The Application of the European Convention on Human Rights* (1969), at 227–32.

[37] Alternatively, art. 13 may simply be a badly drafted *auxiliary* article which is meant to be read in conjunction with 'measures required' in art. 32(4) and 'reparation' envisaged in art. 50. See Fawcett, ibid., at 229; also 'editorial note' in I *HR Rev.*

C. Recourse to '*travaux préparatoires*'

Can the *travaux préparatoires* shed some light on the debate as to whether there exists a legal duty to incorporate the Convention's substantive provisions into the domestic law of contracting states?

The *travaux préparatoires* contain various documents which were used during the drafting of the European Convention on Human Rights and its First Protocol. They include reports of discussions in the Consultative Assembly (now renamed as Parliamentary Assembly) and its committee on legal and administrative questions, in the Committee of Ministers and certain of its committees of experts. These materials were published in 1961-4 in a roneoed edition which remained confidential and could only be referred to by the governments, the Commission, and the Court. However, authorization to publish this collection was obtained in 1972 and to date five of the proposed eight volumes of these documents have been published.[38]

It is, however, unlikely that the publication of the *travaux préparatoires* will shed light on the above discussions. Preparatory work of this type does not appear to constitute an authoritative interpretation of the Convention and is notoriously unreliable as a general guide to treaty interpretation — hence its positioning in the Vienna Convention as a 'supplementary means of interpretation'.[39]

Additionally, as pointed out by Professor Robertson (the former Director of the Human Rights Directorate of the Council of Europe and member of the Council's Secretariat at the time of the Convention's drafting):

... the whole problem of the direct application of the Convention in internal law was (so far as one can tell) not considered by those who drafted it in 1950. The countries which have been most concerned with this problem are Germany and Austria; neither was a member of the Council of Europe in the Spring of 1950. The amendment of the Constitution of the Netherlands (Articles 65-67) only dates from 1956. There is no evidence that any

(1976), 74; and dissenting opinion of Mr Fawcett in applications 7151/75 and 7152/75, *Sporring and Lönnroth* v. *Sweden*, report of Commission, 8 Oct. 1980, at 67-71. (This case is now pending before the Court in Strasbourg.)

   [38] *Collected Editions of the Travaux Préparatoires of the European Convention on Human Rights.* See introduction to 1 (1975).

   [39] See F. G. Jacobs, *The European Convention on Human Rights* (1975), 18. See also report of Commission, Eur. Court HR, ser. B, no. 16, *Golder* (1975), esp. 33-42, and N. S. Marsh, *Interpretation in a National and International Context* (1973), esp. 78-82.

serious thought was given to this matter by the authors of the Convention.[40]

A brief examination of the *travaux préparatoires* would seem to confirm Professor Robertson's views.

While presenting a report on behalf of the Committee on Legal and Administrative Questions to the Council of Europe's Consultative Assembly in 1949, Mr Teitgen, as rapporteur, observed that a list of rights and freedoms was drawn up by the Committee on the basis of the established principle of international law according to which each state is left the right to secure in its own way domestic efficacy of the guaranteed freedoms. In the debate which followed, he emphasized that states parties would be provided a very wide freedom of action in defining the practical conditions for the operation of the proposed list of guaranteed liberties.[41]

A draft Convention was then forwarded to the Committee of Ministers. The Committee of Ministers in turn appointed a committee of governmental experts to look into the Assembly's proposals. As a result a large part of the detailed drafting work was done by this intergovernmental committee early in 1950. Unfortunately, however, although the published *travaux préparatoires* include the various proposals considered by the committee of experts, and the two alternative draft texts of the Convention which emerged from their work, there is no record of the detailed discussions which preceded the adoption of the drafts. This is certainly regrettable in that two of the proposals set out in one of the drafts were later accepted — with certain modifications — as Articles 1 and 57 of the Convention. It appears that these proposals also included a draft provision on the basis of which Article 13 was eventually moulded. This being said, it can be noted that in the committee of experts, meeting in February and March 1950, the UK delegate proposed that Articles 4 to 7 of the recommendation made by the Consultative Assembly be replaced by three articles which, after some alterations and adoptions, became Articles 1, 13, 57, and 15 of the Convention. Here only the first proposed Article is considered:[42]

[40] A. H. Robertson, 'Advisory Opinions of the Court of Human Rights' in *Cassin*, i. 225–40, at 239.

[41] Doc. 77 of the Consultative Assembly, *Coll. Ed. of Travaux Préparatoires* (1975), i. 222, and 230.

[42] Proposals of the UK expert, Sir Oscar Dawson. Cf. *Coll. Ed. of Travaux Préparatoires* (1976), i. 188, and 280. See also R. Beddard, 'The Status of the European

(1) Each State party hereto undertakes to ensure to all individuals within its jurisdiction the rights defined in the Convention. Every deposit of an instrument of access shall be accompanied by a solemn declaration made by the Government of the State concerned with full and complete effect as given by the law of that State of the provisions of the Convention.

(2) Each State party hereto undertakes to ensure:

(a) that any person whose rights and freedoms as defined are violated shall have an effective remedy notwithstanding that the violation has been committed by persons acting in an official capacity;

(b) that any person claiming such a remedy shall have his rights hereto determined by national tribunals whose independence is secured; and

(c) that the police and executive authorities shall enforce such remedies when granted.

The States party hereto declare that they recognise the rights and freedoms set forth in Article 2 hereof, as being among the Human Rights and fundamental freedoms founded on the general principles of law recognized by civilised nations.

The extent to which this proposal apparently influenced the subsequent draft proposals becomes clearer upon an examination of the Committee's preliminary draft Convention of 9 March 1950 and the subsequent final draft of 16 March 1950, both of which provided alternatives, one based on the system of simple enumeration of rights and freedoms and the other on the system of precise definitions of the rights and freedoms.[43]

After considering the report of the committee of experts, the Council of Ministers convened a meeting of senior officers (the Committee of Senior Officials) who prepared a draft Convention incorporating a greater part of the drafts proposed by the committee of legal experts. In its report the Committee of Senior Officials 'considered unanimously that it was useless (*inutile*) to insert into the Convention a solemn declaration by which member states parties would be obliged to give the Convention's provisions full effect in their domestic legal systems'. It was presumed that full effect would be given to the Convention's provisions when a state ratifies the instrument, and in cases where this was deemed impossible, there was included a proposal to the effect that reservations could be made with regard to certain domestic law not in conformity with a particular

Convention on Human Rights in Domestic Law', **16** *ICLQ* (1967), 206–17, and
J. E. S. Fawcett, *The Application of the European Convention on Human Rights* (1969), 227–9.

[43] Cf. CM/WP 1 (15) 14, pp. 1 and 8; and CM/WP 1 (50)15 app., pp. 1, 2, 4, 5.

provision of the Convention.[44] Thus, the following drafts of what eventually concretized into Articles 1 and 13 of the Convention were annexed to the report of the Committee of Senior Officials and forwarded to the Committee of Ministers:

Article 1. The High Contracting Parties undertake to secure to all individuals within their jurisdiction the rights and freedoms defined in Section II of the Convention.

Article 15. The High Contracting Parties undertake to secure that any person whose rights and freedoms herein defined are violated shall have an effective remedy before a national authority notwithstanding that the violation has been committed by persons acting in an official capacity.[45]

To argue that the above proposals provide sufficient 'evidence' to suggest that their drafters intended to impose a clear obligation upon member states requiring them to incorporate the Convention's provisions into their respective legal systems would appear to be rather difficult, to say the least. What does, however, seem clear is that the preparatory work lacks any summary of the debate — if there had at all been such a debate — as to the nature, content, and scope of Articles 1 and 15 of the draft Convention annexed to the Committee's report.

The Committee of Ministers considered the report of the Committee of Senior Officials together with the observations of the Consultative Assembly's legal committee. One of the proposals of the Assembly's legal committee may perhaps be noted: in order to avoid any misunderstanding as to the legal scope of Article 1 of the Convention, the committee considered it desirable that the words 'undertake to secure' be replaced by 'hereby secure'. This originated in a proposal put forward by Mr Rolin. The reasons given for this proposed change were explained in a letter from the chairman of the committee forwarded to the Committee of Ministers:

---

[44] Cf. *Coll. Ed. of Travaux Préparatoires*, **iv**.

[45] Cf. CM/WP 4(50)19, app., pp. 2, 8. It should perhaps be noted that in the report of the senior officials — at p. 14 — special mention was made of the positioning of draft art. 15 (which closely resembled its final form as art. 13): 'This is a question of the right to bring cases before national courts in respect of the rights protected in this Convention. This Article should therefore be placed after the Articles defining these rights'. Thus, it may be suggested that this article deals only with internal remedies rather than with the problem of international collective guarantee. But see further on this subject J. Raymond, 'A Contribution to the Interpretation of Article 13 of the European Convention on Human Rights', **V** *HR Rev.* (1980), 161–75.

. . . the [Legal] Committee [of the Consultative Assembly] however, considers that, in order to avoid any misunderstanding as to the legal scope of the Convention, it would be desirable that the words 'undertake to secure' be replaced by the words 'hereby secure' in respect of the attitude of the High Contracting Parties towards the rights and freedoms enumerated in Section II of the Convention; for the former phrasing appears to imply for each of them a separate action apart from the simple acceptance of the Convention.[46]

Finally, however, upon the suggestion of the UK delegate, the phrase 'shall secure' was chosen by the Committee of Ministers. A revised text of the draft Convention was then submitted to the Assembly. This was again considered by its legal committee whose report was approved by the Assembly. The final text of Article 1 — as amended by the Committee of Ministers — with the exception of a subsequent change made by the Secretariat General of the phrase 'each person' to that of 'everyone', as well as the final draft of Article 13 did not give rise to any discussion in the Assembly and were adopted on 25 August 1950 without amendment in Recommendation 24. The debate at the Assembly's session seems to have clarified at least one ambiguity: the reasons given by Mr Teitgen when he explained why the Assembly's original draft of the Convention was replaced by a list of precisely defined rights and freedoms did *not* include argument supporting the view that the drafters apparently intended to impose upon the contracting parties an obligation to incorporate the Convention's provisions into domestic law. A change of approach was accepted by the Committee of Ministers at the request of the United Kingdom experts who simply preferred the instrument to contain a series of more precise definitions rather than having it couched in broad terms of general principles.[47] The Convention was eventually signed on 4 November 1950 substantially in the same form as it was approved by the Consultative Assembly.

[46] Doc. CM(50)29, 2. At the plenary sitting on 25 Aug. 1950, Mr Rolin was presumably under the mistaken belief that the acceptance of his amendment 'shall recognize' would have the effect of incorporating this instrument — bodily and of its own right— into domestic law of contracting states. See Assembly doc. 1950, III, 914. This view was and still is of course correct in so far as Belgian law is concerned, although *not necessarily* true for other countries: this has been explained in sec. A of this chapter. See also H. Golsong, n. 27 above, esp. at 62, and *Ireland* v. *UK*, Eur. Court HR, judgment of 18 Jan. 1978, ser. A, no. 25, at 90–91, para. 239.

[47] Cf. H. Teitgen, 2nd Session of Consultative Assembly, 16 Aug. 1950 (to be published in *Coll. Ed. of Travaux Préparatoires*, **vi**.). See also Buergenthal, notes 34-5 above, and Beddard, n. 42 above, at 210.

The determination of the disputed meaning of any provision or provisions of the Convention is necessarily open to subjective appreciations which cannot be considered as totally extraneous to the task of interpretation. Consequently, as was pointed out by the Commission in its report in the *Golder* case, the meaning of a text may often be influenced by a particular way of reading what supports the result one wants to reach for other reasons: what one finds in a given text often depends on what one is looking for. The determination of whether or not the contracting states are under an *international* obligation to accord the Convention the status of domestic law is similarly exposed to diverse interpretations, as the above references to the doctrinal debate have illustrated. An apparent lacuna exists in the *travaux préparatoires* since this particular point does not seem to have been adequately (if at all) debated. As a consequence, obvious questions arise: if there would have been general agreement on the need to provide legal effect to the instrument in all member states, why was this not explained, in a clear and simple way? And why did not all the ratifying member states react accordingly? It appears that Professor Fawcett, a member and former President of the European Commission of Human Rights, has correctly interpreted the situation in observing that:

The Convention has left it to each contracting State to secure in its own way domestic efficacy for the provisions of Section I. A requirement that a contracting State must incorporate these provisions in terms into its domestic law is not clearly evidenced either by the terms of the Convention itself, or the preparatory work, or the subsequent practice of the parties. Articles 5(5) and 13, it is true, point towards incorporation of Section I into domestic law, but they do not necessitate it and are . . . difficult to interpret with any certainty on this point.[48]

Subsequent state practice as well as findings of the European Commission and Court of Human Rights appear to confirm this view.

[48] J. E. S. Fawcett, *The Application of the European Convention on Human Rights* (1969), 4; F. Castberg, (former Norwegian member of the Commission) agrees: *The European Convention on Human Rights* (1973), 13-14. Note similar problems in the UN: W. C. Jenks, 'The United Nations Covenant on Human Rights comes to Life' in *Études de droit international en hommage à Paul Guggenheim* (1968), 805-13, at 812.

Conclusions to Part I

Two observations of a general character probably require emphasis:

1. An overview of obligations assumed by the parties to the Convention suggests that the classical distinction between international agreements and domestic law which is based upon the different functions that they are respectively meant to perform in society does not apply in this instance. The European Convention on Human Rights possesses some unique features which are difficult to classify in terms of traditional international law; for, as the European Court of Human Rights has explained in the *Ireland* v. *UK* case: 'Unlike international treaties of the classic kind, the Convention comprises more than mere reciprocal engagements between contracting States. It creates over and above a network of mutual, bilateral undertakings, objective obligations which, in the words of the preamble, benefit from a "collective enforcement".'[1] In many instances the Convention has acquired, with the passing of time, a new meaning which creates the need for an evolutive method of interpretation by the Convention organs so that — to use the late Judge Sørensen's phraseology — there is introduced 'an element of dynamism and progress to keep pace with general social change'.[2] In short, stress is placed on the fact that the Convention is a 'law-making' and 'living instrument' whose basic purpose is to protect individual liberty, promote the rule of law, and prevent the arbitrary use of power; the Convention organs being endowed with the function of safeguarding *'l'ordre public de l'Europe'* occasionally 'accelerating' the harmonious evolution of European standards.[3]

---

[1] Para. 239. This extract was cited in ch. 1, n. 13. Also see the Court's judgments in the *Marckx* case, para. 58, and the *Deweer* case, para. 49 (referred to in ch. 1, sec. B).

[2] M. Sørensen, 'Do the Rights set forth in the European Convention on Human Rights in 1950 have the same significance in 1975?' in *Proceedings of the 4th International Colloquy about the European Convention on Human Rights*, Rome, 5–8 Nov. 1975 (Strasbourg, 1976), 83–109, at 89.

[3] See ch. 1 above, sec. B, *passim*, also Judge Zekia's observations in *The Sunday Times* case, Eur. Court HR, judgment of 26 Apr. 1979, ser. A, vol. 30, 58–66, at 63–4; and in the *Wemhoff* case, Eur. Court HR, judgment of 27 June 1968, ser. A, 7, 35–40, at 38.

2. There exists *no* legal obligation for member states to incorporate the substantive provisions of the Convention into domestic law. Both the Commission and Court appear to accept this proposition to be correct. Thus, for example, in the *Swedish Engine Drivers* case the Court stated unequivocally: '. . . neither Article 13 nor the Convention in general lays down for the Contracting States any given manner for ensuring within their internal law the effective implementation of any of the provisions of the Convention.'[4]

Similarly, in a memorial filed before the Court by the Commission's vice-president and principal delegate, Professor Sperduti, in the case of *Ireland* v. *UK* it was observed that:

. . . the Convention does not formally require Contracting States to incorporate it in their domestic legal systems or to give it a certain position in the hierarchy of sources of domestic law. States are in principle free to choose the means which suit them best for ensuring the effective enjoyment of the rights and freedoms set forth in the Convention. It is, among other things, conceivable that their legal systems, particularly their constitutions, should even go beyond the requirements of the Convention. In any event it must be said that because men live under the sway of domestic law it is domestic law which should ensure for them, through its rules, principles and institutions, the effective enjoyment of the benefits which an international instrument affords them.[5]

Although the European Court of Human Rights had the opportunity to settle this point definitively in its judgment in this case, its approach was rather more subtle and indirect: 'By substituting the words "shall secure" for the words "undertake to secure" in the text of Article 1, the drafters of the Convention [also] intended to make it clear that the rights and freedoms set out in Section 1 would be directly secured to anyone within the jurisdiction of the Contracting States . . . That intention finds a particularly faithful reflection in those instances where the Convention has been incorporated into domestic law.'[6] It is

---

[4] Eur. Court HR, judgment of 6 Feb. 1976, ser. A, vol. 20, 18, para. 50. Also see *Belgian Linguistic* case, judgment of 23 July 1968, ser. A, 6, 35, para. 10; and *Handyside* case, judgment of 29 Apr. 1976, ser. A, 24, 22, para. 48.

[5] Doc. Cour (77)24. Memorial filed on 22 Apr. 1977 on art. 1 of the Convention, para. 3.

[6] Eur. Court HR, judgment of 18 Jan. 1978, ser. A, 25, 90–1, para. 239. (A probable explanation as to why the Court did not treat art. 1 exhaustively is that the issues raised by the parties were in effect covered by art. 24 of the Convention; see p. 91, para. 240 of the judgment. It remains to be seen whether the Court will in the future be prepared to be more specific with regard to states' obligations under art. 1.)

regrettable that the Court was not prepared to be as explicit on this point as had been the Commission's principal delegate; if a reason were to be sought in order to explain this rather elliptical phraseology, a partial answer might be found by studying the composition of the Court.[7]

[7] Apart from the reasons given, n. 6 above, note can be taken for example, of the views held on this subject by Judges Teitgen and Ganshof van der Meersch in their academic capacities. Although the Chamber of the Court did not include either of these judges in the *Swedish Engine Drivers* case, both of them took part in the Court's deliberations in *Ireland* v. *UK.*

PART II

THE CONVENTION'S DOMESTIC STATUS

Preliminary Observations

The law established by the European Convention on Human Rights must undoubtedly in the long run have a significant impact on the majority if not all the legal systems of the member states, and yet surprisingly until very recently little has been known about its domestic status. Perhaps the reason for this is that the study of the Convention's penetration into, and in particular, its growing influence upon the member states happens to be a relatively recent phenomenon. Scholarly work has to date been oriented more to international law, that is to say, concerning itself primarily with the general problems of the relationship between the international and domestic legal orders, and has not sufficiently concerned itself with the impact that this international agreement has made upon the constitutional law and legal systems of the contracting states.[1] This state of affairs compares unfavourably with the very voluminous literature devoted to the relationship between the law of the European Communities and that of its member states which, on the whole, only tangentially concerns itself with the consequences in domestic law of the interaction between the two legal systems.[2] Consequently, what is needed, in the eyes of Professor Buergenthal,

is an assessment of the various ramifications of this development from a comparative law perspective. Such an inquiry would analyze the interaction between national law and new multinational public international law agreements in terms of the impact it has on domestic legal institutions. It might provide valuable comparative law insights about, among other things, the adaptability and transplantability of certain legal institutions, and about the institutional and doctrinal prerequisites and obstacles that make one national legal system more receptive than another to certain externally induced legislative changes or law reforms. These insights might in turn point up the need for, and lead to the development of, general standards for the formulation, interpretation and application of these agreements which would take into account their special nature and functions.[3]

---

[1] Among the noteworthy exceptions are: D. H. M. Meuwissen, *De Europese Conventie en het Nederlandse Recht* (1968), and S. Trechsel, *Die Europäische Menschenrechtskonvention, in Schutz der persönlichen Freiheit und die schweizerischen Strafprozessrechte* (1974).

[2] Th. Buergenthal, 'Human Rights: The European Convention and its National Application', 18 *AJCL* (1970), 233–6. [3] Ibid., at 234.

Unfortunately, it still remains manifestly impossible to make such an assessment and fill the apparent lacuna in this area of the law in the absence of some form of multi-national survey by experts in constitutional and international law. As will become apparent from this survey, there is a variety of methods by which the substantive provisions of international agreements can be incorporated into domestic law: treaties may be given the rank of constitutional law by means of legislative enactment (and also possibly through judicial interpretation to this effect); they can acquire a rank equal to that of other legislation; certain of their provisions may be applied by courts which consider them to be 'directly applicable', or alternatively cited by them as persuasive authority. Likewise, the provisions of international agreements can serve as guidelines for the drafting of bills – to both the legislature and the administrative authorities – and they can also be assumed to form part and parcel of 'general principles of law' or the domestic *'ordre public'* (in certain instances through the medium of customary international law) thereby influencing and modifying not only the practice of domestic courts and tribunals, but also the action of executive and administrative authorities. It follows that there exist substantial differences and diversity of constitutional techniques employed which cannot be dealt with in a study of this length. Thus, Part II of this book is not and does not purport to be an in-depth and exhaustive analysis of the Convention's status under domestic law. Instead, what is here attempted is an overview of the Convention's position in *all* member states of the Council of Europe, with particular emphasis, where possible, on recent developments.

Certain preliminary observations ought to be made prior to the proposed survey. Any attempt at providing an objective and balanced account of the Convention's impact – whether direct or indirect – upon the domestic legal systems of member states is necessarily incomplete, often slightly distorted, and sometimes even inaccurate. There are many reasons for this. For example, although theoretically the provisions of the Convention and its protocols guarantee to all individuals a common denominator of a well-established set of rights and freedoms whose enforcement is ensured by the Convention's relatively advanced form of supervisory machinery, in practice, the system possesses certain in-built drawbacks which can and often do adversely affect a coherent and uniform development of this body of law:

— the right of individual petition to the Commission is *optional* (Article 25). To date Cyprus, Malta, Greece, and Turkey have made no declarations under this article.

— the acceptance of the Court's compulsory jurisdiction is also *optional* (Article 46). Malta and Turkey have made no declarations under this article.

— the member states may restrict the effects of the Convention's law in their respective territories by making specific *reservations* to certain provisions (Article 64). There are at present a number of such reservations deposited with the Secretary-General of the Council of Europe.[4]

— under certain circumstances *derogation* from some of the rights and freedoms enumerated in the Convention is permissible (Article 15).

— the First Protocol remains unratified by Liechtenstein, Spain, and Switzerland, and the Fourth Protocol by Spain and the United Kingdom; the Fourth Protocol remains *unsigned* by Cyprus, Greece, Malta, Switzerland, Turkey, and Liechtenstein.

— there are *no* provisions for the harmonization and uniform interpretation of the Convention's law.[5]

In addition, discussion centred on the Convention's domestic status does not necessarily in itself reflect the real standard of legal protection that a given state affords to an individual. Although political reality obliges one to recognize that the Convention is not considered as an integral part of domestic law in all the contracting states, it does not follow, *mutatis mutandis*, that states which have not incorporated its provisions are necessarily suspected of violating the Convention: the European Convention is but one of the many possible sources — both international and domestic — which may provide individuals redress *vis-à-vis* the state. For instance, in countries where there already exists a catalogue of basic rights, reference to the Convention's provisions need not necessarily be of great importance: the Convention — as stated in its preamble — provides merely the *first steps* for the collective enforcement of

---

[4] See *European Convention on Human Rights. Texts and Documents* (tri-lingual, ed. H. Miehsler, and H. Petzold, 1980), 56–77 (EMRK), 10–23 (EMRK/1.ZP), and 12–13 (EMRK/4.SP).

[5] This subject will be discussed in the General Conclusions below.

certain rights on the regional plane. Article 60 adds weight to this argument: 'Nothing in this Convention shall be construed as limiting or derogating from any of the human rights and fundamental freedoms which may be ensured under the laws of any High Contracting Party or under any other agreement to which it is a party.' Likewise, it may be noted that in certain cases the provisions of the Convention resemble closely and sometimes even correspond exactly with those of national law. This being said, domestic courts perhaps should, and in many cases actually do, take the Convention's provisions into account (as well as the decisions of its organs) when they afford a greater guarantee than does domestic law. Unfortunately, however, if a court or tribunal is able to choose between an international and domestic text in order to motivate its decision, the professional training and natural inclinations of its members more often tend to lead it to select the latter.

Whether or not the actual text of the Convention is incorporated into domestic law, there is no dispute that domestic law must give full effect to the rights guaranteed by the Convention and that contracting parties are obliged, by appropriate means, 'to ensure that their domestic legislation is compatible with the Convention and, if need be, to make any necessary adjustment to this end'.[6] Thus, although the reports of the European Commission and the decisions of the Human Rights Court do not have the value of *res judicata*, they nevertheless do provide precedents for domestic courts in that their authority cannot be disregarded without serious reason, especially in cases in which they clarify concepts found in this instrument.[7]

---

[6] Application 214/56, *De Becker* v. *Belgium*, report of Commission, Eur. Court HR, ser. B, 1962, 48.

[7] For surveys of how the Convention organs influence national tribunals consult H. Rolin, 'L'autorité des arrêts et des décisions des organes de la Convention européenne des Droits de l'Homme', VI *RDH/HRJ* (1973), 729–46; and Ch. Schreuer, 'The Impact of International Institutions on the Protection of Human Rights in Domestic Courts', 4 *Israel Yearbook on Human Rights* (1974), 60–88. See also ch. 10 below. Note may also be taken of art. 57 of the Convention which imposes upon all member states an obligation to furnish, on request from the Secretary General of the Council of Europe 'an explanation of the manner in which its internal law ensures the effective implementation of any of the provisions of this Convention'. It is regrettable, however, that sufficient effort is not made to secure more *adequate* responses to these requests.

Chapter 3
The Benelux Countries and France

A. Belgium[1]

Belgium was one of the original states signatories of the Convention on 4 November 1950. Prior to its ratification, the legislative section of the *Conseil d'État* was consulted. It expressed its opinion that ratification posed no legal difficulties in that the rights and freedoms enumerated in the Convention were either guaranteed by the Constitution of 1831 itself or otherwise enshrined in Belgian law.[2] Thereupon both the Senate and House of Representatives passed the law of approval (*'le Traité . . . sortira son plein et entier effet'*) authorizing the instrument's ratification in accordance with Article 68 of the Constitution. This article stipulates:

The King makes peace treaties, treaties of alliance and commerce. He informs the Chambers and submits all the relevant communications as soon as the interests and security of the State permit him to do so.

Treaties of commerce and those involving the national finances or those which might affect the State or individually become binding on certain Belgians require the consent of the Chambers in order to become effective.

No territorial change shall be effected by virtue of an Act. In no cases may the secret clauses of a treaty render the public clauses null and void.

The Convention and First Protocol were ratified on 14 June 1955, the law authorizing the instrument's 'full and entire effect' having been passed on 13 May 1955 (*Moniteur Belge/Belgisch*

---

[1] In addition to Th. Buergenthal, 'The Domestic Status of the European Convention on Human Rights: A Second Look', 7 *Journal of the ICJ* (1966), 55–96, at 63–6, reference can be made to two articles by W. J. Ganshof van der Meersch, 'Les Droits de l'Homme et la Constitution belge' in *Mélanges Modinos* (1968), 146–80, and 'Les procédés nationaux de mise en vigueur des obligations souscrites et des accords conclus par le gouvernement en droit belge' in *Rapports belges au IX Congrès de l'Académie internationale de droit comparé*, Téhéran, 1974, 627–714. See also, M. Bossuyt, 'The Direct Applicability of International Instruments on Human Rights (with Special Reference to Belgian and US Law)', *RBDI* (1980), 317–43, esp. at 320–5; and J. Velu, *Les effets directs des instruments internationaux en matière de Droits de l'Homme* (1981).

[2] See: *DP: Sénat* (1952–3), no. 279 of 6 May 1953, annex, 36–7.

Staatsblad, 19 Aug. 1955). The text of the Convention was annexed to the law of approval.[3] The optional declarations recognizing the competence of the European Commission of Human Rights to receive individual petitions and accepting the compulsory jurisdiction of the European Court of Human Rights were made on 29 June 1955 and have been renewed ever since. No reservations were made. Belgium ratified the Convention's Fourth Protocol on 21 September 1970.

In accordance with established constitutional practice the European Convention on Human Rights, after its incorporation into domestic law by virtue of parliamentary approval and subsequent publication in the *Moniteur Belge/Belgisch Staatsblad* (the official gazette), obtained the rank of a statute. Its domestic status was considered to be identical to other legislative enactments in that subsequent legislation would supersede it if conflict arose. Belgian constitutional doctrine made no distinction between adopted rules of international treaty law and other domestic legislation, and those provisions of the Convention considered by the courts as 'self-executing' could be invoked before the Belgian courts.[4] Thus, those treaty provisions which according to their nature could bind Belgians 'individually' (Article 68(2) of the Constitution) acquired the force of law without any specific transformation.

Prior to the 1978 *Lootens* case (see below) neither the legislature nor the courts had expressly decided the status of any of the norms enumerated in the European Convention on Human Rights

---

[3] For more detailed explanations as to how treaties are incorporated into Belgian law consult P. F. Smets, *L'assentiment des Chambres législatives aux traités internationaux* (1964); M. Waelbroeck, *Traités internationaux et juridictions internes dans les pays du Marché commun* (1969), 34–6, 102–14, 180–4, and 271–87, as well as an article by the same author entitled 'Considérations sur le rôle du juge belge face au droit international', 56 *Riv. DI* (1973), 499–524; P. De Visscher 'Observations sur l'assentiment parlementaire aux traités et accords internationaux et sur leur publication ', *JT* (1974), 150–1; and J. Masquelin, *Le droit des traités dans l'ordre juridique et dans la pratique diplomatique belge* (1980), and references found therein. It is important to understand that it is the Convention as such and not the law approving the treaty which is applied by the domestic courts. The latter may be called a law in so far as it is a legislative act destined to suspend the effect of prior laws contrary to the Convention's provisions, but *substantively* the approval is not law.

[4] See W. J. Ganshof van der Meersch, 'La Convention européenne des Droits de l'Homme a-t-elle, dans le cardre du droit interne, une valeur d'ordre public?' in *Les Droits de l'Homme en droit interne et en droit international* (1968), 155–251, at 199. Also consult J. Velu and J.-P. Masson, 'L'application et l'interprétation de la Convention européenne des Droits de l'Homme dans la jurisprudence belge'. *JT* (1968), 696–703.

vis-à-vis subsequent domestic legislation. However, recent case-law concerning the relationship between directly applicable (effective) European Community law and conflicting domestic legislation of a later date was instrumental in shedding some light on how this problem was to be tackled. In effect, since the ruling of the *Cour de Cassation* in the *Fromagerie Franco-Suisse 'Le Ski'* case in May 1971, it may be assumed that directly applicable provisions of *all* international agreements will be provided primacy over conflicting national legislation irrespective of the date of the latter's promulgation.[5] This case related to an unsuccessful appeal by the Minister for Economic Affairs to the *Cour de Cassation* in which it was claimed that the Court of Appeal should not have declared that the *SA Fromagerie Franco-Suisse 'Le Ski'* was entitled to claim restitution of certain duties imposed upon it. It was argued, on behalf of the Minister, that the Court of Appeal wrongly refused to apply a law of 19 March 1958 which was of a later date than the law ratifying the EEC Treaty (of which Article 12 prohibits member states from introducing between themselves any new custom duties on imports or any charges having equivalent effect), and that under Belgian law only the legislature was able to test the conformity of laws to the Constitution or to treaties binding Belgium.

In what is considered by Belgian jurists as a landmark decision, the Court rejected the Minister's contentions, and went on to hold that:

Even when the consent to a treaty, required by Article 68, paragraph 2 of the Constitution, is given in the form of a law, the legislature does not exercise a normative function;

The conflict which exists between a rule of law established by an international treaty and a rule of law established by a subsequent statute, is not a conflict between two statutes;

The rule, according to which a law repeals the earlier law in so far as the two conflict, is not applicable in the case of a treaty conflicting with a law;

---

[5] See references in n. 3 above, especially Waelbroeck, 56 *Riv. DI* (1973), 499–524; F. Rigaux, 'Les conflits de la loi avec les traités internationaux', in *Rapports Belges au VIIe Congrès International de droit comparé*, Uppsala, 1966, 269–83; and J. Limpens and G. Schrans in *National Reports*, B. 15–16. It should be noted that, in addition, the delegation of certain powers to international organizations has been approved by a constitutional amendment of 20 July 1970, now art. 25 *bis* of the Constitution. This article reads: 'Either by treaty or by law specific powers may be attributed to institutions created under international law.'

When the conflict is one between a rule of domestic law and a rule of international law having direct effects within the domestic legal order, the rule established by the treaty must prevail; its pre-eminence follows from the very nature of international treaty law;

This is all the more so, when the conflict is one, as in the present case, between a rule of domestic law and a rule of Community law;

In point of fact, the treaties which have created Community law set up a new legal order, in whose favour the member States have restricted the exercise of their sovereign powers in the fields defined by these treaties;

Article 12 of the Treaty establishing the European Economic Community produces direct effect and creates individual rights, which national courts must safeguard.

It follows from the preceding considerations that the court had the duty to reject the application of the provisions of domestic law that are contrary to this provision of the Treaty.[6]

It can therefore be safe to assume that the courts are competent to review the compatibility of any statute with those provisions of a treaty considered to have direct effect in Belgian law if the law is incompatible with the treaty provisions; it naturally follows from this that *mutatis mutandis* those provisions of the European Convention on Human Rights which are considered 'self-executing' in Belgian law must be assumed to have a greater authority than prior or subsequent statutes, on condition that, as provided in Article 60 of the Convention, the domestic law, or any other international agreement to which Belgium is a party, do not provide more favourable guarantees. Surprisingly, however, despite the European Commission's acceptance of this principle[7] and the Belgian Government's confirmation of it,[8] the Belgian courts by and large continue

[6] Text of English translation taken from L. J. Brinkhorst and H. G. Schermers, *Judicial Remedies in the European Communities. A Case Book* (1977), 174–5. *Pas. Bel.* (1971), i. 886–920; *JT* (1971), 471–4, commentary by J. Salmon, at 509–20 and 529–35; and P. Pescatore, 7 *CDE* (1971) 561–86. For a full English translation of the decision: (1972) CMLR 330–76. The *Le Ski* case has since been re-affirmed in the judgment of the *Cour de Cassation*, 14 Jan. 1976, in *SA Indiamex* v. *Fond Social pour les Ouvriers Diamantaires* in *Pas. Bel.* (1976), i. 538–45. For further discussion on this subject see J.-V. Louis, 'La primauté du droit international et du droit communautaire après l'arrêt "Le Ski"' in *Mélanges F. Dehousse* (1979), ii. 235–42.

[7] Applications 6697/74 and 6989/75 (121st Session, 4–12 Mar. 1976). Unpublished.

[8] 'The Convention's provisions governing protection of the rights guaranteed are directly applicable in Belgain law. . . . Furthermore since the Court of Cassation's ruling of 27 May 1971 in the *Fromagerie Franco-Suisse Le Ski* case, there is no longer any doubt that "in the event of conflict between a rule of internal law and a rule of international law which has direct effects within the internal legal system,

to make frequent reference to the Convention's 'self-executing' provisions without indicating this instrument's position in the domestic hierarchy.[9] This attitude may in part be explained by the constitutional repercussions that an express pronouncement to this effect may have — a point to be explained below — as well as by the apparent self-evident nature of the primacy of its provisions over conflicting legislation: see, for example, case-law of both the *Cour de Cassation*[10] and the *Conseil d'État*.[11] This being said, particular attention can be focused on an observation made by the Second Chamber of the *Cour de Cassation* in the *Lootens* case.[12] In determining that a judge could decide that he was empowered to examine the validity of a regulation obliging individuals to wear safety belts when sitting in one of the front seats of a car, the *Cour de Cassation* stated that the *Tribunal Correctionnel* of Antwerp was wrong in rejecting the appellant's argument, that the Convention's provisions are of a hierarchically superior force to ordinary laws, when it mistakenly assumed that *'selon une jurisprudence constante, le juge ne peut apprécier une loi selon le critère*

---

the rule laid down by the treaty must prevail". . . .' This quotation is taken from the Belgian Government's reply to the Secretary General's enquiry relating to the implementation of Articles 8, 9, 10, and 11 of the European Convention on Human Rights, in Council of Europe doc. H(76)15, 15 Oct. 1976: *Implementation of Article 57 of the European Convention on Human Rights*, at 26. See also comments made by Professor De Meyer when representing the Belgian Government before the Court in the *Van Oosterwijck* case, oral hearings of 24 Apr. 1980 (morning session), doc. Cour/misc(80)61 at 12; and para. 33 of the Court's judgment of 6 Nov. 1980, in the same case.

[9] See generally, *Collection* (especially the supplements). For extracts of recent case law consult *Yearbook*, e.g. vol. 18 (1975), 410-20; 19 (1976), 1109-22; 20 (1977), 696-743; and 21 (1978), 681-723.

[10] See n. 13 below. For an exhaustive list of case-law on this subject consult J. Velu, *Les effets directs des instruments internationaux en matière de Droits de l'Homme* (1981).

[11] e.g. case cited in 21 *Yearbook* (1978), p. 688; case no. 18916, *Féd. Belge des Négociants-Détaillants en Combustible* v. *État belge* in *Rec. des Arrêts du Conseil d'État* (1979), 486-498, at 498. See also Velu, n. 10 above. A fascinating debate has developed concerning the self-executing nature of the UN Civil and Political Rights Covenant in Belgian law. On this subject consult papers submitted at a colloquium in Nov. 1980, subsequently published in *RBDI* (1980), 243-354 (esp. articles by M. Bossuyt, at 317-43, J. Verhoeven, at 243-64, and J. Velu, 293-316).

[12] 26 Sept. 1978, *Pas. Bel.* (1979), i. 126-8. In subsequent case-law the 'safety belt legislation' was held to be in accordance with the Constitution and the Convention: see *Poma* case in *JT* (1980), 339; *Rechtskundig Weekblad* (1979/80), 834, with observations by P. Lemmens; 2nd *Lootens* case, *JT* (1980), 195. (The *Poma* case was later taken before the Commission in Strasbourg, application 8707/79, 18, *D&R*, 225-8).

d'un traité international'. The *Cour de Cassation* thereupon emphasized that the lower court's

. . . motivation est contraire au principe de droit susénoncé selon lequel, en cas de conflit entre une règle de droit interne et une norme contenue dans un traité international ayant des effets directs dans l'ordre juridique interne, la norme établie par le traité doit prévaloir; que la prééminence de cette norme résulte de la nature même du droit international conventionnel et entraîne pour le juge, qui serait amené à constater qu'une règle de droit interne est en contradiction avec une disposition d'une convention internationale ayant, comme en l'espèce les articles 5 et 8 de ladite Convention de sauvegarde des droits de l'homme et des libertés fondamentales, des effets directs dans l'ordre juridique interne, l'obligation d'écarter l'application de la règle de droit interne.[13]

The above developments raise an interesting constitutional problem. Until very recently, it has always been accepted that the courts in Belgium had no power to declare statutes or international agreements unconstitutional. Following a strict interpretation of the doctrine of the separation of the judical and legislative powers, the courts have hitherto (with few exceptions) not been prepared to review the constitutionality of legislation, including treaties, once they had been incorporated into domestic law. In effect, Article 107 of the Constitution, which reads '[t]he courts and tribunals shall not apply any general, provincial or local decrees and regulations and orders except in so far as they are in accordance with the law' has been interpreted by a long line of decisions of the *Cour de Cassation* to mean that courts were not competent '*pour vérifier la constitutionnalité des lois'*.[14] There is, however, an indication that the judiciary are having second thoughts on this negative interpretation of Article 107 of the Constitution. The judgment of the *Cour de Cassation* of 3 May 1974, and in particular the opinion expressed in that case by the *Procureur*

---

[13] Ibid., at 127–8. In other cases the *Cour de Cassation* has examined the compatibility of domestic law with the Convention's substantive provisions without attempting to explain the exact position of this instrument's directly applicable provisions in the legal hierarchy. See, for example, cases cited in *Pas. Bel.* (1977), at i. 818–20, 831–3; *Pas. Bel.* (1978), i. 91–3; *JT* (1977), 708; *Pas. Bel.* (1979), i. 128–30, 153–63 (a case discussed at greater length in ch. 10 below), 221–7 (also see ch. 10 below), 337–9, and 367–70; *Pas. Bel.* (1980), i. 619–22. For further reference to Belgian case-law see ch. 8 below, sec. B, and ch 10, sec B.

[14] *Cour de Cassation* decision of 23 July 1849, in *Pas. Bel.* (1849), i. 449; subsequently confirmed by both the *Cour de Cassation* and *Conseil d'État*. See Waelbroeck, n. 3 above, esp. at 271–8, and J. E. S. Fawcett, *The Application of the European Convention on Human Rights* (1969), 9.

Général Ganshof van der Meersch has now shed some doubt on the long established principle that the courts are prevented, in all cases, from reviewing the constitutionality of statutes.[15] This point is worth noting since there now appears to exist a rather interesting situation whereby, in derogation from the well-established principle that the courts possess no jurisdiction to review the compatibility of legislation with the Constitution, the individual is placed in the position where he can ask the courts to review the compatibility of ordinary laws — irrespective of whether they were in force prior to or after incorporation of the European Convention — if and when there appears to have been a breach of his fundamental rights under the European Convention on Human Rights.[16]

Much has already been written about the influence of Convention law upon the Belgian legal system and repetition is unnecessary at this juncture, especially as the substantive provisions of the Convention are often invoked in proceedings before Belgian courts.[17] What is perhaps interesting to note is the fact that although in a number of cases (e.g. *de Becker,* the *Belgian Linguistic* cases, the *Vagrancy* cases, *Marckx, Deweer,* and *Le Compte,* where the Commission and/or the Court have found the Convention to have been breached, the Belgian authorities have been prepared, where necessary, to make appropriate administrative and legislative amendments in order

---

[15] *Le Compte* v. *Ordre des Médecins Pas. Bel.* (1974) i. 910-4; *JT* (1974), 564-71, with a commentary by J. Venwelkenhuyzen, 'L'attribution de pouvoirs spéciaux et le contrôle judiciaire de la constitutionnalité des lois', at 577-84 and 597-608. Also see *Cour de Cassation* decisions of 25 June and 6 Sept. 1974 in *Pas. Bel.* (1974), i, 1114-18, and *Pas. Bel.* (1975), i. 15-9; and L. Moureau, 'Remarques sur le contrôle de la constitutionnalité des lois' in *Administration Publique* (Trimestrielle) (1976/77), i. 16-26.

[16] See *Bull. EC Suppl.* 5/76, 30; P. Wigny, *Cours de droit constitutionnel* (1973), 140. In the case of *Pacheco* v. *Ministre des Finances, Avocat général* J. Velu explained that: '*Lorsqu'un conflit existe entre une norme de droit international conventionnel ayant des effets directs dans l'ordre juridique interne et une norme de droit interne, le juge belge doit faire prévaloir la règle établie par le traité,* [he then referred to the *Le Ski* case, including the conclusions of the *Procureur général* Ganshof van der Meersch, and the case of *Indiamex,* n. 6 above] . . . *il résulte que les juridictions belges, dans les limites de leurs compétences respectives, disposent d'un semblable pouvoir de contrôle à l'égard des lois ou règlements d'exception dérogeant à la Convention* [*européenne des Droits de l'Homme*].' (*Pas. Bel.* (1977), i. 85-96, at 88.)

[17] See references cited in notes 1 and 4 above, and case-law referred to in notes 9, 11, 12, and 13. In addition, chs. 8 and 10 below will deal with aspects of *Drittwirkung* and the authority of findings of the Convention's organs.

to comply with the international obligations undertaken upon the ratification of the Convention.[18]

B. France[19]

Although France was one of the original states signatories to the Convention on 4 November 1950, the country did not in fact ratify the Convention until 3 May 1974.[20] The instrument of ratification was accompanied by two reservations to Articles 5, 6, and 15 (1), and a declaration of interpretation relating to Articles 10 and 63.[21] Also upon ratification of the Convention, a declaration was made under Article 46 recognizing the compulsory jurisdiction of the European Court of Human Rights in all matters concerning the interpretation and application of the Convention. The First and Fourth Protocols were ratified at the same time. On 2 October 1981 France signed, without reservation in respect of ratification, the Second Additional Protocol which confers upon the European Court of Human Rights competence to give, at the request of the Committee of Ministers, advisory opinions on legal questions concerning the interpretation of the Convention,[22] and at the same time made a declaration under Article 25 of the Convention which gives individuals, non-governmental organizations, or groups of individuals the right to petition the Commission on Human Rights (*Décret no.* 81–917, *Journal Officiel*, 14 October 1981, p. 2783).

---

[18] Consult 'Stocktaking', *passim*, and A. H. Robertson, *Human Rights in Europe* (1977), *passim*. Also consult the recent friendly settlement in the *Giama* case, application no. 7612/76, 21 *D&R*, 73–94, commented upon by the author in 4 *TL* (1982), 72–4. Also see ch. 10 below, notes 60–6.

[19] Consult *Bibliography*, 106–7; 'Colloque de Besançon', 3 *RDH/HRJ* (1970), 550–738; A. Pellet, 'La reconnaissance par la France du droit de requête individuelle devant la Commission européenne des Droits de l'Homme', 97 *RDPSP* (1981), 69–103; and P.-H. Imbert, 'La France et les traités relatifs aux Droits de l'Homme', *AFDI* (1980), 31–43.

[20] 17 *Yearbook* (1974), 2. See also A. Pellet, 'La Ratification par la France de la Convention européenne des Droits de l'Homme', 90 *RDPSP* (1974), 1319–9, R. Goy, 'La ratification par la France de la Convention européenne des Droits de l'Homme', 22 *NILR* (1975) 31–51, and A. Cocatre-Zilgien, 'De quelques effets actuels et éventuels de la ratification de la Convention européenne des Droits de l'Homme sur la politique et le droit français', 94 *RDPSP* (1978), 645–78.

[21] Ibid., 2–6. Also see V. Coussirat-Coustère, 'La réserve française à l'article 15 de la Convention européenne des Droits de l'Homme', 102 *Journal de droit international* (1975), 269–93.

[22] See M.-A. Eissen, 'La France et le Protocole 2 à la Convention européenne des Droits de l'Homme' in *Studi in onore di G. Balladore Pallieri* (1978), 249–79.

On 31 December 1973 both the National Assembly and Senate authorized the ratification of the European Convention on Human Rights and its protocols stipulating that '*La présente loi sera exécutée comme loi de l'État*' (*Loi no.* 73-1227, *Journal Officiel*, 3 January 1974, p. 67).[23]

The French Constitution of 1958 provides that:

Peace treaties, commercial treaties, treaties or agreements relative to international organisation, those that imply a commitment for the finances of the State, those that modify provisions of a legislative nature, those relative to the status of persons, those that call for the cession, exchange or addition of territory may be ratified or approved only by a law. [Article 53.]

Treaties or agreements duly ratified or approved shall, upon their publication have an authority superior to that of laws, subject, for each agreement or treaty, to its application by the other party. [Article 55.] [24]

Thus having received legislative approval in the form of a statute, the Head of State duly ratified the Convention whose norms were incorporated into domestic law upon its publication in the *Journal Officiel* on 4th May 1974.[25]

Consequently, from the day of publication the self-executing (directly applicable) provisions of the Convention possess — by virtue of Article 55 of the Constitution — a hierarchically superior position over both prior and subsequent conflicting legislation, subject to the proviso that reciprocity of application can be established.[26] However, this apparently simple rule has been difficult to establish both within the administrative and ordinary court structures, although in the latter case to a lesser extent. Why is this so? Administrative courts determine the legality of

[23] Extracts from debates in the National Assembly and Senate are reproduced in *European Convention on Human Rights, National Aspects*, (Council of Europe, 1975) 5-20. The text of the Convention was annexed to the law authorizing ratification.

[24] A. J. Peaslee, *Constitutions of Nations* (1968), iii. 322-3. Art. 55 is an adaption of art. 26 of the Constitution of 1946 which read: 'Diplomatic treaties duly ratified and published shall have the force of law even when they are contrary to internal French legislation; they shall require for their application no legislative acts other than those necessary to ensure their ratification.'

[25] *JORF*, 4 May 1974, p. 4750 (*Décret no.* 74-360 of 3 May 1974). For further details consult A. Cocatre-Zilgien, n. 20 above, at 650.

[26] For further analysis of the problems concerning the accommodation of international agreements within the French legal system consult J. Rideau, *Droit international en droit interne français* (1971), and P. Reuter, A. Blondeau, N. Questiaux, L. Dubouis, and E. Ruzié, *L'application du droit international par le juge français* (1972), *passim*. Two recent articles are also worth noting: F. Weiss, 'Self-Executing Treaties and Directly Applicable EEC Law in French Courts', *LIEI* (1979/1), 51-84, and G. A. Bermann, 'French Treaties and French Courts: Two Problems in Supremacy', 28 *ICLQ* (1979), 458-90.

acts of administrative authorities and review the compatibility of executive measures with the law. The *Conseil d'État* (the supreme administrative court) thus works on the traditional premiss that as an *administrative* court it has no competence in questioning the legality of legislative action (that is the role of the *Conseil constitutionnel*, to be described below, which determines the constitutionality of statutes). This attitude of unwillingness to review the validity of legislation is reinforced by the more profound unwritten principle that French courts should not be able to question the will of the electorate as expressed by the representative assembly. Even the *Cour de Cassation* (the supreme civil and criminal court) is unable to provide remedies for the enactment of legislation which conflicts with treaty obligations — regrettable as this might be from both the international and constitutional perspectives.[27] Consequently, despite the apparently clear rule of precedence afforded to treaties over ordinary laws, the courts have been reluctant — until very recently — to control or regulate this constitutionally determined hierarchical structure. The classical example is the case of the *Syndicat général de fabricants de semoules en France* (1968) in which the *Conseil d'État* declined to apply an EEC regulation, and instead chose to apply a conflicting French ordinance, on the premiss that it had no power to control legislation which may be of a higher rank (the doctrine of the *souveraineté de la loi*).[28]

It is not often that administrative courts make reference to the European Convention on Human Rights; one reported case was that of *Lahache*, decided by the *Conseil d'État* on 30 October 1980.[29] Having left her husband and being in the process of divorcing him, Mrs Lahache obtained an abortion at the *Centre hospitalier de Dinan*. Her husband petitioned the *Tribunal Administratif* claiming that the abortion was performed in

[27] See G. A. Bermann, n. 26 above, 460-1, and H. Thierry, S. Sur, J. Combacau, and C. Vallée, *Droit international public* (1979), 177-91.

[28] *Dalloz* (1968), Jurisprudence, 285 and note by M. Legrange on 286-9. Cf. C. Eisenmann, 'Le contrôle juridictionnel des lois en France', in *Travaux des sixièmes journées d'Études juridiques Jean Dabin* (Actualité du contrôle juridictionnel des lois, Catholic University of Louvain, 1973), 71-95; and E. Bergsten, *Community Law in the French Courts* (1973), esp. ch. II. But also consult the *Croissant* case of 7 July 1978, *Conseil d'État*, Ass., 292.

[29] *Recueil Dalloz Sirey* (1981), 38, and conclusions of M. Genevois. Also noted in VI *HR Rev.* (1981), 75; and in 97 *RDPSP* (1981), 216-25. (An extract from the decision of first instance is reproduced in 21 *Yearbook* (1978), 737-9).

violation of Article 2 of the Convention which guarantees the right to life. It was held, however, that neither applicable domestic provisions nor the Convention had been violated. Interestingly enough, both the *Tribunal Administratif* and the *Conseil d'État* appeared to have accepted the arguments put forward on behalf of the *Centre hospitalier* to the effect that as the law of 17 January 1975 (concerning abortion) was enacted after the publication of the European Convention on Human Rights it should be given priority in accordance with well-established precedents of the *Conseil d'État* based upon the *lex posterior derogat priori* rule.

In another case the *Conseil d'État* was called upon to consider an issue relating to the publicity of hearings in disciplinary matters.[30] The appellant, a doctor, requested that a decision by the disciplinary section of the *Conseil national de l'Ordre des médecins* be set aside because he had not been judged publicly. In so doing he invoked Article 6 of the European Convention. In its judgment rendered on 27 October 1978, the *Conseil d'État* rejected his argument based on Article 6, and went on to explain *'que les juridictions disciplinaires ne statuent pas en matière pénale et ne tranchent pas de contestations sur des droits et obligations de caractère civil; que, dès lors, les dispositions précitées de l'article 6 de la convention européenne ne leur sont pas applicables.'*[31]

The *Cour de Cassation* (like its administrative counterpart the *Conseil d'État*) had — until the famous case of the *Directeur général des Douanes* v. *Société Cafés Jacques Vabre and J. Weigel & Co.*, 1975, tended to reconcile the directly applicable provisions of treaty law and legislation on the basis of the *lex posterior derogat priori* rule rather than treat the problem from the standpoint that, if and when conflict arises, directly applicable provisions of treaties (whether Community law or other international agreements), must, by virtue of Article 55 of the Constitution, be given priority over legislation. The situation has apparently changed substantially after the *Jacques*

---

[30] *Recueil des décisions du Conseil d'État* (1978), *Début*, 27 Oct. 1978, at 395–7. See also the conclusions of M. Labetoulle, the *commissaire du gouvernement*, at 395–406, in which he refers to the Strasbourg Court's *Ringeisen* case.
[31] Ibid., at 396. More recent case-law before the *Conseil d'État* — in which the Convention is cited — includes *Vimare*, 21 Dec. 1979, *Dalloz* (1980), 225; *Putot*, 14 Jan. 1981, *Section Contentieux*, 38; *Winter*, 15 Feb. 1980, *Dalloz* (1980), 416; and *Dollet*, 25 July 1980, 97 *RDPSP* (1981), 209.

Vabre case, at least in so far as European Community law is concerned.[32] In this case two companies successfully sued the Customs Administration for repayment of tax levied and for compensation for damage suffered due to the deprivation of money paid as such tax, alleging that the tax levied violated Article 95 of the EEC Treaty. The Customs Administration's appeal to the *Cour de Cassation* was unsuccessful. One of the grounds for rejecting the appeal was explained in the following terms:

Mais attendu que le Traité du 25 mars 1957 [the EEC Treaty] qui, en vertu de l'article [Article 55] susvisé de la Constitution a une autorité supérieure à celle des lois, institue un ordre juridique propre intégré à celui des États membres; qu'en raison de cette spécificité, l'ordre juridique qu'il a créé est directement applicable aux ressortissants de ces États et s'impose à leurs juridictions; que, dès lors, c'est à bon droit, et sans excéder ses pouvoirs que la cour d'appel a décidé que l'article 95 du traité devait être appliqué en l'espèce, à l'exclusion de l'article 265 du code des douanes, bien que ce dernier texte fût postérieur; d'où il suit que le moyen est mal fondé . . . [33]

Thus, the *Chambre mixte* of the *Cour de Cassation* held that the EEC Treaty was of a greater authority than both prior and subsequently enacted legislation, that it established its own legal system, which was incorporated into that of member states and, as a result of the specific characteristics of the legal system created, certain of its norms were directly applicable to the nationals of member states and binding upon domestic courts.

However, although the *Jacques Vabre* case is thought to have considerably clarified the relationship between domestic legislation and directly applicable EEC law, firmly establishing the supremacy of the latter, there still appears to be some doubt as to whether the courts would be prepared to extend this control to encompass other international agreements.[34]

---

[32] *Chambre Mixte*, 24 May 1975; *Dalloz*, 497–507; [1975] 2 CMLR 336. In a commentary on the case Professor Ruzié — 64 *Journal de droit international privé* (Clunet, 1975), 801 — explained that this *Cour de Cassation* decision is not limited only to EEC law, since by expressly quoting art. 55 of the Constitution, the Court 'implique . . . sa volonté de faire prévaloir n'importe quel traité ou accord, régulièrement ratifié ou approuvé, sur toute loi postérieure'. See also the subsequent case of *Von Kempis* v. *Geldof, Cour de Cassation*, 3rd Civil Chamber, 15 Dec. 1975; *Dalloz*, 33, and [1976] 2 CMLR 152, commented upon by M. Simon and F. E. Dowrick, 92 *LQR* (1976), 357–9.

[33] *Dalloz* (1975), at 606.

[34] See M. Simon, 'Enforcement by French Courts of European Community Law' I, 90 *LQR* (1974), 467–85, and II, 92 *LQR* (1976), 85–92; and J. Foyer and D. Holleaux, 'Note' in 65 *Revue critique de droit international privé* (1976), 351–61.

It will certainly be interesting to see how the courts will react when faced with an apparent violation of an individual's rights by legislation which has come into force after the incorporation of the European Convention on Human Rights into domestic law, if the former appears to violate a directly applicable (self-executing) norm of the latter.

Judges sometimes have difficulty in understanding the meaning or relevance of a treaty provision; and the European Convention is no exception to this. Thus, for example, in the case of *Glaeser-Touvier* (30 June 1976), the *Cour de Cassation* considered itself incompetent to interpret the provisions of international agreements. It explained that, in so doing, it would have encroached upon governmental prerogatives in the field of *'l'ordre public international'*.[35] Nevertheless, case-law continues to evolve; perhaps slowly, but certainly in an interesting manner. The legal profession is now becoming more aware of the potential that the directly applicable norms of the Convention may have in the domestic forum. In June 1975, for example, in the case of *Respino-Francesco,* the *Cour de Cassation* rejected an appeal based, among others grounds, on the argument that the provisions of the Code of Criminal Procedure were incompatible with Articles 5 and 6 of the Convention.[36] In the same year, the *Tribunal de Grande Instance* of Paris refused to look into the matter of telephone tapping in a case in which Article 8 of the Convention had been pleaded before it, because it felt that the measures in question, even if proven, would be justified under paragraph 2 of the article.[37] Similarly, the *Cour de sûreté de l'État,* in a decision rendered on 22 June 1976 (the *Siméoni* case), was not prepared to consider the relevance of Articles 5, 6, and 13 of the Convention, as it

[35] *La Semaine Juridique* (1977), iii. 18435, together with a note by Mongin. An extract of this case is also reproduced in 19 *Yearbook* (1976), 1126–30. This procedure of suspending proceedings and requesting ministerial interpretation may be used as a device in not deciding issues.

[36] Case no. 75–90 687 -B- *Cour de Cassation* (*Chambre Criminelle*) 3 June 1975; 18 *Yearbook* (1975), 422–5. See further L. Pettiti, 'Une révolution dans l'application de la procédure pénale', 96 *Gazette du Palais* (1976), 397–9, G. Chevalier, 'Au sujet de l'application par les juridictions françaises de la Convention européenne de sauvegarde des droits de l'homme et des libertés fondamentales', 51 *La Semaine Juridique* (1977), Doctrine, 2832, and 19 *Yearbook* (1976), 1128. Also consult G. Roujou de Boubée, 'La protection des Droits de l'Homme en droit pénal français', 47 *Revue intern. de droit pénal* (1976), 93–109.

[37] Case no. 383, 10 July 1975, cited in 18 *Yearbook* (1975), at 425. See also case reported in 123 *The Solicitor's Journal* (1979), 159.

held that existing law already provided greater guarantees to a person lawfully detained.[38] In yet another case, the State broadcasting monopoly had been successfuly challenged on, among other grounds, Article 10 of the European Convention on Human Rights, which guarantees the right 'to receive and impart information and ideas without interference by public authority'.[39]

Particular note should perhaps be taken of a number of cases in which Article 9 of the Convention has been invoked before the courts and which in some instances seem to be plainly contradictory. This article guarantees the freedom of thought, conscience, and religion or belief. A number of persons had refused to take possession of their military papers, i.e. refused call-up for compulsory military service (an offence punishable under Article 133 of the 1971 *'Code de Service National'*) on the ground that they should be considered conscientious objectors by virtue of their philosophical beliefs.[40] In most of these cases the courts were prepared to recognize — expressly or by implication — the primacy of the norms of the Convention over domestic legislation, but differed in their interpretation of the right to change one's beliefs, and of its corollary, the right to manifest such beliefs, guaranteed in Article 9 of the Convention.[41]

For example, in an apparently successful action by the accused in the case of *Ministère Public* v. *Lemesle*, the *Tribunal de Grande Instance* of Béziers held:

---

[38] This was a *special* court, recently abolished, which could try persons charged with a 'crime' or '*délit*' concerning action to substitute some unlawful authority for that of the State. As to divergent views on the importance of this case, consult case-notes of P. Chambon, 50 *La Semaine Juridique* (1976) II Jurisprudence, 18416, and L. Pettiti, 97 *Gazette du Palais* (1977), 117-9. See also the case of *Stuart*, in which the accused unsuccessfully invoked art. 5, 6, and 13 of the Convention before the *Cour de Sûreté de l'État*: decision of 11 July 1979 in 4 *Bulletin du Bâtonnier* (1979), 2-7.

[39] See *Le Monde*, 4-5 Dec. 1977, 26, and *The Times*, 6 Dec. 1977, 4, (article by I. Murray, 'French broadcasting monopoly ruled illegal'). The Government has now amended the law in order to prevent challenges of this sort against the State monopoly: 52 *La Semaine Juridique* (1978), para. 47542. (The Bill was approved on 7 May 1976 by the French National Assembly.) See also case of *Delmas*, 5 May 1978, *CA*, Montpellier, (1979), *Dalloz*, Jurisprudence, 283.

[40] These developments have been closely monitored in the French press. See: *Le Monde* 3 June 1977, 14; 8 June 1977 19; 10 June 1977, 20; 26-7 June 1977, 9; 3 Aug. 1977, 18; 7 Mar. 1978, 19.

[41] See report on the right of conscientious objection to military service (rapporteur Mr Péridier), *Parliamentary Assembly of the Council of Europe* (1977), doc. 4027. 15-16 (discussed in Swiss publication *Cooperation*, 2 Feb. 1978).

Whereas the accused, in claiming the status of a conscientious objector, is merely exercising his freedom to change his beliefs . . .

Whereas this freedom, recognized by international convention, [the European Convention on Human Rights] duly published, thus enjoys authority superior to that of the legal text upon which the prosecution is founded,

Whereas a conviction on the basis of this text would be tantamount to conferring on this text the power to override a legal rule of a higher order . . .

Whereas the individual's freedom to change his opinion, which forms an integral part of his freedom of opinion, may not simply be suppressed on the grounds that nothing has been stipulated as to the way in which it shall be exercised and manifested . . .[42]

In other cases, on the other hand, reference was made to the fact that the rights and freedoms 'specified in Article 9(1) are restricted by the provisions of national law when the latter imposes, as stated in paragraph 2 "limitations . . . necessary in a democratic society in the interests of public safety [and] for the protection of public order"', with the result that 'this international convention does not therefore place any obstacle in the way of enforcement of the internal law which schedules and punishes the offence committed by the accused . . .'[43]

On 9 February 1978 the *Cour de Cassation*, in the case of *Ouin*,[44] considered Article 6 of the Convention without referring to the issue concerning the hierarchical superiority of treaty law *vis-à-vis* domestic legislation. In this case the Court held that a person who had refused the assistance of a lawyer was not entitled to have access to documents in the possession of the

[42] Case no. 1882 of 7 Dec. 1976, English text taken from the report of M. Péridier, ibid., 15; also **20** *Yearbook* (1977), 744-6. A similar decision was given by the *Tribunal de Grande Instance de Montpellier* on 3 Oct. 1977 (Case no. 2413): see case-note by L. Pettiti, in **98** *Gazette du Palais* (1978), Doctrine, 11-12.

[43] As n. 41 above, report of Mr Péridier, 15; case of *P. Lantec, Tribunal de Grande Instance du Havre* (*3ème Chambre*) no. 612 of 14 Feb. 1977. A summary of this case as well as a number of subsequent cases is compiled in **20** *Yearbook* (1977), 746-59, and **21** *Yearbook* (1978), 729-37. In these cases, art. 133 of the 'Code de Service National' was applied on the basis that para 2 of art. 9 permitted limitations upon the rights guaranteed in para. 1, or alternatively on the basis that the courts were unable to '*contrôler la constitutionnalité des lois*'. Also consult two decisions of the *Chambre criminelle* of the *Cour de Cassation*: case of *Lamure*, 4 Jan. 1979 in *Bulletin des Arrêts de la Cour de Cassation*, 9-11, and case of *Coulon*, 5 May 1978 in **99** *Gazette du Palais* (1979), Jurisprudence, 9.

[44] Case no. 76-93.687.B. (*Chambre Criminelle*). Decision pronounced by the Court's President, P. Mongin. See also *Le Monde* of 14 Feb. 1978, 15; and **21** *Yearbook* (1978), 732-3.

Tribunal correctionnel prior to the date of the hearing. The President of the Court explained:

Qu'en effet, ni l'article 6 de la Convention européenne de sauvegarde des Droits de l'Homme et des Libertés fondamentales dont se prévaut la demanderesse, ni l'article 427 du Code de procédure pénale que vise également le moyen n'exigent que les actes écrits constitutifs des dossiers des procédures pas plus que les pièces à conviction, soient matériellement remis en communication à la personne poursuivie; qu'il n'existe aucune exception en faveur de celle qui entend se défendre elle-même; qu'en reconnaissant à tout prévenu le droit d'avoir connaissance de l'intégralité des pièces de la procédure par l'entremise d'un avocat, au besoin commis d'office et à l'assistance duquel il peut d'ailleurs renoncer devant les juges, la loi garantit audit prévenu la possibilité d'assurer sa défense de façon adéquate et satisfait dès lors aux exigences de l'article 6 de la Convention précitée.[45]

More recently the Criminal Chamber of the *Cour de Cassation* invoked *ex officio* Articles 6 and 13 of the European Convention on Human Rights; and what is of importance to note in this context is that it can do so only if the provisions of the instrument are considered part and parcel of *'l'ordre public'*.[46] In this case Baroum, the appellant, successfully petitioned the *Cour de Cassation* which set aside a judgment of the *Cour d'Appel* of Orléans on the ground that, in sentencing him to five years of imprisonment, 3,600 francs fine, and five years' prohibition of residence for illegal commerce of arms and illegal retention of arms and ammunition, it should not have taken into consideration the fact that he had previously been convicted of insulting a public officer.[47] The Court observed that:

Vu les dites articles ensemble les articles 427 et 551 du Code de procédure pénale et les articles 6 et 13 de la Convention européenne de sauvegarde des droits de l'homme et des libertés fondamentales;

Attendu que tout prévenu a droit à être informé d'une manière détaillée de la nature et de la cause de la prévention dont il est l'objet et qu'il doit, par suite, être mis en mesure de se défendre tant sur les divers chefs d'infraction qui lui sont imputés que sur chacune des circonstances aggravantes susceptibles d'être retenues à sa charge; . . .

[45] Ibid., at 733.
[46] It thereby apparently confirmed the view which Ganshof Van Der Meersch expounded in his article 'La Convention européenne des Droits de l'Homme a-t-elle, dans le cadre du droit interne, une valeur d'ordre public?' in *Les Droits de l'Homme en droit interne et en droit international* (1968), 155–251. (This subject is dealt with more fully in ch. 8 below.)
[47] Case no. 78/91.826.B.RA., judgment of 5 Dec. 1978; *Dalloz* (1979), Jurisprudence, 50 (with a note by S. Kehrig, at 50–2). Also reported in *Le Monde*, 20 Dec. 1978, 14.

Attendu cependant que ladite circonstance aggravante [i.e. his previous conviction] n'était pas mentionnée dans l'ordonnance de renvoi et a été révélée d'office par le juge du second degré; qu'il ne résulte d'aucune des énonciations de l'arrêt que le prévenu comparant ait été préalablement informé de cet élément modificatif de la prévention et ainsi mis en mesure de se défendre spécialement sur ce point devant les juges du fond . . .

. . . par ces motifs . . .

. . . casse et annule l'arrêt de la Cour d'appel d'Orléans.[48]

In addition to the administrative and ordinary courts, Article 61 of the French Constitution confers upon the *Conseil constitutionnel* the right to review statutes as to constitutionality. This relates to legislation passed by Parliament which has not yet been published in the *Journal Officiel*, there being no constitutional review of legislation after publication. Article 61 reads:

Organic laws before their promulgation, and regulations of the Parliamentary Assemblies, before they come into application, must be submitted to the *Conseil constitutionnel*, which shall rule on their constitutionality. To the same end, laws may be submitted to the *Conseil constitutionnel*, before their promulgation, by the President of the Republic, the Premier Ministre or the President of one or the other Assembly . . .

The constitutional reform of 29 October 1974 has now considerably strengthened the role of the *Conseil constitutionnel*, in that, in addition to the President, Prime Minister, or Presidents of either the National Assembly or the Senate, 'sixty deputies or sixty senators' can now also submit matters to this court for determination.[49]

In an initiative taken by eighty-one members of the National Assembly, the *Conseil constitutionnel* was invited to declare Article 4 of the French Abortion Law of 20 December 1975 (*Loi relative à l'interruption volontaire de grossesse*) to be unconstitutional and incompatible with Article 2 of the European Convention, whose domestic status had been ensured in

---

[48] Ibid., at 51-2.

[49] Amendment of art. 61(2) of the French Constitution by *Loi Constitutionnelle* of 29 Oct. 1974, *JORF*, 11035, 30 Oct. 1974, *Keesing's Contemporary Archives* (1975), 27109. A. It can also be added that art. 54 of the Constitution stipulates: 'If the Constitutional Council, the matter having been referred to it by the President of the Republic, by the Premier, or by the President of one or the other assembly, shall declare that an international commitment contains a clause contrary to the Constitution, the authorisation to ratify or approve this commitment may be given only after amendment of the Constitution.'

May 1974. Article 2 of the European Convention guarantees to everyone the right to life save in the execution of a capital sentence pronounced by a court. The *Conseil constitutionnel* was therefore confronted with the problem of whether an international treaty — in this case the European Convention on Human Rights — formed part of 'the Constitution'. In its important decision of 15 January 1975 the *Conseil constitutionnel* made it clear that, as far as the European Convention on Human Rights is concerned, the incompatibility of legislation with this treaty cannot be regarded as a case of unconstitutionality.[50] It therefore refused to incorporate the European Convention into the constitutional criteria for review for the purposes of the procedure under Article 61:

Article 61 of the Constitution only authorises the *Conseil constitutionnel* to pronounce on the conformity of statutes submitted to its examination with the Constitution; that while the provisions of Article 55 of the Constitution confer upon treaties an authority superior to that of statutes, these provisions do not imply that respect for this principle has to be enforced by the *Conseil constitutionnel*, and whereas decisions taken by virtue of Article 61 of the Constitution have absolute and final authority, preventing publication and enforcement of any provisions declared unconstitutional; and whereas, on the contrary, the superiority of Treaties to statutes is of a relative and contingent nature, relative because limited to the scope of the Treaty and therefore non-applicable to non-signatory States, contingent because dependent on reciprocity of enforcement by the other party.[51]

The position of the European Convention, as interpreted by domestic tribunals — still remains unclear and, as Dr Golsong has observed,[52] '*les effets de la Convention en droit interne*

---

[50] For further discussion on this subject consult: L. Favoreu, 'Le Conseil constitutionnel et le droit international', 23 *AFDI* (1977), 95–125; G. Ress, 'Der Rang völkerrechtlicher Verträge nach französischen Verfassungsrecht, Überlegungen zur Entscheidung des Conseil Constitutionnel vom. 15. Januar 1975 über den Rang der Europäischen Konvention zum Schutze der Menschenrechte und Grundfreiheiten nach Artikel 55 der französischen Verfassung', 35 *ZRV* (1975), 445–501; and H. Golsong, 'L'effet direct, ainsi que le rang en droit interne, des normes de la Convention européenne des Droits de l'Homme et des décisions prises par les organes institués par celle-ci' in *Les recours des individus devant les instances nationales en cas de violation du droit Européen (Communautés Européennes et Convention européenne des droits de l'Homme* 1978), 59–83, at 70–3.

[51] *JORF* of 16 Jan. 1975. Translation taken from Simon, n. 34 above, 74. The reasoning in this case appears unsatisfactory with regard to at least one particular matter: how can the 'reciprocity principle' be applied to the Convention? See ch. 1 above, sec. B, *passim*. See also decision of *Conseil constitutionnel* of 27 July 1978, in *JORF*, 29 July 1978, 2949.

[52] Golsong, n. 50 above, at 80.

français restent très limités; ils ne peuvent . . . pratiquement pas
avoir une portée réelle notamment à l'égard d'une loi contraire
à la Convention surtout s'il s'agit d'une loi postérieure.' This
state of affairs is most unfortunate. A conflict between ordinary
laws and domestically enforceable treaty provisions is not,
strictly speaking, a conflict of 'constitutionality' and cannot
therefore be determined by the *Conseil constitutionnel*. However,
both the ordinary courts (*Cour de Cassation*) and administrative
tribunals (*Conseil d'État*) are empowered, in theory at least, to
control and regulate the superiority of international treaties
over ordinary laws: '*la Convention a, théoriquement au moins,*
en droit français, une valeur infra-constitutionnelle mais supra-
législative.'[53] Thus, if there were to exist an apparent divergence
between a Convention norm and subsequent legislation, the
courts should be able to give priority to the provisions of the
Convention; and now that France has made a declaration under
Article 25 of the Convention, the courts may be more willing —
as they apparently are in so far as European Community law is
concerned — to affirm the superiority of directly applicable
provisions of the Convention over both prior as well as subsequent
conflicting legislation. In all probability they will now have to
take greater notice of judicial decisions in Strasbourg. Thus,
Louis Pettiti, member of the European Court of Human Rights
and former *Bâtonnier de l'Ordre des Avocats de Paris*, con-
veniently summarized the present situation when he said, '*Après*
une longue hésitation les magistrats français ont tiré les consé-
quences de la ratification de la Convention par la France et par
référence à l'art. 13 de ce texte ont confronté les principes de
la Convention au droit interne'.[54]

C. Luxembourg

The Grand Duchy of Luxembourg was an original state signatory
of the Convention on 4 November 1950, and of the First
Protocol on 20 March 1952. Both were ratified on 3 September
1953. Declarations of recognition of the competence of the

[53] Pellet, n. 19 above, 70. Also see H. Batiffol, *Droit international privé* (1974) i.
40–41, and Ch. Rousseau, *Droit international public* (1970), i. 174–80. Perhaps the
French Constitution is in need of amendment or clarification? See F. Hamon and J.
Buisson, 'Le Traité et la loi postérieur' in *Service Public et Libertés. Mélanges R.-E.*
Charlier (1981), 131–41.
[54] Pettiti, no. 42 above, at 77.

European Commission of Human Rights in respect of individual applications and of acceptance of the compulsory jurisdiction of the European Court of Human Rights were deposited with the Secretary-General of the Council of Europe on 28 April 1958, and both have been regularly renewed since then.[55] A reservation was made with regard to Article 1 of the First Protocol. This concerns the liquidation of certain ex-enemy property rights and interests provided in an Act of 1951. The Fourth Protocol was ratified on 2 May 1968.

When the Luxembourg Government submitted the Convention for parliamentary approval in 1953 it explained that the instrument was designed to protect the same basic rights and freedoms which were already guaranteed to Luxembourg citizens by the country's Constitution (Articles 12-28). It further stated that ratification of the Convention would extend to foreigners the guarantee of rights formerly provided only to citizens, and that the Convention 'would be binding in internal law and would take precedence over any existing provisions which might be in conflict with it.'[56]

The first paragraph of Article 37 of the Constitution stipulates: 'The Grand Duke shall conclude treaties. No treaty shall enter into force until it has been approved by law and published in the manner prescribed for the publication of laws.'[57] It follows that the House of Deputies controls international treaties; i.e. they can become effective only if approved by statute.[58] This prior approval by the legislature (*'est approuvé le traité'*) must not, however, be confused with legislative competence: *'elle se définit comme une compétence de simple contrôle et de simple approbation différente de la législation'*.[59] The law of approval permits the given treaty to have effect in domestic law, although the instrument is applicable — both on the

---

[55] 1 *Yearbook* (1958-9), 70 and 76; *Mémorial du Grand-Duché*, no. 20, 441.

[56] Council of Europe doc. H(67)2, 26.

[57] A. J. Peaslee, *Constitutions of Nations* (1968), iii. 558. Note may also be taken of art. 49 *bis* of the Luxembourg Constitution which reads: 'The exercise of the attributes reserved by the Constitution to the legislative, executive and judicial authorities may be temporarily derogated by treaty to institutions of international law.' This article was introduced upon the revision of the Constitution in 1956. Such a treaty must be approved like a constitutional amendment, i.e. by a two-thirds majority of the legislature. See Pescatore, n. 59 below, esp. 67-73.

[58] See P. Pescatore, in *National Reports*, L. 47-52, at 48.

[59] See K. Holloway, *Modern Trends in Treaty Law* (1967), at 155. See also P. Pescatore, *Conclusion et effet des traités internationaux selon le droit constitutionnel, les usages et la jurisprudence du Grand-Duché de Luxembourg* (1964), *passim*.

international as well as domestic planes – *only* upon ratification.[60] Therefore, although the European Convention on Human Rights obtained legislative approval on 29 August 1953 it did not become an integral part of the domestic law of Luxembourg until the country actually ratified the instrument on 3 September 1953.[61] From this latter date the rights and freedoms guaranteed by the Convention were considered to have a status equivalent to internal rules which could be invoked directly by individuals before domestic courts.

The Constitution of the Grand Duchy of Luxembourg, as revised in 1956, does not contain any specific provisions on the relationship between international agreements that have become an integral part of domestic law and other statutory provisions. Until a reversal of the legal practice initiated by the Supreme Court in the case of *Huberty* v. *Ministère Public* in 1950 in which it was held that 'in the case of a conflict between the provisions of an international agreement and the provisions of subsequent domestic law, international law must prevail over domestic law',[62] the Luxembourg courts refused to review domestic law by reference to international treaties and to recognize the latter's priority if conflict arose.

The determination of whether a provision of an international agreement is directly applicable (self-executing) is made by the courts. Consequently, although there exists a rule of interpretation whereby, until the contrary is proven it is presumed that the legislature did not intend to violate international obligations, it is important to appreciate that this principle of interpretation is based entirely upon judge-made law: only if and when the provisions of an international agreement are

---

[60] P. Pescatore, 'Note' in *JT* (1954), 697. In a later article entitled 'L'autorité en droit interne des traités internationaux selon la jurisprudence Luxembourgeoise', **XVIII** *Pas. Lux.* (1960-2), 97-115, the same author explained (at 104) that 'La loi approbative n'est pas un acte de législation au sens matériel du terme, mais bien un acte du contrôle politique et juridique de la part du parlement et des autre corporations qui participent à l'exercise du pouvoir de législation'.

[61] Law of 29 Aug. 1953, *Mémorial du Grand-Duché* no. 53, 1009-110. Art. 1, para. 2 of this law stipulates that it be 'executed and observed by all those whom it may concern'.

[62] Judgment of 8 June 1950, in **XV** *Pas. Lux.* (1950-3), 41. In a judgment of 14 July 1954, in the case of *Chambre des Métiers* v. *Pagani*, **XVI** *Pas. Lux.* (1954-6), 150, the Supreme Court reaffirmed the precedence of international agreements by holding that 'a treaty is a law of a higher nature, of a nobler origin than the will of a national body'. It can now therefore be assumed that a *jurisprudence constante* exists on this point.

considered *by the courts* to be directly applicable are they given precedence over national statutes, irrespective of the date of their coming into force.[63] In practice the putting into effect of this principle of interpretation has surprisingly given rise to a number of difficulties, and in contrast to the other Benelux countries, the result has been that many of the Convention's provisions have been denied precedence over apparently conflicting national legislation. Probably the most often cited example is the case of *Ministère Public* v. *Von Halem,* decided by the *Tribunal Correctionnel* on 24 October 1960 when the court explained that:

The rights and principles set out in the Convention may not be appealed against or invoked directly before national courts but may only be the subject of the international remedy as provided for and defined in the Convention. Hence Article 6 of the Grand-Ducal Decree of 8th November 1944 retains its full legal and executive force. The Court cannot examine whether or not the principle laid down in Article 6 of the Grand-Ducal Decree of 8th November 1944 is compatible with Article 6 of the Convention.[64]

An explanation for this attitude may be found:

As international agreements become an integral part of municipal law in Luxembourg, the rights guaranteed by the European Convention are to be treated as equivalent to internal rules which can be invoked directly by private individuals.

In practice, however, putting this principle into effect can give rise to difficulties whenever the rule recognised does not at the same time establish an obligation which is specific enough to be enforceable. There are thus cases where more precise internal rules are needed in order to ensure full enforcement of a rule laid down in the Convention.

It is, however, true that a general principle whose methods of implementation are not directly specified by the Convention is none the less highly effective, owing to the fact that internal law, over which the provisions of the international treaty have priority, cannot be contrary to the international rule.[65]

[63] See *Bull EC Suppl.* 5/76, 41. Also see Pescatore, n. 59 above, and 'L'effet direct du droit communautaire' by the same author, **XXII** *Pas. Lux.* (1972), 1–19.

[64] An extract from this decision can be found in 4 *Yearbook* (1961), 622–30. This case concerned an unsuccessful appeal against a fine imposed upon the defendant for charging rental prices for films at a higher rate than was permitted by law. Alternatively, the courts have tended to refer to a provision of the Convention without alluding to its position in the domestic hierarchy, e.g. judgment of 26 June 1972 of the Supreme Court in **XXII** *Pas. Lux.* (1972-4), 216–22; and that of 25 Jan. 1958, in **XVII** *Pas. Lux.* (1957-9), 248 at 252.

[65] Reply of Luxembourg to the Secretary General's enquiry, Council of Europe doc H(76)15 Oct. 1976. *Implementation of Article 57 of the European Convention on Human Rights,* 103–10, at 104.

Despite the above-mentioned hesitation of the Luxembourg courts to apply the Convention's norms in domestic proceedings, there are indications that there has of late been a slight reassessment in approach: one can cite, for example, the case-law of the *Cour Supérieure de Justice* when Article 6 has been invoked in a number of cases relating to the payment of interpreter's fees.[66] In one of these interpreter's-fees cases, dated 17 January 1972, the Court held that the Convention's *'dispositions doivent prévaloir sur celles de la loi interne, s'opposant à la mise à charge du prévenu acquitté des frais de citation ainsi que des taxes des témoins . . .'*[67] Similarly, in another decision of the *Cour Supérieure de Justice*, dated 5 May 1975, it was considered that the taking of a blood test against the wishes of a motorist did not violate any of the provisions of the Convention or its Protocol.[68] Finally, mention can be made of a decision of the *Cour Supérieure de Justice* of 2 April, 1980 in which an order of an investigating magistrate was annulled. In so doing the court stated *'qu'il est . . . certain que les droits reconnus par la Convention sont d'application directe et immédiate'* and *'. . . que le texte de l'article 8 est péremptoire'*.[69] It followed that the tapping of a person's telephone was unacceptable unless it was done within the context of specifically circumscribed exceptions provided by law.

Time will tell if this recent tendency of the courts to provide the Convention's 'self-executing' provisions a hierarchically superior status *vis-à-vis* other legislation will be maintained;[70] certainly, an acceptance of this instrument as 'higher internal law' appears to conform with the intention of the Luxembourg legislature in that parliamentary approval of the Convention had

[66] See cases cited in **19** *Yearbook* (1976), 1137–41.

[67] Ibid., 1139. To determine which provisions are 'directly applicable' the courts look (i) to the intention expressed by the parties, and (ii) the purpose of the agreement: Pescatore, in article in **XVIII** *Pas. Lux.* cited in n. 60, at 106.

[68] **XXIII** *Pas. Lux.* (1975–7), 182–9, esp. at pp. 185–6. In a letter to the author dated 12 Sept. 1978, the *Procureur Général d'État* (who is also a member of the Strasbourg Court), Mr L. Liesch, explained that *'L'arrêt du 5 mai 1975 . . . affirme seulement que la protection recherchée par l'intéressé va au-delà de la sphère d'application de la Convention invoquée. La Cour aurait dès lors appliqué directement la Convention, à supposer qu'une prise de sang y fût contraire.'*

[69] *JT* (1980), 489–92, at 491.

[70] The Luxembourg courts are faced with similar problems as are their Belgian counterparts concerning constitutional control: see A. Bonn, 'Le contrôle de la constitutionnalité des lois', **XXII** *Pas. Lux.* (1972–4), 1–29, esp. 13–16; and L. Liesch, 'Bestand und Bedeutung der Grundrechte in Luxembourg', **9** *EGZ* (1981), 84–8.

originally been obtained after the *Conseil d'État* had given a reasoned opinion on its apparently undisputed domestic position:

D'après la jurisprudence actuelle, un traité international revêt, sous un certain rapport, une efficacité supérieure même au texte constitutionnel . . . une loi interne sera toujours primée par les dispositions convention-nelles. En effet, une jurisprudence récente admet qu'en cas de conflit entre les dispositions d'un traité international et celles d'une loi interne, même postérieure, le traité doit prévaloir sur la loi interne.[71]

D. The Netherlands

The Convention and First Protocol were signed by the Nether-lands on 4 November 1950 and 20 March 1952 (*Tractatenblad* (Bulletin of Treaties) nos. 154 (1951) and 80 (1952)). Both re-ceived approval by the law of 28 July 1954 (*Staatsblad van het Koninkrijk der Nederlanden* (Bulletin 'of Acts, Orders, and De-crees) 1954 no. 335, 942-3). Ratification of both the Convention and First Protocol took place on 31 August 1954. The com-pulsory jurisdiction of the European Court of Human Rights was recognized at the same time. On 1 December 1955, in accordance with Article 63 of the Convention, the Netherlands extended the application of the Convention and its protocol to the territories for whose international relations it was responsible.[72] A declaration recognizing the right of individual petition in accordance with Article 25 was deposited with the Secretary General of the Council of Europe on 5 July 1960.[73] Both declarations under Articles 25 and 46 have been regularly renewed since their initial acceptances. The Fourth Protocol was signed on 15 November 1963; ratification took place on 23 June 1982.

The following articles of the Dutch Constitution (as amended

---

[71] See: Séances de la Chambre des Députés. Session ordinaire de 1952-3 of 23 June 1953, vol. ii annexes, 423 (projet de loi no. 44(466)); see also debate of 7 July 1953 in vol. 1, col. 1722-29. A recent innovation — art. 443(5) of the Criminal Code — provides for re-trial when a person has been convicted in breach of a provision of the European Convention. See ch. 10 below, sec. B, for further discussion on this point.

[72] Note reservation concerning art. 6(3): letter of 29 Nov. 1955, 1 *Yearbook* (1955-7), 45. (The Convention is a 'closed' instrument: the Republic of Surinam's declaration of succession was therefore refused in Jan. 1977: M.-A. Eissen, 'Surinam and the European Convention on Human Rights', 49 *BYIL* (1978), 200-1. But see Y. Dinstein, 'The European Convention . . . from an Israeli Perspective', III *RDH/HRJ* (1975), 493-504.)

[73] 3 *Yearbook* (1960), 62.

in 1953 and again revised in 1956) are concerned with the relationship between the Netherlands domestic law and international agreements:

Article 60:
Agreements with other Powers and with organizations based on international law shall be concluded by or by authority of the King. If required by such agreements they shall be ratified by the King. The agreements shall be communicated to the States-General as soon as possible; they shall not be ratified and they shall not enter into force until they have received the approval of the States-General. The judges shall not be competent to judge the constitutionality of agreements.

Article 61:
Approval shall be given either explicitly or implicitly. Explicit approval shall be given by an Act . . .

Article 63:
If the development of the international legal order requires this, the contents of an agreement may deviate from certain provisions of the Constitution.
In such cases only explicit approval can be given; the Chambers of the States-General shall not approve a Bill to that effect except with a two-thirds majority of the votes cast.

Article 65:
The provisions of agreements the contents of which may be binding on anyone shall have this binding effect as from the time of publication. Rules with regard to the publication of agreements shall be laid down by law.

Article 66:
Legal regulations in force within the Kingdom shall not apply if this application should be incompatible with provisions — binding on anyone — of agreements entered into either before or after the enactment of the regulations.

Article 67:
Subject, where necessary, to the provisions of Article 63, certain powers with respect to legislation, administration and jurisdiction may by or in virtue of an agreement be conferred on organizations based on international law.
With regard to decisions made by organizations based on international law, Articles 65 and 66 shall similarly apply.[74]

Consequently, those provisions of the European Convention on Human Rights which, according to their substance are directly

---

[74] A. J. Peaslee, *Constitutions of Nations* (1968), iii. 659-61. (Some sections as well as arts. 62 and 64 are not relevant to the present study and have therefore been omitted.) It should be noted, in this context, that the Constitution — including the above cited articles — is in the process of being amended.

applicable, possess direct binding force within the Dutch legal system from the date of the Convention's publication. In the words of Brinkhorst and Lammers:

Publication should not be considered as a governmental act *by virtue of which* the agreement (or decision) takes binding effect and therefore does not transform the agreement (or decision) into municipal law. The 'binding effect on anyone' of the agreement or decision is the direct consequence of the international law obligation which the State has accepted. According to the Government the publication indicates only *the point of time after* which the binding effect occurs. Therefore, the mere fact of publication does not mean that the agreement or decision contains provisions which have direct effect. This can only be surmised from the contents of the agreement or the decision.[75]

It should be noted in particular that Articles 65 and 66 of the Dutch Constitution are concerned with the internal applicability of international agreements and their superiority over domestic legislation. By virtue of these articles, the judiciary has to give precedence to directly applicable (self-executing) provisions of treaties if they conflict with the Constitution itself or with prior or subsequent legislation.[76] This precedence over the Constitution as well as over Acts of Parliament and delegated legislation relates not only to directly applicable provisions of international agreements but also to decisions of international governmental organizations (Article 67(2) of the Constitution).[77]

The Constitution itself therefore authorizes the courts to apply the directly applicable provisions of this treaty, even against conflicting domestic norms if there are any, without requiring any further implementation by legislative or administrative action.[78] Were the Convention to have been formally

[75] See n. 76 below, 566-7. (Emphasis original.)

[76] See especially H. F. van Panhuys, 'The Netherlands Constitution and International Law', 47 *AJIL* (1953), 537-8, and 'The Netherlands Constitution and International Law — A Decade of Experience' 58 *AJIL* (1964), 88-108; L. J. Brinkhorst and J. G. Lammers, 'The Impact of International Law, Including European Community Law, on the Netherlands Legal Order' in *Introduction to Dutch Law for Foreign Lawyers* (eds. D. C. Fokkema, J. M. Chorus, E. G. Hondius, and E. Ch. Lisser, 1978), 561-84; L. Erades and W. L. Gould, *The Relation between International Law in Municipal Law in the Netherlands and in the United States* (1961), *passim*; D. H. M. Meuwissen, *De Europese Conventie en het Nederlandse Recht* (1968), esp. 5-74; and E. A. Alkema, 'The Application of Internationally Guaranteed Human Rights in the Municipal Order' in *Essays on the Development of the International Legal Order in Memory of H. F. van Panhuys* (eds. F. Kalshoven, P. Kuyper, and J. G. Lammers, 1980), 181-98.

[77] Brinkhorst and Lammers, ibid., at 574-76. This subject is further discussed in ch. 10 below, sec. B.

[78] See M. J. van Emde Boas, 'The Impact of the European Convention on Human

implemented into domestic law in the guise of a legislative enactment — as was the procedure followed in the case of the 1965 UN Convention on the Elimination of All Forms of Racial Discrimination — it may have retained precedence *as such*, although it is unlikely that its provisions would be deemed 'self-executing'. In other words, the courts are very reluctant to hold that implementing legislation violates treaty norms even though in theory they can and must review the conformity of the legislative enactment with treaty provisions.[79]

The European Convention on Human Rights can be considered (together with the two 1966 UN Covenants) as the main *international* source *within* the Dutch legal system with regard to the protection of human rights. Even though the rights defined in this instrument are to a large extent expressly or impliedly also enunciated in the Netherlands Constitution, its practical value, as far as the courts are concerned, lies in the fact that statutes (as distinct from lower legislation) cannot be reviewed for their conformity to the Constitution (the courts are prohibited to do so under Article 131); whereas such review is possible — and indeed obligatory since 1953 — when the courts examine conformity of legislation to those provisions of ratified treaties which are directly applicable.[80] And, in the absence of any other authority, it is the courts themselves which determine whether a given provision of the Convention is directly applicable or not. The courts have not been slow in applying their role of interpreting the domestic status of such provisions: already in 1960 the *Hoge Raad* (Supreme Court) pronounced that 'all Netherlands laws *must* be examined by the courts for their compatibility with the (directly applicable) provisions of the Convention . . .'[81] And Dutch case-law since that time tends to

Rights and Fundamental Freedoms on the Legal Order of the Netherlands', 13 *NILR* (1966), 337–73, at 343, and 14 *NILR* (1967), 1–32.

[79] See *Hoge Raad*, 8 Nov. 1968, *Argus Steamship Co.* v. *Hanno* (*The Portalon* case) (1969) no. 10, in *NJ* (1969), 33. The 1965 UN Covenant was 'transformed' into domestic law: Act of 18 Feb. 1971 (see 4 *NYIL* (1973), 431–3). Most ILO Conventions also fall into this category of 'implemented' legislation. Also consult Alkema, n. 76 above, at 187–90 and 195–6.

[80] See, for example, E. A. Alkema, *Studies over Europese Grondrechten* (1978), 242–4, and 'Fundamental Human Rights and the Legal Order of the Netherlands' in *International Law in the Netherlands* (eds. H. F. van Panhuys, W. P. Heere, J. W. Josphus Jitta, K. Swan Sik, and A. M. Stuyt, 1980). iii. 109–46. Also consult: D. H. M. Meuwissen, and E. A. Alkema, *De Europese Conventie en het Nederlandse Recht* (1976), *passim*; and Erades and Gould, n. 76 above, 307–25.

[81] Quotation taken from 3 *Yearbook* (1960), 650. (Emphasis added.) See also

confirm the view that most of the provisions of the Convention have now secured for themselves hierarchically superior status of directly applicable treaty norms.[82] A few examples can be given. In a case dated 10 October 1978 the *Hoge Raad* upheld the decision of a Court of Appeal which suspended the application of Articles 423 and 424 of the Code of Criminal Procedure, due to the fact that the person concerned, when charged with a criminal offence, had not been informed in a language which he understood, the latter right being guaranteed by Article 6, paragraph 3 of the European Convention.[83] Similarly, the Arnhem Tribunal, in a case dated 14 November 1978, found that Article 6(1) had been breached by the authorities as they had taken more than 13 months to formulate a coherent case against the accused.[84] In a judgment dated 31 May 1978 in the case of *Voerman* v. *Municipality of Riderkerk* the *Raad van Staat* (Council of State) upheld the appellant's plea that the prohibition to permit him to install an aerial violated Article 10 of the Convention.[85] Lastly, in a more recent judgment of 23 September 1980 the *Hoge Raad* indicated that if the 'reasonable time' provision in Article 6(1) of the Convention — which has no equivalent in Dutch law — were to have been violated in the case before it, the prosecution would have been dimissed.[86]

The relationship between directly applicable provisions of international agreements, and in particular those of the European Convention on Human Rights and the Dutch Constitution, does not appear very clear. Whereas Article 60, paragraph 4 declares that the courts are not competent to pronounce on the constitutionality of international agreements, Article 63 nevertheless

---

Hoge Raad judgments in 4 *Yearbook* (1961), 602, 640; and in 7 *Yearbook* (1974), 503. It is interesting to note that the *Hoge Raad* does not regard art. 13 as self-executing: *NJ* (1960) no. 483; for comments on this case consult Brinkhorst and Lammers, n. 76 above, esp. 568–74.

[82] See *Yearbook* and *Collection, passim.* In 1980, for example, there were 55 cases in which Dutch courts referred to the Convention: see list compiled by L. A. N. M. Barnhoorn in 6 *Bulletin of the NJCM* (1981), 394–413.

[83] *NJ* (1979), no. 144, 441-3. (A similar case was reported in 21 *Yearbook* (1978), 764.) See also *NJ* (1978), no. 595, 1971-4, *NJ* (1978), no. 664, 2216-19, *NJ* (1979), no. 8, 26-8, and 10 *NYIL* (1979), 484-4.

[84] *Bulletin of the NJCM* (1979), no. 14, 23.

[85] Also in *Bulletin of the NJCM* (1978), no. 12, 27; and in VII *European Law Digest* (1979), 56. Also consult the notes by D. H. M. Meuwissen, E. A. Alkema, and Th. L. van Bennekom, in 23 *NILR* (1976), 314-37. (Other cases are mentioned in chs. 8 and 10 below.)

[86] *NJ* (1981), no. 116, and commentary by E. Myjer, in *Ars Aequi* (1981), 302-11.

accepts the position that the contents of treaties may — if the development of the international order thus requires — deviate from certain constitutional provisions of the *Grondwet* (the Constitution). In such cases, however, an agreement must be enacted into law by a special two-thirds majority of the two chambers of the States General. Consequently, as the Convention was neither enacted into law in accordance with Article 63, nor was it implemented with the special two-thirds majority, it would appear that the Convention does not enjoy a constitutionally guaranteed supremacy equivalent to that of the Constitution itself; rather, its directly applicable provisions possess a unique 'extra-constitutional' status.[87] It may be added that the purpose of Article 60(4) is not to confer upon treaties the status of constitutional law, but rather to assign to the legislature rather than the courts the task of determining whether an international agreement possesses or does not possess that status.[88]

When the Convention was ratified, both the Government and the States-General considered that Dutch law conformed to the norms set out in the instrument, and no constitutional amendments were deemed necessary. However, certain subsequent legislation, in particular relating to the treatment of aliens, to extradition, and to the retirement of female civil servants, was altered in order to avoid possible conflict with certain provisions of the Convention.[89]

More recent examples of the Convention's domestic influence are the amendment of the Code of Penal Procedure limiting the duration of the period of detention pending trial and the revision of certain laws concerning the military disciplinary system.[90] The latter changes were obtained as a direct result of a set of applications which had been brought before the Strasbourg organs and which terminated in an adverse finding against the Netherlands by the Court of Human Rights: *Engel & others* v. *The Netherlands*.[91] Likewise, the Court's judgment in the

---

[87] Cf J. E. S. Fawcett, *The Application of the European Convention on Human Rights* (1969), 14–16; Meuwissen, n. 76 above, 263; and Meuwissen n. 80 above, 68 ff.

[88] Fawcett, ibid., at 16. For a critical appraisal of recent suggestions to amend the Dutch Constitution see Alkema, n. 89 below, 239–71.

[89] van Emde Boas, n. 78 above, 360-73. Also consult E. A. Alkema, *Studies over Europese grondrechten* (1978), *passim*; and Evans, 'Written Communication', 109–97, at 161 and 163.

[90] See Alkema, n. 76 above, at 186.

[91] Eur. Court HR judgement of 8 June/23 Nov. 1976, ser. A, no. 22. The legislative

Winterwerp case will lead to legislative amendments.[92] In this connection note may be taken of an official circular dated 16 April 1980 from the Netherlands Minister of Justice to the Public Prosecutors at the Courts of Appeal. In this circular the Minister recalled that legislation and certain administrative practices need adaptation to the Court's findings with respect to Articles 5(4) and 6(1) of the Convention and that — pending legislative action — 'the judgment of the Court shall be considered as guidelines for legal practice', adding 'I invite you to see to it that the above is complied with'.[93]

An interesting legal issue has arisen as a consequence of these developments. Article 67(2) of the Constitution — read in conjunction with Articles 65 and 66 — gives directly applicable decisions of international organizations (e.g. regulations of the Community organs), the force of domestic law. The question may now therefore arise, especially in the light of the Strasbourg Court's decisions in the *Engel* and *Winterwerp* cases, of whether the Dutch courts will be prepared to interpret this article in such a way as to give similar domestic status to judgments of international tribunals. And, if prepared to do so, would they limit such an interpretation to the decisions of judicial organs only or would it also encompass the findings of quasi-judicial bodies such as the European Commission of Human Rights?[94]

revisions actually took effect *prior* to the Court's judgment, pending a total revision of military law. See on this subject Alkema, n. 89 above, esp. 147-237; and Council of Europe, *Information Bulletin on Legal Activities* (1974), no. 4, 41.

[92] Eur. Court HR judgment of 24 Oct. 1979, ser. A, no. 33.

[93] Reproduced in *Bulletin of the NJCM* (1980), no. 5, 233-6. (English translation provided by Mr F. Hondius.)

[94] See Brinkhorst and Lammers n. 76 above, at 574-6. This subject is more fully discussed in ch. 10 below. (Note should perhaps be taken of the report issued by the Netherlands Ministry of Internal Affairs: *Towards a Basic Law* (*Grondwet*), (1977), two volumes.) See comments by Alkema, n. 89 above, esp. 239-71, with a summary in English at 294-6.

Chapter 4
Austria, Federal Republic of Germany, Liechtenstein, and Switzerland

A. Austria[1]

Austria did not participate in the drafting of the European Convention on Human Rights nor was the country among the original contracting parties. However, it became a member of the Council of Europe in April 1956, and signed the Convention and First Protocol on 13 December 1957. These were ratified by the President on 3 September 1958 after the approval of the two chambers of the Austrian Federal Parliament *Nationalrat* (National Council) and *Bundesrat* (Federal Council) had been obtained in accordance with Section 50 of the 1929 text of the Constitutional Act (*Bundes-Verfassungsgesetz*). With the publication of the Convention and its Protocol in the Federal Law Gazette (*Bgbl. Nr.* 210/1958), the Convention obtained the status of domestic law.[2] At the same time, Austria recognized both the competence of the European Commission of Human Rights to receive individual petitions and the compulsory jurisdiction of the European Court of Human Rights. These declarations have since been renewed every three years. Austria ratified the Convention's Fourth Protocol on 18 September 1969 (*Bgbl. Nr.* 434/1969).

When ratifying the Convention, Austria made certain reservations with regard to Articles 5 and 6 of the Convention and Article 1 of the First Protocol, later adding another with regard to Article 3 of the Fourth Protocol.[3]

---

[1] See two recent studies: A. Khol, 'The Influence of the Human Rights Convention on Austrian Law', 18 *AJCL* (1970), 237–58, and K. Berchtold, 'The European Convention on Human Rights and the Austrian Legal Order: Some Experiences', VIII *RDH/HRJ* (1975), 383–405. For further references consult *Bibliography* 99–101, and W. Berka, 'Die EMRK und die österreichische Grundrechtstradition', 34 *ÖJZ* (1979), 365–75 and 428–32.

[2] i.e. the *Bundesgesetzblatt*, no. 60, 24 Sept. 1958.

[3] See *Collected Texts*, 605. (See also recent application of *X* v. *Austria*, no. 8180/78, 20 *D&R*, 23–8). For the authentic German text of the reservation see the forthcoming publication of H. Miehsler and H. Petzold, *European Convention on Human Rights. Texts and Documents* (1982), (Trilingual.)

In accordance with the principle of general incorporation of state treaties by which Austrian constitutional law was governed up to 1964, the Convention and First Protocol became part of Austrian domestic law. The Convention was considered to have the status of 'constitutional law', binding on all administrative and judicial bodies. The rights enumerated by the Convention were considered to exist concurrently with the already well-established catalogue of fundamental rights and other domestic legal texts although, as explained by the Government at the time, not all the provisions of the Convention were to be considered as necessarily immediately applicable (self-executing) by the authorities or by the courts.[4] However, although the Austrian legislature approved the conclusion of the Convention in the belief that by so doing it gave this instrument the status of constitutional law — which takes precedence over both prior and subsequent ordinary legislation — the Austrian Constitutional Court (*Verfassungsgerichtshof*) ruled in 1961 that the Convention lacked this status:

In view of the fact that the decision of the National Council approving the Convention for the Protection of Human Rights, and consequently the text promulgated in the official Federal Gazette do not carry the mention of 'constitutional' as required by Article 50(2) taken jointly with the second part of Article 44(1) of the Constitution, neither the Convention itself nor any part of it have the status of constitutional law.[5]

The effect of this decision was to reduce the Convention's position to that of an 'ordinary' law.

In order to understand the *Verfassungsgerichtshof's* decision, reference must be made to certain sections of the Austrian Constitution (*Bundes-Verfassungsgesetz*) of 1920 revised in 1929 and reinstated in 1945. Article 50(1) of this Constitution gives the federal organs of the State power to conclude treaties: 'Political treaties and other treaties only in so far as they contain provisions modifying or completing existing laws, shall require

[4] See n. 1 above: Khol, at 24, and Berchtold, at 384. See also report of the Federal Government, 22 June 1966, reprinted in 9 *Yearbook* (1966), 666-83.
[5] Constitutional Court decision of 14 Oct. 1961 GS/61, in *Vfgh.* (1961), 488-93. Translation from 4 *Yearbook* (1961) 604-17, at 616. For comments on this case — as well as other pre-1964 developments — see V. Liebscher, 'Austria and the European Convention for the Protection of Human Rights and Fundamental Freedoms', IV *Journal of the ICJ* (1961), 282-93; and G. Winkler, 'Der Verfassungsrang von Staatsverträgen', 10 *Österreichische Zeitschrift für öffentliches Recht* (1960), 514-39. (The article by Winkler actually lead to the Constitutional Court's decision, although the Court did not refer to this fact in its judgment.)

for their validity the approval of the *Nationalrat* [the National Council].'[6] In order for a treaty to obtain the rank of constitutional law a procedure stipulated in the then operative Article 50(2) of the Constitution had to be followed: 'The provisions of Article 42, paras. (1) to (4) and, if a constitutional law be modified by a treaty, those of Article 44(1) are applicable, *mutatis mutandis*, to resolutions of the *Nationalrat* regarding approval of treaties.' For present purposes, Article 44(1) is of particular importance in that it includes a stipulation that the promulgation of constitutional laws and amendments — including the enactment of treaties as constitutional law — may be enacted 'by the *Nationalrat* only in the presence of at least one half of its members and by a majority of two-thirds of the votes cast. They shall be explicitly designed as such ("constitutional law", "constitutional provision").'[7]

Thus, although at the time when the Convention and First Protocol were incorporated into domestic law and subsequently published, it was believed that the *Nationalrat* was enacting constitutional law — the requirement of a two-thirds majority of at least one half of the *Nationalrat* members being complied with — the fact that there had been *no express* mention that the Act in question constituted a constitutional amendment, was reason enough for the *Verfassungsgerichtshof* not to attribute to the Convention constitutional status.[8]

Reaction to this decision was relatively swift: the Federal Constitution (Amendment) Act of March 1964 (*Novelle zur Bundesverfassung*) revised the procedure for the incorporation of treaties into Austrian law (*Bgbl. Nr.* 59/1964). The relevant article — which gave the Convention the status of federal constitutional law with retroactive effect to the time of the Convention's promulgation in Austria — reads as follows:

Article II
There are hereby approved, in application of Article 50(2) taken together with Article 44(1) of the Federal Constitutional Law (text of 1929), even though they were not expressly declared as modifying the Constitution either in the decision of the National Council or in their publication in the Official Journal the State Treaties and the following treaty provisions which

---

[6] A. J. Peaslee, *Constitutions of Nations* (1968), iii. 38–9.
[7] Ibid.
[8] See I. Seidl-Hohenveldern, 'Transformation or Adoption of International Law into Municipal Law', 12 *ICLQ* (1963), 124, at 106, and 'Relations of International Law to Internal Law in Austria', 49 *AJIL* (1955), 451–76.

were considered by the National Council as modifying the Constitution
and which have been approved by a majority of two-thirds of the National
Council, more than half of its members being present . . .
. . . The Convention for the Protection of Human Rights and Fundamental
Freedoms.[9]

Thus, the new procedure for the incorporation of international
agreements was amended *generally*, with effect as to the future
(Article I) and at the same time the position was retroactively
clarified with regard to certain treaties, including the Human
Rights Convention (Article II).[10] It may be interesting to add

[9] *Bundesverfassungsgesetz vom 4. März 1964, mit den Bestimmungen des Bundes-
Verfassungsgesetzes in der Fassung von 1929 über Staatsverträge abgeändert und
ergänzt werden, Bgbl. Nr.* 59/1964. English translation from 7 *Yearbook* (1964),
444. (Special note should be taken of the revised wording of the former art. 50(2)
which by the amendment — *Bgbl. Nr.* 59/1964 — was renumbered para. 3; see Peaslee,
n. 6 above. This also applies to the 2nd, 3rd, 4th, and 5th Protocols of the Convention — *Bgbl. Nr.* 329/1970; *Nr.* 330/1970; *Nr.* 434/1969; *Nr.* 84/1972 — in that
the texts accompanying their publication made explicit reference to their status as
constitutional law, in accordance with the new art. 50(3)). A certain problem of
terminology should be explained: what is considered by an Austrian constitutional
lawyer as 'general transformation' would probably be classified by most international
lawyers as 'incorporation' in that by this method of implementation 'treaties become
part of the domestic Austrian legal order upon their entry into force, without any
further action being necessary' per W. P. Pahr, 'How International Treaties are
Implemented in EFTA Countries', 12 *EFTA Bulletin* (1971), 9-10, at 9. When an
Austrian lawyer refers to 'special transformation', an international lawyer may
understand this to mean simply 'transformation', in that the 1964 amendment of art.
50 of the Constitution provides for such an eventuality. That is, the implementation
of treaty norms by means of separate legislation (which must be distinguished from
legislative approval) deprives the said provisions of their direct effect in domestic
law. For more detailed examination of this subject consult A. Verdross and B. Simma,
Universelles Völkerrecht (1976), 435-42, Th. Öhlinger, *Der völkerrechtliche Vertrag
im staatlichen Recht* (1973), *passim*, I. Seidl-Hohenveldern, *Völkerrecht* (1980),
121-9, R. Walter, *Österreichisches Bundes-Verfassungsrecht* (1972), 177-83, and
Rack, *Das Völkerrecht im staatlichen Recht* (1979), *passim*. The constitutional
amendment of 1964 produced some fascinating doctrinal debates: see Khol, n. 1
above. Also see R. Novak, 'Probleme des Bundesverfassungsgesetzes vom 4. März
1964 über Staatsverträge', *Juristische Blätter* (1969), 307-15, R. Walter, 'Die Neu-
regelung der Transformation völkerrechtlicher Verträge in das österreichische Recht',
19 *ÖJZ* (1964), 449-54, von Grünigen, 'Die österreichische Verfassungsnovelle über
Staatsverträge vom März 1964', 25 *ZRV* (1965), 76 ff., H. Miehsler, 'Alfred Verdross'
Theorie des gemässigten Monismus und das Bundesverfassungsgesetz vom 4. März
1964, *Bgbl. Nr.* 59', 87 *Juristische Blätter* (1965), 566-73, H. R. Klecatsky, 'Die
Bundesverfassungsnovelle vom 4. März 1964 über die Staatsverträge', 86 *Juristische
Blätter* (1964), 349-58.

[10] In a letter to the author, 21 Dec. 1981, Professor H. Miehsler questioned this
interpretation. He explained that 'One may come to this conclusion but an Austrian
lawyer would not. He understands Article 49(1) of the Federal Constitution regulating
the publication of statutes and treaties as the provision enacting a treaty as part of
domestic law. In addition I must point out that some authors consider art. 9(1) of
the Federal Constitution ("The generally recognised rules of international law are

in this connection, that there is actually no express provision in the Austrian Constitution which makes international agreements (ratified in accordance with Article 50) part of domestic law; there does however exist well-established case-law which indicates that they have this effect. And, as the 1964 amendment of Article 50 provides for a special procedure whereby the *National-rat* may decide that a treaty can be implemented by separate legislation,[11] it is generally understood that in the absence of such a decision the provisions of an international agreement — approved in accordance with Article 50(1) — are directly applicable in domestic law.

To summarize the above developments: the 1964 amendment secured the Convention a normative rank equivalent to the Constitution, i.e. the rank of federal constitutional law. Thus, in Austria human rights can be said to be guaranteed by the Constitution of 1920 as amended in 1929, the Basic Law on General Rights of Citizens and legislation relating thereto, the Peace Treaty of St. Germain of 1918, the Treaty of Vienna of 1955, as well as by the European Convention on Human Rights. They all possess the rank and force of constitutional law.[12]

The *Verfassungsgerichtshof* possesses exclusive jurisdiction to decide on the validity of any law or regulation. It is the only judicial instance competent to decide upon any alleged infringements of constitutionally protected fundamental human rights by the legislature, international agreements entered into by Austria, regulations, or any other decisions or orders of

regarded as integral parts of Federal Law.") as a general rule of incorporation. This reading, however, is challenged by many other scholars (including myself). In my view a concept of incorporation primarily referring to art. 9(1) which is obviously ambiguous in many respects is not based on solid grounds.'

[11] Art. 50(2) (an addition made to the Austrian Constitution in 1964) stipulates that 'At the time of its approval of a treaty falling under para. (1), the *Nationalrat* may decide that such a treaty should be implemented by the promulgation of laws.' In other words, the provisions of a treaty implemented in this way do *not* have direct effect. This procedure was used beforehand in the case of the 1961 European Social Charter. See Khol, n. 1 above, at 247. The 1966 Covenant on Civil and Political Rights, ratified by Austria on 10 Sept. 1978 was also transformed in the same way. See *Bundesgesetzblatt Nr.* 591/1978. Also consult UN doc. E/CN4 1098/Add.6. (This also applies to the Covenant on Economic, Social, and Cultural Rights: *Bgbl. Nr.* 590 and 591/1978.)

[12] See A. Khol, 'The Protection of Human Rights in Relationships between Private Individuals: — the Austrian Situation', in *Cassin,* iii. 195-213, at 197. See also E. Melichar, 'Der Schutz der Menschenrechte im Verfassungsrecht der Republik Österreiches' in *Österreichische Länderreferate zum IX. Internationalen Kongress für Rechtsvergleichung in Teheran* (Vienna, 1974), 121-34.

administrative authorities. Consequently, when in the course of proceedings before another court a question as to whether a law is unconstitutional or whether a regulation is contrary to law arises, and the court believes that there are doubts as to the constitutionality of the provision, the matter must be referred to the *Verfassungsgerichtshof* for decision.[13] In other words, when dealing with the competence to decide on the validity of statutes (Article 140), regulations (Article 139), or treaties (Article 140(a)), the question may arise whether such a norm is inconsistent with the European Human Rights Convention and, if the answer is affirmative, the norm in question is annulled. It was in the course of one such case − concerning the question of whether an arbitration court appointed to decide a claim for compensation under a statute (Burgenland Hunting Law) was a dispute relating to 'civil rights' within the meaning of Article 6(1) of the Convention − that the *Verfassungsgerichtshof* had the opportunity to confirm the Convention's constitutional status. In this judgment, rendered on 14 October 1965, the Court recognized that Article 6 was not only a programmatic principle for the legislature, but a binding norm of constitutional significance. It then went on to say that:

By virtue of Section II of the Constitutional Law (BG Bl No. 59/1964), the Convention on Human Rights has constitutional status and as clearly emerges from the introductory sentence of the said Section II, this has been the case ever since it became part of the Austrian legal system (3rd September 1958) and not merely since the promulgation on 6th April 1964 of the Constitutional Law . . . [and a claim under Article 6 of the Convention] must henceforth be considered as based on a constitutional provision, and in this respect is comparable to the right that everyone has to a hearing before a tribunal established by law [a lawful judge] in accordance with Section 83, para. 2 of the Constitutional Law.[14]

Since that time, the *Verfassungsgerichtshof* has developed a quite remarkable case-law in which it has made frequent

---

[13] Until of late an individual could not himself lodge an appeal before the *Verfassungsgerichtshof*. See R. Walter, *Österreichisches Bundesverfassungsrechtsystem* (1972), *passim*; and Evans, 'Written Communication', 113-28, esp. at 119-21. The Court is now competent to decide on individual applications alleging infringements of 'constitutionally protected rights' (i.e. including rights guaranteed by the European Convention) by decisions or actions of administrative authorities (art. 144). As to recent developments see n. 31 below; and the admissibility decision of the European Commission of Human Rights, application 8142/78, *X* v. *Austria* 18 *D&R* 88-99.

[14] Case no. G.28/64, 30 *Vfgh.*, no. 5100, 619-24; *ÖJZ* (1966), 248-9. Translation from 9 *Yearbook* (1966), 734-45, at 736-8.

reference to the Convention's provisions.[15] Recent examples in which the *Verfassungsgerichtshof* has taken the substantive provisions of the Convention into consideration include a judgment of 17 June 1977 in which it was held that the appellant's constitutionally guaranteed right under Article 2 of the Convention had not been violated when the police used firearms in order to arrest him after he had driven through a road block;[16] a case decided on 6 October 1977 in which the *Verfassungsgerichtshof* considered that the police had violated Article 3 of the Convention (degrading treatment) because of the manner in which they had made the arrest;[17] a judgment delivered on 9 March 1978 in which the Court held that action considered to be immoral did not in itself justify an interference with a person's right to privacy unless this were also 'necessary in a democratic society';[18] and lastly, in a case decided on 23 June 1977, in which a ministerial decision to dissolve an association that had contravened a Press Act was deemed unconstitutional as it had violated Article 11 of the Convention.[19]

However, although the Convention's substantive provisions most certainly impose immediately binding obligations upon individuals when and if the *Verfassungsgerichtshof* so determines, it is nevertheless of importance to note that the Court has on occasion preferred to rely upon older constitutional provisions in order to support its reasoning in particular cases rather than refer to the Convention. A vivid example of such an instance can be found in the Court's reluctance to interpret the meaning of the term 'civil rights' in Article 6 of the Convention:

[t]he Constitutional Court is not unaware that a better solution could be found from the point of view of the Convention. It did not feel

---

[15] See, for example, surveys made in the *ÖJZ* by G. Schantl, and M. Welan, 'Betrachtungen über die Judikatur des Verfassungsgerichtshofes zur Menschenrechtskonvention', in **25** (1970), 617–25 and 647–55; and two articles by W. Groiss, G. Schantl, and K. Welan 'Betrachtungen zur Verfassungsgerichtsbarkeit' in **31** (1976), 253–60 and 287–97, *passim*, and again in **33** (1978), 119 ff. Extracts of decisions and references to case-law are also published irregularly in *Yearbook*, e.g. **17** (1974), 628–34; **18** (1975), 407–9; **20** (1977), 674–8, 686–91, and 693–6; and **21** (1978), 667–77 and 679–80. The problem of self-executing provisions of the Convention is discussed below.

[16] Case B.425/75 in **100** *Juristische Blätter* (1978), 311, Vfgh. 8082/1977. An extract of this judgment can be found in **20** *Yearbook* (1977), 693–6.

[17] Case B.350/76 in **100** *Juristische Blätter* (1978), 312; Vfgh. 8145/1977. See also case B.15/73 in **38** *Vfgh.* (1975) no. 7081, 434–9.

[18] Case G.63/77 in *Vfgh.* 8272/1978; **34** *ÖJZ* (1979), 300; and 5 *EGZ* (1978), 245–7.

[19] Case B.209/76 in *Vfgh.* 8090/1977.

justified, however, in declaring a system unconstitutional which has existed for so long and has proved generally satisfactory. To declare the Austrian provisions contrary to the Convention of Human Rights would have far-reaching and profoundly disruptive consequences for Austrian law. In view of the widely differing notions found in the legal systems of the Contracting States on the meaning of a 'judicial tribunal' and a 'fair hearing', the Court is unable to reach the conclusion that the Austrian system violates the Convention.[20]

Although at first sight such an approach can be considered inadequate, an explanation may be found. It appears that the Court was simply not prepared to take responsibility for short-comings in domestic law which if found inappropriate, could require profound changes. In such cases, therefore, the Court shifts the onus upon the Government of the day to pass the necessary legislation to implement in a more adequate fashion certain of the Convention's provisions.

Particular note must be taken of the *Verfassungsgerichtshof's* readiness to consider the findings of the Convention organs.[21] In an important judgment of 29 June 1973 the Court based a decision of annulment — that a provision of the Tyrol Real Property Sales Act concerning the composition of the Tyrol Real Property Sales Commission was not an 'independent and impartial tribunal' — not only upon Article 6(1) of the Convention, but also upon a judgment rendered by the European Court of Human Rights.[22] It referred to the findings of the Strasbourg Court in the case of *Ringeisen* v. *Austria* in which it was held that although the decision of the Austrian Real Property Sales Commission applied rules of administrative law, the fact that the decision not to approve a contract of sale was decisive for the relations in civil law between the seller and buyer of the property in question, it followed that the matter concerned the civil rights and obligations of the parties to the

---

[20] This passage is quoted by Khol, n. 1 above, at 256. Case G.6/65 of 14 Oct. 1965; *Vfgh*. 5102/1965; also in 21 *ÖJZ* (1966), 409. (This decision later constituted the subject of an application before the European Commission of Human Rights. See application no. 2076/63, 10 *Yearbook* (1967), 136–69.) The *Verfassungsgerichtshof* used similar terms in case G.28/64, cited n. 14 above, at 744 in the *Yearbook*.

[21] Recent case-law is cited in ch. 10 below. See also Ch. Schreuer, 'Beschlüsse internationaler Organe im Österreichischen Staatsrecht' ('Decisions of International Institutions in Austrian Law'), 37 *ZRV* (1977), 468–503, and *Die Behandlung internationaler Organakte durch staatliche Gerichte* (1977), *passim*.

[22] Case G.15/73, 38 *Vfgh*. (1973), no. 7099, 516–25; commented upon by H. Petzold, 'The European Convention on Human Rights in the Austrian Constitutional Court', 46 *BYIL* (1972–1973), 401–4. See also *Collection*, art. 6(1), 151.

contract within the meaning of Article 6(1).[23] Similarly, the Court has recently indicated that it would probably be prepared to review its previous case-law concerning Article 6 of the Convention in the light of developments in Strasbourg. In an interesting passage, the *Verfassungsgerichtshof* held that:

[Although it] has repeatedly stated, the punishment of the failure to observe the personal and professional duties of civil servants does not fall under Article 6 of the Convention for the protection of Human Rights and Fundamental Freedoms . . .

According to the judgment of the European Court of Human Rights of 8 June 1976 in *Engel and others*, this statement is now no longer entirely unqualified. The Court of Human Rights stated that the Convention required the appropriate authorities to allow the accused the benefit of the guarantees of Article 6 [of the Convention] in the field of disciplinary proceedings in cases where severe sentences of imprisonment were imposed.[24]

However, the *Verfassungsgerichtshof* did not find it necessary to examine the Strasbourg Court's judgment and the consequences of its decision in domestic law, since the case before it did not concern an appeal against a domestic judgment imposing a sentence of imprisonment.

The constitutional importance of the Convention's substantive provisions (and probably also the decisions of the Convention organs) cannot be underestimated in Austrian law; and it is inevitable that the findings of the Constitutional Court will increasingly influence the case-law of other domestic jurisdictions. This being said, it must be pointed out that in Austria, by contrast with the Federal Republic of Germany — where the Federal Constitutional Court (*Bundesverfassungsgericht*) can hear appeals against decisions of both the Federal Court of Justice (*Bundesgerichtshof*) and the Federal Administrative Court (*Verwaltungsgerichtshof*) — the Austrian Supreme Court of Justice (*Oberster Gerichtshof*) and the Administrative Court (*Verwaltungsgerichtshof*) are independent from, and neither superior nor subordinate to one another or the *Verfassungsgerichtshof*. It follows that although the *Verfassungsgerichtshof*

---

[23] Eur. Court HR, *Ringeisen* case, judgment of 16 July 1971. For a more profound discussion of this subject consult D. J. Harris, 'The Application of Article 6(1) of the European Convention on Human Rights to Administrative Law', 47 *BYIL* (1974-5), 157-200.

[24] Case B.55/76, 15 Oct. 1976; *Vfgh.*, 7807/1976; and 4 *EGZ* (1977), 54-9; translation from 20 *Yearbook* (1977), 686-91, at 688-9.

has exclusive jurisdiction to review the application and scope of the constitutionally guaranteed rights and freedoms defined in the Convention, it does not have the competence to control the *acts* of the ordinary or administrative courts as to their constitutionality and compliance with human rights; it only possesses jurisdiction to decide on the validity of a law or regulation if and when it is requested to do so by a judicial instance in a particular case.[25]

Although the *Verfassungsgerichtshof* possesses exclusive jurisdiction to decide on the validity of domestic law, including its compatibility with the constitutionally guaranteed rights enumerated in the Convention, it does not necessarily follow that the *Oberster Gerichtshof* — and to a lesser extent the *Verwaltungsgerichtshof* — do not make reference to this instrument's provisions. The *Oberster Gerichtshof*, the highest court in civil and criminal matters, has rendered a number of important decisions in which it has taken the Convention's provisions into account when reviewing the findings of subordinate courts, and this is especially true in so far as penal matters are concerned.[26] It may be noted, for example, that on several occasions the Court has stressed the importance of the right to be provided free legal aid (Article 6(3)(c) of the Convention), and has ordered new proceedings to be instituted in the presence of a lawyer.[27] More important perhaps are decisions in which it has emphasized that the provisions of the Convention must always be taken into consideration when the Code of Penal Procedure is interpreted.[28] However, what appears to be unfortunate — at

[25] This form of 'norm-control' is regulated in part by arts. 89, 130, 131, 139, 140, and 141 of the Constitution. Further explanations of the working of the Austrian legal system can be found in *Encyclopedia of Comparative Law, National Reports*, 'Austria' by F. Schwind and H. Zemen, A.67–73; 'The Austrian Judicial System' in *Judicial Organisation*, 3–11; and Evans, 'Written Communication', 115–28, *passim*. See also n. 13 above.

[26] See Khol, and Berchtold, n. 1 above, *passim*. Extracts of selected cases can be found in 19 *Yearbook* (1976), 1105–8; 20 (1977), 681–6 and 691–3; and 21 (1978), 677–9. (Actually, *all* the ordinary courts have, in principle, to control themselves as to the constitutionality — and conformity with the Convention — of their individual acts. Control of regulations is referred to the *Verfassungsgerichtshof*.)

[27] See *European Convention on Human Rights: National Aspects* (Council of Europe, 1975), 32–4.

[28] See, for example, the *Oberster Gerichtshof's* judgment of 30 Nov. 1966 and 26 Apr. 1967 (extracts of which can be found in *Collection*, art. 6, 64–71), and that of 30 Apr. 1964 (in 7 *Yearbook* (1964), 512–4). Consult also J. Gebert, F. Pallin, and M. Pfeiffer, *Das Österreichische Strafverfahrensrecht: Strafprozessordnung* iii/1, n. 108(a) to sec. 1 (Code of Penal Procedure).

least in the eyes of one knowledgeable observer — is the fact that the *Oberster Gerichtshof* possesses a strong conservative inclination generally, with an attitude of particular reserve towards the Convention.[29] The fact that the Court's decisions are final and that violations of the Constitution (including the Convention's norms) occurring within the system of criminal and civil justice cannot be appealed by individuals to the *Verfassungsgerichtshof* probably unduly restricts the impact which the major provisions of the Convention — especially Articles 5 and 6 — may otherwise have upon the ordinary courts. And, although visibly influenced by the case law of the *Verfassungsgerichtshof* (as well as the findings of the Convention's organs), the *Oberster Gerichtshof* and all the ordinary courts appear to refer to the Convention's provisions only when they are specifically invoked by the parties, whereas this instrument should be constantly applied on its own motion.

In contrast, the *Verfassungsgerichtshof* is often the court competent to decide appeals against decisions of the administrative authorities in cases in which the appellant alleges violation of his constitutional rights (which include his rights under the Convention). This probably accounts for the rather limited use that the *Verwaltungsgerichtshof* makes of the Convention's provisions.[30] Thus, although the *Verwaltungsgerichtshof* has jurisdiction in matters relating to appeals lodged by certain public agencies alleging violations of 'public law' and by individuals alleging violations of their rights on the basis of administrative authorities' lack of competence, unlawfulness of action, and failure to act, most interesting case-law in this area of 'public law' is regulated by the *Verfassungsgerichtshof*, which has exclusive jurisdiction, once all remedies in the administrative hierarchy are exhausted, to decide whether or not an administrative authority has violated the individual's constitutionally protected rights.[31]

[29] Khol, n. 1 above, at 246 and 251. Dr Khol suggests (at 250) that the *Oberster Gerichtshof* may, in addition, be reluctant to assume the role of an applicant before another court, and submit to its jurisdiction. See art. 140 of the Austrian Constitution. The situation may now have improved; cf., for example, the attitude of the *Oberster Gerichtshof* in *X* v. *Austria*, Application 9167/80 (admissibility decision of 15 Oct. 1981).

[30] See written communication of A. Kobzina, in *Human Rights in National and International Law* (ed. A. H. Robertson), 61–4; and Council of Europe doc. H(76) 15, 21–2. Also consult R. Walter and H. Mayer, *Grundriss des österreichischen Verwaltungsverfahrensrechts* (1978), *passim*.

[31] See Khol, n. 1 above, esp. 252–7. It should perhaps be mentioned that there

Although the rights enumerated in the Convention must be effectively secured in the Austrian legal system, it does not necessarily follow that its provisions have in all cases direct effect (i.e. that they are necessarily 'self-executing') at the constitutional level. The *Verfassungsgerichtshof* referred to this problem in a judgment rendered on 14 October 1965 (case G6/65) when it stressed that the Convention was first and foremost a component part of 'a constitutional order which binds the *legislative* power directly',[32] and that when the compatibility of ordinary legislation with the Convention is examined by it in accordance with Article 140 of the Austrian Constitution, there is no need for the Court to consider that all the substantive provisions of this instrument are directly enforceable by individuals. This particular issue was also brought to light by the Federal Chancellor in his report relating to the measures taken by the Austrian authorities to meet the obligations incurred upon the ratification of the Convention. In this report he explained that:

... from the point of view of municipal law it is *not* imperative that the Convention shall *in all cases* be made *directly applicable at constitutional level.* ... A distinction must be drawn between the question of the level at which the Convention is to be applied in municipal law and that of the rank to which it is entitled in itself. ... The Convention has the rank of federal constitutional law in Austria. Under international law it ranks even higher; for being a rule that is binding on Austria as a State subject to the law, it also binds the authorities responsible for federal constitutional legislation, who are an organ of Austria.[33]

exists a possibility of *parallel* appeals, one before the *Verwaltungsgerichtshof* (legality) and the other before the *Verfassungsgerichtshof* (constitutionality of administrative act). An individual may, since the coming into force of a constitutional amendment in July 1976, immediately file an application before the *Verfassungsgerichtshof* to annul a law (without the exhaustion of all available administrative remedies beforehand) when and if the alleged violation of fundamental human rights affects him *directly* and where *no* judgment or administrative ruling has been pronounced. See Th. Öhlinger, 'Die Verfassungsentwicklung in Österreich seit 1974', 37 *ZRV* (1977), 399–467. (English summary on 466–7.) The text of this constitutional amendment can be found in *Bgbl. Nr.* 302; Federal Constitutional Act of 1975, translation in A. P. Blaustein and G. H. Flanz, eds., *Constitutions of the Countries of the World* (Austria, Cumulative Supplement, 1976) 3–13.

[32] In 30 *Vfgh.* (1965), no. 5102, 628–33. Translation taken from 9 *Yearbook* (1966), 679. (Emphasis added.) It is interesting to note that this judgment, G.6/65, was delivered on the same day as the famous judgment G.28/64 referred to in n. 14 above.

[33] See 9 *Yearbook* (1966), 666–83 at 676. (Emphasis added.) Also consult A. Verdross, 'Die Stellung der Europäischen Konvention zum Schutz der Menschenrechte und Grundfreiheiten im Stufenbau der Rechtsordnung', *Juristische Blätter* (1966), 1–5.

It is interesting to observe that at that time the specific problem relating to the question of 'self-execution' was closely tied to the quite separate issue of the Convention's status in the domestic legal hierarchy.[34] Nevertheless, this problem still continues to persist today although admittedly it has lost much of its force; it seems to be generally accepted that the Convention's provisions are by and large 'self-executing'. Thus, although in principle the Convention confers rights and obligations upon the individual which he can enforce when the *Verfassungsgerichtshof* is seised in the matter in dispute, there remains an exception to this general rule: in cases where certain fundamental well-established Austrian legal institutions may be jeopardized if a provision were to be interpreted as giving an individual directly enforceable constitutional rights, the *Verfassungsgerichtshof* — whose function is to resolve such conflicts — tends to apply the Convention in such a way as to leave the ultimate decision to the legislature.[35] (In this context it may be important to appreciate the distinction made in Austrian law between the internal validity of the Convention and its internal applicability to individuals (direct effect) because the *Verfassungsgerichtshof* appears to reject the notion that the intentions of contracting parties should serve as a criterion establishing the direct application or otherwise of the Convention's norms *vis-à-vis* individuals, and instead tends to rely on domestic legal considerations.)

The overall effect of the Convention on the Austrian legal system has been substantial, and the Convention's rank of federal constitutional law secures it an additional dimension which is absent in *all* the other contracting States. Special attention is given to draft laws, to ensure conformity with the Convention and domestic tribunals are increasingly aware of its internal impact. What is perhaps of more importance, in cases where specific laws have been found not to conform with the Convention's provisions, as for example, in the cases of *Pataki & Dunshirn* v. *Austria* (nos. 596/59 and 789/60) and *Stögmüller. Matznetter, Neumeister* v. *Austria* (nos. 1602/62, 2278/64 and 1936/63), the Austrian Government has always

---

[34] Further references can be found in the report of the Federal Government, n. 33 above, at 668–70. ('Self-execution' and 'direct applicability' possess the same meaning for the purposes of this study.)
[35] See Khol, n. 1 above, esp 242–45.

taken steps to amend domestic law and bring it into conformity with the Convention. Further examples of changes in domestic law can be found in connection with friendly settlements in *Simon-Herold* (no. 4340/69), *Gussenbauer* (nos. 4897/71 and 5219/71), and more recently in *Peschke* (no. 8289/78), and in cases in which some form of arrangement had taken place: *Rebitzer* (3245/67) and *Vampel* (4465/70).[36] In addition, particular note may be taken of the Federal Act of 26 March 1963 by which the Austrian authorities permitted certain individuals, who had applications pending before the European Commission of Human Rights concerning the domestic appeals procedure, to have proceedings reopened before the Austrian courts.[37]

In 1964 a special Committee of Human Rights Experts was set up to draft a codified catalogue of fundamental human rights. To date, it has only succeeded in producing a number of alternative drafts for two rights — the rights to life and freedom of information. It has apparently found it extremely difficult to improve upon the simple guidelines provided in the Basic Law and the European Convention on Human Rights and replace them with a new detailed code which may subsequently be difficult to alter.[38] In these circumstances, it appears to be unfortunate that the Austrian Government, in June 1966, abandoned the idea of passing a Supplementary Act to make appropriate domestic legal adaptations in order to meet the requirements of the Convention.[39]

B. Federal Republic of Germany

The European Convention was signed on behalf of the German Federal Republic on 4 November 1950. The Convention was subsequently approved by the legislature in the form of an enactment on 7 August 1952.[40] The instrument of ratification

[36] For more details concerning the above-cited cases consult A. H. Robertson, *Human Rights in Europe* (1977), *passim*; and 'Stocktaking', *passim*. The case of *Peschke* is discussed by the author in a case-note in 4 *TL* (1982), 71–8, at 75–6.

[37] See 6 *Yearbook* (1973), 804–6; and Ch. Schreuer, 'The Impact of International Institutions on the Protection of Human Rights in Domestic Courts', 4 *Israel Yearbook on Human Rights* (1974), 60–88, at 65.

[38] See Evans, n. 25 above, at 6; and *UN Yearbook on Human Rights* (1967), 19; and subsequent references to this Committee's work in *Yearbook* (1965–72).

[39] See report of the Federal Government, n. 33 above.

[40] Ratification Act of 7 Aug. 1952, in *Bundesgesetzblatt* (Federal Gazette of Legislation), II (1952), 685 and 953.

was deposited with the Secretary-General of the Council of Europe on 5 December 1952. Declarations under Articles 25 and 46 were made on 5 July 1955 and have been renewed without interruption ever since. The First Protocol was ratified on 13 February 1957 and the Fourth on 1 June 1968. A reservation was made concerning Article 7(2) of the Convention.[41]

The relationship between the norms of public international law and their application within the German legal system is catered for in the following provisions of the Basic Law of the Federal Republic of Germany:

Article 24:
(1) The Federation may, by legislation, transfer sovereign powers to intergovernmental institutions.
(2) For the maintenance of peace, the Federation may enter a system of mutual collective security; in doing so it will consent to such limitations upon its rights of sovereignty as will bring about and secure a peaceful and lasting order in Europe and among the nations of the world.
(3) For the settlement of disputes between states, the Federation will accede to agreements concerning a general, comprehensive and obligatory system of international arbitration.

Article 25:
The general rules of public international law are an integral part of federal law. They shall take precedence over the laws and shall directly create rights and duties for the inhabitants of the federal territory.

Article 31:
Federal law shall override *Land* law.

Article 32:
(1) The conduct of relations with foreign states shall be the concern of the federation . . .

Article 59:
(1) The federal President shall represent the Federation in its international relations. He shall conclude treaties with foreign states on behalf of the Federation. He shall accredit and receive envoys.
(2) Treaties which regulate the political relations of the Federation or relate to matters of federal legislation shall require the consent or participation, in the form of a federal law, of the bodies competent in any specific case for such federal legislation. For administrative agreements the provisions concerning the federal administration shall apply *mutatis mutandis*.[42]

---

[41] See *Collected Texts*, 606. The FRG also made three interpretative declarations, see 612-16.
[42] Translation from A. J. Peaslee, *Constitutions of Nations* (1968), iii. 366-9 and 373.

Interestingly enough, once the European Convention on Human Rights had been drafted, all the political parties initiated a bill for this instrument's approval even before the Government of the day could do so formally.[43] Approval by the legislature naturally followed. This took the form of an enactment (*Zustimmungsgesetz*: 'the Treaty . . . is hereby approved') in accordance with Article 59(2) of the Basic Law (the legislature gave its 'consent or participation': *Zustimmung order Mitwirkung*) whereby the Convention acquired for itself the status of federal law.[44]

German doctrine appears divided as to the exact legal effect of the *Zustimmungsgesetz*. Most authors adhere to the doctrine of transformation, whereby the norms of a given treaty are transformed into the domestic plane by the legislature's law of approbation, with the result that they may reach officials and individuals alike. Others believe that a treaty is not as such transformed into domestic law, but that the law of approbation permits internal applicability without necessarily altering the legal basis of these norms.[45] Although it is generally assumed that the former view continues to prevail, it is nevertheless a well-established fact that the courts consider that such legislative approval implies an order addressed to the domestic authorities and to the courts to give effect to treaty provisions on the domestic plane.[46]

It follows that, as Article 59 of the Basic Law secures the Convention the status of *at least* federal law, the directly applicable provisions of this instrument have precedence over all legislation of the *Länder*, whether prior or subsequent to the Convention's incorporation into domestic law; and by virtue of

[43] K. J. Partsch, 'Die europäische Menschenrechtskonvention vor den nationalen Parlamenten', 17 *ZRV* (1956/57) 93-132 at 99.

[44] According to the Federal Constitutional Court (*Franco-German Commercial Treaty* case, 1 *Bverfg.* (1952), 372 at 395) the 'consent or participation' must be 'a governmental act in the form of a statute'.

[45] For further references on this subject consult M. Waelbroeck, *Traités internationaux et juridictions internes dans les pays du Marché commun* (1969), 61-79; P. Lardy, *La force obligatoire du droit international en droit interne* (1966), 41-94; and L. Wildhaber, *Treaty-Making Power and Constitution* (1971), 215-18.

[46] See B. Vatányi, 'Some Reflections on Article 25 of the Constitution of the Federal Republic of Germany', 24 *NILR* (1977), 578-88; H. Rupp, 'International Law as Part of the Law of the Land: Some Aspects of the Operation of Article 25 of the Basic Law of the Federal Republic of Germany', 11 *Texas International Law Journal* (1976), 541-7, and his 'Judicial Review of International Agreements: Federal Republic of Germany', 25 *AJCL* (1977), 286-302.

the principle *lex posterior derogat legi priori*, its provisions also take precedence over all prior federal legislation. This was explained unequivocally by the *Bundesverwaltungsgericht* (Federal Administrative Court) in December 1955: 'The Convention has the status of federal law. After its entry into force the Convention is applicable to all proceedings instituted subsequently and also to cases pending at that date'.[47]

Since its entry into force on 3 September 1953, therefore, those provisions of the Convention which are considered by the courts to be directly applicable, i.e. those which grant substantive rights to individuals, are part of German law and can be invoked before the German courts.[48] The sole exception to this appears to be Article 13 of the Convention which, due to its specific nature, has been interpreted by the *Bundesgerichtshof* (Federal Court of Justice) not to be in itself a directly enforceable right.[49] And, as the courts have not been too rigorous in determining that the majority of the instrument's provisions are in fact 'self-executing', there has ensued an immense wealth of case-law on this subject:[50] Up to the end of 1974 the Council of Europe had recorded about 170 cases in which the Convention had been referred to by the courts.[51]

The Convention does not, however, have the status of constitutional law and cannot be invoked by way of constitutional appeal before the Federal Constitutional Court. In its decision of 14 January 1960 the *Bundesverfassungsgericht* (Federal Constitutional Court) held that 'An appeal to the Constitutional

---

[47] Judgment of 15 Dec. 1955, 3 *Bverwg.* 48–61.

[48] See H. Golsong, 'The European Convention on Human Rights before Domestic Courts', 38 *BYIL* (1962), 445–56 at 449; and P. Seidel, 'Der Rang der EMRK in den Mitgliedstaaten', 19 *Deutsches Verwaltungsblatt* (1975), 747–53, at 749. See also 2 *Yearbook* (1958–9), 578.

[49] Decision of 20 July 1964 *NJW* (1964), 2119–20; *Collection*, art. 13, 4. There exists a well recognized rule of interpretation whereby the courts try to give German statutes an interpretation which is in line with the FRG's obligations in public international law.

[50] See *Collection* and *Yearbook, passim.* In addition to two basic works which deal with this subject extensively — H. Guradze, *Die Europäische Menschenrechtskonvention* (1968), and K. J. Partsch, *Die Rechte und Freiheiten der Europäischen Menschenrechtskonvention* (1966) — particular note may be taken of a forthcoming looseleaf handbook for German-speaking practising lawyers: *Internationaler Kommentar zur Europäischen Menschenrechtskonvention* (to be edited by H. Miehsler, H. Petzold, and others, 1980–).

[51] See Evans, 'Written Communication', 142–56, at 152. An interesting survey of earlier case-law is provided by A. L. Del Russo, *International Protection of Human Rights* (1971), at 222–9.

Court cannot be based on the Convention of Human Rights (Article 90 of the Federal Constitutional Court Act . . .) . . .'[52] A rather more difficult question to answer is whether the Convention's provisions may possess a hierarchically superior status to federal legislation.[53] This problem is likely to receive renewed consideration in the light of the Human Rights Court's finding that the Federal Republic of Germany had violated certain articles of the Convention in the *König* and *Luedicke, Belkacem, and Koç* cases.[54] In this connection note may be taken of a case that came before the *Bundesverfassungsgericht* in 1971. In that case the Court ruled that as Article III of the General Agreement on Tariffs and Trade was a provision of an international agreement and not a general rule of international law within the meaning of Article 25 of the Basic Law, it obtained the rank of a federal statute upon its incorporation and consequently did not take precedence over a subsequent turnover tax law.[55] What appears particularly interesting in this case is the fact that the Court indicated that it may be prepared to give priority to certain well-established 'general rules of public international law' (apparently whether they be customary or codified in international agreements) which presumably possess a hierarchically superior status over federal laws generally. It could therefore be argued — at least before the ordinary and administrative courts[56] — that certain norms of the Convention are an integral part of these 'general rules of public international law' referred to in Article 25 of the Basic Law, and may consequently take precedence over both prior and subsequent federal legislation. Perhaps, in this context, the

---

[52] *NJW* (1960), 1243–4. Translation from 3 *Yearbook* (1960), 628–32 at 632. (This decision was discussed by H. Guradze and R. Herzog, see 3 *Yearbook* (1960), n. at 628.) The same court, in its decision of 14 Mar. 1973 (*Baader-Meinhof* case, *Collection*, art. 6, 160), was likewise not prepared to uphold a constitutional complaint based on art. 6 of the Convention on the ground that a constitutional complaint could not be based upon the provisions of the Convention.

[53] See Partsch, n. 50 above; H. Guradze, 'Written Communication' in *Human Rights in National and International Law* (ed. A. H. Robertson, 1968), 56–9; and T. Buergenthal, 'The Domestic Status of the European Convention on Human Rights: A Second Look', 7 *Journal of the ICJ* (1966), 55–96, at 67–72.

[54] Eur. Court HR, judgment of 28 June 1978, ser. A, no. 27; and judgment of 28 Nov. 1978, ser. A, no. 29.

[55] Judgment of 9 June 1971, 31 *Bverfg.*, case no. 15, 145–80, at 177–8.

[56] In a case decided on 20 Oct. 1976 the *Bundesgerichtshof* explained that if an inconsistency were to occur between an international legal norm and subsequent legislation, the latter 'withdraws' without becoming unconstitutional or violating art. 25 of the Constitution: *Juristenzeitung* (1977), 67, at 68.

astute observation made by Dr Golsong in 1957 deserves to be cited:

From a purely legal point of view [however] it cannot be said that the provisions of the Convention invariably take precedence over federal laws enacted after the promulgation of the Convention if these laws are incompatible with the said provisions. But it may be assumed that the legislature will feel obliged to honour the engagement undertaken by ratifying the treaty and that the judge, in case of conflict, will apply the treaty provisions on the assumption that the legislature did not intend to derogate from the international engagement.[57]

The important role that the *Bundesverfassungsgericht* has in the German legal system in safeguarding individuals' basic rights needs to be stressed. It is generally accepted that its interpretation and upholding of the rights guaranteed in the Republic's Basic Law has ensured the protection of individuals' human rights in a manner unparalleled in former German constitutions or in comparable foreign constitutions.[58] Of special significance in this connection is the constitutional right of complaint (*Verfassungsbeschwerde*). Anyone can lodge such a complaint with the *Bundesverfassungsgericht* alleging that his fundamental rights have been violated by the public powers, an administrative court or a legislator. It can therefore come as no surprise that as the Basic Law in general provides a better standard of protection than does the European Convention on Human Rights (which does, after all, lay down *minimum* guarantees which are internationally supervised), the relevant provisions of the Basic Law are invoked to a much greater extent before the courts than are those of the European Convention.[59]

The German Constitution does not expressly state whether international agreements are subject to judicial review of their constitutionality. Article 100, paragraph 2, of the Basic Law merely stipulates that 'If, in the course of litigation, doubt exists

---

[57] H. Golsong, 'The European Convention for the Protection of Human Rights and Fundamental Freedoms in a German Court', 33 *BYIL* (1957), 317-21, at 320. But see the *Bundesverfassungsgericht* decision in 21 *Yearbook* (1978), 745-7.

[58] *Bull. EC* Suppl. 5/76, 33-4. For more detailed studies see H. Saeker, *Der Bundesverfassungsgericht* (1975).

[59] See, for example, cases cited in *Juristenzeitung* (1977), 21-4; and in 21 *Yearbook* (1978), 745-7. Also consult the writings referred to in notes 50 and 58 above. The *Bundesverfassungsgericht* can also look into the compatibility of *Land* law with the Convention: See Evans, n. 51 above, at 150-1. Failure to raise a constitutional appeal, in many instances, precludes an applicant from pursuing his case in Strasbourg; see *X* v. *FRG*, application 8408/78, in 18 *D&R*, 209-15; and *X* v. *FRG*, application 8499/79, in 21 *D&R*, 176-9.

whether a rule of public international law is an integral part of federal law and whether such a rule directly creates rights and duties for the individual (Article 25), the court shall obtain the decision of the Federal Constitutional Court.' The *Bundesverfassungsgericht* has however held that treaties are subject to such review by invoking the dualist transformation doctrine whereby review is made not of the treaty itself but of the statute approving and transforming the agreement.[60] The Court has interpreted its role of constitutional review very rigorously: it has, for example, held in the famous *Internationale Handelsgesellschaft* case that it will accord priority to constitutionally guaranteed fundamental rights even though this could result in a breach of European Community law.[61] If faced with a similar dilemma *vis-à-vis* the European Convention, it is probable (but of course not certain) that a similar line of reasoning will be taken.[62]

As already explained, German courts often refer to the Convention's provisions. A few decisions of the *Bundesgerichtshof* (Federal Supreme Court) may be cited as examples. On 29 September 1977 the Civil Chamber of the *Bundesgerichtshof* considered that the helping of a person to escape from the German Democratic Republic was not contrary to *boni mores* and it did not necessarily follow that a contract to that effect was null and void.[63] In so holding the court referred to Articles 2(2) and 3(2) of the Convention's Fourth Protocol in order to substantiate its reasoning.[64] In another case a criminal sentence

---

[60] See Wildhaber, n. 45 above, at 355.

[61] Judgment dated 29 May 1974, 37 *Bverfg.*, 271–305. (The Court so held despite its acceptance of European Community law as 'an independent system of law flowing from an autonomous legal source'. This subject is further discussed in ch. 9 below.) Among a large number of commentaries on this case are W. R. Edeson and F. Wooldridge, 'European Community Law and Fundamental Rights: Some Recent Decisions of the European Court and National Courts', *LIEI* (1976), 1–54; M. Hilf, E. Klein, and A. Bleckmann, 'Sekundäres Gemeinschaftsrecht und Deutsche Grundrechte, Zum Beschluss des Bundesverfassungsgerichts vom 29. Mai 1974', 35 *ZRV* (1975), 51–107; and U. Scheuner, 'Der Grundrechtsschutz in der Europäischen Gemeinschaft und in der Verfassungsrechtsprechung', 100 *Archiv des Öffentlichen Rechts* (1975) 30–52.

[62] But what if a right guaranteed by the Convention — as interpreted by the Strasbourg Court — were to provide a higher standard of protection than does the Basic Law? Note must be taken — in this connection — of the *Eurocontrol* case (9 *EGZ* (1982), 172–81) in which the Court indicated that it would control the compatibility of domestic statutes with binding rules of public international law (this case is further discussed in ch. 10 below, n. 81.)

[63] See 69 *Bgh.*, case no. 38, 295–302.   [64] Ibid., at 298.

was set aside by the *Bundesgerichtshof* as the delay in proceedings violated the guarantee of a trial within 'a reasonable time' provided by Article 6(1) of the Convention;[65] while a few months later the same court set aside a decision of a regional court as the latter had given undue consideration to the unreasonable length of the accused's trial (Article 6 of the Convention) without abiding by certain statutory conditions prescribed by the German Criminal Code in which specific criteria for the discontinuance of a trial are laid down.[66]

Generally speaking, all domestic courts — whatever their position in the internal hierarchy — are competent not only to determine infringements of the *Grundrechtskatalog* (Bill of Rights) but also those of the European Convention on Human Rights. Here again, case-law is quite substantial. Suffice it for present purposes to concentrate on one particular issue for illustrative purposes.[67] In the case of *Luedicke, Belkacem, and Koç* before the European Court of Human Rights, all three applicants had argued unsuccessfully before various German courts that their payment of interpreter's fees upon conviction conflicted with Article 6(3)(e) of the European Convention which provides that 'everyone charged with a criminal offence has . . . [the right] . . . to have the free assistance of an interpreter if he cannot understand or speak the language used in court'.[68] In all three cases the domestic courts considered that this provision related only to an obligation to provide provisional exemption from interpretation costs.[69] Similarly, the administrative courts (whose jurisdiction extends to all disputes of a public-law nature unless jurisdiction of another court has been expressly provided for by federal legislation), when reviewing the manner in which public authorities observe the Constitution, often refer to the Convention's provisions as well as written and

---

[65] See 21 *Yearbook* (1978), 744. [66] Ibid., 748–50.

[67] Reference to other cases may be found in *Collection* and *Yearbook, passim*, and in writings referred to in n. 50 above. See also U. Hoffman-Remy, *Die Möglichkeiten der Grundrechtseinschränkung nach den Art. 8–11 Abs. 2 der EMRK* (1976).

[68] See n. 54 above.

[69] In this case the Court in Strasbourg held that the contested decisions of the German courts were in breach of art. 6(3)(e). (An extract from the Cologne Court of Appeal decision in the *Koç* case is reproduced in 19 *Yearbook* (1976), 1125–6; the other German court decisions are cited in the Strasbourg Court's judgment, paras. 17 and 22.) New amendments to the Court Costs Act (*Gerichtskostengesetz*, see annex i, no. 19040), in force as of 1 Jan. 1981, have been implemented as a consequence of these proceedings in Strasbourg.

unwritten constitutional norms, i.e. rights guaranteed in the *Grundrechtskatalog* and such notions as the principle of proportionality and the rule of law.[70] In this context it will be fascinating to observe how the administrative courts will interpret Article 6 of the Convention in the light of the findings of the European Court of Human Rights which considered that this Article was applicable to certain matters which come before the German administrative courts.[71]

Although the provisions of the European Convention on Human Rights appear to be invoked before German courts to a greater extent than in any other contracting state and the impact of this instrument is far from negligible, the fact that its norms are not given the status of constitutional law and that subsequent federal legislation may supersede any of its provisions does at least theoretically limit its impact on domestic law. This does not, however, in itself adversely affect the Convention's impact achieved on the international plane: over one thousand individual applications against the Federal Republic of Germany had been lodged before the Commission in the first ten years of its life,[72] a number of friendly settlements have been achieved in accordance with Articles 28 and 30 of the Convention,[73] unofficial arrangements have taken place in several cases, and law amending the country's Code of Criminal Procedure[74] as well as an extradition treaty with the German Democratic Republic have been altered as a direct consequence of action taken before the Strasbourg organs.[75]

---

[70] See, for example, *Collection*, art. 6, pp. 21 and 101; art. 8, pp. 1, 4, 6, 7, 19, and 24; and art. 10, pp. 2 and 4. It should be noted that the *Bundesverwaltungsgericht* (Federal Administrative Court), like its counterpart in the 'ordinary courts', the *Bundesgerichtshof*, is subject to the jurisdiction of the *Bundesverfassungsgerichtshof* in so far as the constitutionality of formal statutes is concerned.

[71] See n. 54 above, esp. paras. 89 ff. of the Court's judgment. (Compare this to previous domestic law developments: *Collections*, art. 6, pp. 1, 2, 4, and 6.)

[72] See in this connection a fascinating study undertaken at the Erasmus University of Rotterdam entitled *Complaints about Violations of Human Rights* (Sept. 1981, interim report, ed. P. W. C. Akkermans, H. Elffers, W. G. Verkruisen, and A. Th. Walterbeek-Matlung), esp. 17–29.

[73] See 'Stocktaking', 84–100 *passim*, the latest being *X* v. *FRG*, application 6699/74, report of Commission, 11 Oct. 1979, 17 *D&R*, 21–34.

[74] See Eur. Court HR, *Wemhoff* case, judgment of 27 June 1968, ser. A, no. 7; (also ser. B., vol. 6 (1969) in the same case); and 'Stocktaking', 44–5. See also D. Sattler, *Wiederaufnahme des Strafprozesses nach Feststellung der Konventionswidrigkeit durch Organe der Europäischen Menschenrechtskonvention* (Ph.D. dissertation, University of Freiburg, 1973). Also see n. 69 above.

[75] Application 6242/73, *Bruckmann* v. *FRG*, 6 *D&R*, 57–61. (The Commission's

It should perhaps be added that the Convention's provisions may be elevated to the status of constitutional law either by means of legislative enactment or by judicial interpretation to that effect, although to date these suggestions do not seem to have found sufficient support.[76]

C. Liechtenstein

The Principality of Liechtenstein became the 21st member state of the Council of Europe on 23 November 1978. Upon the deposit of its instrument of accession the country signed the European Convention on Human Rights.[77] This was done shortly after the Parliamentary Assembly had given a favourable opinion to the Committee of Ministers in which it welcomed, *inter alia*, Liechtenstein's willingness to fulfill the provisions of Article 3 of the Statute of the Council of Europe and welcomed the country's intention to sign the Human Rights Convention simultaneously when acceding to the organization.[78]

Article 8(2) of the Principality's Constitution of 1921 specifies that 'Treaties which . . . dispose of rights of sovereignty or state prerogatives, assume any new burden for the Principality or its citizens . . . shall not be valid unless they have been approved by the Diet.'[79] To date, the European Convention on Human Rights has not been approved by the Diet and promulgated in the National Legal Gazette (*Landesgesetzblatt*), and does not as yet possess the status of domestic law. Therefore it is too early to determine with any certainty the extent to which the Convention's norms will be taken into consideration by the

report adopted on 14 July 1976, 'noted . . . with satisfaction' that a Mutual Assistance Act had been amended.)

[76] See E. Menzel, 'Verfassungsrang für die Normen der Europäischen Menschenrechtskonvention nach dem Recht der Bundesrepublik Deutschlands?' in *Festbuch für P. Guggenheim* (1968), 573-604, at 573. Also consult G. Dronsch, *Der Rang der Europäischen Menschenrechtskonvention im deutschen Normensystem* (doctoral dissertation, University of Göttingen, 1964).

[77] Chart Showing Signatures and Ratifications of Council of Europe, Conventions and Agreements (15 Dec. 1981), 17-18. See also Council of Europe Press Releases F(78)45 and C(78)48, 23 Nov. 1978; and *Le Monde*, 28 Nov. 1978, 4.

[78] Opinion 90 (1978) adopted on 28 Sept. 1978. See also Parliamentary Assembly docs. 4193 (10 July 1978) and 4211 (13 Sept. 1978). But also consult C. Zanghi, 'L'Ammissione del Liechtenstein al Consiglio d'Europa (Una "associazione" mancata?)', 20 *Riv. DE* (1980), 240-53.

[79] Translation taken from A. J. Peaslee, *Constitutions of Nations* (1968), iii. 532. (See also arts. 62(6), 65, and 66.)

Liechtenstein courts.[80] An exchange of correspondence with a lawyer in Liechtenstein suggests that the Convention will probably be ratified by the end of 1982 or early in 1983. It is understood that both the penal code and the code of criminal procedure are in need of revision prior to ratification and a draft project for their revision is being circulated amongst lawyers for comments and observations. This draft is modelled on the Austrian codes and it is envisaged that it will likewise be adopted by the Diet at the end of 1982 or in the spring of 1983.[81]

The Liechtenstein Government has acquired the services of a human rights expert as *'conseiller juridique'* specifically in order to advise it on the subject of ratification of the Convention, and more specifically on its relationship with Liechtenstein law, as well as on such matters as reservations and declaratory interpretations.[82] A governmental report to the legislature on this subject is due to be published in the spring of 1982.[82a]

D. Switzerland[83]

Switzerland became a member state of the Council of Europe on 6 May 1963. The Convention on Human Rights was signed on 21 December 1972 and ratified on 28 November 1974.

[80] But see generally: W. Kranz, ed., *The Principality of Liechtenstein* (1973, a documentary handbook); and S. G. Kohn, 'The Sovereignty of Liechtenstein', in 61 *AJIL* (1967), 547–57. Consult also the interesting case of *X & Y* v. *Switzerland*, application nos. 7289/75 and 7349/76, in 9, *D&R*, 57–94, and criticism of this decision by J. Andrews, in 2 *EL Rev.* (1977), 486–457. See also D. J. Niedermann, *Liechtenstein und die Schweiz. Eine völkerrechtliche Untersuchung* (1976); and L. Wildhaber, 'Liechtensteinische Gerichtsentscheide zum Völkerrecht' in 24, *ASDI* (1978), 163–166.

[81] Letter of 23 Dec. 1981 from Mrs M. Gassner-Hemmerlé (Vaduz). Liechtenstein has historically followed the Austrian example in this field because legal notions and traditions are oriented towards Austria in this respect: see *Neue Züricher Zeitung* 13 Nov. 1980, 24.

[82] The expert concerned is Professor L. Wildhaber (University of Basel), a judge on the Liechtenstein Supreme Court since 1975.

[82a] The Convention and its Second Protocol were ratified on 8 Sept. 1982. Reservations were made in respect of Articles 2, 6, and 8. Liechtenstein also made declarations under Articles 25 and 46 of the Convention.

[83] Recent publications concerning the domestic status of the Convention in the Swiss legal system include: G. Malinverni, 'L'application de la Convention européenne des Droits de l'Homme en Suisse', XV *Journée Juridique* (1976), 1–51; J. B. Reimann, 'La Convention de sauvegarde des Droits de l'Homme et des libertés fondamentales et la Suisse', VIII *RDH/HRJ* (1975), 407–16; 94 *Revue de droit Suisse* (1975), special issue: 'La Convention européenne des Droits de l'Homme et son application en droit Suisse', see, in particular, articles by D. Schindler, 357–72, J. P. Müller, 373–405, M. Schubarth, 465–510, L. Wildhaber, 511–44; and bibliography, at 545. Consult also S. Trechsel, *Die europäische Menschenrechtskonvention, ihr Schutz der persönlichen*

Declarations under Articles 25 and 46 were made at the same time, and reservations were made in respect of Articles 5 and 6 of the Convention.[84] Prior to ratification of the Convention, the Swiss authorities considered that certain constitutional provisions were not in conformity with the Convention, and they made appropriate amendments to the Federal Constitution: votes for women in federal elections were secured by the amendment of 7 February 1971 and the denomination articles (discriminating against Jesuits and Catholic convents) were repealed on 20 May 1973.[85] The First Protocol was signed on 19 May 1976 but as yet has not been ratified. The Fourth Protocol remains unsigned.[86]

Articles 8 and 85(5) of the Swiss Federal Constitution of 1848 (as amended and revised in 1874 and 1964), read as follows:

Article 8:
The Confederation has the sole right to declare war and conclude peace, and to make alliances and treaties, particularly customs and commercial treaties, with foreign states.

Article 85 [Powers of the Federal Assembly]:
The following matters in particular are within the competence of the two councils [i.e. the National Council and the Council of State] . . .
(5) Alliances and treaties with foreign states, as also the approval of treaties made by the cantons between themselves or with foreign states; nevertheless, treaties between cantons shall only be brought before the Federal Assembly when the Federal Council or another canton raises objection.[87]

Thus, the Federal Constitution confers upon the Federal Assembly powers to make alliances and treaties with foreign states, and upon their approval by the Federal Assembly, such

Freiheit und die schweizerischen Strafprozessrechte (1974); D. Poncet, *La protection de l'accusé par la Convention européenne des Droits de l'Homme* (1977); and B.-F. Junod, *La Suisse et la Convention européenne des Droits de l'Homme* (Ph.D. thesis, Neuchâtel, 1968).

[84] See 17 *Yearbook* (1974), 2, 6–8, and 18. Consult also extracts of and references to parliamentary debates in *Yearbook*: vol. 12 (1969), 500–78; 14 (1971), 912, 940–56; and 15 (1972), 742–8. Interpretative declarations were also made in respect of art. 6, paras. 1 and 3(c) and (e); see *Collected Texts* at 614. See, in this connection, *Temeltash* v. *Switzerland*, application 9116/80, declared admissible in Oct. 1981.

[85] See Reimann, n. 83 above, 410–12. The second amendment was technically voted upon *after* the Swiss signature of the Convention.

[86] Chart showing signatures and Ratifications of Council of Europe Conventions and Agreements (15 Dec 1981) at 17 and 18.

[87] Translation from A. J. Peaslee, *Constitutions of Nations* (1968), iii. 933 and 956–7. Also see L. Wildhaber, *Treaty-Making Power and Constitution* (1971), 52–9.

international agreements become a source of domestic law like all other legislation. (Mention should also be made of the now-amended Article 89(4) of the Constitution which provided a stipulation to the effect that treaties that have been concluded for an indefinite duration or for a period of more than fifteen years are subject to an optional referendum.[88]) This domestic validity of treaties is acquired by Article 113(3) of the Constitution which gives them, for the law enforcement organs, a rank equivalent at least to that of statutes.[89] Article 113 provides:

The Federal Tribunal has also jurisdiction in regard to: . . .
(3) Complaints in respect of violation of constitutional rights of citizens, and complaints by individuals in respect of violation of concordats or treaties.
Administrative disputes to be determined by federal legislation are excluded.
In all the cases above mentioned, the Federal Tribunal shall administer the laws passed by the Federal Assembly and such ordinances of that Assembly as are of general application. It shall likewise act in accordance with treaties ratified, by the Federal Assembly.[90]

Consequently, the 'incorporation' of international agreements into Swiss law is considered to be automatic in that there is no need for them to be enacted as statutes. Usually, the Executive (Federal Council) negotiates and signs a given international agreement, it then submits the treaty for approval by the Federal Assembly which, by means of an *arrêté fédéral*, approves the document ('The treaty . . . is approved. The Federal Council is authorized to ratify it.') When an international agreement is subject to a referendum a second article is added stipulating that the 'present *arrêté* is subject to the optional referendum, in accordance with Article 89(4) of the Federal Constitution'.[91] It is important to note, in this context, that legislative approval is not a law but that it is a legislative authorization to ratify the given instrument which binds Switzerland

---

[88] See G. Malinverni, 'Democracy and Foreign Policy: The Referendum on Treaties in Switzerland', 49 *BYIL* (1978), 207–19. (As the European Convention on Human Rights contains a 'denunciation' clause (art. 65) the procedure was deemed unnecessary.)
[89] Z. Giacometti, *Schweizerisches Bundesstaatsrecht* (1949), 829, para. 80.
[90] Peaslee, n. 87 above, at 961.
[91] See P. Guggenheim, *Traité de droit international public* (1967), i. 73, W. G. Rice, 'The Position of International Treaties in Swiss Law', 46 *AJIL* (1952), 641–66, and J.-F. Aubert, 'L'autorité, en droit interne, des traités internationaux', in 81 *Revue de droit suisse* (1962), 265–87.

and its officials internationally upon its ratification and entry into force. However, although there exists no requirement of promulgation — for the agreement is as such (*ipso jure*) valid and binding domestically before publication — official publication *is necessary* in order to extend its binding effect upon individuals.[92] It is in accordance with the above procedure that the European Convention on Human Rights became an autonomous source of law upon its ratification on 28 November 1974 (*RO* (Federal Gazette) (1974), 2148).[93]

As the Convention forms an integral part of Swiss law, those of its provisions deemed by the courts to be directly applicable (self-executing) have attained for themselves a standing of 'at least the rank of federal law'.[94] It follows that the interpretation and application of guarantees of constitutional rights as well as the rights protected by the European Convention are within the competence of all Swiss courts, but in the majority of cases they tend to apply constitutional norms to a much greater extent. This is so because the courts are naturally more familiar with rights enumerated in the Federal Constitution and with case-law relating to them. Only when the relevant written and unwritten constitutional norms have been invoked are the courts prepared to consider whether the result reached is compatible with the Convention's provisions. Thus, rather than apply the European Convention directly, the judiciary, not unnaturally, try to interpret constitutional guarantees so that they conform to the Convention's provisions; this *verfassungskonforme Auslegung* is probably a frequent occurrence even in those cases where no express reference to the Convention is made. From an interpretation of conformity with the Swiss constitution, the courts then turn to an examination of conformity with the Convention. This happens very often and unconspicuously because constitutional and 'European' guarantees

[92] Wildhaber, n. 87 above, at 205-6.

[93] *Recueil officiel des lois fédérales* (1974), 2148-79. See L. Caflisch, 'La pratique suisse en matière de droit international public 1974' 31 *ASDI* (1975), 155-269, esp. 158-73; and Malinverni, n. 83 above. The actual publication took place on 23 Dec. 1974: see 20 *Yearbook* (1977), 791. See also message from the Federal Council to the Federal Assembly relating to the European Convention on Human Rights, 4 Mar. 1974, *Feuille Fédérale* (1974), i. 1020-54; and previous report of 9 Dec. 1968, *Feuille Fédérale* (1968), ii. 1069-98.

[94] Swiss Government's reply of 24 Sept. 1975 in *Implementation of Article 57 of the European Convention on Human Rights*, Council of Europe doc. H(76)15, 15 Oct. 1976, at 131. See also case-law noted in *Yearbook*: vol. 17 (1974), 677-80; 18 (1975), 430-2; 19 (1976), 1153-8; 20 (1977), 780-813; and 21 (1978), 779-83.

may be invoked by *'staatsrechtliche Beschwerde'* in the same proceedings and on the basis of the same reasoning. It is therefore quite surprising to observe — especially when one considers that Switzerland has only relatively recently ratified the European Convention — that there already exists an impressive amount of case-law in which reference is actually made to the Convention's provisions (even though by and large, the courts have done so in order only to substantiate a finding that neither domestic law nor international obligations have been breached).[95]

Although doctrine — supported by case-law — tends to indicate that international agreements possess a superior status *vis-à-vis* conflicting legislative provisions (this is of course certainly true in so far as prior federal law is concerned), the actual positioning of the European Convention on Human Rights within the domestic legal hierarchy has not as yet been clearly determined.[96] In connection with this problem, the role played by the *Tribunal Fédéral* needs emphasis. This court acts as a constitutional court when it hears appeals in public law (*staatsrechtliche Beschwerde*) relating to the jurisdiction and competence of public authorities, including the alleged infringement of inter-cantonal agreements and directly applicable provisions of international agreements. It also possesses chambers which deal with, *inter alia*, criminal law appeals (*Cour de Cassation pénale*) and appeals against decisions applying federal administrative law (*Cour de droit public et de droit administratif*). Consequently, its pronouncements on this subject carrry considerable weight.

In an important decision rendered on 19 March 1975 in the case of *Diskont- und Handelsbank AG*, the *Tribunal Fédéral*

---

[95] See references in n. 94 above and compilations of case-law in the latest issues of the *ASDI*: vol. 31 (1975), 158–73; 32 (1976), 89–117; 33 (1977), 157–96; 34 (1978), 176–224; 35 (1979), 181–222; and 36 (1980), 239–72. Also consult L. Wildhaber, 'Erfahrungen mit der Europäischen Menschenrechtskonvention', 98 *Revue de droit Suisse* (1979), 230–379, esp. 327–79.

[96] See Ch. Dominicé, 'La Convention européenne des Droits de l'Homme devant le juge national', 28 *ASDI* (1972), 9–40, esp. at 31–6; Malinverni, n. 83 above, esp. 16–35; Evans, 'Written Communication', 95–116, at 179–80; and L. Wildhaber, 'Verfassungsrecht der EMRK in der Schweiz?', 105 *Revue de la Société des juristes bernois* (1969), 249–67. Note, however, the unanimous opinion of the Standing Commission of the National Council, in 1974, that the Convention *must* have priority *vis-à-vis* subsequent federal statutes: see Wildhaber, n. 95 above, at 329.

It may be worth noting that in a federal system such as exists in Switzerland — as opposed to a unitary state — a sharper distinction is made between different kinds of law ('higher', 'general principles') in the country as a whole because, in a sense, the federal system itself is 'international'.

determined that, *for procedural purposes*, it considered certain provisions of the European Convention on Human Rights as granting to individuals rights of equal value to the rights guaranteed in Swiss written and unwritten constitutional law; and, as their *content* relates *ipso facto* to issues of constitutional appeal, the use of the Convention for the purposes of such an appeal before the *Tribunal Fédéral* necessitates the prior exhaustion of all cantonal remedies in accordance with Article 84(1)(a) and 86(2) of the 1943 Judicature Act.[97] In this case, cantonal remedies had not been exhausted and the court was consequently not prepared to hear the constitutional appeal alleging violations of Articles 6(1), 13, and 17 of the Convention. The *Tribunal Fédéral* went on to say:

As it [the Convention] is a treaty, it might be deduced from S.86(3) of the Judicature Act (in conjunction with S.84(1)(c)), that it was not necessary to exhaust the available judicial remedies before bringing a constitutional appeal based on a breach of the Convention. This interpretation of the rules of procedure, however, fails to take into account the special nature of the Convention and would entail a number of disadvantages.
Whereas most treaties oblige a Contracting State to behave in a certain way towards the other state or its citizens, the Convention requires Switzerland to grant the rights it guarantees to her own citizens and third parties. These rights have *per se* a *constitutional content*. By enumerating them the Convention adopts and further elaborates provisions frequently found in the section of a constitution dealing with fundamental freedoms, or which the Contracting States recognize as unwritten constitutional rights. Moreover, the protection afforded by the Convention is only of independent significance in so far as it goes beyond that provided by the constitutions of the Federation and of the cantons. This means that rights protected by the Convention have to be determined in conjunction with the corresponding individual rights guaranteed in our written and unwritten constitutional law. This close relationship of subject-matter between constitutional rights and those protected by the Convention makes it possible to treat violations of the Convention in the same way, *for procedural purposes*, as a violation of constitutional rights as treated under S.84(1)(a) of the

---

[97] In **101** *ATF* (1975), I(a), 67–71, at 70. Arts. 84(1)(a) and 86(2) provide that the *Tribunal Fédéral* can consider appeals from judgments of cantonal tribunals relating to constitutionally guaranteed citizens' rights *after* the exhaustion of all available cantonal remedies. Art. 86(3) read in conjunction with Art. 84(1)(c) provides for a determination of an alleged violation of treaty provisions *without* the necessity of exhausting cantonal remedies: see *Loi fédérale d'organisation judiciaire* of 16 Dec. 1943 in *Recueil systématique de droit fédéral*, 173.100, pp. 28–9. Malinverni, n. 83 above, at 20, explains the court's decision: '*c'est le contenu de la disposition qui est déterminant pour la question de la subsidiarité relative du recours, beaucoup plus que la circonstance que celle-ci se trouve être incorporée dans un traité international.*'

Judicature Act and insist that constitutional appeals are also submitted to the requirement of exhausting the available cantonal remedies . . .[98]

Developments subsequent to the famous *Diskont- und Handelsbank AG* case are thus of particular interest and need close monitoring. Recent case-law on this subject includes a decision of the *Tribunal Fédéral* of 3 November 1976, which referred to two judgments of the European Court of Human Rights in order to clarify the meaning of certain provisions in the Convention which were considered an extension of recognized principles of constitutional law.[99] Likewise, in a decision dated 9 March 1977 the *Tribunal Fédéral* considered that Article 8 of the Convention had been violated by the public prosecutor's office in the Canton of Zürich, when the office did not permit the forwarding of a letter written by the appellant to a person held in prison. In so holding, the court stated that '[by] their nature the rights guaranteed by the European Convention on Human Rights form part of constitutional law'.[100] In yet another decision of 2 May 1979 the *Tribunal Fédéral* equated certain provisions of the Convention with the unwritten constitutional norm of proportionality when it upheld an appellant's argument that the Fribourg authorities had acted unconstitutionally when they prevented the appellant from communicating orally with his lawyer before the examining magistrate had concluded his investigations.[101]

For the present, the situation may be summarized as follows: There appears to be in the Swiss legal system an absence of any constitutional provision that expressly determines the relationship between domestically applicable provisions of international agreements and subsequent legislation, even though case-law has given the former a relative supremacy. As a consequence — and in particular in the light of the recent tendency to equate the provisions of the European Convention on Human Rights with individual rights guaranteed in written and unwritten

[98] Translation from 19 *Yearbook* (1976), 115–16. (Emphases added.)

[99] *Burger* case, no. 55, 120 *AFT* (1977) i(a), 379–86. (English translation available in 20 *Yearbook* (1977), 801–9.) See ch. 10 below, sec. B, for the facts of this case and extracts from the actual judgment.

[100] See 20 *Yearbook* (1977), 812–13; also 32 *ASDI* (1976), 90–1, and 6 *EGZ* (1979), 3–6.

[101] See 105 *AFT* (1979), I(a), 98–103; and further, J.-F. Aubert, 'Les droits fondamentaux dans la jurisprudence récente du Tribunal fédéral suisse' in *Mélanges Kägi* (1979), 1–30.

constitutional law — the law-enforcing authorities may be unable to examine the conformity of federal statutes with the Convention's norms, in that by so doing they would in effect be determining the constitutionality of federal laws, which they are prohibited from doing (Article 113(3) of the Constitution). A way of circumventing this problem would be to introduce a system of judicial review of constitutionality; and the fact that the *Tribunal Fédéral* may have a more limited control over Swiss law than does the Human Rights Court in Strasbourg might be a decisive factor in favour of such a proposal when the present debate concerning the total revision of the Federal Constitution is concluded.[102] Alternatively, if the courts were to interpret Article 113(3) of the Constitution as clearly giving the Convention a hierarchically superior status over both prior and subsequent federal statutes, such an interpretation would in effect result in an indirect control of constitutionality. This would be further accentuated by the fact that the rights and freedoms found in the European Convention on Human Rights are by and large the same as those enumerated in the Federal Constitution.[103]

Much has recently been written about the influence of Convention law upon the Swiss legal system and repetition is here not necessary.[104] It is sufficient to note that in the *Schiesser* case, the first to come before the European Court of Human Rights against Switzerland, the Strasbourg Court in effect confirmed an earlier decision reached by the *Tribunal Fédéral* when it held that there had been no breach of Article 5(3) of the Convention,[105] while the *Eggs* case has brought about an early revision of military law in the light of the Commission's

---

[102] See Malinverni, n. 83 above, 34-5 and 48-50. The *Eggs* case, n. 106 below, provides a good example of how a decision of the Strasbourg Court (the *Engel* case) may influence Swiss law: see F. Blaser, 'Arrêts militaires: les tribunaux jugeront', *Journal de Genève*, 3 Mar. 1977; and commentary by Malinverni, and Wildhaber, 34 *ASDI* (1978), at 181-8.

[103] See n. 83 above: Trechsel, 158 and 167, and Malinverni, at 35. For further information concerning the revision of the Swiss Constitution see note by Wildhaber, IV *HR Rev.* (1979), 47-50, and a special set of articles published in 97 *Revue de droit suisse* (1978), 229-528.

[104] See J. Raymond, 'La Suisse devant les organes de la Convention européenne des Droits de l'Homme', 98 *Revue de droit suisse* (1979), 1-108, and references there.

[105] Eur. Court HR, judgment of 4 Dec. 1979, ser. A, no. 34 (case no. 28 of 14 July, 102 *ATF* (1976) I(a), 179-85). See also *Tribunal Fédéral*, case of *Zimmermann*, *Neue Züricher Zeitung*, 7 Apr. 1979, at 23.

finding that there had been a violation of the Convention.[106] In two other cases, *Peyer*[107] and *Geerk*,[108] friendly settlements have been reached. In fact, as a direct result of the *Peyer* case, an amendment of the Swiss Civil Code came into effect, as of 1 January 1981, in order that 'exhaustive regulations governing deprivation of liberty for purposes of assistance, in conformity with the provisions of the Convention' be established.[109]

[106] Application 7341/76, 15 *D&R*, 35–69. (Changes in domestic law are explained in the *Information Bulletin on Legal Activities within the Council of Europe and Member States*, 5 (1980), 53–4.)

[107] Application 7397/76, 15 *D&R*, 105–19.

[108] Application 7640/76, 16 *D&R*, 56–67.

[109] See n. 107 above, at 119. The Swiss reservation was withdrawn upon the modification of the Civil Code — effective as of 1 Jan. 1982. See 34 *ASDI* (1978), 188–200. Also see O. Jacot-Guillarmod, 'Intérêt de la jurisprudence des organes de la CEDH pour la mise en œuvre du nouveau droit suisse de la privation de liberté à des fins d'assistance', 36 *Zeitschrift für Vormundschaftswesen* (1981), 41–58; and *Neue Züricher Zeitung* 20 Feb. 1982, 26.

Chapter 5
The Scandinavian Countries and Iceland

A. Denmark

The Kingdom of Denmark was one of the original states signatories of the Convention on 4 November 1950. Prior to ratification, which took place on 13 April 1953, the Danish authorities reviewed the compatibility of Danish law with its provisions. The review showed domestic law to be consistent with the provisions of the Convention, although a few relatively minor provisions in a statute of social assistance were amended (statute no. 33 of 25 February 1953). This statute abolished the right to detain a person who failed to support his family or to pay alimony or maintenance as the said provisions were considered to be contrary to Article 5 of the Convention.[1]

Article 19, paragraphs 1 and 3, of the Danish Constitution of 1953 stipulates that:

(1) the King shall act on behalf of the Realm in international affairs. Provided that without the consent of the Folketing the King shall not undertake any act whereby the territory of the Realm will be increased or decreased, nor shall he enter into any obligation which for fulfilment requires the concurrence of the Folketing, or which otherwise is of major importance; nor shall the King, except with the consent of the Folketing, terminate any international treaty entered into with the consent of the Folketing. . . .
(3) The Folketing shall appoint from among its Members a Foreign Affairs Committee, which the government shall consult prior to the making of any decision of major importance to foreign policy. Rules applying to the Foreign Affairs Committee shall be laid down by Statute.[2]

In accordance with these provisions, the *Folketing* approved ratification by a resolution which, unlike the passing of a law,

---

[1] See O. Espersen, 'Denmark and the European Convention on Human Rights', 18 *AJCL* (1970), 293–304, esp. 298–301. See also papers by Espersen, N. E. Holm, and J. Færkel, at the Turku-Åbo Colloquy, Finland, June 1974, published in VIII, *RDH/HRJ* (1975) at 139–43, 167–78, and 237–49. It is of interest to note that legislative amendments were also made before Denmark ratified the 1966 UN Covenant on Civil and Political Rights: see Danish report to the Human Rights Committee under art. 40 of the International Covenant on Civil and Political Rights, UN docs. CCPR/C/1/Add.4, 29 Mar. 1977, and CCPR/C/1/Add.19, 3 Jan. 1978.

[2] A. J. Peaslee, *Constitutions of Nations* (1968), iii. 255.

did *not* confer domestic status on the Convention. This means that the Danish Government, upon ratification of the Convention and its First Protocol on 13 April 1953, undertook an *international* obligation to secure everyone within its jurisdiction the rights and freedoms enumerated in the Convention. At the time of ratification Denmark also made declarations under Articles 25 and 46 which have always been renewed since that date. No reservations to the Convention have been made by Denmark. The Fourth Protocol was ratified on 30 September 1964.

The Constitution of Denmark contains no express provision relating to the domestic effect of a validly concluded international agreement.[3] The provisions of a treaty are not, generally speaking, directly enforceable by the courts or administrative authorities. When and if conflict arises, the domestic rules of law and not the treaty provision must be applied by the Danish law-enforcing authorities: the provision of a treaty cannot apparently be relied on in Danish courts, even by way of persuasive legal authority. Consequently, an international agreement would need to be incorporated into internal law if Danish courts were to be allowed to enforce any of its provisions.

Note should, however, be taken of Article 20 of the Constitution which permits the transfer of sovereignty to supranational organizations.[4] Article 20 reads:

(1) Powers vested in the authorities of the Realm under this Constitution Act may, to such extent as shall be provided by Statute, be delegated to international authorities set up by mutual agreement with other states for the promotion of international rules of law and cooperation.
(2) For the passing of a Bill dealing with the above a majority of five-sixths of the Members of the Folketing shall be required.
If this majority is not obtained, whereas the majority required for the passing of ordinary Bills is obtained, and if the government maintains it, the Bill shall be submitted to the Electorate for approval or rejection in accordance with the rules for Referenda laid down in section 42.[5]

---

[3] See Holm, 'The Protection of Civil and Political Rights in Denmark', n. 1 above, 167–78, at 169. Also consult his recent article 'Konventionens praktiske betydning i Danmark' in 50 *Nordisk Tidsskrift for International Ret* (1981), 118–42. For general information relating to the Danish legal system consult *National Reports*, 'Denmark' by M. Koktvedgaard, D.23–35 and references there.

[4] See I. Foighel, 'Denmark', 12 *EFTA Bulletin* (Sept.–Oct. 1971), 11; and M. Sørensen, 'Compétences supranationales et pouvoirs constitutionnels en droit danois' in *Miscellanea W. J. Ganshof van der Meersch* (1972), ii. 481–92.

[5] Peaslee, n. 2 above, at 256. See also A. Ross, *Dansk Statsfortningsret* (1966) [Danish Constitutional Law], 398–403; and M. Sørensen, 'Spørgsmålet om den umiddelbare anvendelse af traktater som bestanddel af dansk ret' [Direct Application

The procedure provided for in paragraph 2 of Article 20 was followed when Denmark joined the European Communities. Thus, certain decisions of institutions set up within the framework of European Community law possess immediate and direct effect within the Danish legal system.[6]

The traditional method for incorporating treaties into Danish law is by transforming them — or rather, to be more accurate, reformulating that part of the treaty which needs implementation — either by the promulgation of a statute or in the form of an administrative regulation. Although neither the text of the Constitution nor constitutional practice provide for automatic domestic validity of treaties, mention should perhaps be made of the possibility of 'adoption' in so far as specific legislative provision for this is provided: an example of such an adoption is statute no. 252 of 1968 on diplomatic relations (incorporating the provisions of the 1961 Vienna Convention on Diplomatic Relations into domestic law). The difference between the two forms of incorporation is that with the less frequently used adoption method the courts refer to international principles of interpretation in contradistinction to the 'transformed' treaties where the courts apply *domestic* rather than international principles of interpretation.[7] However in the case of the European Convention on Human Rights the Danish authorities considered that incorporation was not needed since domestic law already conformed to the norms laid down in the Convention.

The fact that incorporation was not considered necessary does not, however, indicate that the European Convention is without legal impact in Denmark: its provisions serve as a basis, binding upon Denmark under international law, for a corresponding set of domestic rules of law.[8] In the event of ambiguity or possible conflict between the state's international obligation and a corresponding domestic provision, legal opinion is agreed upon a rule of interpretation based on the assumption that the courts will interpret the domestic rules in accordance with Denmark's international obligations. This interpretation is

of Treaties as Part of Danish Law], in Danish with an English summary, *Nordisk Administrativt Tidsskrift* (1966) 107–24.

[6] See M. Sørensen, 'Die Anwendung des Rechts der Europäische Gemeinschaften in Dänemark' in *Die Erweiterung der Europäischen Gemeinschaften* (1972), 1–25, and N. Gangsted-Rasmussen, 'Primauté du droit communautaire en cas de conflit avec le droit danois', 11 *RTDE* (1975), 700–7.

[7] Espersen, n. 1 above, at 295.

[8] See Council of Europe doc. H(76)15, Danish reply, 54.

further reinforced by the so-called 'rule of presumption' whereby, in the absence of any specific indications to the contrary, it is 'presumed' that Parliament did not intend to pass legislation contrary to Denmark's international obligations; and any new provision of legislation should be so interpreted even if the tenor of the new provision is clearly at variance with the treaty. A recent Ministry of Justice memorandum — relating to certain constitutional problems in connection with Denmark's entry into the European Communities — acknowledges this to be the correct interpretation: '. . . In the Ministry's view, Danish law courts would in all probability prefer a more *ad hoc* application of the law to a literal interpretation if the latter would make the State of Denmark responsible under international law for an unintentional violation of a treaty.'[9]

This extensive formulation of the 'rule of interpretation' has already been relied upon by the Danish Government before the European Commission of Human Rights in the case of *Kjeldsen* v. *Denmark*.[10] Similarly, one unreported case has been found in which the Copenhagen City Court, in a case brought against an Algerian citizen who had been convicted of a penal traffic offence, held that 'the cost of the interpreter must be borne by the state, cfr. art. 6(3)(e) in the Convention for the Protection of Human Rights and Fundamental Freedoms, which has been ratified by Denmark. . . .'[11] This decision is of some interest in that Section 1008 of the 1969 Danish Administration of Justice Act stipulates that 'if the accused is convicted . . . he shall be required to pay to the state the necessary expenses of the trial'.

One additional point may be worth noting. The above Ministry of Justice memorandum states that administrative

[9] Quoted by Holm, 'The Protection of Civil and Political Rights in Denmark', n. 1 above, at 107. This passage was also quoted by the Danish Government in its report submitted to the UN Human Rights Committee, see UN doc. CCPR/C/1/Add.4, n. 1 above, 3.

[10] Application 5095/71, 43 *Coll. of Dec.*, 44–56, at 50. This case (joined with others) later went before the Court: Eur. Court HR, case of *Kjeldsen, Busk Madsen, and Pedersen*, judgment of 7 Dec. 1976, ser. A, no. 23. See also bi-annual report submitted to the UN Committee on Racial Discrimination in accordance with art. 9 of the 1965 Convention on Elimination of All Forms of Racial Discrimination, doc. CERD/C/R 77/Add.2.

[11] Judgment of 25 Apr. 1966, case no. 21472/1965, I, cited by Espersen, n. 1 above, at 299–300. (Also noted in *Collection*, art. 6, 60.) Whether this is an application of the rule of interpretation or the rule of presumption is an open question. This decision was followed by a circular from the Ministry of Justice to public prosecutors and the courts stating that costs of interpretation are to be borne by the state.

authorities should exercise discretionary powers in such a way that administrative acts, whether they be specific decisions or general regulations, conform to validly contracted international obligations. As a consequence the 'rule of interpretation' appears to have been expanded to the extent that the courts should now take due regard of certain provisions of the Convention when determining questions that bear upon the powers of administrative authorities.[12]

B. Iceland

The country was one of the original states signatories of the Convention on 4 November 1950. The deposit of the instruments of ratification, of both the Convention and First Protocol took place shortly afterwards, on 29 June 1953. On 29 March 1955 Iceland recognized the competence of the European Commission to receive individual applications, and on 3 September 1958 a declaration recognizing the jurisdiction of the Court was deposited. Both declarations have been renewed since those dates. No reservations to the Convention have been made by Iceland. The Fourth Protocol was ratified on 16 November 1967.

Successive governments of Iceland have considered it unnecessary to give the Convention domestic status in that the Constitution of Iceland (technically referred to as Constitutional Law no. 33 of 17 June 1944, as amended by Constitutional Laws nos. 51/1959 and 9/1968) is assumed to give full effect to the fundamental rights and freedoms guaranteed therein.[13]

Article 21 of the Icelandic Constitution stipulates: 'The President concludes treaties with other states. Except with the consent of the Althing, he may not make such agreements if they entail renouncement of or servitude on territory or territorial waters or if they imply constitutional changes.[14]

---

[12] See UN doc. CCPR/C/1/Add.4, n. 1 above, at 3-4. Art. 63 of the Danish Constitution authorizes the Danish courts to determine all questions that bear upon the scope of the powers of administrative authorities: see Holm, n. 1 above, 117-6. (Administrative courts have not been introduced into the Danish legal system although the Constitution expressly permits the establishment of such courts.)

[13] Reply of the Government of Iceland: *Implementation of Article 57 of the European Convention on Human Rights*, Council of Europe doc. H(67)2, 10 Jan. 1967, 20. see also T. Vilhjalmsson, 'The Protection of Human Rights in Iceland', **VIII** *RDH/HRJ* (1975), 221-33.

[14] A. J. Peaslee, *Constitutions of Nations* (1968), iii. 451.

Consequently, international agreements do not acquire the status of domestic law unless and until they are transformed into statutes, thereby obtaining the force of an Act of Parliament. Often, as an alternative procedure, incorporation of the contents of an international agreement is secured by the amendment of existing statutes without the treaty itself acquiring the force of law.[15] The European Convention on Human Rights does not fall under either of these categories; it has *not* been given the force of law by a special statute nor has there been a systematic revision of older statutes aimed at achieving a compatibility between existing legislation and the Convention's provisions.[16] The *Althing* merely adopted a resolution on the matter prior to ratification.

Although in theory the European Convention on Human Rights, as other ratified treaties, is not part of Icelandic law it can nevertheless be used by the courts as an instrument for the interpretation of statutes which are presumed to be in conformity with it.[17] However, despite the fact that the Convention is occasionally cited in judgments of the lower courts, its impact upon the higher courts, including the Supreme Court, seems to be negligible. Thus, in June 1960 the Town Court of Reykjavik, in rejecting a plaintiff's arguments based upon a claim that the Convention entitled him to be released from a tax provision which imposed a capital tax of up to 25% of the value of taxable property, held that:

In so far as the European Convention on the Protection of Human Rights and Fundamental Freedoms is concerned, Althing has by a parliamentary resolution of 19th December 1952 granted authority to the government to become a party to it, and on the part of Iceland a document of ratification was delivered on the 29th of July 1953. On the other hand, this Convention has not been legalised in this country, neither as general law nor as constitutional law. Plaintiff cannot, therefore, base his claims here in Court upon the said Convention granting him any such right to a release from the tax provisions of Law No. 44/1957 as according to the foregoing he does not enjoy according to Icelandic constitutional law.[18]

[15] This procedure was used when Iceland joined EFTA. See note by H. G. Andersen, 12 *EFTA Bulletin* (1971), at 7.
[16] See Vilhjalmsson, n. 13 above, at 222. He feels that certain of the rights listed in the Convention (e.g. freedom of movement) are not adequately protected under Icelandic law (discussion at 235).   [17] Ibid., at 223.
[18] *Olafsson* v. *Ministry of Finance*, judgment of 28 June 1960, in 3 *Yearbook* (1960), 642–7 at 646. This Icelandic revenue law was – in an application lodged by two Icelandic citizens at approximately the same time as the *Olafsson* case – held by the European Commission of Human Rights not to have infringed art. 1 of the Convention's First Protocol: see 3 *Yearbook* (1960), 394–427.

Similarly, the *Hæstiréttur* (Supreme Court) in a decision dated 25 June 1963, held that the seizure of a boat on grounds of illegal fishing in Icelandic territorial waters, and the sale thereof to cover the fine imposed on the person responsible, was in conformity with Icelandic law and that it did not contravene Article 1 of the Convention's First Protocol.[19]

A case declared inadmissible by the European Commission of Human Rights in 1976 provides probably the most recent example of an instance in which the *Hæstiréttur* has made reference to the Convention.[20] An application had been brought before the Commission with the argument that regulations prohibiting the keeping of dogs in one's home were contrary to the provisions of Article 8 of the Convention (respect for private life). The applicant, prior to the lodging of his unsuccessful case before the Commission, had appealed to the Supreme Court of Iceland on this matter. His appeal was rejected on 18 June 1975. The Court held that the Convention on Human Rights had no relevance to the applicant's case, in that it had not been given the force of domestic law and, besides, that the prohibition of dogs in Reykjavik was not in conflict with Article 8 of the Convention.

C. Norway

An original member state signatory of the Convention on 4 November 1950 and of the First Protocol on 20 March 1952, Norway ratified both soon afterwards, on 15 January 1952 and 18 December 1952 respectively. Before ratifying the Convention, however, the Norwegian authorities considered that Article 2 of the Constitution, which prohibited the activity of Jesuits on Norwegian soil, was incompatible with Article 9 of the Convention and a reservation was made in this respect. The Constitution was subsequently amended and the reservation was withdrawn.[21] Declarations under Articles 25 and 46 were deposited on 13 December 1955 and 30 June 1964.[22] The Fourth Protocol was ratified on 12 June 1964.

[19] See *Collection*, art. 1 of the First Protocol, 4. For an explanation of the Icelandic legal system consult *Judicial Organisation*, 61–6, and *National Reports*, 'Iceland', by T. Vilhajalmsson, I 1–16.

[20] *X* v. *Iceland*, application 6825/74, 19 *Yearbook* (1976), 342–72.

[21] See 1 *Yearbook* (1955–57), 41–2. See also C. Morrisson, *The Developing European Law of Human Rights* (1967), 188–9.

[22] 1 *Yearbook* (1955–57), 54, and 7 *Yearbook* (1964), 22.

The generally accepted view is that Norway adheres to the dualistic theory of the relationship between international law and domestic legislation. Thus, treaties do not automatically become part of domestic Norwegian law and in the event of a conflict between the provisions of an international agreement and the rules of domestic law, the courts and the administrative authorities are obliged to base their decisions on the latter.[23] Traditional Norwegian doctrine has so interpreted Article 26 of the 1814 Constitution. This article reads:

The King shall have the right to assemble troops, to commence war in the defence of the Kingdom and to make peace, to conclude and denounce treaties, to send and to receive diplomatic envoys.
Treaties on matters of special importance and, in any case, treaties the implementation of which, according to the Constitution, necessitates a new law or decision on the part of the *Storting* [Parliament], shall not be binding until the Storting has given its consent thereunto.[24]

Consequently, as the European Convention has *not* been enacted into Norwegian law, it appears not to be an integral part of the Norwegian legal system.

However, despite the absence of express incorporation, the question of the Convention's domestic status remains a controversial issue. It has been argued, for instance, that Norwegian legislation which might possibly contravene the Convention's provisions should not be applied. This view is based on the assumption that the Convention, according to its contents, established individual rights which necessarily have a greater internal penetration power than state treaty rights.[25] In addition,

---

[23] See Council of Europe doc.H(67)2, Norwegian reply, p. 30. See also: F. Castberg, *Norges Statsforfatning* [Constitutional Law of Norway] (1964), ii. 125–31; C. Smith, 'International Law in Norwegian Courts', 12 *Scandinavian Studies in Law* (1968), 151–201; and two articles by E. Hambro: 'The Theory of the Transformation of International Law into National Law in Norwegian Law' in *Law, State and International Legal Order* (Essays in honour of H. Kelsen, eds. S. Engel and R. A. Métall, 1964), 97–106, and 'The New Provision for International Collaboration in the Constitution of Norway', in *Hommage à P. Guggenheim* (1968), 557–72. An important point, stressed by Professor T. Opsahl, n. 27 below, is that a statutory amendment of 1969 provides for the *reopening of civil and criminal proceedings* where a domestic court's judgment is based directly or indirectly on a point of international law or a treaty provision which has been interpreted differently by an international tribunal whose determinations bind Norway internationally. (Ch. 10 below returns to this subject.)

[24] A. J. Peaslee, *Constitutions of Nations* (1968), iii. 692–3.

[25] See T. Wold, 'Den europëiske menneskerettskonvensjon og Norge' in *Legal Essays in honour of Frede Castberg* (1963), 355–73 (with a summary in English). Also consult forthcoming article by T. Opsahl, in *Festskrift Johs Andenaes* (1982); and ch. 10 below, sec. C, n. 185.

the Norwegian Government has recently expressed the opinion that the Convention 'has been implemented in Norway through an "ascertainment of legislative harmony"'. There is said to exist a strong presumption that Norwegian law may not contravene the Convention's law, and that the authorities do in fact consider this international instrument as a source of law in Norwegian legal practice. The courts, and in particular the *Høyesterett* (Supreme Court) do not appear to have committed themselves on this issue.[26] The Norwegian member of the European Commission of Human Rights has explained the situation in the following terms:

. . . it is probably generally recognized that the Convention is a legitimate and important aid to the interpretation of domestic law. The courts, when faced with such issues, so far have avoided deciding them. Rather than expressly disregarding the Convention, however, the courts have stated that the domestic provisions and the Convention as interpreted by them, did not conflict with each other. Modern legal thought in Norway does not accept only a limited number of 'sources of law', formally recognized. Although not everybody is willing to accept the view — argued by some — that the Convention is on such grounds 'part of the law of the land', it can be said to have considerable and substantial force, in particular because the authorities seem to have assumed that Norwegian domestic law generally is in conformity with its requirements, in substance if not in form or explicit terms. There is no rule of the Constitution requiring formal legislation for the imposition of obligations on the state and the recognition of corresponding rights of individuals.
2. It follows that the provisions of the Convention, although in the traditional 'dualistic' view not formally a source with the force of domestic law, may be said to enjoy a precarious legal status as a relevant guide and perhaps even limitation to the application of domestic law by domestic authorities.[27]

---

[26] Norwegian Reply, n. 23 above, at 118. See also T. Opsahl, 'The Protection of Civil and Political Rights in Norway', VIII *RDH/HRJ* (1975), 179-191. It appears that the Ministry of Justice, in the case of *X* v. *Norway*, application 5923/72 (decision of 30 May 1975, an extract of which can be found in 3, *D&R*, 43-5) actually considered the Convention as a *source of domestic law*. A similar approach was taken by the Norwegian Government when it ratified the 1966 UN Covenant on Civil and Political Rights: see Norwegian report submitted under art. 40 of the Covenant to the Human Rights Committee, UN doc. CCPR/C/1/Add. 5, 6 Apr. 1977, esp. 1-2. See also report to the Storting (Parliament) no. 93 (1976-7), 'Norway and the International Protection of Human Rights' (Royal Ministry of Foreign Affairs, Oslo).

[27] T. Opsahl, 'Legal Protection for Human Rights in Norway', unpublished paper presented at a symposium organized by the British Institute of Human Rights in Northampton, England, June 1976. (The author is indebted to Professor Opsahl for providing him with this paper.) Also consult publication of the *Norges Offentlige Utredninger* 1972: 16 entitled *Gjennomføring av Lovkonvensjoner i norsk rett*; and Opsahl, 'Human Rights Today: International Obligations and National Implementation', 23 *Scandinavian Studies in Law* (1979), 149-76, esp. at 165-6 and 173-6.

Thus, in the *Iversen* case (which later became a much noted application before the Commission in Strasbourg), the *Høyesterett* was not prepared to enter into the question of whether a Norwegian Act of Parliament or the Convention should prevail in the event of a conflict.[28] In this case, the Supreme Court held that Articles 1 and 4 of a provisional act on compulsory civilian service by dentists did not violate Article 4 of the Convention. Judge Hiorthoy, speaking for the majority, ruled:

It seems hardly doubtful to me that the prohibition in the Convention against subjecting anyone to perform 'forced or compulsory labour' cannot reasonably be given such a wide construction that it includes instructions to perform public service of the kind in question here. The present case concerns brief, well-paid work in one's own profession in immediate connection with completed professional training. Although such injunctions may in many cases be in conflict with the interests of the individual as he sees them in the moment, I find it manifest that they cannot with any justification be characterized as an encroachment on, still less a violation of any human right. Accordingly, as I cannot see that there is any contradiction between the Convention and the Norwegian Act in question, I need not enter into the question as to which of these shall prevail in the event of conflict.[29]

Again, in a decision dated 28 March 1966, the Norwegian Supreme Court held that the Provisional Act mentioned above is contrary neither to Section 105 of the Constitution nor Article 4 of the Convention which prohibits forced or compulsory labour. In this connection the Court referred to *Iversen's* inadmissible application before the European Commission of Human Rights.[30]

More recently, the Supreme Court considered whether a measure of preventive detention had violated Article 6 of the Convention although, as it found that the article had not been violated in the particular case before it, it was not prepared to express its opinion on the Convention's domestic status, if any.[31]

---

[28] *Public Prosecutor* v. *Iversen*, judgment of 16 Dec. 1961, *Norsk Retstidende* **II** (1961), 1350; case-note by E. Hambro, 90 *JDI* (1963), 788–90; Th. Buergenthal, 'The Domestic Status of the European Convention on Human Rights: A Second Look', 7 *Journal of the ICJ* (1966), 55–96, at 89–90. Iversen's application before the European Commission of Human Rights was declared inadmissible: 6 *Yearbook* (1963), 278–332.

[29] English quotation taken from Buergenthal, ibid., 89.

[30] See *Collection*, art. 4, 8.

[31] Decision of 8 Oct. 1974, *Norsk Rettstidende* (1974), 935. A commentary on the case by Professor Brotholm can be found in 17 *Yearbook* (1974), 673–7.

A report by a Government expert committee on implementation of international agreements, *Norges Offentlige Utredninger* (1972: 16), touched upon the general problems of reform within the existing Norwegian legal system, but did not recommend any particular solution in the area of human rights. It has, nevertheless, recently been suggested by a prominent jurist that the present situation is in need of clarification.[32] He suggests that there should be either a review of all domestic legislation or an incorporation of appropriate international conventions into domestic law. Alternatively, if sufficient support is mobilized, the allegedly outdated provisions of the Constitution should be completely rewritten and priorities reassessed in order to provide a more complete protection of individual human rights in the light of Norway's international obligations in this field.[33]

D. Sweden

The Convention and First Protocol were signed by Sweden on 28 November 1950 and 20 March 1952. Both were duly ratified on 4 February 1952 and 22 June 1953. A declaration in accordance with Article 25 was made — for an unspecified period of time — when the Convention was ratified. The Swedish Government considered that certain of its domestic legal provisions were inconsistent with Article 2 of the First Protocol; accordingly, a reservation was made at the time of the Protocol's ratification.[34]

[32] Opsahl, n. 26 above, 185 and 191, and more recently in his 1979 article, n. 27 above, at 173-6.

[33] In this connection it should be observed that in 1962 a new article was inserted into the Norwegian Constitution: art. 93. This article reads: 'In order to secure international peace and security, or in order to promote international law and co-operation between nations, the *Storting* may, by a three-fourths majority, consent that an international organization of which Norway is or becomes a member, shall have the right, within a functionally limited field, to exercise powers which in accordance with this Constitution are normally vested in the Norwegian authorities, exclusive of the power to alter this Constitution. For such consent as provided above at least two-thirds of the members of the *Storting* — the same quorum as is required for changes in our amendment to this Constitution — shall be present. The provisions of the preceding paragraphs do not apply in cases of membership in an international organization, the decisions of which are not binding on Norway except as obligations under international law.' This quotation is taken from Peaslee, n. 24 above, 703. See also art. 112 of the Norwegian Constitution. The procedure in art. 93 would have been used if Norway had joined the European Communities: see T. Opsahl, 'Constitutional Implications in Norway of Accession to the European Communities', 9 *CML Rev.* (1972), 271-92.

[34] See 1 *Yearbook* (1955-7), 44. (Note can be taken of a Swedish court's judgment of 28 June 1974 which referred to the application of this article.)

A declaration recognizing the compulsory jurisdiction of the European Court of Human Rights was not made until 13 May 1966.[35] The Fourth Protocol was ratified on 13 June 1964.

Under Article 12(1) of the former Swedish Constitution of 1809 (now repealed by the new Instrument of Government which came into force on 1 January 1975) international agreements which dealt with matters requiring the concurrence of the *Riksdag* (Parliament) or which were of major importance 'shall contain a reservation making their validity dependent upon the sanction of the *Riksdag*'. In all other cases, the King could enter into international agreements 'after the Council of [Cabinet] had been heard upon the subject'.[36] Thus, in so far as the former Swedish Constitution is concerned, the country adhered to the principle that international agreements do not automatically become part of the domestic legal system. The domestic implementation of treaties had usually been secured by the passing of a corresponding statute which *transforms* international obligations into national law. However, such a procedure of transformation was not considered necessary in the case of the European Convention on Human Rights. Both the Government of the day as well as the Parliament were of the opinion that existing domestic law already indirectly ensured the Convention's implementation. Consequently, the courts and administrative authorities did not directly apply the provisions of the Convention but instead, where necessary, applied synonymous provisions of Swedish law which embodied the same rights and freedoms as found in the Convention.[37]

A characteristic feature of the new Instrument of Government which entered into force on 1 January 1975 is that both the established doctrine of parliamentary sovereignty and the long-standing constitutional principle that rules of public international law do not automatically become part of the domestic legal system unchanged, although certain innovations· concerning a limited transfer of powers to an international

---

[35] See 9 *Yearbook* (1966), 12.

[36] See O. Espersen, 'Indgåelse og opfyldelse af traktater i Sverige' ['Conclusion and Enforcement of Treaties in Sweden'] in *Nordisk Tidsskrift for Rettsvitenskap* (1968), 257–317.

[37] See Swedish Government reply of 1964 in *Implementation of Article 57 of the European Convention on Human Rights*, Council of Europe doc. H(67)2, 10 Jan. 1967, at 32; and the more recent reply in 1975 on the same subject in doc. H(76) 15, 15 Oct. 1976, at 122. See further H. Danelius, *Human Rights in Sweden* (1982); and L. Kellberg, 'Sverige och Europarådets Konvention om de mänskliga rättigheterna', in *Svensk Juristtidning* (1961), 503–7.

organization or an international tribunal have been added (Chapter 10, Articles 1–9 of the Instrument of Government).[38] Of particular relevance are Articles 1, 2, and 5 which read as follows:

Article 1. An agreement with another state or with another organisation shall be concluded by the Government.

Article 2. The Government may not conclude any international agreement binding upon the Realm without the *Riksdag* having approved thereof, if the agreement presupposes any amendment or abrogation of any law or the enactment of new law, nor if it otherwise concerns a matter in which the *Riksdag* shall decide.

If in such a case as is referred to in the preceding paragraph a special procedure has been prescribed for the requisite decision of the *Riksdag*, the same procedure shall be followed in connection with the approval of the agreement.

Nor may the Government in any case other than such as is referred to in the first paragraph of this Article conclude any international agreement binding on the Realm without the *Riksdag* having approved thereof, if the agreement is of major importance. The Government may, however, omit obtaining the *Riksdag's* approval of the agreement if the interest of the Realm so requires. In such a case the Government shall instead confer with the Foreign Affairs Advisory Council before the agreement is concluded.

Article 5. The right to make a decision which under the present Instrument of Government devolves on the *Riksdag*, on the Government, or on any other organ referred to in the Instrument and which does not relate to the enactment, amendment or abrogation of a fundamental law may to a limited extent be entrusted to an international organisation for peaceful cooperation of which Sweden is or is to become a member of an International Tribunal. In any such matter the *Riksdag* shall decide in the matter prescribed for the enactment of fundamental laws or, if a decision under such procedure cannot be abided, by way of a decision agreed upon by not less than three-fourths of the *Riksdag* members.

Any judicial or administrative function which does not under the present Instrument of Government devolve on the *Riksdag*, on the Government, or on any other organ referred to in the Instrument, may be entrusted to another state, to an international organisation or to a foreign or international institution or community, if the *Riksdag* so determines by a decision in which not less than three-fourths of those present and voting have concurred, or a decision taken in the manner prescribed for the enactment of fundamental laws.

---

[38] Constitutional Documents of Sweden (published by the Swedish *Riksdag* 1975) 26 and 55–6. See also Swedish Government's report submitted to the Human Rights Committee under art. 40 of the International Covenant on Civil and Political Rights: UN Docs. CCPR/C/1/Add.9, 7 Apr. 1977, and CCPR/C/1/Add.42, 8 May 1979.

In addition, it should be noted that, although the newly drafted chapter on fundamental freedoms and rights (Chapter 2, Articles 1-20) guarantees citizens and aliens certain constitutional basic rights, this guarantee is *not* entrenched, in that some of these rights and freedoms may in fact be restricted by subsequent ordinary legislation.[39]

The Swedish courts have rarely made reference to the provisions of the European Convention on Human Rights. In 1963 the *Svea Hovrätt* (Court of Appeal) referred to Article 7 of the Convention (which prohibits retrospective imposition of criminal offences and/or penalties) when it held that Article 3 of the Financial Offences Act, 1961, extending the time-limit for instituting proceedings from two to five years, was not retroactive in that the two years' limitation period remained applicable to acts committed before 1 July 1961.[40] Also in that year, the same Court expressed the opinion that by ratifying the Convention, Parliament had recognized that Swedish penal law did not present any obstacle to the application, within the Realm, of the fundamental principles governing freedom of opinion as guaranteed by Article 10 of the Convention, including freedom to impart information and ideas without interference by a public authority.[41]

Similarly, reference was made to the Convention's provisions — in particular Article 11 which guarantees the right to freedom of association with others, including the right to form and join a trade union for the protection of one's interests — in two cases which came before the *Arbetsdomstolen* (Swedish Labour Court) in February 1972[42] and before the *Högsta Domstolen* (Supreme Court) in October 1973.[43] In the former judgment the petitioner, the Swedish Engine Drivers Union, claimed that

---

[39] See S. Jägerskiöld, 'Civil and Political Rights in Sweden', **VIII** *RDH/HRJ* (1975), 193–200, at 196; also G. Petren, 'The Protection of Economic, Social and Cultural Rights in Sweden', ibid., 263–74; 17 *Yearbook* (1974), 624–5; and H. Danelius, *Mänskliga rättigheter* [Human Rights] (1981). Ch. 8, art. 15 stipulates that 'any fundamental law shall be adopted by way of two decisions of identical wording. The second decision may not be taken until elections for the *Riksdag* have been held in the entire Realm after the first decision and the newly-elected *Riksdag* has convened. The *Riksdag* may not as pending adopt any proposition for a fundamental law which is incompatible with any other pending proposition for such law, unless at the same time the *Riksdag* rejects the proposition first adopted.'

[40] *Collection*, art. 7, 3; *Nytt Juridiskt Arkiv* (1963), 284.

[41] *Collection*, art. 10, 10.

[42] Labour Court decision of 18 Feb. 1972, no. 5/72, *Swedish Engine Drivers* v. *Sweden; Collection*, art. 11, 7.   [43] See n. 45 below.

the Swedish National Collective Bargaining Office, by refusing to conclude a new collective agreement with it, had not only violated certain sections of a 1936 Act regarding the right to organize and to negotiate, but also a number of international texts including Articles 11, 13, and 14 of the European Convention on Human Rights. The Court rejected the request of the petitioner. Of the invoked treaty provisions, the Court said:

. . . With specific regard to the provisions of international agreements as touched upon earlier, [with reference to, *inter alia*, Articles 11, 13, and 14 of the European Convention], it is the accepted view in Sweden that such provisions — insofar as they do not already have their counterparts in our legislation or customary law — do not become applicable Swedish law except through the medium of legislation. They can, however, clarify the meaning of laws enacted in Sweden, which must be assumed to be in conformity with Sweden's international undertakings. However, the submissions made in the case in this respect do not in any way cause the Labour Court to change its judgment of the questions in dispute between the parties.[44]

In its decision of 2 October 1973 the *Högsta Domstolen* (Supreme Court) held that neither a retroactive clause in a collective agreement in itself nor its application to the plaintiff was improper or unfair. This case concerned the legal validity and effect of a clause which was included in a collective agreement between the National Collective Bargaining Office and four federations of trade unions representing state employees and which stipulated that increased salaries were not to be given retrospectively to members of trade unions which had been on strike during a part of the period of negotiations. And, as the plaintiff was a member of a trade union which had not been a party to the agreement, he was not entitled to receive retroactive benefits in spite of the retroactivity clause provided in the collective agreement. Reference was made before the Court to the European Convention on Human Rights, although the judgment made only indirect allusion to this instrument:

[44] This extract from the judgment was provided to the author by the Registry of the European Court of Human Rights. The Swedish Engine Drivers' Union later petitioned the European Commission of Human Rights in this matter, which in turn brought the case before the Court in Strasbourg. See Eur. Court HR, judgment of 6 Feb. 1976, ser. A, vol. 20, and ser. B, no. 18 (pleadings, oral arguments and documents). See also a similar case brought against Sweden: Eur. Court HR, *Schmidt and Dahlström* case, judgment of 6 Feb. 1976, ser. A, vol. 21, and ser. B, no. 19. Reference to another application concerning an alleged violation of art. 11 by Sweden (brought before the European Commission of Human Rights) can be found in 'Stocktaking', 147–8; and in *Collection*, art. 11, 6.

Even if Sweden had assented to an international agreement, this would not be applicable for the state within the existing application of the law. To the extent that the agreement gives expression to principles which have not earlier prevailed here in this country, corresponding legislation ('transformation') will be necessary. Such legislation had, however, not been considered necessary when Sweden ratified the agreements referred to by Mr. Sandström. In that respect it should be noticed that these agreements cannot be considered as having the content to which Mr. Sandström refers.[45]

Finally, note can be taken of an important judgment of the *Regeringsträten* (Supreme Administrative Court) in which the court made it quite clear that the European Convention is not 'directly applicable' in the Swedish legal system.[46]

It follows that the basic protection of the rights and freedoms dealt with by the provisions of the Convention are considered to be adequately secured by Chapter 2 (Articles 1-20) of the new Instrument of Government although the courts may possibly be prepared to refer to the provisions of international agreements when attempting to clarify the meaning of domestic law.

It must be accepted that prima facie there may often be no need to invoke the Convention's provisions in Swedish courts for the simple reason that there now exists a catalogue of basic rights which are constitutionally entrenched: see Chapter 2 of the Instrument of Government. This being said, the attempts to formulate a set of constitutionally guaranteed basic rights and freedoms acceptable to the majority of the political parties in the *Riksdag* turned out to be one of the most difficult tasks during the elaboration of the new Swedish Constitution.[47] As a consequence it was decided that the list provided in the new Constitution would remain provisional subject to the possibility of accepting, at a future date, proposals of a Governmental Commission which had been appointed early in 1973 and which was at the time analysing the possibilities of a more detailed constitutional protection of human rights. The recommendations of this Commission were embodied, with some minor changes, in a

[45] Case D/T 113/71 *Swedish State* v. *Sandström*, judgment of 2 Oct. 1973, in *Nytt Juridiskt Arkiv* (1973), 423. The extract from this decision was provided to the author by the Registry of the European Court of Human Rights. A summary of the case is provided in *European Convention on Human Rights. National Aspects* (Council of Europe, 1975) at 60. See also Eur. Court HR, ser. B, no. 18, n. 44 above, 109 and 133-6. Express reference to art. 11 of the Convention was, however, made by the Court of Appeal in this case.
[46] See *Regeringsrättens årsbok* (1974), ref. 61, 121-2.
[47] See G. Petren, n. 39 above, 269.

Bill which was approved by the *Riksdag* on 4 June 1976.[48] These were finally adopted in the autumn of 1976 and entered into force on 1 January 1977. A new Governmental Commission was then set up and submitted its proposals in 1976,[49] which were thereupon adopted by the *Riksdag*. These new constitutional amendments, in force as of 1 January 1980, substantially amend and strengthen the protection of individual rights. For example, when the *Riksdag* enacts legislation which may appear to limit fundamental rights and freedoms, the courts now possess the power, in certain circumstances, to decide upon the constitutionality of laws (Chapter 11, Article 14).[50]

[48] *Medborgerliga fri-och rättigheter*: Sou 1975: 75. See 25 *ICLQ* (1976), 456 and 923. This Commission also published, at the request of the Ministry of Foreign Affairs, a report concerning the functioning of the European Convention on Human Rights and the European Social Charter: Swedish Government Official Reports 1974: 88 (in Swedish).

[49] SOU 1978: 34. (A short explanation of the present domestic hierarchy of legal norms in Sweden is provided at 21 of the *Riksdag* publication referred to in n. 38 above.)

[50] For a more detailed discussion on this and related subjects consult O. Nyman, 'Some Basic Features of Swedish Constitutional Law', in *An Introduction to Swedish Law* (ed. S. Strömholm, 1981, 2 vols.), i. 45–71, esp. 56–8.

Chapter 6

Greece, Italy, Portugal, Spain, and Turkey

A. Greece

The Convention was signed by Greece on 28 November 1950. In accordance with Article 32 of the then operative Constitution of 1952 the Convention was simultaneously approved by Parliament and brought into force domestically by Act no. 2329 of 18 March 1953. This was followed by ratification of the Convention and the First Protocol on 28 March 1953. Greece did not recognize the compulsory jurisdiction of the Court of Human Rights nor did it make a declaration under Article 25. A reservation was made in respect of Article 2 of the First Protocol.[1] Accordingly, the Convention and its First Protocol were considered an integral part of Greek domestic law which could be invoked directly before the administrative and judicial state organs by individuals. It was considered to have been 'transformed' into domestic law and to have acquired the status of an ordinary law which abrogated prior inconsistent legislation and which in turn could be superseded by subsequent conflicting legislation.[2]

The country's resignation from the Council of Europe and denunciation of the Convention on Human Rights shortly before the Committee of Ministers adopted by resolution (Resolution DH 70/1 of 15 April 1970) the Commission's opinion that Greece had violated several articles of the Convention will not be discussed here.[3] Although this was certainly

---

[1] 1 *Yearbook* (1955-57), 44.

[2] See T. Buergenthal, 'The Domestic Status of the European Convention on Human Rights: A Second Look', 7 *Journal of the ICJ* (1966), 55-96, at 72-5. Also consult Ph. Vegleris, *The European Convention on Human Rights and the Greek Constitution* (1977, in Greek, with a summary in French), esp. 17-55, and his 'Statut de la Convention des Droits de l'Homme dans le droit grec', in *Mélanges dédiés à R. Pelloux* (1980), 299-318. Reference to case-law in which the Convention was cited can be found in Buergenthal, at 72-5, in Vegleris at 31-55, and in 9 *RHDI* (1956), 206-7.

[3] See *The Greek* case 21 *Yearbook* (1969), supplementary volume. For analyses of this case consult: A.-Ch. Kiss and Ph. Vegleris, 'L'affaire grecque devant le Conseil de l'Europe et la Commission européenne des Droits de l'Homme', 17 *AFDI* (1971),

a major happening in the Convention's short history — it was apparently the first and only inter-state case not motivated by the applicants' self-interest, or political, religious, or ethnic links with the population of the state against which the application had been lodged — such a study would go beyond the ambit of present discussions. Happily, Greece renewed its ratification of the Convention and the First Protocol when the country rejoined the Council of Europe on 28 November 1974.[4] This was done after the transitional Government of National Unity, formed on 23 July 1974, had taken the necessary domestic measures (DL no. 53 of 19 September 1974).[5] Although the Second, Third, and Fifth Protocols were in fact ratified on 8 January 1975, it was explicitly declared that the ratification would be retroactive to 28 November 1974. This time no reservation was made. Greece has again made no declaration under Article 25 but has done so in respect of Article 46 of the Convention.[6] The Fourth Protocol remains unsigned by Greece.

It is as yet too early to judge the domestic impact that the Convention is having or will have in the foreseeable future. With the coming into force of the new Greek Constitution on 11 June 1975 (Greek Government Gazette, Fasc. A. no. 111 of 9 June 1976), it now appears that rules of international law possessing domestic status supersede both prior *and* subsequent legislation. If this is so, the resultant importance of the distinction between the Convention's self-executing and non-self-executing provisions may now need to be examined more closely by the courts.[7] This subject was not raised in the parliamentary debates

889-931; and H. D. Coleman, 'Greece and the Council of Europe. The International Legal Protection of Human Rights by the Political Process', 2 *Israel Yearbook on Human Rights* (1972), 121-41.

[4] See 17 *Yearbook* (1974), 2 (also published in the Greek Official Journal: 38/ 1975). Also consult A. Manin, 'La Grèce et le Conseil de l'Europe du 12 décembre 1969 au 28 novembre 1974', 20 *AFDI* (1974), 875-85; and the Commission's report in the 2nd *Greek* case, application 4448/70, adopted on 4 Oct. 1976, and Committee of Ministers resolution in 17 *Yearbook* (1974) at 618.

[5] Published in the Official Journal on 20 Sept. 1974, no. 256. See 28 *RHDI* (1975), 370. (Parliamentary elections took place soon afterwards, on 17 Nov. 1974.)

[6] See Chart Showing Signatures and Ratifications of Council of Europe Conventions and Agreements, 15 Dec. 1981, 17.

[7] See A. A. Fatouros, 'International Law in the New Greek Constitution' 20 *AJIL* (1976), 492-506. The importance of paras. 2 and 3 of art. 28 of the Greek Constitution is discussed by D. Evrigenis in his article 'Legal and Constitutional Implications of Greek Accession to the European Communities', 17 *CML Rev.* (1980), 157-69.

which preceded adoption of the new Constitution and past Greek practice provides no indicators as to how the Greek courts will treat this novel concept of determining which treaty provisions are directly enforceable by the individual (self-executing).[8]

The Convention's superior status *vis-à-vis* other domestic legislation seems to be secured by Article 28(1) of the 1975 Greek Constitution: 'The general rules of international law as well as international treaties, duly ratified by the legislature, and entered into force in accordance with their provisions, form an integral part of Hellenic domestic law and are superior to any contrary legal provision.'[9] In addition, Article 100 of the Constitution provides for the setting-up of a special supreme tribunal competent to rule, *inter alia*, in disputes concerning the applicability of provisions of international law which have obtained domestic status in accordance with Article 28(1) of the Constitution. The decisions of this tribunal are irrevocable, and a provision declared unconstitutional by it ceases to have effect.[10]

Thus, although it appears that the provisions of the new Greek Constitution more or less fall into and correspond to the provisions of other relatively recent constitutional texts (e.g. Article 24(1) of the Basic Law of the Federal Republic of Germany, Article 67 of the Netherlands Constitution, and Article 55 of the French Constitution), it does not necessarily follow that they will be interpreted in a similar fashion. It would be premature to say, with any certainty, how domestic courts and tribunals will apply those provisions of the Convention which are deemed directly enforceable. Certainly a recent case in which the European Convention was unsuccessfully invoked before the Council of State is not very encouraging in this respect.[11] The case concerned the marriage of a policeman

[8] Cf. articles by Vegleris, n. 2 above, and D. Y. Evrigenis, 'Les conflits de la loi nationale avec les traités internationaux en droit hellénique' **18** *RHDI* (1965), 354–7. Also see Fatouros, n. 7 above, at 503. Prior to the 1975 Constitution, treaty provisions were deemed to have been transformed into Greek law.

[9] Text provided by N. Kambalouris, *Proceedings of the Fourth International Colloquy about the European Convention on Human Rights,* Rome, 5–8 Nov. 1975 (Council of Europe, 1976), at 269.

[10] See V. Perifanaki Rotolo, 'La Corte Suprema Speciale nella Costituzione greca del 1975', **30** *Rivista trim. di diritto pubblico* (1979), 183–204.

[11] Case no. 4590/1976. The facts of this case have been obtained from an article by N. Patouris, 'Prisoners' Rights in Greece: A Comparative Analysis of the Greek Code of Corrections and the Council of Europe Standards', **IV** *Journal of the Hellenic*

despite the refusal of his superiors to give him permission to do so. The refusal was based on Law 1970/72 which stipulates that a policeman applying for permission to marry must be at least 26 years old and have completed two years in service since he was drafted, and that his future wife 'should be a Greek citizen, of unblameworthy conduct, analogous education and social position, as well as devoted to the national ideals. To grant permission, there should also be examined the element of the devotion to the national ideals of [the wife's] relatives to the second degree of consanguinity'. As the policeman concerned was suspended from service for two months he appealed to the Council of State. The Court held this law to be compatible with Article 12 of the Convention — which protects the right of men and women 'to marry and to found a family according to national law governing the exercise of this right' — by assuming that the article permitted domestic law to subject the exercise of this right to the previous approval of administrative authorities. This interpretation of Article 12 has been criticized by Greek jurists as difficult to reconcile with the position taken by the Strasbourg Court.[12]

Despite the unpromising start of the Convention's domestic existence, it must be stressed that if and when conflict arises between the Convention's norms and both prior *and* subsequent legislation (and the court in question recognizes this to be the case), it appears, at least upon an initial reading of Article 28(1) of the new Greek Constitution, that priority must be given to the former.

B. Italy

The European Convention of Human Rights was signed by the Republic of Italy on 4 November 1950, and the First Protocol 20 March 1952. They were both ratified on 26 October 1955. Declarations relating to Articles 25 and 46 were made on

---

Diaspora (1979), 17–63, at 32. The case is also cited by Ph. Vegleris, n. 2 above, at 123.

[12] See ibid. The Council of State did *not* question the superior status of treaty norms *vis-à-vis* prior and subsequent legislation: all it did was to hold that no inconsistencies existed in this case. See Vegleris, n. 2 above, at 86–7 and 96 ff. But note the recent proposals for change, reported in *Information Bulletin on Legal Activities within the Council of Europe and member states*, no. 7 (June 1980), 31–2.

1 August 1973.[13] Italy has made no reservations to this instrument or its protocols. The Fourth Protocol has recently been ratified (on 27 May 1982).

Under Italian constitutional law a treaty once ratified and executed by the legislature becomes an integral part of domestic law. Consequently, from the date of its ratification by Italy (26 October 1955), the Convention constitutes an integral part of the legal system (Law no. 848 of 4 August 1955). The legislative act of incorporation (order of execution) remains distinct from the separate function of legislative approval. But despite this substantial distinction, both authorization to ratify and transformation of a treaty into domestic law are usually included in the same legislative text. Thus, Article 1 of Law 848/1955 authorized ratification — which took place shortly afterwards — and Article 2 ordered execution of the Convention into domestic law: '*E fatto obbligo a chiunque spetti di osservarla e di farla osservare come legge delle Stato.*' A verbatim copy of the French text of the Convention and First Protocol then followed.[14]

There appears to be no express provision in the Italian Constitution which regulates the problem of the implementation or the hierarchical positioning of international agreements in domestic law, although the following articles of the 1947 Italian Constitution (as amended in 1953 and 1963) touch upon the relationship between the Italian legal order and international law generally:

Article 10, paragraph 1
Italy's legal system conforms with the generally recognized principles of international law.

---

[13] See Chart Showing Signatures and Ratifications of the Council of Europe Conventions and Agreements (15 Dec. 1981), 17. See also Bari Conference: *Les clauses facultatives de la Convention européenne des Droits de l'Homme*, 17–8 Dec. 1973 (1974), esp. articles by D. Giuliva, 107–31, and G. Sacerdoti, 133–45; V. Starace, 'Italian Acceptance of the Optional Clauses of the European Convention on Human Rights', *IYIL* (1975), 42–51; G. M. Palmieri, 'L'esperienza italiana in tema di ricorsi individuali alla Commissione europea dei diritti dell'uomo', **63** *Riv. DI* (1980), 45–74. (Domestic case-law also cited at 294–307.)

[14] *Gazetta Ufficiale* no. 221 (4 Aug. 1955), 3372, 'full and entire execution shall be given to the treaty'. It should be noted that the effects of the second clause were tacitly subject to the condition of the enforcement of the treaty on the international plane (art. 11 of the Constitution). The probable reason why both the *ordine d'esecuzione* and authorization to ratify are included on the same legislative text is to avoid the promulgation of two different legislative acts concerning the same international agreement.

Article 11
Italy condemns war as an instrument of aggression against the liberties of other peoples and as a means for settling international controversies; it agrees, on conditions of equality with other states, to such limitation of sovereignty as may be necessary for a system calculated to ensure peace and justice between Nations: it promotes and encourages international organizations having such ends in view.

Article 80
The Chambers authorize, by law, ratification of international treaties of a political nature, or which provide for arbitration or judicial regulation, or imply modifications to the nation's territory or financial burdens or to laws.

Article 87
The President of the Republic is the Head of the State and represents the unity of the Nation . . . ratifies international treaties, provided they be authorized by the Parliament whenever such authorization is necessary.[15]

Thus, although Article 10(1) provides for the automatic absorption of international legal values into the Italian legal system, this provision confines itself to the field of general principles of international law and to the rules of general customary law. International agreements, on the other hand, are transformed by means of an 'order of execution' in conformity with Article 80 which requires that the President of the Republic be authorized to ratify a given treaty *by means of a law*. And, as the European Convention on Human Rights was transformed into domestic law by the legislature's order of execution in accordance with Article 80, this agreement obtained the force of an ordinary law.[16] It follows that if and when a conflict arises between the incorporated provisions of the Convention and subsequent legislation, the well-established rule of *lex posterior derogat legi priori* would appear to apply, for (unlike in the case of general international law) the Convention's provisions do not *per se* have any priority *vis-à-vis* ordinary legislation.[17]

---

[15] A. J. Peaslee, *Constitutions of Nations* (1968), iii. 501, 512, and 513–14.

[16] At the time of the Convention's promulgation by the Italian Parliament there appeared a certain amount of disagreement as to whether this instrument created directly enforceable rights for individuals. See K. J. Partsch, 'Die europäische Menschenrechtskonvention von der nationalen Parlamenten', 17 *ZRV* (1956-7), 93–132, at 127–31. Subsequent case-law has now clarified this problem: see below.

[17] For relatively recent studies on this subject see K. Holloway, *Modern Trends in Treaty Law* (1967), 172–7 and 284–8, L. Ferrari Bravo and A. Giardina, 'Les procédés nationaux de mise en vigueur des obligations souscrites et des accords conclus par les gouvernements' in *Italian National Reports to the IXth International Congress of Comparative Law*, Tehran, 1974, 474–90.

Although the Italian courts have in recent years made reference to the European Convention on Human Rights on a number of occasions, the fact that its provisions overlap to a great extent with those of the fundamental human rights already protected in the Italian Constitution of 1948, as well as with other internal legislation, probably explains in part why the judiciary tends to use this instrument only as a supplementary aid when interpreting domestic law.[18] The explanation provided by the Italian Government in the course of its pleadings before the European Commission of Human Rights in the *Pfunders* (*Austria* v. *Italy*) case illustrates this point:

Since the date of ratification by Italy (26th October 1955), the Convention constitutes an integral part of the Italian legal system because Article 2 of Law No. 848 of 4th August 1955 makes it compulsory to observe the Convention and to cause it to be observed as 'law of the land'; that, as a result, the provisions of the Convention are to be invoked before Italian courts in the same way as the Constitution, the Codes and any other municipal law, ignorance of the law and, consequently, of the Convention being no valid excuse . . .[19]

An additional reason why the Convention's norms have not yet acquired a predominant domestic position may also be better understood when an appreciation is made of the specific characteristics of the Italian legal system generally, and in particular the manner in which the instrument is referred to by the *Corte Costituzionale*, on the one hand, and the administrative and ordinary courts, on the other.

The observance of the Constitution is ensured primarily by the *Corte Costituzionale* (Article 134 of the Constitution).[20] However, the constitutionality of a law may only be questioned in the course of a trial *incidenter tantum* (whether in relation to civil, penal, or administrative matters) and when the court has decided that the constitutional issue is not manifestly unfounded

---

[18] See V. Grementieri and N. Trocker, 'The Protection of Human Rights in Constitutional Law: Italy' in *Italian National Reports to the IXth International Congress of Comparative Law*, Tehran, 1974, 491–504. For extracts of Italian case-law in which the Convention has been cited consult various volumes of *Yearbook* and *Collection, passim*.

[19] Reprinted in 4 *Yearbook* (1961), 154.

[20] See A. Pizzorusso, 'Cour constitutionelle italienne', 33 *RICD* (1981), 395–416; G. Astuti, 'Bestand und Bedeutung der Grundrechte in Italien', 9 *EGZ* (1981), 77–84; and M. Evans, 'The Italian Constitutional Court', 17 *ICLQ* (1968), 602–33. The functioning of this court was recently scrutinized by the European Commission: see *Crociani et al.* v. *Italy*, applications 8603-8722-23-29/79, 22 *D&R*, 147-235.

(*non manifesta infondatezza*) and is relevant to the decision of the case before it. The protection of fundamental rights is therefore not secured by means of a direct individual appeal by way of objection on grounds of constitutionality, as in the Federal Republic of Germany, but only incidentally, or alternatively by a procedure *in via principale* which concerns specific requests for review of constitutionality of a statute or legislation of a region.[21] It follows that the jurisdiction of the *Corte Costituzionale*, in so far as the protection of human rights is concerned, is limited to cases referred to it by courts in matters specifically falling within the ambit of the rights and freedoms guaranteed by the Italian Constitution.

It should be noted that the Court itself determines the parameters of its interpretative power 'concerning the constitutional legitimacy of laws and acts having the force of law emanating from central and regional government', and that in so doing it has made occasional reference to the Convention's norms. The following cases may be cited as examples: the famous *San Michele* case, in which the Court referred to Article 6 of the Convention when it confirmed that the right to a fair trial was one of man's inviolable rights guaranteed in Article 2 of the Constitution;[22] a decision rendered on 6 July 1972, when it held that an acquittal 'for insufficient proof' (Article 479(2) of the Code of Criminal Procedure) was not incompatible with Article 27(2) of the Constitution or with the European Convention on Human Rights;[23] and its decision of 12 December 1972 when it decided that Articles 135 and 376 of the Code of Criminal Procedure were compatible with Articles 3 and 24 of the Constitution (which guarantee equality before the law and the right of defence) as well as Article 6(3)(c) of the European Convention on Human Rights.[24]

---

[21] See P. Biscaretti di Ruffia, *Diritto Costituzionale* (1977), 570 ff.; and V. Starace and C. De Caro, *La Giurisprudenza della Corte Costituzionale in materia internazionale* (1977), *passim*.

[22] Case no. 98 (1965), decision of 27 Dec. 1965, *Il Foro Italiano* (1966), i, col. 8–14, at col. 13.

[23] Case no. 124, *Il Foro Italiano* (1972), i, col. 1897–8; *Collection*, art. 5(1) and 6, 48. The Court added that the provisions of art. 6(2) when read together with art. 5(1)(b) and (c) permitted detention on remand, and that such action was not incompatible with a presumption of innocence and can only be reconciled with one of the absence of guilt.

[24] Case no. 178, *Il Foro Italiano* (1973) i, col. 15–16; *Collection*, art. 6(3)(c), 166. More recently arts. 8 and 14 of the Convention were unsuccessfully invoked before the Court, see *Il Foro Italiano* (1979) i, col. 1624–5.

Thus 'It is important to note that in raising questions of constitutionality judges refer to the rights guaranteed by both the Constitution and the Convention,'[25] and that the *Corte Costituzionale* appears to accept the view, at least implicitly, that the Convention's provisions embody the same category of fundamental human rights which are constitutionally protected and which fall essentially within the ambit of constitutional law.[26]

In the Italian judicial system a distinction is made between the court's competence to determine rights in the strict sense (*diritti soggettivi*) and legitimate interests (*interessi legittini*). In cases of violations of private interests (subjective rights) the ordinary courts, with the *Corte Suprema di Cassazione* (Supreme Court) at their head, are competent; while if a person complains of a rule made in the public interest, the administrative courts are competent (Article 113 of the Constitution). (It should perhaps be added that despite the fact that the *Consiglio di Stato* (Council of State) is the highest administrative court, it is not completely independent of the ordinary courts, in that in conflicts of jurisdiction, the *Corte Suprema di Cassazione* decides in the last instance.)[27] Consequently, the Convention's provisions are not usually pleaded before the administrative courts, because individuals, once a *diritto soggettivo* is established, must take public officials before the ordinary courts (with a few statutory exceptions) in disputes such as those concerning liability arising from certain contracts, recovery of property, and liability in tort, even though the official in question had been acting in his official capacity. In such cases the 'subjective rights' of individuals may be protected as against administrative action in the ordinary courts.

In the ordinary courts, decisions referring to the provisions of the Convention appear not infrequently, especially in criminal

---

[25] V. Grementieri and N. Trocker, n. 18 above, at 494. See also comment of F. Capotorti in *Human Rights in National and International Law* (ed. A. H. Robertson, 1968), 42-3.

[26] The European Commission of Human Rights was prepared to accept this line of reasoning in application 6452/74, *Sacchi* v. *Italy*, 5 *D&R* 43-57, at 51.

[27] Judicial review of administrative action which violates 'legitimate interests' is basically conferred upon the administrative courts, while the protection of 'subjective rights' against administrative action — except in certain cases concerning the exclusive jurisdiction of the *Consiglio di Stato* and the *Corte dei Conti* — is entrusted to the ordinary courts.

cases.[28] For example, in a case decided by the *Corte Suprema di Cassazione* on 17 November 1973, it was held that a judge's failure to admit an application by the defence for the hearing of witnesses who could refute the evidence of the prosecution witnesses, violated Article 6(2)(d) which stipulates that 'Everyone charged with a criminal offence has the right . . . to obtain the attendance and examination of witnesses on his behalf under the same conditions as witnesses against him'.[29] Similarly, in a more recent case dated 10 July 1976, the Court held that:

. . . The interests protected by Article 5(3) of the European Convention for the Protection of Human Rights and Fundamental Freedoms . . . which require that a person should not be deprived of his freedom except for a limited period unless he has appeared for trial, are taken into account by the existing Italian criminal procedure provisions by the institution of release after expiration of the maximum periods allowed for detention on remand (which does not permit the maintenance of a person in detention to a discretionary decision by the court).[30]

However, despite an impressive amount of case-law before the ordinary courts in which reference is made to the Convention, the *Corte Suprema di Cassazione* rejects the view that the Convention may possess some form of constitutional significance. Thus, in 1967, it held that the constitutionality of a provision of municipal law cannot be contested by reference to the Convention, as the latter was incorporated into the Italian legal system in pursuance not of Article 10 of the Constitution but by means of an ordinary law.[31] This view was reiterated by the *Corte Suprema di Cassazione* in July 1974 when it held that:

It is manifestly ill-founded to claim that Article 510 of the Code of Criminal Procedure which governs the judgment consequent on an appeal against a penal order is unconstitutional because it conflicts with·Article 10 of the Constitution (the Italian legal system conforms to the recognised

---

[28] See n. 18 above. D. Giuliva, of the University of Bari, has compiled a list of over seventy cases in which mention has been made of the Convention's norms.

[29] An extract of this case is reproduced in **19** *Yearbook* (1976) 1135. See also M. Chiavario, 'Le garanzie fondamentali della persona umana nella Convenzione di Roma e nel processo penale italiano', **8** *Rivista del diritto matrimoniale e dello stato delle persone* (1966), 501–12; and M. Chiavario, *La Convenzione Europea dei diritti dell'uomo nel sistema delle fonti normative in materia penale* (1969).

[30] Extract of decision taken from **20** *Yearbook* (1977), 767. See also the decision cited in **21** *Yearbook* (1978), 760–3.

[31] In **6** *CDE* (1970), 343–4; *Collection*, art. 8, 17. In this case it was held that art. 72 of the Code of Civil Procedure, which authorizes the Attorney-General's Department to enter an objection to decisions concerning a marriage, was not contrary to art. 8 of the Convention.

rules of international law). On the one hand, Act No. 848 of 4 August 1955, which brought into force the European Convention on the Protection of Human Rights and Fundamental Freedoms, whose Article 6 stipulates that judgments shall be independent and impartial, did not introduce such principles into the Constitution. On the other hand, in cases consequent on an appeal against a penal order, the judge passes judgment on the basis of new evidence that has emerged from the hearing, in which the accused takes part, with all the facilities for defence he is entitled to at this stage in the proceedings.[32]

Although it would appear from the above cited case-law that the *lex posterior derogat legi priori* rule applies with regard to all 'transformed' treaties (as the provisions of such instruments do not *per se* possess a hierarchically superior status to ordinary legislation), an important exception appears to have been made with regard to the norms of the European Communities.[33] Despite their initial hesitance to break with traditional dualist thinking, the Italian courts have slowly been able to consolidate the presence of European Community law within the Italian legal system, at least regarding the question of the direct applicability of Community law.[34] Thus, in the relatively recent case of *Frontini* v. *Ministero delle Finanze*, the *Corte Costituzionale* appears to have elevated the rank of the Italian EEC Treaty Ratification Act (no. 1203 of 14 October 1957), when it held as not founded the request to examine the constitutionality of Section 2 of this Act, in so far as it was claimed that by making Article 189 of the EEC Treaty effective in Italy, the Act had contravened Articles 23 and 70 of the Italian Constitution. In an interesting passage of the decision, it was explained that:

. . . as this Court has already stated in *Costa* v. *ENEL*, Article 11 [of the Constitution] means that, when its pre-conditions are met, it is possible to sign treaties which involve limitations of sovereignty and to make them executory by an ordinary statute.

. . . This Court has already had occasion to declare the autonomy of the Community order as compared with the internal order (*Soc. Acciaierie San Michele Spa* v. *High Authority*). The regulations issuing from the

[32] Extract taken from 19 *Yearbook* (1976), 1136.

[33] See L. Ferrari Bravo, 'European Communities and the Italian Legal System' in *Multitudo Legum Ius Unum* (Essays in honour of W. Wengler, 1973), i, 135–54; S. Neri, 'Le droit communautaire et l'ordre constitutionnel italien', 2 *CDE* (1966), 363–87; R. Monaco, *Diritto delle Comunità europee e diritto interno* (1967); and a number of articles in *Studi di Diritto europeo in onore di R. Monaco* (1977).

[34] See P. Pescatore, 'Address on the Application of Community Law in each of the Member States' *Judicial and Academic Conference*, 27–8 Sept. 1976 (Luxembourg, 1976), report VI, esp. 24–7. Also see *Simmenthal* case [1978] *ECR* 629; [1978] *CMLR* 620.

organs of the EEC within the meaning of Article 189 of the Treaty of Rome belong to the Community's own order: its laws and the internal law of the individual member States can be described as autonomous and distinct legal systems, albeit co-ordinated in accordance with the division of power laid down and guaranteed by the Treaty. Fundamental requirements of equality and legal certainty demand that the Community norms, which cannot be characterised as a source of international law, nor of internal law of the individual States, ought to have full compulsory efficacy and direct application in all the member States, without the necessity of reception and implementation statutes, as acts having the force and value of statute in every country of the Community to the extent of entering into force everywhere simultaneously and receiving equal and uniform application in all their addressees.[35]

In this case, therefore, the *Corte Costituzionale* in effect accepted the view that Article 11 of the Italian Constitution allows for a partial transfer of sovereignty to international organizations by means of an ordinary statute without the need to express constitutional amendment in accordance with the specific conditions laid down in Article 138 of the Constitution.

This development is worth recording in the context of the European Convention's domestic status, as it indicates that Italian courts may in certain circumstances give treaty provisions a hierarchically superior status to statute law: certainly, the possibility of the ordinary courts accepting the directly applicable norms of the European Convention on Human Rights as possessing a status higher than that of ordinary legislation cannot be ruled out in the light of the *Corte Costituzionale's* implicit recognition of this instrument's 'quasi-constitutional rank'. Alternatively, some of the Convention's norms may be deemed by the courts to reflect 'generally recognized principles of international law' as embodied in Article 10(1) of the Italian Constitution. The courts could likewise accept the Convention as *lex specialis* thereby securing its provisions a superior status over subsequent conflicting legislation: *lex posterior generalis non derogat priori specialis*.

Italy recognized the competence of the European Commission of Human Rights to receive individual applications in 1973, and

---

[35] Case no. 183, 18–27 Dec. 1973, **XVIII** *Giurisprudenza Costituzionale* (1973), 2401–20. Translation from 14 *CMLR* [1974], ii. 372–90, at 386–7. The Court made an important reservation in relation to constitutionally protected fundamental human rights: See W. R. Edeson and F. Wooldridge, 'European Community Law and Fundamental Rights: Some Recent Decisions of the European Court and National Courts', *LIEI* (1976), 1–54, esp. 48–52. Also see note of P. Gori, 6 *EL Rev.* (1981), 222–7.

it will probably take some time before an appropriate assessment of the Convention's domestic impact can be made. Certainly, the Strasbourg Court's adverse findings in the *Artico*[36] and *Guzzardi*[37] cases, as well as the two cases now pending before the Court (in the Commission's *opinions*, in both sets of cases, court proceedings exceeded the 'reasonable time' limit guaranteed by Article 6(1) of the Convention)[38] will undoubtedly arouse a certain amount of interest in legal circles, and will probably lead to at least some changes in the Italian Code of Criminal Procedure.[39]

C. Portugal

The Republic of Portugal signed the European Convention on Human Rights on 22 September 1976, on the same day as the country became the nineteenth member state of the Council of Europe.[40] The Convention and its two protocols were subsequently ratified on 9 November 1978 after legislative approval had been acquired in accordance with Article 8 of the new Portuguese Constitution, which came into force on 25 April 1976 (Law no. 65/78 of 13 October 1978).[41]

Article 8 of the new Portuguese Constitution stipulates that:

1. The rules and principles of general or ordinary international law shall be an integral part of Portuguese law.

---

[36] See Eur. Court HR, judgment of 13 May 1980, ser. A, no. 36. (The Court held that there had been a breach of art. 6(3)(c) of the Convention.) Commented on by G. M. Palmieri, 20 *Riv. DE* (1980), 345–61.

[37] Eur. Court HR, judgment of 6 Nov. 1980, ser. A, no. 39. (The applicant was a victim of a breach of art. 5(1) of the Convention.) It is of interest to note that the *Guzzardi* case originally came before Judge Siclari who considers that the Convention possesses the status of ordinary law: see B. Siclari, *Le Misure di prevenzione* (1974), at 223. Also see UN doc. CCPR/C/6/Add.4 of 21 May 1980, at 30 and 65–7 (Italian report to the Human Rights Committee under art. 40 of the 1966 Civil and Political Rights Covenant).

[38] i.e., *Corigliano* v. *Italy*, report of Commission, 16 Mar. 1981; and *Foti, Lentini, Cenerini, Guli* v. *Italy*, report of Commission, 15 Oct. 1980.

[39] Academic interest in the Convention is rapidly growing: see the bibliographical lists compiled in I *IYIL*, (1975), 351–7; II (1976), 521–3; and III (1977), 611–15; and recent lengthy articles in which the Strasbourg mechanism is explained to Italian lawyers in 22 *Riv. Italiana di Diritto e Procedura Penale* (1979), articles by G. Gregori, at 1209–325, and M. De Salvia, at 1403–30; and also vol. 23 (1980), 93–128. There also exists a useful handbook for the practising lawyer: G. Gregori, *La Tutela Europea dei Diritti dell'Uomo* (1979).

[40] See 19 *Yearbook* (1976), 2.

[41] *Diário da República*, no. 236, 2119.

2. Rules derived from international conventions duly ratified or approved shall, following their official publication, apply in municipal law in so far as they are internationally binding on the Portuguese State.

Thus, upon ratification, the European Convention on Human Rights obtained the status of domestic law. At the time of ratification Portugal also recognized both the competence of the European Commission of Human Rights to receive individual petitions and the compulsory jurisdiction of the European Court of Human Rights.[42] Portugal also formulated reservations in respect of Articles 4, 5, 7, 10, and 11 of the Convention and Articles 1 and 2 of the First Protocol.[43]

The domestic status of the European Convention was confirmed by the Lisbon Court of Appeal on 17 November 1978. As this appears to be the first case in which a Portuguese court has referred to this instrument, an extract of its judgment, translated into French, merits citation:

. . . L'expropriation devrait viser à satisfaire un besoin actuel de l'expropriant et non pas un besoin passé.

Par ailleurs, le Portugal a ratifié la Convention européenne des Droits de l'Homme, dont les dispositions — article 8, No. 1 de la Constitution — font partie intégrante du droit portugais.

L'article 6 de ladite Convention dispose que: 'toute personne a droit à ce que sa cause soit entendue équitablement'. Il serait contraire à toute équité de priver d'habitation celui qui en a besoin en faveur de celui qui n'en a plus besoin.

C'est pour cette raison qu'il convient de tenir compte de la situation actuelle. . . .[44]

Although the court did not make reference to the Convention's positioning in the domestic hierarchy, it is generally assumed that the relationship between directly applicable norms of international agreements and statute law remains what it was

[42] See n. 6 above, 17-18. Applications against Portugal have already been considered by the Commission: see applications 8560/79 and 8613/79, *X & Y* v. *Portugal* **16** *D&R* 209-12.

[43] See *Collected Texts*, 607-9, and **21** *Yearbook* (1978), 12-18. There has been some interesting correspondence, concerning Portugal's reservation in respect of art. 1 of the First Protocol, between the Secretary General of the Council of Europe and the UK, West German, and French governments: see Council of Europe docs. DH(79)2, at 15, DH(79)6, at 16, and DH(79)7, at 24.

[44] Provided to the author by Ms J. Dinsdale of the Council of Europe's Human Rights Directorate. The European Convention on Human Rights and the case-law of the Commission were also referred to in a judgment of the Constitutional Commission on 24 June 1979, *Boletim do Ministério da Justiça*, no. 291 (Dec. 1979), 163-91, at 344 and 351. (More details about this case are provided in ch. 10 below.)

prior to the coming into force of the new Constitution. That is
to say:

At first sight it might be said that we have here [in Portugal] a system of
implicit transformation. But in actual fact the system is one of general
adoption. The internal validity of a treaty is not founded on its approval
by Parliament or the Government, but on its rank in international law;
just like its publication, its approval is reduced to an enforcement *conditio*
of norms which in themselves are already binding. . . .

Treaties possess a power greater than laws (but that does not imply *ipso
facto* invalidity of contrary laws). This conclusion results not only from
the primacy of international law, but also from the wording of the Constitution itself. . . .[45]

It follows that if a conflict were to arise between a provision of
the Convention and a subsequent Act of Parliament, it is not
certain that the former would prevail. Such an occurrence is
considered doubtful, however, for the simple reason that the
presumed inconsistent legislation would probably also violate
a constitutional provision and be struck down accordingly.

This somewhat delicate problem was discussed at length in a
recent report which Portugal submitted to the UN Human Rights
Committee in Geneva, an extract of which merits citation:

. . . Let us assume that a right prescribed in the Covenant is not provided
for in the Constitution and that a provision of law supervening after the
entry into force of the Covenant[46] infringes one of its provisions. *Quid juris?*

The provisions in question may have the same standing, and this may
justify the abrogation of the provision of international law by the provision of internal law supervening subsequently. This, however, would
probably entail an infringement of article 8 of the Constitution. Paragraph 2 of this article states that, provided certain conditions are fulfilled,
the provisions of international conventions shall have effect internally
in so far as they are internationally binding on the Portuguese State. If
they can be abrogated by subsequent internal legislation, would this
not be tantamount to denying that such provisions have effect?

In any event, the solution is rather questionable. The Constitution is
not explicit enough on this point, with the result that there are many explanations and interpretations of it. Part of case law nevertheless recognizes the
primacy of the provision of international law over that of internal law.

[45] Quotation taken from J. Miranda, 'How International Treaties are Implemented
in EFTA Countries: Portugal', 13 *EFTA Bulletin* (1972), 5–6, at 6. For further
discussion consult A. Gonçlaves Pereira, *Curso de Direito Internacional Público*
(1970), esp. 87–114.
[46] 'If this provision of internal law precedes it, the repeal of the provision can
always be defended by the supervening provision of international law.' [Note to the
report.]

With this end in view, it defends the principle of immediacy: the national judge automatically applies international law, regardless of any change or acceptance effected by an internal legislative act. According to this interpretation, international law, by reason of its inherent validity, is part of the internal legal order and its conversion into internal law, by whatever change or acceptance, is not determined by the way in which it is adopted.

The general provision embodied in article 8 concerning the acceptance of international law is, according to this argument, entirely unrelated to the problem outlined, because it does not permit the inference that this law is automatically integrated on account of the way in which it has been adopted.

Article 8, paragraph 2, establishes only one requirement for effectiveness, namely, official publication (see art. 122, para. 2(b), of the Constitution), which alone would not permit the inference that international law becomes internal law.

The inherent validity of international law therefore precludes it from being challenged by internal law. Accordingly, if a provision of the Covenant was called in question by a provision of internal law supervening subsequently, it could nevertheless be invoked in the national courts.[47]

As the new Portuguese Constitution came into force on 25 April 1976, it is still too early to make any significant assessment of its functioning or to draw on learned opinion or case-law. Thus, in the absence of such information only brief and rather superficial reference is made here to certain of the Constitution's provisions. Part I of the 1976 Constitution provides an exhaustive list of constitutionally guaranteed fundamental rights and duties (Articles 12–79).[48] These appear to provide a standard of guarantee far superior to that provided by the Convention's norms. Appropriate provision is also made for the preventive scrutiny of constitutionality as well as judicial determination of constitutionality by a Constitutional Commission whose

---

[47] Portuguese report to the Human Rights Committee under art. 40 of the International Covenant on Civil and Political Rights, UN doc. CCPR/C/6/Add.6 4 Oct. 1980. It can be added that the fundamental rights enunciated in the Portuguese Constitution do not exclude any other rights deriving from the law and the applicable provisions of international law (art. 6(1)). The provisions of the Constitution and laws relating to fundamental rights (and the other rights enunciated in art. 17) must, in addition, be interpreted and applied in accordance with the Universal Declaration of Human Rights (art. 6(2)). (See p. 7 of the report; also p. 22.)

In the recent oral hearings in the application of *Guincho* v. *Portugal*, no. 8990/80, held on 16 Dec. 1981, the direct applicability of the Convention was accepted by the Government although it appears that this instrument's *exact* positioning within the legal system remains unclear: see press release C(81)71, 22 Dec. 1981.

[48] Recent literature on this subject includes L. M. Cazorla Prieto, 'Las libertades públicas en la nueva Constitución portuguesa', no. 176 *Documentación Administrativa* (1977), 43–68, and A. M. Pereira, *Direitos do Homem* (1979).

judgments are final (Articles 277 and 282).[49] In addition, Article 280, paragraph 3, lays down: '. . . Organic or formal unconstitutionality in international conventions shall not prevent application of their provisions in Portuguese municipal law unless such application is impossible in the municipal law of the other party or parties'.[50] Here again, it is too early to assess the significance of the provisions cited as no case-law is as yet available on this subject.

In a recent publication a Portuguese academic lawyer, when presenting a report outlining the extent to which human rights are protected by Portuguese criminal procedure, wrote '. . . *Je crois même que la nouvelle Constitution protège les droits de l'homme dans la procédure pénale d'une façon plus* étendue *que ce qui est habituel dans la plupart des* États, *et qu'elle dépasse les exigences de la Déclaration Universelle et de la Convention Europeénne des Droits de l'Homme'.*[51] Most Portuguese lawyers would, it seems, confirm this to be true with regard to all the human rights norms enumerated in the new Portuguese Constitution when compared with the substantive provisions of the European Convention. Certainly, Portugal's willingness to be subjected to the international supervisory machinery in Strasbourg, both in respect of the right of individual petition and the compulsory jurisdiction of the European Court of Human Rights, appears to confirm the country's confidence in its new democratic institutions.

D. Spain

Spain became a member state of the Council of Europe on 24 November 1977 and at the same time signed the European Convention on Human Rights.[52] This was done after the Par-

---

[49] The respective roles of the Council of the Revolution and the Constitutional Commission are described in the Portugese report, n. 47 above, at 11–14, and by A. Thomashausen, 'Basic Rights, Liberty and their Protection under the New Portuguese Constitution of 1976', I *HRLJ* (1980), 182–208. It is understood that the present revision of the Constitution will lead to the abolition of the above two bodies and the creation of a Constitutional Court. See the *Financial Times*, 21 Mar. 1981, 2; and *The Times*, 30 Oct. 1982, 5.

[50] The various provisions on the Portuguese Constitution referred to can be consulted in vol. xii, *Constitutions of the Countries of the World* (ed. A. P. Blaustein and G. H. Flanz, loose-leaf publication.)

[51] Y. De Figueiro Dias, 'La protection des Droits de l'Homme dans la procédure pénale portugaise', no. 291 *Boletim do Ministério da Justiça* (1979) 163–91, at 167. (Emphasis original.)   [52] See 20 *Yearbook* (1977), 2.

liamentary Assembly of the Council of Europe had provided the Committee of Ministers with a recommendation that the country be invited to join the organization.[53] The Convention was subsequently ratified by Spain on 4 October 1979 after the Government of the day had obtained authorization to do so from the *Cortes Generales* on 28 June 1979 (*Boletín Oficial de las Cortes/Congreso de los Diputados*, of 5 July 1979, no. 5-III). The text of the Convention was subsequently published on 22 December 1979 (*Boletín Oficial*, no. 213, 5525). At the time of ratification Spain recognized for a period of three years from 4 October 1979, on condition of reciprocity, the compulsory jurisdiction of the European Court of Human Rights;[54] and this was followed by the acceptance of the right of individual petition, effective as of 1 July 1981.[55] The First and Fourth Protocols have been signed but not yet ratified. The Second Protocol was ratified on 6 April 1982.

The domestic application of treaties — as well as their relation to constitutional law — is governed by Articles 93-6 of the new Spanish Constitution which entered into force on 29 December 1978.[56] The relevant provisions of these articles read:

Article 93
By means of an organic law, authorization may be established for the conclusion of treaties which attribute to an international organization or institution the exercise of competences derived from the Constitution. It is the responsibility of the Cortes Generales or the Government, depending on the cases, to guarantee compliance with these treaties and the resolutions emanating from the international or supranational organizations who have been entitled by this cession.

Article 94
1. The giving of the consent of the State to obligate itself to something by means of treaties or agreements shall require prior authorization of the Cortes Generales in the following cases: . . .
   c) Treaties or agreements which affect the territorial integrity of the State or the fundamental rights and duties established in Title I.
   d) Treaties or agreements which imply important obligations for the public treasury. . . .
2. The Congress and the Senate shall be immediately informed of the conclusion of the treaties or agreements.

---

[53] Recommendation 820 (1977), adopted on 12 Oct. 1977.

[54] See n. 6 above, 17. Reservations were also made in respect of arts. 5, 6, and 11, and interpretative declarations in respect of arts. 10, 15, and 17: see *Collected Texts*, 609 and 613. [55] *Boletín Oficial*, 30 June 1981.

[56] The text of the new Constitution is reproduced in *Boletín Oficial*, 28 Oct. 1978, 3701 (English translation in *Constitutions of the Countries of the World* ed. A. P. Blaustein and G. H. Flanz, vol. iii).

Article 95
1. The conclusion of an international treaty which contains stipulations contrary to the Constitution shall require a prior constitutional revision.
2. The Government or either of the Chambers may request the Constitutional Court to declare whether or not such a contradiction exists.

Article 96
1. Validly concluded international treaties once officially published in Spain shall constitute part of the internal (legal) order. Their provisions may only be abolished, modified or suspended in the manner provided for in the treaties themselves or in accord with general norms of international law.
2. To denounce international treaties and agreements, the same procedure established for their approval in Article 94 shall be used.[57]

It follows that those provisions of the European Convention on Human Rights which are considered to be directly applicable by the Spanish courts have attained the force of domestic law as of 10 October 1979 (date of its publication in the *Boletin Oficial del Estado*). To date no case-law is available on the subject. And, although it is not clear how the courts will react were a conflict to arise between a directly applicable provision of the Convention and a subsequently enacted statute, there is reason to believe that the domestic courts may have a duty, under Article 10, paragraph 2 of the Constitution, to provide priority to the former:

Article 10
1. The dignity of the person, the inviolable rights which are inherent, the free development of the personality, respect for the law and the rights of others, are the foundation of the political order and the social peace.
2. The norms relative to basic rights and liberties which are recognized by the Constitution, shall be interpreted in conformity with the Universal Declaration of Human Rights and the international treaties and agreements on those matters ratified by Spain.

Certainly, both legal literature[58] as well as previous Spanish

[57] Taken from Blaustein and Flanz, ibid., at 21. (Art. 93 was drafted with Spain's eventual accession to the European Communities in mind.) In addition, art. 62(2) of the Constitution stipulates that 'It is incumbent on the King to express the consent of the State to oblige itself internationally through treaties in conformity with the Constitution and the laws'. Art. 96, para. 1 must be read in conjunction with art. 1, para. 5 of the Spanish Civil Code. See S. Riesenfeld, editorial comment 74 *AJIL* (1980), 892–904, at 896.

[58] See E. Linde, L. I. Ortega, and M. Sánchez Morón, *El sistema europeo de protección de los derechos humanos* (1979), esp. ch. 7, entitled 'Eficacia de la Convención en el derecho español', 141–74, at 146–52 and 152–4; and A. F. Panzera, 'La costituzione Spagnola del 1978 e il diritto internazionale', **LXII** *Riv. DI* (1979), 340–52. For a more general study consult J. D. González Cámpos and Sanchez Rodrigues, *Curso de Derecho internacional público* (1980).

case-law[59] suggest that the Convention's directly applicable norms (as similar provisions of other international human-rights agreements)[60] possess a hierarchically superior status *vis-à-vis* both prior and subsequent conflicting legislation.

It may be noted that the drafters of the new Spanish Constitution were directly influenced by and took into consideration a number of the substantive norms enumerated in the European Convention when the provisions on fundamental human rights were drawn up for the Constitution. As in Portugal, it is assumed by most commentators that the protection of human rights afforded to individuals in the newly drafted Spanish Constitution is of a far higher standard than provided by the Convention.[61] In actual fact, one Spanish jurist has been critical of developing case-law in Strasbourg, and has indicated that not too much notice of these developments should be taken by the Spanish courts or legislators, adding a proviso that it might nevertheless be advisable to be kept aware of 'minimum standards' maintained in Strasbourg.[62]

In an attempt to obtain information on recent developments concerning the domestic status of the European Convention on Human Rights in Spain, the author has received the following reply:

. . . je ne connais aucun développement législatif ou jurisprudentiel jusqu'à présent. La ratification par l'Espagne de la Convention est très récente et son développement demande un certain temps. D'autre part, et à mon avis, la Constitution espagnole est dans ce domaine plus progressive que la Convention elle-même et par conséquence cette dernière a un valeur très

[59] See J. L. Iglesias-Buigues, 'Algunas Reflexiones en torno a las relaciones entre el derecho internacional y el derecho interno', I *Anuario de Derecho Internacional* (1974), 381–401. But also see recent case-law cited in *European Law Digest* (1981), at 195 and 204.

[60] See Spanish report submitted to the UN Human Rights Committee under art. 40 of the Civil and Political Rights Covenant, UN docs. CCPR/C/4Add.1, 8 Sept. 1978, and CCPR/C/4Add.3; and esp. CCPR/C/SR141, 4 May 1979, 6, para. 23. Consult, for example, Supreme Court judgment of 3 July 1979 in the case of *Gran Oriente Español* [1979] RA 3182. This subject is further dealt with by J. A. Corriente Córdoba, 'España y los Convenios internacionales de protección de los derechos humanos'. III *Anuario de derecho internacional* (1976), 129–72.

[61] See *Una Costituzione democratica per la Spagna* (ed. de Vergottini, 1978); commentaries in 6 *EGZ* (1979), at 229–35 and 237–9; and *Lecturas sobre la Constitución Española* (ed. T. R. Fernandez Rodriguez, 2 vols., 1978), *passim*.

[62] D. Liñan Nogueras, *El Detenido en el Convenio Europeo de Derechos Humanos. Estudio del Convenio y su jurisprudencia para un análisis comparativo con la Constitución Española* (1980), at 107–9. Also consult V. F. Guillén, 'Algunos problemas procesales suscitados par el articulo 6° de la Convención Europea de los Derechos del Hombre', 7 *Revista de Instituciones Europeas* (1980), 553–68.

faible en Espagne. En outre, les domaines où la Convention a pu avoir une plus grande importance vis-à-vis du droit interne espagnol sont les points qui ont été réservés (Régime de la Radiodiffusion, etc. . . .) dans la ratification espagnole.[63]

A study of the relevant provisions of the Spanish Constitution appears to substantiate this claim, although of course case-law has not as yet confirmed it.[64]

E. Turkey[65]

A member of the Council of Europe since 9 August 1949, Turkey signed the Convention of Human Rights on 4 November 1950 and its First Protocol on 20 May 1952. Both were ratified simultaneously on 18 May 1954. Turkey has made no declarations under either Article 25 or Article 46, and the Fourth Protocol remains unsigned.[66] A reservation has been made in respect of Article 2 of the First Protocol.[67] Turkey has also — in accordance with Article 15 of the Convention — often availed itself of the right to derogation from certain of the Convention's provisions.[68]

The Turkish Constitution in force at the time of the Convention's ratification (as amended in 1944) contained no explicit reference to the domestic status of international agreements. Article 26 provided that 'the Grand National Assembly alone exercises such functions as enacting, modifying, interpreting, and abrogating laws; concluding conventions and treaties and making peace with foreign states. . . .' In addition, Article 27 stipulated that treaties concluded by the Government 'become effective, in regard to Turkey, upon ratification by the Grand National Assembly'.

---

[63] Letter to the author by Dr D. Liñan Nogueras, 1 Aug. 1980 (as academic lawyer at the Dept. of International Law, Faculty of Law, University of Granada).

[64] See arts. 10–35 of the Spanish Constitution in Blaustein and Flanz, n. 56 above, at 3–12. For recent studies on this subject consult special issue of *Revista de la Facultad de Derecho de la Universidad Complutense*, vol. ii (1979), entitled *Los Derechos Humanos y la Constitución de 1978*, 3–284; and L. Aguiar de Luque, 'Las Garantías constitucionales de los derechos fundamentales en la Constitución española', 10 *Revista de Derecho Politico* (1981), 107–29.

[65] There appears to be very little bibliographical material available concerning the Convention's influence and status in the Turkish legal system: see Th. Buergenthal, 'The Domestic Status of the European Convention on Human Rights: A Second Look', 7 *Journal of the ICJ* (1966), 55–96, at 90–2; and *Bibliography*, 122.

[66] See n. 6 above, 17.   [67] See 1 *Yearbook* (1955-7), 43.

[68] Turkey appears to have used (abused?) this right of derogation on numerous occasions: see *Yearbook, passim*.

Thus it was assumed that upon the entry into force of the Convention and Turkish ratification of it, this instrument 'became effective' in (was incorporated into) the domestic legal system, securing for itself at least a superior status to any prior conflicting legislation (Law no. 6366 of 10 March 1954).[69]

The present domestic rank of international agreements appears unclear.[70] The relevant paragraphs of Articles 65 and 97 of the 1961 Turkish Constitution read:

Article 65
1. The ratification of treaties negotiated with foreign States and international organisations on behalf of the Turkish Republic is dependent upon its approval by the Turkish Grand National Assembly through the enactment of a law. . . .
4. The provisions of paragraph 1 shall apply in all treaties involving amendments to Turkish legislation.
5. International treaties duly put into effect carry the force of law. No recourse to the Constitutional Court can be made as provided in Articles 149 and 151 with regard to these treaties.

Article 97
1. The President of the Republic is the head of the State. In this capacity he shall represent the Turkish Republic and the integrity of the Turkish Nation.
2. The President of the Republic shall preside over the Council of Ministers whenever he deems it necessary, shall send representatives of the Turkish State to foreign states, shall receive the representatives of foreign states, shall ratify and promulgate international treaties. . . .[71]

Consequently, although these new provisions may certainly be interpreted as giving international agreements a hierarchically superior status over prior and subsequent ordinary legislation, it would appear that the courts have not as yet been directly confronted with such an issue. As a result, the exact situation of the European Convention of Human Rights is also rather difficult to ascertain. Whereas ordinary legislation may be annulled by the *Ana Yasa Mahkemesi* (Constitutional Court) if the Court deems such legislation unconstitutional, this cannot be the case with regard to the provisions of the Convention (Article 65(5)

---

[69] See A. R. Güllü, *Les Droits de l'Homme et la Turquie* (1958), esp. 63–74. (He believed that the Convention also ranked above *subsequent* legislation: 73–4.)
[70] Cf. K. Holloway, *Modern Trends in Treaty Law* (1967), at 186–8; E.Çelik, 'La formation des traités en droit international et en droit turc', 20 *Annales de la Faculté de Droit d'Istanbul* (1970), 1–50, at 48; and A. Güriz, 'Sources of Turkish Law' in *Introduction to Turkish Law* (ed. T. Ansay and D. Wallace, 1978), 1–21, at 7–8.
[71] English translation from Blaustein and Flanz, n. 56 above, **xiv**. 27–8 and 43.

of the Constitution).[72] In addition it has been explained that: '. . . since the Constitution provides for a more extensive list of fundamental rights, the question of whether the provisions of the European Convention on Human Rights have direct applicability in domestic law becomes an academic question rather than a practical one; i.e. if the law is not compatible with the provisions of ECHR it must a *fortiori* be in contradiction with the Constitution and therefore be annulled through judical review'.[73]

The *Ana Yasa Mahkemesi* has nevertheless made reference to the Convention on a couple of occasions.[74] In July 1963, for instance, the Court, when deciding that Article 11(1) of the Turkish Penal Code (dealing with the death penalty) was not incompatible with the Constitution, referred to Article 2 of the Convention in the following terms:

. . . The question can be further clarified by referring to the relevant provisions of an international convention which, as is evident from the report of the Constitutional Committee and the proceedings of the Constituent Assembly, was taken into consideration during the drafting of the Constitution. Article 2(1) of the Convention for the Protection of Human Rights and Fundamental Freedoms, to which Turkey acceded in 1954, stipulates that 'everyone's right to life shall be protected by law' and that 'no-one shall be deprived of his life intentionally save in the execution of a sentence of a court following his conviction of a crime for which this penalty is provided by law'. This also shows clearly that the death penalty is not incompatible with fundamental rights and freedoms.[75]

Similarly, in a decision dated 18–19 June 1968, the *Ana Yasa Mahkemesi* mentioned both Article 17 of the Universal Declaration of Human Rights and Article 1 of the Convention's First Protocol (the right to property) when it held that certain provisions of the Act on Entries in the Land Register were not contrary to the Constitution.[76]

[72] Cf. H. N. Kubali, 'Les traits dominant de la Constitution de la seconde République Turque', 17 *RIDC* (1965), pp. 855–72, and P. Arik, 'La Cour constitutionnelle turque', 14 *RIDC* (1962), 401–12. As to recent case-law consult the Council of Europe's *Newsletter on legislative activities*, no. 21 (1975) at 9, and no. 22 (1976), at 6; and Ş. Müftigil, 'Bestand und Bedeutung der Grundrechte nach türkischen Verfassungsrecht', 8 *EGZ* (1981), 423–7.

[73] R. Aybay, 'International Human Rights Instruments and Turkish Law' in *Turkish Yearbook of Human Rights* (1979), 17–25, at 22.

[74] See B. N. Esen, 'Système turc de protection des droits de l'homme dans les rapports entre personnes privées' in Cassin, iii. 163–76, at 173–4; and Aybay, ibid., at 23.

[75] Case no. 1963/207E, 1 July 1963, 6 *Yearbook* (1963), 820–6, at 824–6. See also comments by B. N. Esen in *Human Rights in National and International Law* (ed. A. H. Robertson, 1968), 149–50.

[76] Case no. 13412, *Resmî Gazete* (Official Journal of the Republic of Turkey), 28 Jan. 1970; *Collection*, art. 1 to the First Protocol, 8.

The infrequent use of the European Convention's provisions by domestic courts was critically examined by Professor Dogan in a paper presented at an international symposium organized on the occasion of the 100th anniversary of the Istanbul Bar Association in April 1978. In his estimation, not only is there *'insuffisance de la connaissance du contenu de la Convention et de sa valeur juridique dans l'ordre juridique turc*, [whereby] *les juristes turcs ne s'y fondent pas du tout comme il le faut devant les tribunaux . . .* [but also] *. . . même malgré l'effort déployé par les juristes, ils n'arrivent pas à faire accepter à la Cour Constitutionnelle ou aux tribunaux de rendre leurs décisions en se fondant sur les dispositions des Conventions ou des traités en général'.* He then goes on to explain that an international agreement duly incorporated into Turkish law possesses a hierarchically superior status to ordinary legislation and that its provisions cannot be subjected to constitutional review. Thus, when incompatibility exists, *'La Convention restera valable et le juge doit appliquer les dispositions de la Convention par préférence en omettant celle de la loi* ou même de la Constitution.'[77]

Until and unless the Turkish authorities are prepared to recognize the compulsory jurisdiction of the Human Rights Court and accept the right of individual petition before the Commission, it will remain difficult to determine the real extent to which human rights guaranteed by the Convention are actually respected.[78] Such action appears even more urgent in the light of the two sets of applications brought before the Strasbourg instances by Cyprus,[79] not to mention developments inside the country itself.[80]

[77] M. Dogan, 'L'influence de la Convention de sauvegarde des Droits de l'Homme et des libertés fondamentales sur l'ordre constitutionnel turc', quotations from pp. 7 and 8. (Emphasis added.) Another important passage from this text is reproduced in ch. 10 below, sec. B. (This paper was forwarded to the author by Mr Beygo of the Council of Europe's Human Rights Directorate.)

[78] An Amnesty International report of June 1980 claimed that torture is widespread in Turkey (see *The Times*, 10 June 1980, at 9). See also M. Simon, 'The Trial of the Turkish Workers Party before the Constitutional Court of Turkey', 21 *Review of the ICJ* (1980), 53–64, esp. at 64, and recent applications, dated 1 July 1982, brought against Turkey by Denmark, France, the Netherlands, Norway and Sweden.

[79] See applications 6780/74 and 6950/75, *Cyprus* v. *Turkey*, report of Commission, 10 July 1976, and Committee of Ministers resolution DH(79)1, 20 Jan. 1979; and application 8007/77, *Cyprus* v. *Turkey*, 13 *D&R*, 85–230.

[80] See ICJ 'Commentary' in 26 *Review of the ICJ* (1981), 24–40, esp. 30–2. Turkey now has a new Constitution, see *Financial Times*, of 14 Oct. 1981, 2; and *The Times*, 22 July 1982, 8.

Chapter 7

Cyprus, Ireland, Malta, and the United Kingdom

A. Cyprus

Shortly after becoming a member state of the Council of Europe the Republic of Cyprus acceded to the European Convention on Human Rights and its First Protocol by signing them both on 16 December 1961. This was approved internally by the passage of the European Convention for the Protection of Human Rights (Ratification) Law (no. 39 of 1962) in accordance with paragraph 2 of Article 169 of the 1960 Constitution. Article 169 reads:

Subject to the provisions of Article 50 and paragraph 3 of Article 57 [concerning the President's and/or Vice-President's right to veto certain legislation, including the conclusion of treaties within a specified time-limit]:
1. Every international agreement with a foreign State or any International Organisation relating to commercial matters, economic cooperation (including payments and credit) and *modus vivendi* shall be concluded under a decision of the Council of Ministers;
2. Any other treaty, convention or international agreement shall be signed under a decision of the Council of Ministers and shall only be operative and binding on the Republic when approved by a law made by the House of Representatives whereupon it shall be concluded;
3. Treaties, conventions and agreements concluded in accordance with the foregoing provisions of this Article shall have, as from their publication in the official Gazette of the Republic, superior force to any municipal law on condition that such treaties, conventions and agreements are applied by the other party thereto.[1]

The instrument of ratification was deposited with the Secretary General of the Council of Europe on 6 October 1962.[2] Cyprus has not signed the Fourth Protocol nor has it made any decla-

---

[1] A. J. Peaslee, *Constitutions of Nations* (1968), iii. 201.
[2] See C. G. Tornaritis, 'The European Convention on Human Rights in the Legal Order of the Republic of Cyprus', **IX** *Cyprus Law Tribune* (1976) 1–19. See also Z. Nedjati, *Human Rights and Fundamental Freedoms* (1972).

rations under Article 25. The country has, however, recently accepted the Court's jurisdiction.[3]

When the European Convention on Human Rights was signed in 1950, it contained an article known as the 'colonial clause' (Article 63). Paragraph 1 of this article provides that 'Any State may at the time of its ratification or at any time thereafter declare by notification addressed to the Secretary-General of the Council of Europe that the present Convention shall extend to all or any of the territories for whose international relations it is responsible'. The United Kingdom made such a declaration on 23 October 1953 (declaration no. 61/48/53) thereby extending the Convention's applicability to, among others, the then Colony of Cyprus. However, upon the independence of Cyprus on 16 August 1960 the UK ceased to be responsible for the international relations of the country and the Convention automatically ceased to apply to the newly independent Republic. The Republic's Constitution came into force on the same day.

In its report recently submitted to the Human Rights Committee under Article 40 of the 1966 UN Covenant on Civil and Political Rights, the Cyprus Government provided an excellent overview of developments subsequent to independence:

Under the Treaty of Establishment of the Republic of Cyprus, Article 5, it is provided that the Republic of Cyprus 'shall secure to everyone within its jurisdiction human rights and fundamental freedoms comparable to those set out in Section I of the European Convention for the Protection of Human Rights and Fundamental Freedoms, signed at Rome on the 4th of November, 1950, and the Protocol to that Convention signed at Paris on the 20th March 1952. Thus, the Rome Convention and the Protocol have served as the prototypes for drafting the relevant provisions in the Cyprus Constitution. The Republic of Cyprus ratified the Rome Convention and its First Protocol in 1962 by means of the European Convention on Human Rights (Ratification) Law, 1962 (Law 39/1962). By virtue of such ratification and by virtue of the provisions of Article 169(3) of our Constitution, the actual provisions of the Rome Convention and its First Protocol have superior force to any municipal law in Cyprus; thus, these provisions have become part of the law of Cyprus alongside with the Fundamental Rights and Liberties provisions in Part II of our Constitution. The same applies to the International Covenant on Civil and Political Rights ratified by Law of the Republic 14/69.[4]

---

[3] See Chart showing Signatures and Ratifications of Council of Europe Conventions and Agreements (Dec. 1981), 17.

[4] UN doc. CCPR/C/1/Add.6, 6 Apr. 1977, 1. Also see J. E. S. Fawcett, *The Application of the European Convention on Human Rights* (1969), 9-10. (It appears that Professor Fawcett was not correct in saying that 'the provisions of the Convention have not been incorportated as such into the law of Cyprus'.)

It can be said that the substantive provisions of the Convention — with slight modifications and additions — were incorporated into the Cypriot legal order prior to the country's accession to the Council of Europe.

The domestic status of the Convention in Cyprus had been explained by the country's present Attorney-General in the following terms:

> . . . the European Convention on Human Rights . . . as from its publication in the official Gazette of the Republic, that is to say the 24th May 1962, forms part of the law of Cyprus and has under paragraph 3 of (the aforesaid) Article 160 superior force to any municipal law on condition that such Convention is applied by the other party thereto. Taking into consideration that such Convention, as far as the other parties thereto are concerned, it is applied as from the date of the deposit of the ratification, that is to say as from the 6th October 1962, then as from that date the Convention has in Cyprus the force provided in the aforesaid Article . . . The Convention is of a status superior to any other law either prior or subsequent, that is to say 'a law of the Republic', but inferior to its Constitution.[5]

As a result of the Convention's incorporation into domestic law, this instrument may and has been invoked before the Cypriot courts as a supplementary aid in interpreting corresponding articles of the Constitution. Additional reference is also made, if need be, to the findings of both the Commission and Court in Strasbourg.[6] In other words, the courts apply the Constitution as highest law, using the Convention and decisions of the Convention organs as guidelines.

Thus, in several cases the Supreme Court has made reference to the Convention's provisions in order to substantiate its reasoning based upon the relevant sections of the Republic's Constitution.[7] Reference to decisions of the Convention's

[5] Tornaritis, n. 2 above, at 8. He also quotes case-law of the Supreme Court of Cyprus to substantiate his reasoning.

[6] See n. 2 above: Nedjati, 20, and Tornaritis, 9–15. Two earlier decisions worth noting are case no. 50/61 in 1 Reports of Cases decided by the Supreme Constitutional Court of Cyprus (1960-1), 121–6; and case no. 272/62 CLR (1964), 336–46 in which references were made to the European Commission of Human Rights' interpretation of art. 6(1)(d) of the Convention. Also consult C. G. Tornaritis, 'The Human Rights as Recognised and Protected by Law with Special Reference to the Law of Cyprus' in *International Round-Table Discussion on Human Rights*, Berlin 3–8 Oct. 1966 (1968), 119–55.

[7] See, for example, in CLR: case no. 157/68 (1968) Part 3, 406–10, case no. 8/67, (1971), Part 1. 211–25, case no. 51/71 (1971), Part 3, 317–44; also case no. 3626, 2 Judgments of the Supreme Court of Cyprus (1976), 302–85, and case no. 5601/72, in vol. 3 (1976), 496–509.

organs has been frequent. For example, in the *Kannas* case, in 1968, Triantafyllides J. made reference to the applications of *Nielsen* and *Ofner* in order to substantiate the Court's finding that an appellant had not been deprived of the possibility of adequately preparing his defence,[8] while in a number of subsequent cases, note has also been taken of judgments of the European Court of Human Rights.[9] A recent example of the latter is the case of *Kouppis* v. *The Republic* in which Kouppis, the appellant, had been convicted of homicide. In his separate opinion, Judge Triantafyllides observed that Articles 30(2) and 12(5) of the Cypriot Constitution both corresponded closely to Article 6(1) of the European Convention on Human Rights and, after referring to Article 169(3) of the Constitution and to domestic case-law which confirmed this instrument's 'superior force to any municipal law' he went on to hold: 'It follows from the foregoing that the interpretation and mode of application of the aforesaid provisions of the European Convention on Human Rights (by the European Commission of Human Rights and the European Court of Human Rights) can provide most useful guidance as regards the interpretation and application of the corresponding provisions of our Constitution which have, already, been quoted in this judgment'.[10] He then referred to over twelve decisions of the Commission as well as two judgments of the Court, namely those of *Neumeister* and *Delcourt*.

In view of the present unstable situation in Cyprus, a legal analysis of the Cypriot legal system remains to a certain extent an artificial one, even more so when discussing the normative rank of the Convention and its usefulness as an additional domestic remedy whose provisions are directly enforceable in the Republic's courts. Mention must therefore be made of the third *Cyprus* v. *Turkey* inter-state application now pending

[8] Case no. 2975 CLR (1968), Part 2, 29–39, at 35–6; an extract from this decision is reproduced in 11 *Yearbook* (1968), 1084–7. Other judgments referring to the Commission's case-law include: case no. 3220 CLR (1971), Part 2, 40–145; case no. 56 CLR (1971), Part 3, 176–84; case no. 3487, CLR (1973), Part 2, 204–10; and case no. 3/77, 6 Judgments of the Supreme Court of Cyprus (1977), 1043–58. (This subject is dealt with at greater length in ch. 10 below.)

[9] See, for example, case no. 3211, CLR (1971), Part 2, 229–38; and case no. 3487, CLR (1973), Part 2, 204–10. A summary of the latter case can be found in *European Convention of Human Rights. National Aspects* (1975), 45–6. (Also see ch. 10 below.)

[10] Case no. 3797, judgment of 31 Oct. 1977 in 11 Judgments of the Supreme Court of Cyprus (1977), 1860–998, at 1879–80.

before the Convention organs,[11] as well as the recent efforts to create the Turkish Federated State of Cyprus.[12]

B. Ireland

The Convention was signed by Ireland on 4 November 1950 and the First Protocol on 20 March 1952. Both were ratified shortly afterwards on 25 February 1953. Upon ratification Ireland also recognized, for an unspecified period, the competence of the European Commission to receive individual applications, and recognized the compulsory jurisdiction of the European Court of Human Rights. At the same time a reservation was made concerning the interpretation of Article 6(3)(c) of the Convention.[13] In July 1957 the Republic of Ireland availed itself of the right of derogation as provided by Article 15 of the Convention. This derogation remained operative until March 1962.[14] The Fourth Protocol was ratified on 29 October 1968.

Ireland has not incorporated the Convention into domestic law. The rights and freedoms guaranteed under the Convention and its First Protocol are considered to be sufficiently well protected by the provisions of the Irish Constitution of 1937, and in particular in the section of the Constitution which relates to 'Fundamental Rights' (Articles 40–44). These provisions are supplemented by parliamentary enactments, administrative regulations, and by various remedies provided under the common law (customary and non-statute law) as well as by the criminal law.[15]

---

[11] Application 8007/77, 13 *D&R* 85-230.

[12] Recent accounts of the political and constitutional problems facing Cyprus include two publications by C. G. Tornaritis, *The Council of Europe and the Republic of Cyprus* (1978), and *Cyprus and its Constitutional and Other Legal Problems* (1980); also two articles in 21 *German Yearbook of International Law* (1978): D. S. Constantopoulos, 'Die Türkische Invasion in Zypern und ihre völkerrechtlichen Aspekte', 272-310 (with a summary in English), and Y. Alkuğ, 'The Cyprus Question', 311-34; and see also Z. M. Nedjatigil, *The Cyprus Conflict — A Lawyer's View* (1981), esp. 105-27.

[13] See *Collected Texts*, 606; also declarations on 613. See also interesting observation of K. Vasak, 'Le contrôle parlementaire des actes de l'exécutif concernant la ratification de la convention et l'acceptation de ses clauses facultatives' in *La protection internationale des Droits de l'Homme dans le cadre européen* (1961), 321-9, at 323.

[14] See 5 *Yearbook* (1962), 6.

[15] Council of Europe doc. H(67)2, Irish reply, 21. See also J. M. Kelly, *The Irish Constitution* (1980), and *Fundamental Rights in the Irish Law and Constitution* (1967); also D. Costello, 'Aspects of a Judicially Developed Jurisprudence of Human Rights in Ireland' in *Understanding Human Rights: An Interdisciplinary & Interfaith Study* (ed., A. D. Falconer, 1980); and J. P. Clarke, *The European Convention on Human Rights and Fundamental Freedoms and Irish Law* (1981).

Articles 15 and 29 of the Irish Constitution of 1937 lay down in explicit terms the conditions necessary for the enactment of laws and domestic implementation of international agreements. Article 15(2), paragraph 1, stipulates that 'The sole and exclusive power of making laws for the State is hereby vested in the Oireachtas: no other legislative authority has power to make laws for the State'.[16] Article 29 of the Constitution, as amended in 1972, reads as follows:

1. Ireland affirms its devotion to the ideal of peace and friendly cooperation amongst nations founded on international justice and morality.
2. Ireland affirms its adherence to the principle of the pacific settlement of international disputes by international arbitration or judicial determination.
3. Ireland accepts the generally recognised principles of international law as its rule of conduct in its relations with other states.
4. (1) The executive power of the State in or in connection with its external relations shall in accordance with Article 28 of this Constitution be exercised by or on the authority of the Government.

(2) For the purpose of the exercise of any executive function of the State in or in connection with its external relations, the Government may to such extent and subject to such conditions, if any, as may be determined by law, avail of or adopt any organ, instrument, or method of procedure used or adopted for the like purpose by the members of any group or league of nations with which the State is or becomes associated for the purpose of international cooperation in matters of common concern.

(3) The State may become a member of the European Coal and Steel Community (established by Treaty signed at Paris on the 18th day of April 1951), the European Economic Community (established by Treaty signed at Rome on the 25th day of March, 1957) and the European Atomic Energy Community (established by Treaty signed at Rome on the 25th day of March 1957). No provision of this Constitution invalidates laws enacted, acts done or measures adopted by the State necessitated by the obligations of membership of the Communities or prevents laws enacted, acts done or measures adopted by the Communities, or institutions thereof, from having the force of law in the State.

5. (1) Every international agreement to which the State becomes a party shall be laid before Dail Eireann.

(2) The State shall not be bound by any international agreement involving a charge upon public funds unless the terms of the agreement shall have been approved by Dail Eireann.

(3) This section shall not apply to agreements or conventions of a technical and administrative character.

6. No international agreement shall be part of the domestic law of the State save as may be determined by the Oireachtas.[17]

---

[16] A. J. Peaslee, *Constitutions of Nations* (1968), iii. 469.
[17] Text taken from L. J. Brinkhorst, and H. G. Schermers, *Judicial Remedies in the European Communities. A Casebook* (1977), 205. In order to eliminate possible

Thus, as the provisions of the Convention have not been specifically enacted by the *Oireachtas* in the form of legislation, the instrument has no legal value as against domestic law: the Convention is binding *on* the State but not *within* the State. In the famous case of *Ó'Laighléis* v. *O'Sullivan & Minister of Justice* (the *Lawless* Case) the Irish Supreme Court confirmed this interpretation in unequivocal terms:

> The Oireachtas has not determined that the Convention of Human Rights and Fundamental Freedoms is to be part of the domestic law of the State, and accordingly this Court cannot give effect to the Convention if it be contrary to domestic law or purports to grant rights or impose obligations additional to those of domestic law.
>
> No argument can prevail against the express command of Sec. 6 of Article 29 of the Constitution before the judges whose declared duty is to uphold the Constitution and the Laws.
>
> The Court accordingly cannot accept the idea that the primacy of domestic legislation is displaced by the State becoming a Party to the Convention for the Protection of Human Rights and Fundamental Freedoms. Nor can the Court accede to the view that in the domestic forum the Executive is in any way estopped from relying on the domestic law. . . .[18]

The question of whether or not the Convention can be used before the courts as persuasive legal authority when, for example, there appears to be a lacuna in domestic law, or alternatively, when the courts are faced with a doubtful or uncertain point of Irish law, has as yet not been determined. However, an *obiter* by O'Higgins CJ in a case before the Irish Supreme Court in July 1976 suggests that there may possibly arise a development in case-law similar to that which has already occurred in the United Kingdom.[19] In this particular case, O'Higgins CJ made reference to the European Convention on Human Rights when quashing the conviction and sentences imposed upon two

conflict between the Irish Constitution and the European Community legal system, a third sub-paragraph to para. 4 of art. 29 was added. This amendment was adopted by the *Oireachtas* and subsequently approved by referendum in May 1972. For further discussion on this topic see J. Temple Lang, 'Legal and Constitutional Problems for Ireland of Adhesion to the EEC Treaty', 9 *CML Rev.* (1972), 167–78; M. T. W. Robinson, 'The Irish European Communities Act 1972', 10 *CML Rev.* (1973), 352–4.

[18] Judgment of 3 Dec. 1957, [1960] IR 93 at 125; 2 *Yearbook* (1958–9), 608–27, at 624. The case was later taken before the Strasbourg organs: see A. H. Robertson, 'The First Case before the European Court of Human Rights. *Lawless* v. *The Government of Ireland*', 36 *BYIL* (1960), 343–54, and 37 *BYIL* (1961), 536–47. See also R. J. O'Hanlon, 'The Guarantees Afforded by the Institutional Machinery of the Convention' in *Privacy and Human Rights* (ed. A. H. Robertson, 1973), 307–15.

[19] See case-notes in 1 *The Human Rights Review* (1976), 1–2, and in 92 *LQR* (1976), 33–6. This subject is further discussed in ch. 10 below, sec. C.

accused persons who had been tried in the absence of their lawyers. After referring to the Irish Constitution's Preamble, O'Higgins CJ went on to say:

... Even Article 38 [of the Constitution] makes it mandatory that every criminal trial shall be conducted in accordance with Justice, and that the person accused be afforded every opportunity to defend himself. If this were not so, the dignity of the individual would be ignored, and the State would have failed to indicate his personal rights. Because of ignorance, or lack of education, justice may require that an accused should have legal assistance, and that if necessary the state should aid him. According to ... [established case-law] ... Justice requires that a person charged must be afforded the opportunity by the State of being represented — otherwise the Court would tolerate injustice. This is specifically confirmed by the wording of Article 6(3)(c) of the European Convention on Human Rights ratified by Ireland on 25 February 1953....[20]

Similarly, in the case of *the State (at the Prosecution of C.)* v. *Frawley* in which the High Court rejected the applicant's claim that his detention in prison was not 'in accordance with the law' within the meaning of Article 40(4)(2) of the Irish Constitution, an attempt by counsel for the applicant to base part of his arguments on Article 3 of the Convention (freedom from torture and from inhuman and degrading treatment and punishment) was considered unnecessary because the rights guaranteed there were sufficiently well-protected by Irish constitutional law.[21]

There have been two more recent cases in which the Convention's provisions have been cited, namely *Shaw* v. *DPP*[22] and *the State (DPP)* v. *Walshe and Conneely*,[23] but unfortunately both remain as yet unreported. Of particular interest is a statement made by Mr Justice Henchy in the *Walshe and Conneely* case when he said:

In upholding the current position, to the extent of saying that it is for a judge and not a jury to say if the established facts constitute a major criminal contempt, I would stress that, in both the factual and legal aspects

---

[20] *The State (Healy and Foran)* v. *The Governor of St. Patrick's Institution et al.*, 70 *Gazette of the Incorporated Law Society of Ireland* (1976), 28; extract reprinted in **19** *Yearbook* (1976), 1130–1; also in [1976] IR 325. It is of interest to note that the Convention had been cited by an Irish court even *before* Ireland ratified the instrument: see *The State (Duggan)* v. *Tapley* [1952] IR 62 at 83; 18 *ILR* (1951), 336.

[21] Judgment of 13 Apr. 1976 in [1976] *IR* 365, at 371 and 374; also in **21** *Yearbook* (1978), 750–4.

[22] Supreme Court, 17 Dec. 1980.

[23] Supreme Court, 6 Feb. 1981. Both these cases are cited by Clarke, n. 15 above, at 32–4 and 149.

of the hearing of the charge, the elementary requirements of justice in the circumstances would have to be observed. There is a presumption that our law in this respect is in conformity with the European Convention on Human Rights, particularly Articles 5 and 10(2).[24]

The case of *Norris* v. *Ireland & A.-G.*, decided by Mr Justice McWilliam on 10 October 1980, is also of interest to note.[25] In this case counsel for the plaintiff argued unsuccessfully that Irish law discriminates against homosexuals. In so doing he made reference to the *Dudgeon* v. *UK* case which was at the time pending before the European Court of Human Rights. (In the *Dudgeon* case a majority of the Commission was of the *opinion* that the laws in force in Northern Ireland prohibiting homosexual activities between male consenting adults over the age of 21 violated Article 8 of the Convention.)[26] This case is now pending on appeal before the Supreme Court.

Although the European Convention on Human Rights does not possess the status of domestic law, this instrument's impact upon the Irish legal system has as of late come to the notice of many legal practitioners.[27] In this connection, it can be mentioned that there has recently been political debate concerning the Convention's possible incorporation,[28] as well as a relative increase of applications brought against the Republic of Ireland before the European Commission of Human Rights.

---

[24] Ibid., quotation taken from Clarke, n. 15 above, at 149. After quoting this passage of Mr Justice Henchy, Ms Clarke raised a pertinent point: 'A rebuttable or irrebuttable presumption — only time will tell, either way.'

[25] Unreported judgment of the High Court, Dublin. Noted in *The Times*, 11 Oct. 1980, at 4. Also consult Clarke, n. 15 above, at 123–5.

[26] Application 7525/76. Report adopted on 13 Mar. 1980. In its judgment of 22 Oct. 1981 the European Court of Human Rights, by 15 votes to 4, found that art. 8 of the Convention had been breached. (Interestingly enough one of the dissenters was Mr Justice Walsh who is also a judge on the Irish Supreme Court!)

[27] See, for example, July-Sept. 1978 and Jan. 1980 issues of *The Irish Law Times*; and Clarke, n. 15 above, *passim*.

[28] See *A Bill of Rights* (pamphlet published by the Irish Association of Democratic Lawyers 1976); M. Giblin, 'Rights of Man', *The Irish Times*, 23 Mar. 1978; and Clarke, n. 15 above, esp. at 5, 144, and 150–3. In Nov. 1981 the Attorney-General, Mr Sutherland, set up a Constitutional Review Committee in response to Dr Garret Fitzgerald's 'Crusade on the Constitution'. See *The Times*, 2 Oct. 1981, at 2. In this context it has been suggested that there may be an attempt to revive the idea of incorporating the Convention with reference back to the proposals mooted at the Sunningdale Agreement of 1975. (For a commentary on the latter consult C. K. Boyle and H. Hannum, 'Ireland in Strasbourg', 7 *The Irish Jurist* (1972), 329–48.) For suggestions as to how Irish law should be up-dated *vis-à-vis* the Convention, consult Clarke, at 109–35, and M. Robinson, 'Human Rights in the Republic of Ireland', in *Do We Need a Bill of Rights?* (ed. C. Campbell, 1980), 50–76, esp. at 69–75.

The case of *Airey* v. *Ireland*,[29] decided by the European Court of Human Rights in October 1979, is of particular interest. In this case both the Commission and the Court upheld the applicant's complaint that she had been refused access to the High Court in order to obtain a judicial separation (divorce *a mensa et thoro*), due to prohibitive costs of civil proceedings. In response to this judgment the Irish Government introduced a civil aid and advice scheme in January 1980.[30]

C. Malta

By a declaration on 23 October 1953, in pursuance of Article 63 of the Convention, the United Kingdom extended the applicability of the Convention to a number of territories for whose international relations it was responsible at the time. Malta was included among these territories.[31]

Malta attained independence on 21 September 1964 (Malta Independence Order, 1964). On the same day the Constitution of Malta became effective (Malta Government Gazette no. 11, 688, 18 September 1964). Under the terms of an agreement between the Maltese Government and the United Kingdom on 31 December 1964, Malta assumed, as from 21 September 1964, many international obligations and responsibilities which had rested with the Government of the United Kingdom, but these did not include obligations under the European Convention on Human Rights.[32]

Malta acceded to the Council of Europe on 29 April 1965. This was followed by signature of the Convention and First Protocol on 12 December 1966. At the time of signing the Convention, the Government of Malta made declarations and reservations with regard to the interpretation of Articles 2, 6(2), and 10 of the Convention and Article 2 of the First Protocol.[33]

[29] Eur. Court HR, judgment of 9 Oct. 1979. ser. A, no. 32. For a recent commentary on this case consult P. Thornberry, 'Poverty, Litigation and Fundamental Rights – A European Perspective', 29 *ICLQ* (1980), 250–8.

[30] See Committee of Ministers Resolution DH(81)8 of 22 May 1981, and appended information provided by the Irish Government. Seven law centres staffed by solicitors, employed full-time by the Legal Aid Board, were established in Aug. 1980 (see parliamentary document prl.8543), and additional measures were taken in order to provide cheaper, quicker, and more convenient access to the courts. Also consult Legal Aid Board Annual Report, 1980.

[31] 1 *Yearbook* (1955–7), 46–7.

[32] See M.-A. Eissen, 'The Independence of Malta and the European Convention on Human Rights', 41 *BYIL* (1965–6), 401–10, at 404–5.

[33] 9 *Yearbook* (1966), 24–5.

On ratifying the Convention on 23 January 1967, Malta did not make declarations under Articles 25 and 46. This is still the position today. In addition, the Fourth Protocol of the Convention also remains unsigned.

Articles 66(1) and 73 of the Maltese Constitution of 1964 (as amended in 1974) read:

Article 66. para. 1
Subject to the provisions of this Constitution, Parliament may make laws for the peace, order and good government of Malta.

Article 73
(1) The power of Parliament to make laws shall be exercised by bills passed by the House of Representatives and assented to by the President.
(2) When a bill is presented to the President for assent, he shall without delay signify that he assents.
(3) A bill shall not become law unless it has been duly passed and assented to in accordance with this Constitution.
(4) When a law has been assented to by the President it shall without delay be published in the Gazette and shall not come into operation until it has been so published, but Parliament may postpone the coming into operation of any such law and may make laws with retrospective effect.[34]

Thus, in accordance with established constitutional practice, international agreements must be transformed by means of an Act of Parliament in order to obtain the status of Maltese domestic law. Likewise, subsequently enacted law overrides prior conflicting legislation with the proviso that it is in conformity with the Constitution which is the supreme law of the land. The European Convention on Human Rights has *not* been so transformed. However, there exists a Constitutional Court which hears appeals from decisions of lower courts on applications for redress in respect of human rights protected in Chapter IV of the Constitution (Articles 33–48).[35] In this connection it is of interest to observe that, although to date there appears to be no case-law which refers directly to the Convention on Human Rights, many of the provisions of the

[34] Text provided by Department of Information, Valletta. The Constitution was amended in 1965, 1966, 1970, 1972, and 1974. Act LVIII of 1964 (Constitutional Amendment Act of 13 Dec. 1974) proclaimed Malta a Republic. The amendments of 1974 were largely based on the work of A. Sceberras Trigona, *Constitutional Change and the Maltese Constitution* (Doctorate in Laws, Royal University of Malta, 1972–3).
[35] These were modelled on the European Convention on Human Rights. See J. Cremona, *Human Rights Documentation in Malta* (1966), esp. 47–66; and E. Busuttil, *The Frontiers of Human Rights* (1966).

Constitution are taken verbatim from corresponding articles of the Convention.[36]

Consequently, although the provisions of the Convention have not been incorporated into domestic law most of the rights and freedoms enumerated in the latter are in fact constitutionally guaranteed. However, Malta's failure to make declarations regarding individual applications, and its non-acceptance of the compulsory jurisdiction of the European Court of Human Rights, prevent the Convention organs from assessing the practical quality and force of these norms; and it would certainly be most interesting to know what prevents the Maltese Government from making these declarations.[37]

D. The United Kingdom[38]

The United Kingdom was one of the original states signatories of the Convention on 4 November 1950, and of its First Protocol on 8 March 1952. Prior to ratification, the Convention was ordered 'to lie upon the Table' of the House of Commons on 23 January 1951. This was done in accordance with the constitutional usage (which is possibly a binding constitutional convention), whereby the texts of international agreements are laid before both Houses of Parliament for the duration of twenty-one days prior to ratification.[39] On 5 February 1951, the Minister of Foreign Affairs stated that 'if no objections are raised, the instrument of ratification will be prepared on or after 21st February'. The instruments of ratification of the Convention and subsequently its First Protocol were deposited with the Secretary General of the Council of Europe on 8 March

[36] Consult, for example, the following law reports printed in *The Times of Malta*: case no. 78 (3 Nov. 1969), no. 126 (24 Apr. 1972), no. 168 (6 Aug. 1973), no. 176 (8 Oct. 1973), no. 302 (21 June 1976), and no. 306 (19 July 1976).

[37] In the present Government's *Labour Party Manifesto* of 1971 a pledge was made to accept the right of individual petition (at p. 13). This 'pledge' was omitted in the *Labour Party Manifesto* 'Forward in Peace' of 1976.

[38] This subject has recently been studied at considerable length in an excellent article by P. J. Duffy, 'English Law and the European Convention on Human Rights', 29 *ICLQ* (1980), 585–618. An exhaustive treatment is therefore unnecessary in this section. For a thorough overview of case-law in which the Convention has been cited in domestic courts see a publication by the author, 'British Courts and the European Human Rights Convention: An Unsatisfactory Situation', *TL* (1979), 38–54. Also see report of the Standing Advisory Commission on Human Rights, Northern Ireland, entitled *The Protection of Human Rights by Law in Northern Ireland*, Cmnd. 7009 (1977).

[39] This is called the 'Ponsonby' rule: HC Deb. 2001 (1 Apr. 1924). The practice was begun in 1924, then abandoned, and restored in 1929.

1951 and 3 November 1952, respectively.[40] A reservation was made with regard to Article 2 of the Protocol: the states' duty to provide education facilities in accordance with parental convictions was 'accepted by the UK only in so far as it is compatible with the provisions of efficient instruction and training, and the avoidance of unreasonable expenditure'. On 23 October 1953 a declaration was made under Article 63(1) extending the Convention's force to certain territories for whose international relations the UK was responsible. On 14 January 1966, the UK recognized the competence of the European Commission of Human Rights to receive individual applications, and recognized the compulsory jurisdiction of the Court of Human Rights.[41] The right of derogation, provided under Article 15(3) of the Convention, has been used on several occasions in respect of certain territories for whose international relations the UK has been responsible, and when internment was introduced in Northern Ireland.[42] The Fourth Protocol has been signed but not as yet ratified.[43]

In accordance with well-established British legal and constitutional practice based upon the concept of Parliamentary sovereignty, the provisions of international agreements ratified by the UK have no internal effect unless they are transformed into domestic law by Parliament.[44] Such implementing legislation was not considered necessary in the case of the European Convention on Human Rights. At the time of ratification the Government of the day assumed that domestic law was in full conformity with the Convention's provisions, and successive governments have since that time expressed the opinion that the rights and freedoms enumerated are in all cases already secured by domestic law.[45] As a consequence the European Convention on Human Rights has not acquired a domestic status in the UK,

---

[40] 1 *Yearbook* (1955-7), 98 and 100.

[41] See *Yearbook* vol. 1 (1955-7), 45-6, and vol. 9 (1966), 8 and 14.

[42] See, for example, *Yearbook* vol. 1 (1955-7), 48; vol. 14 (1971), 32, and vol. 18 (1975), 18.

[43] See 'Legislation on Human Rights with Particular Reference to the European Convention' (Inter-departmental discussion paper published by the Home Office 1976), para. 3.01; and *Hansard*, HL Debs., vol. 389, cols. 468-9 (28 Feb. 1978).

[44] Lord McNair, *The Law of Treaties* (1961), 81-2.

[45] See UK reply of 13 Sept. 1966 in 'Implementation of Article 57 of the European Convention on Human Rights', Second Addendum to Council of Europe doc. H(69)9, 1. Also consult R. Beddard, 'The Status of the European Convention on Human Rights in Domestic Law', 16 *ICLQ* (1967), 206-17; and H. W. Shawcross, 'UK Practice on the European Convention on Human Rights', 1-2 *RBDI* (1965), 297-305.

and individuals cannot directly rely upon it before the courts. The unwritten UK Constitution differs in many ways from the legal systems of other contracting states. The sovereignty of the Westminster Parliament is absolute, and a later Act of Parliament always overrides former legislation if direct conflict arises. The legal safeguards against infringements of human rights are not contained in any 'basic law' but can be found in specific Westminster statutes and judge-made common law.[46] However, a close relationship between domestic law and international law is maintained by a principle of judicial interpretation to the effect that international law forms part of the law of the land.[47] This principle is supplemented by the rule of construction under which the judiciary, while recognizing the overriding effect of Acts of Parliament, interprets legislation in such a manner as to avoid conflict with international agreements ratified by the UK.[48]

It is through this rule of construction that the courts have been prepared to make reference to the Convention; for, although it is not considered as a formal source of internal law, this instrument is nevertheless used by the judiciary as a persuasive authority when there appears to exist a lacuna in domestic law, the clarification of an ambiguity is needed, or if the courts are faced with a doubtful or controversial point of law. The case of *Waddington* v. *Miah*[49] was apparently the first reported case in which the UK courts actually relied on the European Convention on Human Rights in the interpretation of a statute. In this case both the Court of Appeal and the House of Lords concluded that certain words of section 34, paragraph 1 of the 1971 Immigration Act were ambiguous and that the penal legislation in question could not be retrospective, on the presumption that legislation is consonant with treaty obligation. In support of this presumption Stephenson LJ in

[46] See UK reply ibid.; T. C. Daintith, 'The Protection of Human Rights in the UK', 1 *RDH/HRJ* (1968), 275–302 and 407–52; and C. Palley, 'The Protection of Human Rights in Constitutional Law in the UK', delivered at the 9th International Congress of Comparative Law in Tehran, 1974. For a more general work consult E. C. S. Wade and G. G. Phillips, *Constitutional and Administrative Law* (9th ed. by A. W. Bradley, 1977).

[47] See P. J. Duffy, n. 38 above, esp. 599–613. Also consult vol. 18, Halsbury's Laws of England 4th ed. (1977), para. 1403; D. P. O'Connell, I *International Law* (1970), at 56–8; and J. Dutheil de La Rochère, 'Le droit international fait-il partie du droit anglais?' in *Mélanges Offerts à Paul Reuter* (1981), 243–69, esp. at 263–8.

[48] See K. Holloway, *Modern Trends in Treaty Law* (1967), at 288–94. Also Duffy, esp. 586–99; and case-law referred to in ch. 10 below, sec. C.

[49] [1974] I WLR 683.

the Court of Appeal and Lord Reid in the House of Lords made specific reference to Article 7 of the Convention which expressly prohibits retrospective criminal legislation. As Lord Reid said after quoting Article 7, '. . . [s]o it is hardly credible that any government department would promote or that Parliament would pass retrospective criminal legislation'.[50]

In *Birdi* v. *Secretary of State for Home Affairs*[51] Lord Denning MR stated in effect that he might be inclined to hold an Act of Parliament invalid if it did not conform to the Convention: 'The courts could and should take the Convention into account in interpreting a statute. An Act of Parliament should be construed so as to conform with the Convention.' This case concerned an unsuccessful appeal to the Court of Appeal by Ram Chand Birdi who applied for a writ of habeas corpus on the ground that by virtue of his arrival in England before 1 January 1975, he was an illegal immigrant entitled to Her Majesty's pardon because of an amnesty announced by the Home Secretary in April 1974. Considering both Articles 5 and 6 of the Convention, the Master of the Rolls — in dismissing the appeal — made a distinction between: (i) giving the right to liberty and security of persons (guaranteed by Article 5) in that this provision did not apply to a case in which there had been a lawful arrest of a person against whom action was being taken with a view to deportation or extradition (Article 5 paragraph 1(f) of the Convention); and (ii) the provisions, of Article 6, paragraph 1, entitling a person to a 'fair and public hearing' in the determination of his civil rights or in criminal charges brought against him, which did not apply to administrative procedures or licences such as the immigration procedure. Geoffrey Lane LJ concurred, stating that the Home Secretary's announcement relating to a pardon conferred as such no right upon the applicant.

R. v. *Secretary of State for Home Affairs, ex parte Bhajan Singh*[52] shed new light on this problem in so far as Lord Denning retracted, to a certain extent, what he had said in *Birdi*. The *Singh* case related to an appeal to the Court of Appeal on the basis of Article 12 of the European Convention on Human Rights which states 'Men and women of marriageable age have the right to marry and to found a family, according to the national laws governing the exercise of this right.' The Court of Appeal dismissed the appeal holding that this article did not

[50] Ibid., at 694.   [51] [1975] 119 *Solicitor's Journal*, 322; 61 ILR, 250.
[52] [1975] 3 WLR 225.

require the Home Secretary to release a man detained as an illegal entrant under the Immigration Act 1971, pending deportation, in order to marry a girl in Wolverhampton before his removal. The Master of the Rolls said:

What is the position of the Convention in our English law? I would not depart in the least from what I said in the recent case of *Birdi* v. *Secretary of State for Home Affairs.* The courts can and should take the Convention into account.
They should take it into account whenever interpreting a statute which affects the rights and liberties of the individual. It is to be assumed that the Crown, in taking its part in legislation would do nothing which was in conflict with treaties.[53]

Lord Denning went on to explain that he thought that he had gone too far in one sentence in *Birdi*, when he had said that if an Act of Parliament did not conform to the Convention he might be inclined to hold it invalid. The Master of the Rolls then proceeded to explain that in many former cases the court has stated that a treaty did not become part of English law except and in so far as it was made such by Parliament. So the Convention was not part of English law; but on the other hand it could be considered by the courts, the Home Office, and other authorities when they were dealing with problems concerning human rights, the implication being that there existed a tendency to adhere to and not contravene it. Lord Denning subsequently reiterated certain remarks made by Lord Reid in *Waddington* v. *Miah* and agreed with his reasoning that it was hardly credible that Parliament would pass any legislation contrary to the Convention. Browne and Geoffrey Lane LJJ concurred. (It is of interest to observe, in this connection, that an illegal immigrant may now be released in order to be married when detained pending his deportation (Schedule 3 to the Children Act, 1975).)

In two cases joined on appeal, *R.* v. *Secretary of State for Home Affairs, ex parte Phansopkar,* and *R.* v. *Secretary of State for the Home Department, ex parte Begum*[54] the Court of Appeal (Lord Denning MR and Lawton and Scarman LJJ), allowed appeals by Mrs Phansopkar and Mrs Begum, both wives of patrials — whose countries of origin were India and Bangladesh — to obtain certificates of patriality in accordance with certain sections of the 1971 Immigration Act in order that they be permitted to enter the UK immediately and not be sent back to

---

[53] Ibid., at 230-1.   [54] [1975] 3 All ER 497.

Bombay and Dacca for the same purpose. In their judgments, both Lord Denning MR and Scarman LJ referred to Article 8 of the European Convention on Human Rights which secures the right to respect for family life, interference with this right being permitted only if made in accordance with the law and when considered to be necessary in a democratic society. In addition, Scarman LJ went on to say:

. . . Delay of this order appears to me to infringe at least two human rights recognised, and therefore protected, by English law. Justice delayed is justice denied: 'We will not deny or defer to any man either justice or right': Magna Carta. This hallowed principle of our law is now reinforced by the European Convention for the Protection of Human Rights 1950 to which it is now the duty of our public authorities in administering the law, including the Immigration Act 1971, and of our courts in interpreting and applying the law, including the Act, to have regard: see *R.* v. *Secretary of State for Home Affairs, ex parte Bhajan Singh* in this court. [He then quoted Article 8 of the Convention before continuing.] . . . It may, of course happen under our law, that the basic rights to justice undeferred and to respect for family and private life have to yield to express requirements of a statute. In my judgment it is the duty of the courts, so long as they do not defy or disregard clear and unequivocal provision, to construe statutes in a manner which promotes, not endangers, those rights. Problems of ambiguity or omission, if they arise under the language of the Act, should be resolved so as to give effect to, or at the very least so as not to derogate from, the rights recognised by Magna Carta and the European Convention.[55]

Another interesting case was that of *Ahmad* v. *Inner London Education Authority*[56] in which the court of Appeal (Scarman

----

[55] Ibid., 510–11. However, in a case decided not long after the above two cases, *R.* v. *Chief Immigration Officer, Heathrow Airport and another, ex parte Salamat Bibi* [1976] 3 All ER 843, the Court of Appeal rejected a claim based on art. 8. In this case the applicant, who was not a person entitled to enter the UK as of right as had been Mrs Phansopkar and Mrs Begum, did not satisfy the immigration officer that she only intended to visit her husband and not remain in the country as required by the relevant immigration rules applicable to her as a non-patrial. Certain *dicta* by Lord Denning in *ex p. Singh* and by Scarman LJ in *ex p. Phansopkar* were disapproved by the Court; Lord Denning 'amended' a statement he had previously made in the *ex p. Bhajan Singh* case: see 847–8. In addition, Roskill LJ agreed with Lord Denning that the Convention was not part of the law of England, and went on to disagree with *obiter dicta* of Scarman LJ — on this particular subject — in the cases of *Phansopkar* and *Pan American World Airways Inc.* v. *Department of Trade* [1976] 1 Lloyd's Rep. 257. (In the latter case, Scarman LJ referred to the Convention at 261: '. . . such a convention, especially a multilateral one, should then be considered by Courts even though no statute expressly or impliedly incorporates it into our law.') Geoffrey Lane LJ concurred with the other two members of the Court.

[56] [1978] 1 All E574. His subsequent petition to Strasbourg was unsuccessful: see application 8160/78, admissibility decision of 12 Mar. 1981.

LJ as he then was, dissenting) upheld decisions of the Employment Appeal Tribunal and an industrial tribunal, that Mr Ahmad, a Muslim schoolteacher, had not been unfairly dismissed or forced to resign his position as a full-time teacher with the Inner London Education Authority by being refused leave to take time off on Friday afternoons to attend prayers at a mosque. Both Lord Denning MR and Orr LJ held that Mr Ahmad was not entitled, either by the Education Act 1944 or by the European Convention on Human Rights, to preferential treatment over other teachers to enable him to attend mosque during school hours on Friday afternoons, and that he could not rely upon Article 9 of the Convention — which provides for everyone the right to freedom of thought, conscience, and religion — because the Convention was not a part of English law. Scarman LJ did not agree with the majority and, referring to the elaborate statutory protection of the individual from discrimination arising from race, colour, religion, or sex, and against the background of the European Convention, he considered that the choice which the Inner London Education Authority had forced upon Mr Ahmad was tantamount to dismissal from full-time employment.[57]

The Convention has also been cited by the courts in Northern Ireland as well as in Scotland.[58] For example, in the case of *R.* v. *Deery*[59] Sir Robert Lowry LCJ delivering judgment of the Court of Criminal Appeal on 13 May 1976, accepted the argument put forward by counsel for the appellant and expressly recognized the European Convention as a source of legal interpretation. Deery had been charged and convicted on two counts of possessing firearms and ammunition under suspicious circumstances contrary to Section 19A of the Firearms (NL) Act 1969, as amended in 1971. However, as between the date of the offence and the date of Deery's trial, a Firearms Amendment Order (NL 1976), had been made increasing the maximum term of imprisonment for the offence from five to ten years, the trial judge considered that this order applied in Deery's case, and accordingly sentenced him to six years of imprisonment. The Court of Appeal allowed the appeal and held that the trial judge

---

[57] Ibid., at 583–5.
[58] See, for instance, *R.* v. *McCormick* [1977] NI 105; *R.* v. *McGrath* [1980] NI 91; and *Kaur* v. *Lord Advocate* (1980) CMLR 79, commented upon by W. Finnie, 25 *Journal of the Law Society of Scotland* (1980), 434–9.
[59] 20 *Yearbook* (1977), 827–31.

had erred in holding the appellant liable for heavier penalties than provided by law at the time he had committed the offences. In his judgment Sir Robert Lowry referred to Article 7(1) of the Convention and its counterpart, Article 15(1) in the UN Covenant on Civil and Political Rights, as well as domestic case-law: *R.* v. *Miah, ex parte Bhajan Singh* and *Pan-Am*. Citing Diplock LJ in *Salamon* v. *Commissioners of Customs and Excise* [1966] 3 All ER 871, at 875, he held that although there is no rule of law which invalidates Acts of Parliament which conflict with binding treaties, treaty obligations (in this case the European Convention and the UN Covenant) are a strong guide to the meaning of ambiguous provisions, as the Government is presumed to intend to comply with such obligations. As the presumption that law is not retrospective and that treaty obligations imposed upon the UK were not rebutted – either expressly or by implication – the appeal was allowed and sentence reduced from six to three years of imprisonment.

In a number of cases the courts have referred to the possibility of using the Convention to try to resolve uncertainties in the common law. In the case of *R.* v. *Lemon & Gay News Ltd.,*[60] in which the House of Lords reaffirmed the conviction of the appellants for publishing a blasphemous libel, it is of interest to note that Lord Scarman referred to Articles 9 and 10 of the Convention in order to justify the court's reasoning[61] whereby the character of the words published and not the motive of the author or publisher was considered to be the necessary ingredient to secure a conviction; whereas Lord Diplock considered that by rejecting the 'subjective test' of the accused's intention, blasphemous libel would revert to the exceptional category of crimes of strict liability, and that such a retrograde step could not be justified by *any* considerations of public policy.[62]

Although Lord Diplock did not make express reference to the European Convention in the *Lemon* case, he certainly considered this instrument to be of undoubted authority in the case of *Gleaves* v. *Deakin & Others*[63] a few months later. In this case a private citizen instigated a prosecution alleging that the criminal offence of defamatory libel had been committed against him. The defendants claimed that they should have been able to

[60] [1979] 1 All ER 898.　　　　[61] Ibid., at 927.　　　　[62] Ibid., at 905.
[63] [1979] 2 All ER 497.

provide evidence of the general bad reputation of the prosecutor before the magistrate at committal proceedings, although their appeal on this point failed both before the Court of Appeal and the House of Lords. In expressing his concern about the unsatisfactory state of affairs in the English legal system, Lord Diplock was of the opinion that the criminal offence of defamatory libel retained anomalies involving serious departure from accepted principles upon which the modern criminal law of England is based which was also difficult to reconcile with the UK's international obligations under the European Convention. He explained that

. . . under art. 10(2) of the European Convention, the exercise of the right of freedom of expression may be subjected to restrictions or penalties by a contracting state, only to the extent that those restrictions or penalties are necessary in a democratic society for the protection of what (apart from the reputation of individuals and the protection of information received in confidence) may generically be described as the public interest. In contrast to this the truth of the defamatory statement is not in itself a defence to a charge of defamatory libel under our criminal law; so here is a restriction on the freedom to impart information which states that are parties to the Convention have expressly undertaken to secure to everyone within their jurisdiction. No onus lies on the prosecution to show that the defamatory matter was of a kind that it is necessary in a democratic society to suppress or penalise in order to protect the public interest. On the contrary, even though no public interest can be shown to be injuriously affected by imparting to others accurate information about seriously descreditable conduct of an individual, the publisher of the information must be convicted unless he himself can prove to the satisfaction of a jury that the publication of it was for the public benefit. This is to turn art. 10 of the Convention on its head. Under our criminal law a person's freedom of expression, wherever it involves exposing seriously discreditable conduct of others is to be repressed by public authority unless he can convince a jury ex post facto that the particular exercise of the freedom was for the public benefit, whereas art. 10 requires that freedom of expression shall be untrammelled by public authority except where its interference to repress a particular exercise of the freedom is necessary for the protection of the public interest.[64]

He then went on to suggest that in order to 'avoid the risk of our failing to comply with our international obligations under the European Convention' the consent of the Attorney-General should be required before a prosecution for criminal libel is instituted, and that in deciding whether to grant his consent in a specific instance 'the Attorney-General could then consider

[64] Ibid., at 498–9.

whether the prosecution was necessary on any of the grounds specified in Article 10(2) of the Convention and unless satisfied that it was, he should refuse his consent'.[65]

Proposals to incorporate the European Convention on Human Rights into domestic UK law either in the form of an Act of Parliament or by the enactment of an entrenched Bill of Rights (even for Northern Ireland alone), without introducing a formal written constitution, have in recent years received widespread attention in academic circles as well as in Parliament.[66] Without entering into the detailed discussions on the various issues raised by these debates it is sufficient to note for present purposes that certain eminent personalities in the UK consider that fundamental human rights of the individual are inadequately ensured against excessive executive and administrative power and that the incorporation of the Convention could help to redress this balance in favour of the individual.[67] It has also been argued that if the European Convention were to have the status of domestic law, the individual would in most instances not have to seek redress before the Strasbourg organs; this way the alleged violations of the Convention's norms would be adequately and immediately available to him in the domestic legal order.

Whether or not the Convention will in the foreseeable future be incorporated into domestic law, it is undeniable that this instrument has had a substantial impact upon the UK: changes have been made in prison rules (*Knechtl,*[68] *Golder*[69]); immi-

---

[65] Ibid. Also see, in this context, the cases of *Malone* v. *Commissioner of Police of the Metropolis* (no. 2) [1979] 2 All ER 620; and *A.-G.* v. *BBC* [1980] 3 WLR 109 (discussed at greater length in ch. 10 below, sec. C); and three House of Lords decisions: *Cassell* v. *Broome* [1972] 1 All ER 801, esp. Lord Kilbrandon at 876; *Science Research Council* v. *Nassé* [1979] 3 All ER 673, esp. Lord Wilberforce at 682; and *Morris* v. *Beardmore* [1980] 3 WLR 283, esp. Lord Scarman at 296.

[66] See, for example, House of Lords report of the Select Committee on a Bill of Rights, paper 176 (1978); Standing Advisory Commission's report, n. 38 above; J. Jaconelli, *Enacting a Bill of Rights* (1980), esp. 246-81; P. Wallington and J. McBride, *Civil Liberties and a Bill of Rights* (1976); M. Zander, *A Bill of Rights?* (1979); J. E. S. Fawcett, 'A Bill of Rights for the United Kingdom?' 1 *HR Rev.* (1976), 57-64; J. McBride, 'Civil Liberties and a Bill of Rights: Incorporating the European Convention', *TL* (1979), 28-37; and *Do We Need A Bill of Rights?* (ed. C. Campbell, 1980).

[67] For further references consult the bibliography in Wallington and McBride, ibid., at 142-6.

[68] Application 4115/69, report of the Commission, 24 Mar. 1972; 13 *Yearbook* (1970), 730-72 (friendly settlement).

[69] Eur. Court HR, judgment of 21 Feb. 1975, ser. A, vol. 18. Note also that the case of *Silver & Others* v. *UK* is pending before the Court in Strasbourg: see report of

gration procedures have been ameliorated (*Alam & Khan,*[70] the *East African Asian* cases[71]); certain interrogation techniques used with detainees in Northern Ireland have been abandoned (*Ireland* v. *UK*[72]); compensation has been paid for various degrees of administrative miscarriages of justice (*Amekrane,*[73] *A.* v. *UK*[74]); the Contempt of Court Act 1981 has been enacted, in order, among other reasons, to comply with the Strasbourg Court's judgment in *The Sunday Times* case;[75] and the Mental Health (Amendment) Act was passed by Parliament in 1982 to amend and up-date the Mental Health Act of 1959 in the light of an adverse finding by the European Court of Human Rights in the case of *X* v. *UK*.[76] Legislation which prohibits homosexual relations between male consenting adults in Northern Ireland has likewise been changed: Homosexual Offences (N.I.) Order 1982.[77] In addition, there are a number of important cases pending before both the Commission and the Court in Strasbourg.[78]

the Commission, adopted 11 Oct. 1980, and comments in *PL* (1981), 435–41 and *LAG Bulletin* (1981), 280–3.

[70] Application 2991/66, 11 *Yearbook* (1968), 788–94 (friendly settlement).

[71] See 'Stocktaking', 117–9; see also case-note by the author in 41 *MLR* (1978), 337–42; and 3 EHRR, 76.

[72] Eur. Court HR, judgment of 18 Jan. 1978, ser. A, vol. 25.

[73] Application 5961/72, 16 *Yearbook* (1973), 356–88 (friendly settlement).

[74] Application 6840/74, report of Commission, 16 July 1980 (friendly settlement), 20 *D&R*, 5–18.

[75] Eur. Court HR, judgment of 26 Apr. 1979, ser. A, no. 30. Also see Committee of Ministers resolution DH(81)2 of 2 Apr. 1981.

[76] Eur. Court HR, judgment of 5 Nov. 1981, ser. A, no. 46. Also consult paras. 16 and 64 of the Court's judgment. Arguably, the proposed legislative amendments concerning the closed shop may be linked with the case of *Young, James, & Webster* v. *UK*, Eur. Court HR, judgment of 13 Aug. 1981, ser. A, no. 44. see case-note by the author and F. Wooldridge, 'The Closed Shop Case in Strasbourg', 31 *ICLQ* (1982), 396–402.

[77] See *Dudgeon* v. *UK*, Eur. Court HR, 22 Oct. 1981, ser. A, no. 45. While this case was pending before the Commission the law was changed in Scotland: see paras. 18 and 46 of the Court's judgment.

[78] See *Annual Review* 1981 (European Commission of Human Rights, 1982), recent issues of *HR Rev.* and *HRLJ*.

Conclusions to Part II

In the above survey attention has been placed upon the different modes by which the Convention enters into domestic law — if at all — and its rank in the domestic legal hierarchy. In so doing, emphasis has been placed on the role played by domestic courts in determining this instrument's legal significance. A comparative study of this type must remain tentative, incomplete, and often distorted: the optional nature of the right of individual petition and of the Strasbourg Court's compulsory jurisdiction, the right of states to derogate from certain of the Convention's norms, and to make reservations, all complicate and often confuse an already complex situation. The difficulty in assessing the Convention's domestic status is still further complicated by the ambiguity of constitutional law and the existence in most states of a largely unexplained principle that international law, including international agreements, has a higher rank than internal law; the ambiguity of this principle is reflected in the often confused ways in which the domestic courts attempt to deal with it, and this confusion is in turn reflected in any attempt to monitor and assess domestic developments with any degree of accuracy. To this must of course be added the self-evident fact that the domestic implementation of this rather unique instrument does not necessarily involve express or implied reference to the Convention's provisions by the domestic courts; not to mention the state's discretion of whether or not to incorporate its substantive provisions into internal law. The existence of various legal traditions, legislative and judicial approaches, can mean that in practice the same or a higher level of protection of human rights may be provided in a number of other ways. The international obligations found in the European Convention reflect propositions and standards which in many legal systems are self-evident. In certain cases, for instance protection afforded by constitutionally entrenched fundamental human rights provisions, detailed legislation, penal codes, and unwritten principles of law, such as the principle of legality and that of proportionality, provide protection to individuals which can be of an infinitely superior quality than the Convention's list of 'common rights'. Article 60 of the Convention bears witness to this truism.

It therefore follows that the result of a comparative survey of the Convention's domestic status in all the member states of the Council of Europe must be assessed on an *ad hoc* basis. It has been found that from the twenty-one countries which have ratified the Convention, *fourteen* of them have secured this instrument the status of domestic law.

Austria, Switzerland, and Italy

In Austria the Convention possesses the status of constitutional law, while in Switzerland its substantive provisions appear to possess — at least to the *Tribunal Fédéral* — a 'constitutional content'. Likewise, in Italy, although given the status of a statute, the *Corte Costituzionale* has implicitly recognized the Convention's 'quasi-constitutional rank'. All three of these countries have accepted the right of individual petition and the Court's compulsory jurisdiction.

Belgium, Cyprus, France, Greece, Luxembourg, the Netherlands, Portugal, Spain, and Turkey

The directly applicable provisions of the Convention appear to possess a hierarchically superior status to ordinary legislation in these countries although they remain subordinate to constitutional norms. This generalization must, however, be qualified by the fact that in some of these countries, namely Belgium, Luxembourg, the Netherlands, and possibly Turkey, the lack of constitutional review and control of constitutionality may in practice allow the courts to determine the compatibility of statute law *vis-à-vis* the Convention's provisions, thereby in effect securing this instrument a unique extra-constitutional significance. The courts' appreciation of the above situation differs substantially from country to country, although it is opportune to stress that the Belgian and Dutch courts have been particularly active in this field. Note must, however, be taken of the fact that whereas optional declarations under Articles 25 and 46 have been made by Belgium, the Netherlands, and Portugal (Cyprus and Greece have made declarations only in respect of Article 46), the right of individual petition has not been accepted by Cyprus, Greece, and Turkey, nor has the Court's compulsory jurisdiction been accepted by Turkey.

Federal Republic of Germany

In the FRG the Convention is considered to have the same legal value as other federal statutory provisions. The country has accepted both the right of individual petition and the compulsory jurisdiction of the European Court of Human Rights.

Denmark, Iceland, Norway, Sweden, Ireland, Malta, and the United Kingdom

The Scandinavian countries and most of the common-law countries have not incorporated the European Convention on Human Rights into their domestic law, although in all these states there appears to exist a presumption upon which the judiciary will, in the absence of express statutory indications to the contrary, interpret domestic law to be compatible with the country's international obligations. All these states have, with the exception of Malta, made declarations under Articles 25 and 46.

Liechtenstein

Liechtenstein has recently ratified the Convention which, in accordance with constitutional stipulations, has obtained the status of domestic law. Declarations have also been made under Articles 25 and 46.

If any general conclusion can be made relating to the Convention's domestic status it is simply this: although the Convention is domestic law in fourteen countries, there is great confusion in many of these states as to this instrument's *exact status* within the internal legal hierarchy.

Without again entering into the debate whether Article 13 of the European Convention on Human Rights *obliges* states to incorporate its norms into domestic law (this subject has been dealt with in Part I), one particular point may perhaps be brought out in the light of the present study: how or why should an individual plead a breach of the Convention in the domestic courts, where in effect he cannot ensure that its provisions will be *directly* applied by the courts? In other words, although in the early days of the Convention's existence it was strongly argued that there was a legal duty to incorporate the Convention's substantive provisions, this argument appears to a certain extent too theoretical — and possibly also superfluous — for the simple reason that in *practice* the vast majority of domestic courts consider it unnecessary to *directly* apply the Convention's provisions when examining alleged violations of individuals' human rights in the domestic forum.

Has incorporation of the Convention really made much of a difference, at least in countries that possess similar or better drafted constitutional provisions? The answer is probably a qualified 'no'. In the majority of cases the fact that the Convention possesses the status of domestic law appears to be only of marginal importance. The possibility of using the Convention's provisions as persuasive sources of law, however, where otherwise there appears to exist a lacuna in domestic law, or where courts are faced with a doubtful or uncertain point of internal law, has self-evident advantages.

Finally, it must again be stressed that discussion centred on the Convention's domestic status and the position its provisions have secured for themselves in the domestic hierarchy does not necessarily in itself reflect the real standard of legal protection that a given state affords to individuals. Although the incorporation of the Convention's substantive provisions may be deemed desirable (even though not obligatory), of *much greater significance* appears to be the right of individual petition and the submission to the Strasbourg Court's compulsory jurisdiction.

PART III

SELECTED ASPECTS OF THE CONVENTION'S AUTHORITY IN DOMESTIC COURTS

Preliminary Remarks: Delimitation of the Topic of Study

The impact of the European Convention on Human Rights has in recent years been quite substantial. For instance, Norway has amended its Constitution to secure complete religious freedom and Switzerland amended its Constitution in order to give votes to women and greater freedom to Jesuits. In addition, when the constitutions of Cyprus, Greece, Malta, Turkey, Spain, and Portugal were drafted, specific regard was taken of the Convention's provisions. Likewise, the institution of the procedure for inter-state and individual applications is considered to have transformed the general principles of the Universal Declaration of Human Rights into concrete obligations which have rendered effective the regional protection of human rights. Thus, the positive aspects of this instrument's effect on the legal systems of member states cannot be underestimated. A brief and yet thorough evaluation of domestic changes brought about as a direct consequence of case-law in Strasbourg was provided in a letter recently published in *The Times*:

Austria has modified three important sections of its code of criminal procedure, as well as its instructions as to treatment of prisoners in hospitals and the whole system of legal aid fees for lawyers. Belgium has amended its penal code, its vagrancy legislation, measures for subsidizing French-speaking schools in the Flemish area, and the civil code in order to give equal rights to legitimate and illegitimate children. Denmark has amended the law on custody of illegitimate children and the Federal Republic of Germany has modified its code of criminal procedure on the length of pre-trial detention, has taken measures to expedite criminal and civil proceedings and has legally recognized trans-sexuals. The Netherlands have amended the military criminal code and the law on detention of mental patients. Sweden amended the law of compulsory religious instruction and Switzerland has completely reviewed its judicial organization and criminal procedure as applied to the federal army and has amended the civil code regarding deprivation of liberty in reformatory centres. Many cases have also been formally or informally settled with the commission's approval following some concessionary measure taken by the government concerned.[1]

---

[1] Extract from a letter of A. B. McNulty, Director of the British Institute of Human Rights (formerly Secretary of the European Commission of Human Rights), *The Times*, 19 Aug. 1980, at 11. To this list can be added changes which have occurred in the UK: see ch. 7 above, sec. D.

But how efficacious has this regional system really become? Upon an examination of recent applications it can be observed that, apart from the six sets of inter-state applications, *only* some 270 out of over 9,650 registered applications have in fact been considered admissible by the Commission. Out of this sum total of about 270 applications, just under 55 cases (involving a total of about 80 applications) have been referred to the European Court of Human Rights for determination, and some 80 (involving some 170 applications) have been referred to the Committee of Ministers. The Court has held in 27 cases that violations of the Convention's provisions have in fact taken place;[2] while in 13 sets of cases the Committee of Ministers has expressed its satisfaction with legislative or other measures taken by states against which complaints were originally considered at least partially justified.[3] Consequently, although it may be certainly wrong to measure the achievements of this regional mechanism purely in terms of available statistical data, this form of crude factual evaluation none the less provides a rather less satisfactory overview of the Convention's effectiveness than was perhaps indicated by observers in a stock-taking of the instrument's impact during the first twenty-five years of its existence.[4]

A variety of questions probably need examination. Are enough rights protected by the Convention?[5] Now that all member states of the Council of Europe have ratified the Convention should not the facultative declarations concerning the right of individual petition and the acceptance of the Court's compulsory jurisdiction be made mandatory? Should not the principle of non-discrimination in the exercise of human rights

[2] See statistical charts provided in *Yearbook* plus recent Council of Europe press releases, *passim*.

[3] See *Collection of Resolutions Adopted by the Committee of Ministers in Application of Article 32 of the European Convention for the Protection of Human Rights and Fundamental Freedoms.* 1959–1979. (1979, Council of Europe doc. H(79)7). For a recent overview of case-law in Strasbourg consult R. Beddard, *Human Rights and Europe* (1980), *passim*; or recent issues of *EGZ* or *HRLJ*.

[4] See *Proceedings of the Fourth International Colloquy about the European Convention on Human Rights*, Rome, 5–8 Nov. 1975 (Council of Europe, 1976), *passim*. Also consult F. Newman, written communication in *Privacy and Human Rights* (ed. A. H. Robertson, 1973), 413–24.

[5] An additional draft protocol is being completed. This protocol may include such rights as freedom to seek information, equality of rights and responsibilities between spouses, and the principle of *non bis in idem*. See also A. H. Robertson, 'The Promotion of Human Rights by the Council of Europe', **VIII** *RDH/HRJ* (1975), 545–85, at 547–67.

be upheld independently of whether a given right is actually guaranteed by other provisions in the Convention?[6] Does it not appear that the individual's inability to bring an application before the Court violates the 'equality of arms' principle enshrined in Article 6(1) of the Convention?[7] Should not incorporation of the Convention's norms into domestic law become obligatory? Why cannot a substantial number of social and economic rights guaranteed by the 1961 European Social Charter be included in the Convention?[8] Should not more frequent and effective use be made of Article 57 in order to restrict the scope of certain reservations to the Convention as well as to draw attention of the states parties to the possible defects in their legislation or administrative practices, and to induce elimination of them?

Although these and many other questions most certainly merit analysis, Part III is primarily concerned with the *domestic impact* the Convention's norms have had and possibly may have in the near future: the Convention's application on the international plane is therefore intentionally omitted.[9] Three specific subjects are discussed. The first relates to one particular aspect of the Convention's domestic application which appears not to have been foreseen at the time of the instrument's creation, namely, the Convention's application by domestic courts in inter-individual relations (Chapter 8). The second is to note whether this instrument could be referred to by domestic courts of the ten member states of the European Communities

---

[6] See M.-A. Eissen, 'L'autonomie de l'article 14 de la Convention européenne des Droits de l'Homme dans la jurisprudence de la Commission' in *Mélanges Modinos* (1968), 122-45, and M. Bossuyt, *L'interdiction de la discrimination dans le droit international des droits de l'homme* (1976), esp. at 129-65.

[7] For a recent discussion on this subject see W. J. Ganshof van der Meersch, 'Aspects de la mise en œuvre d'une sauvegarde collective des Droits de l'Homme en droit international − La Convention européenne', *Mélanges F. Dehousse* (1979), i. 193-208, at 193-7.

[8] See F. Jacobs, 'The Extension of the European Convention on Human Rights to Include Economic, Social and Cultural Rights', III *HR Rev.* (1978), 166-78; and H. Wiebringhaus, 'La Convention européenne des Droits de l'Homme et la Charte Sociale européenne', VIII *RDH/HRJ* (1975), 527-44. Also consult Eur. Court HR, *Airey* case, judgment of 9 Oct. 1979, ser. A, no. 32, esp. para. 26 at 15.

[9] Material concerning the latter subject is plentiful: see *Bibliography*, esp. 49-90, and 123-54; and Beddard, n. 3 above. This form of categorization may certainly be considered unduly arbitrary in that the 'international supervisory machinery' was set up to ensure that the contracting parties secure to everyone within their jurisdiction the rights and freedoms set out in this instrument. What is here attempted, however, is to avoid too much discussion of developments in Strasbourg, and instead to pay attention to the Convention law's impact on and penetration into domestic law, with particular emphasis on its influence upon domestic courts and tribunals.

on the ground that some of the Convention's substantive provisions form part of the corpus of European Community law (Chapter 9). Lastly, a comparative study will be made, on a country by country basis, in order to examine the extent to which the decisions of the Convention's organs actually influence *domestic* courts, either in domestic proceedings to give effect to their findings or as guidelines which serve to clarify the extent and nature of resulting obligations (Chapter 10).

Chapter 8

Convention Rights and Obligations Between Individuals

A. The problem posed

The duty or obligation not to infringe constitutionally protected fundamental human rights which have hitherto been owed by state organs towards individuals may now have been extended, in certain countries, to encompass relationships between individuals. This particular development — also referred to as an issue relating to third parties (*Drittwirkung*) or alternatively as one concerning the 'horizontal' or 'inter-individual' application of fundamental human rights — appears to have its origins in the German doctrine of the so-called 'absolute effect of human rights', whereby fundamental human rights which are defined in constitutions are considered to be enforceable by individuals against other private persons as well as by public authorities.[1]

Without delving into and analysing the complex problem surrounding the *Drittwirkung* (third party effect) theory, it is sufficient to note for present purposes that it has received considerable attention in the German-speaking countries, especially in the Federal Republic of Germany. In general, the fundamental rights enumerated in the German *Grundgesetz* (Basic Law) concern the public-law relationship between the authorities and the individual, protecting the latter's rights against the legislature, executive, administrative, and other public authorities. (Private law is a separate branch of the law governing inter-individual relations in such matters as tort, contract, personal property, succession, and commercial law

---

[1] See A. Khol, 'The Protection of Human Rights in Relationships between Private Individuals: the Austrian Situation' in *Cassin* iii. 195–213, at 198. This legal development was apparently little known outside the German-speaking countries at the time of the Convention's drafting. It probably explains the very widespread use, even outside of the German-speaking countries, of the expression *Drittwirkung der Grundrechte*. See J. De Meyer, 'The Right to Respect for Private and Family Life, Home and Communications in Relations between Individuals, and the resulting Obligations for State Parties to the Convention' in *Privacy and Human Rights* (ed. A. H. Robertson, 1973), 255–75, at 264.

This chapter is an expanded version of an article published in **24** *NILR* (1979).

generally.) Nevertheless the courts have applied these basic rights clauses to bear upon relations between private persons because private law has apparently been unable to adequately protect individuals against other 'social power'.[2] Broadly speaking, this *Drittwirkung* theory has been interpreted in two ways: the direct ' (*unmittelbar*) approach encompasses the application of constitutionally guaranteed fundamental human rights to private legal relations (e.g. by the use of the principles of equality and non-discrimination), while the indirect (*mittelbar*) approach is more cautious and is based upon such notions as 'law and order', *boni mores* (good morals), *Treu und Glauben* (good faith) and *ordre public* (public order). It is also important to understand that the *Drittwirkung* effect upon inter-individual relations has grown out of the *Bundesverfassungsgericht's* (Federal Constitutional Court's) interpretation of 'constitutionally protected freedoms' as an expression of a 'value order' (*Wertordnung*) which should be taken into consideration when applying and interpreting law, particularly law of a general character.[3] This *Drittwirkung* theory has also taken root — although to a lesser degree — in Austria and Switzerland.[4]

The application of constitutionally guaranteed human rights provisions in relations between individuals has also been noted in other countries.[5] In many cases domestic tribunals appear

---

[2] See H. C. Nipperdey, 'Freie Enthaltung der Persönlichkeit', IV/2 *Die Grundrechte* (1962), 742 ff., at 752–3. For a historical account consult W. Leisner, *Grundrecht und Privatrecht* (1960), esp. at 1–112. These authors support the theory of the so-called *unmittelbare Drittwirkung* (direct horizontal effect). The predominant theory, that of *mittelbare Drittwirkung* (indirect horizontal effect) is supported by G. Dürig. See his 'Grundrechte und Zivilrechtssprechung' in *Festschrift für Nawiasky* (1956), 157–77; see also H. Gamillscheg, 'Die Grundrechte im Arbeitsrecht', 164 *Archiv für die zivilistische Praxis* (1964), 385–403, and J. Schabe, *Die sogenannte Drittwirkung der Grundrechte* (1971). For succinct explanations concerning the basic differences between public and private law consult R. David, and J. E. C. Brierley, *Major Legal Systems in the World Today* (1978), 74–86, and Ch. Szladitz, 'The Civil Law System', ii *International Encyclopaedia of Comparative Law* ('The Legal Systems of the World. Their Comparison and Unification', ed.-in-ch. R. David, 1969) 15–76. This classification has not taken root in common-law countries: see C. Harlow, '"Public" and "Private" Law: Definition without Distinction', 43 *MLR* (1980), 241–65.

[3] The *Lüth* case, 7 *Bverfg* (1958), 198–230. Other cases are cited by K. M. Lewan, 'The Significance of Constitutional Rights for Private Law: Theory and Practice in West Germany', 17 *ICLQ* (1968), 571–601, esp. 579–91.

[4] See references in Khol, n. 1 above; J. P. Müller, *Die Grundrechte der Verfassung und der Persönlichkeitsschutz des Privatrechts* (doctoral dissertation, University of Berne, 1964); and P. Saladin, *Grundrechte im Wandel* (1975).

[5] See M. J. Horan, 'Contemporary Constitutionalism and Legal Relationships between Individuals', 25 *ICLQ* (1976), 848–67; H. Waldock, 'The Legal Protection of Human Rights — National and International' in *An Introduction to the Study of*

increasingly prepared to draw inspiration from human rights principles which were originally thought to apply purely to disputes with public authorities. This is due to a large extent to the fact that structural innovations in contemporary society have in many instances obliged states to share their power with influential groups of individuals, large-scale private organizations which hold considerable economic and political power (e.g. corporations, trade unions, political parties), and other institutions. Thus in Belgium, for example, certain human rights provisions of the Constitution may be invoked not only against public authorities but also against individuals, groups, and organizations; traditional human rights are considered to be increasingly threatened by new dangers from multinational corporations, the mass media, mechanical devices (such as data banks), and other phenomena of a private nature which give rise to a need for protection *erga omnes*.[6] Similarly, the Italian courts also appear prepared to take into consideration constitutional provisions when balancing out interests in inter-individual cases, such as those concerning religious, political, and trade-union freedoms.[7]

It should perhaps be stressed that in some member states of the Council of Europe the differences between 'public' and 'private' law are either non-existent or unimportant, and that as a consequence no distinction is made concerning the legal responsibilities of persons acting on behalf of state authorities

Human Rights (ed. F. Vallat, 1972), 83-98; and Ch. Dominicé, report presented at the *Parliamentary Conference on Human Rights*, Vienna, 18-20 Oct. 1971 (Council of Europe, 1972), 64-74. It appears that the first serious attempt to study this subject on a comparative basis was not made prior to 1969: see *Cassin*, iii, esp. Part II ('Protection of Human Rights in Relations between Private Individuals', 149-322). Of particular interest are articles by N. Esen, at 163, O. Espersen, at 177, A. Favre, at 189, A. Khol, at 195, J. D. B. Mitchell, at 235, U. Scheuner, at 253, C. Zanghi, at 269, and J. Rivero, at 311.

[6] See Evans, 'Written Communication', 109-97, at 137. See also W. J. Ganshof van der Meersch, 'La Convention Européenne des Droits de l'Homme a-t-elle, dans le cadre du droit interne, une valeur d'ordre public?' in *Les Droits de l'Homme en droit interne et en droit international* (1968), 155-251; an English summary is reproduced in *Human Rights in National and International Law* (ed. A. H. Robertson, 1968), 97-143.

[7] See C. Nickel-Lanz, 'Les effets des droits fondamentaux dans les relations entre personnes privées: étude comparative', submitted to the Colloquium on the Protection of Human Rights in the European Community held under the auspices of the European University Institute, Florence, 14-17 June 1978, esp. pp. 9-13; and C. Zanghi, 'La protection des Droits de l'Homme dans les rapports entre personnes privées (Italie)' in *Cassin*, iii. 269-78.

and other individuals or private organizations. Also, the idea of protecting individuals' rights against other social groupings or private power-holders is certainly in itself not a novel development, in that one of the basic functions of state authority has always been the balancing of divergent individual interests within the confines of what are considered the fundamental interests and values of the society at large. However, what appears to be different in the *Drittwirkung* theory is that domestic courts have on a number of occasions been compelled to make recourse to constitutional or quasi-constitutional norms in order to intervene in interpersonal relationships when the rights and freedoms of individuals have been threatened. And, what may be of particular importance to understand in the context of this study is the fact that the domestic judiciary — at least in those countries in which the European Convention on Human Rights possesses the status of domestic law — may have at its disposal not only written and unwritten constitutional norms but also an extensive category of common/human rights provisions which form the embryo of a common constitutional order by which states are bound. In other words, domestic courts may be prepared to assume that certain rights and freedoms guaranteed by the Convention can be invoked by individuals against other private persons or organizations because the subject-matter covered by this international instrument falls within the conceptual framework of the nature and scope of the obligations imposed upon the states parties to the Convention which necessarily extends to *all legal activity* within the state's internal legal order. Such a creative use of the Convention's provisions certainly cannot be dismissed: the instrument already possesses an extra-constitutional status in the Netherlands,[8] forms part of the constitutional law of Austria,[9] is interpreted as having a 'constitutional content' in Switzerland,[10] and possibly also in Italy,[11] and there is reason to believe that its norms may be considered part and parcel of the *ordre public* of the francophone member states of the Council of Europe.[12]

---

[8] See ch. 3 above, sec. D.   [9] See ch. 4 above, sec. A.
[10] See ch. 4 above, sec. D.   [11] See ch. 6 above, sec. B.
[12] See Ganshof van der Meersch, n. 6 above, and ch. 3 above, *passim*. It is important to appreciate that legal norms and values endowed with the status of *ordre public* can be invoked and applied *ex officio* by the domestic courts: 'The function of *ordre public* is to permit an exception to a general rule for the sake of a superior interest. Thus in public law it permits the restriction of individual liberty in the interests of society as a whole.' This quotation is from A. C. Evans, 'Ordre Public in French

Even in states in which the Convention does not possess the status of domestic law, courts may — and possibly should — secure the effective implementation of the rights and freedoms guaranteed in the Convention by referring to its substantive norms in inter-individual cases when purely domestic criteria may indicate a solution which might be at variance with developments in Strasbourg. Should it not, after all, be assumed that in situations where there appears to exist a lacuna in domestic law, or where courts are faced with a doubtful or uncertain point of law in cases concerning two private parties (e.g. in Ireland, the UK, or one of the Scandinavian countries), the law ought to be interpreted so as not to contravene the Convention's provisions? In particular, it may be noted that the freedoms enumerated in Articles 8, 9, 10, and 11 of the Convention legally bind states parties to ensure by all appropriate means at their disposal that the rights therein may actually be exercised without risk of physical harm or some form of violent action; does there not exist a corollary to this, namely, that the courts must likewise ensure that domestic law does not violate international agreements which engage the responsibility of the state under the Convention?[13]

A basic aim of this chapter will be to indicate that the domestic courts (as well as the Commission and possibly also the Human Rights Court in Strasbourg) may be prepared to extend the reach of the Convention to interpersonal relations in the same way as some of them are prepared to make recourse to constitutional or quasi-constitutional norms to intervene in such relationships. However, this relatively new and apparently creative use of the Convention's provisions is difficult to determine with any accuracy, and a search for parallel developments must necessarily make allowances for probable distortions of analysis based upon the incoherent evolution of the concepts described and divergence of legal thinking generally. For the present, it suffices to underline the fact that this particular development, whereby constitutional provisions may be considered by the courts to impose duties upon individuals in inter-individual relations — and in particular the extension of

Immigration Law', *Public Law* (1980), 132–49, at 133. Also consult A.-Ch. Kiss, 'Permissible Limitations on Rights' in *The International Bill of Rights. The Covenant on Civil and Political Rights* (ed. L. Henkin, 1981), 291–310, esp. 299–302.

[13] The notion of state responsibility to regulate individual behaviour under the Convention is discussed at greater length in section C below.

this concept to the substantive provisions of the European Convention on Human Rights — has only recently come to the attention of a wider audience of legal scholars.[14] It has also at the same time blurred to a certain extent the distinction made in civil law countries between the conceptual categories of public and private law. This being said, it must be stressed that there actually does exist a clearly discernible development whereby constitutional and quasi-constitutional norms have been used 'in order to control the actions of non-governmental persons and institutions who behave in ways that may not be outside the bounds of the ordinary law, but that nevertheless are believed to be inimical to the fundamental interests or values of the community'. Also, express constitutional provisions banning, among other evils, slavery, discrimination in public accommodation, and certain labour practices, may be lacking or insufficiently comprehensive in scope; then 'egalitarian-minded courts have been sufficiently resourceful to find the requisite prohibitory authority in the interstices of the constitution or civil code. Judicial sensitivity to the freedom of conscience and expression appears to be producing a like tendency towards those protections of human rights.'[15]

In short, domestic courts appear prepared to ensure that private persons, groups, and organizations do not infringe a set of constitutionally protected fundamental human rights which bind state organs by superimposing duties or obligations upon inter-individual relationships. And, as in many countries the Convention's provisions possess a hierarchically superior position *vis-à-vis* other statutes, a similar extension of these obligations may also have been established in respect of some of the Convention's provisions.

B. Developments in the domestic forum

The 'horizontal' extension of the Convention's application

---

[14] See U. Scheuner, 'Fundamental Rights and the Protection of the Individual Against Social Groups and Powers in the Constitutional System of the Federal Republic of Germany' in *Cassin*, iii. 253–68.

[15] M. J. Horan, n. 5 above, at 866–7. A variant of the problem has been developed by the courts in the USA in the so-called 'State action' cases. For further comments on this subject see Horan, *passim*; T. Koopmans, 'Comparative Analysis and Evaluation' in *Constitutional Protection of Equality* (ed. Koopmans, 1975), 213–55, at 227–30; H. Abraham, *Freedom and the Court* (1972), esp. at 348–67; and P. G. Polyviou, *The Equal Protection of the Law* (1980), esp. at 536–635.

within the domestic legal structures of member states is most likely to arise where the courts are prepared to accept its provisions either as sources of internal law or as directly applicable norms of international law. In such instances the question of whether or not a state has made declarations under Article 25 and/or Article 46 does not appear to be of importance.

Although it may certainly be argued that the authors of the Convention did not intend this instrument to possess a third party effect, it must be acknowledged that the Convention does not forbid contracting parties to allow for this interpretation within their domestic jurisdictions. It has been argued that quite the reverse may be true, i.e. that the possibility of taking legal action against private persons as well as public authorities may be the 'effective remedy' provided within the meaning of Article 13.[16] After all — as pointed out by the Registrar of the European Court of Human Rights — the word 'notwithstanding' [*alors même que*] does not limit the application of Article 13 to government officials but instead 'admits implicitly, but inevitably, that breaches of the Convention may be committed by private individuals'.[17] More recently, the Deputy Secretary to the European Commission of Human Rights has indicated that, at least in his eyes, the meaning which best reconciles the French and English texts of Article 13 'is that the States Party are obliged by Article 13 to provide a remedy in domestic law against violations committed by private persons or by public authorities'.[18] Irrespective of whether domestic courts accept this interpretation, these arguments based on Article 13 are more difficult to sustain on the international plane, for the simple reason that such an interpretation may involve an unforeseen and undue extension of the notion of state responsibility under the Convention. (The extent to which a state may be held responsible for an individual's behaviour under the Convention is a problem to which section C of this chapter will revert).

---

[16] Art. 13 of the Convention reads: 'Everyone whose rights and freedoms as set forth in this Convention are violated shall have an effective remedy before a national authority notwithstanding that [*alors même que*] the violation has been committed by persons acting in an official capacity.' See further, comments by P. Mertens, and numerous publications of M.-A. Eissen, noted in sec. C below.

[17] M.-A. Eissen, 'The European Convention on Human Rights and the Duties of the Individual', 32 *Nordisk Tidsskrift for International Ret* (1967), 229–53, at 237.

[18] J. Raymond, 'A Contribution to the Interpretation of Article 13 of the European Convention on Human Rights', V *HR Rev.* (1980), 161–75, at 170. He added that this view finds support in the *travaux préparatoires* of the 1966 Covenant on Civil and Political Rights.

It could also possibly be argued that Article 17 of the Convention may impose a specific duty upon individuals: the duty not to destroy any of the rights and freedoms set forth in the Convention or to limit these rights to a greater extent than provided in the instrument.[19]

But how does the situation present itself in practice? An overview of domestic case-law tends to suggest that there certainly exists an inclination, on the part of national tribunals, not to rule out the possibility of applying the Convention's norms in cases between private persons.

Austria

In Austria where the European Convention on Human Rights has the rank of constitutional law, the Supreme Court (*Oberster Gerichtshof*) in a decision dated 16 January 1963 considered that Articles 304 to 307 of the Code of Civil Procedure (relating to the presentation of documents) did not violate Article 6 of the Convention.[20] Similarly, in a case decided by the same court in December 1975, it appears that were the penal law not to have regulated the unauthorized tape-recording of telephone conversations by individuals, Article 8 of the Convention would probably have served this purpose.[21] Case-law still, however, remains rather conservative in this respect, especially that of the *Verfassungsgerichtshof* (Constitutional Court).[22] However, the *Drittwirkung* issue was recently raised in a debate in the *Nationalrat* in relation to the right to life in the context of abortion legislation; and there is reason to believe that were the European Court and Commission of Human Rights to develop case-law in this direction, the Austrian courts would probably follow suit.[23]

[19] See sec. C below. In art. 17 reference to individuals is usually understood to mean that 'no individual or group may use the Convention as a shield for activities which will undermine it': J. E. S. Fawcett, *The Application of the European Convention on Human Rights* (1969), at 254.

[20] Mentioned in *Collection,* art. 6, 32; 7 Ob. 354/1962. For reference to other case-law consult Moser, n. 23 below, 89–90.

[21] Case no. 186 of 9 Dec. 1975 in *ÖJZ* (1976), 359 ff; extract also reproduced in 20 *Yearbook* (1977), 678-9. (In this case a man installed a listening device to record a telephone conversation of his wife.) Interestingly enough, reference to para. 2 of art. 8 appears not to have been made.

[22] See A. Saxer, 'Bestand der Grundrechte in Österreich', 462-7, and W. Rozenzweig, 'Bedeutung der Grundrechte in Österreich', 5 *EGZ* (1970), 467-75.

[23] Evans, 'Written Communication', at 125. See further B. Moser, *Die Europäische*

Belgium

The Brussels Conciliation Board of Appeal or Labour Court (*Conseil des Prud'hommes d'Appel*), recognized that Article 3 of the Convention could be invoked in relations between private persons.[24] In this case a female employee was dismissed from her work for practising prostitution by making clearly comprehensible signs to motorists. She claimed compensation in lieu of notice and alleged that the Convention guarantees to everyone the right to dispose freely of his person and the right to have one's private life respected, which implies that everyone has the right to live as he sees fit. The court considered that the practice of prostitution in a place where her employer's clients and staff could see her amounted to a public act liable to cause damage to the firm, and that such behaviour in public could not be considered as pertaining exclusively to the private life of the person concerned.

A Belgian jurist was also able to find (from 1967 to 1969) that the Brussels civil court rendered some ten judgments in cases between private persons in which the judgments were based, among other sources, on Article 6 of the Convention.[25] According to these decisions, the rights safeguarded by Article 6 were binding on both physical and artificial persons. Other Belgian judgments which have relied on the Convention's provisions in relations between private individuals and/or private institutions include the use of Article 6(1) in a case concerning the enforcement of a foreign judgment for the payment of maintenance;[26] Article 8, in a case of an alleged

---

Menschenrechtskonvention und das bürgerliche Recht. Zum Problem der Drittwirkung von Grundrechten (1972), esp. 86-124 and 125-286; and G. Dahm, *Völkerrecht,* iii (1961), who wrote, at 196: 'The State can be held responsible for the fact that its organs cause, promote or − contrary to duty − do not prevent the activities of private persons that are contrary to law.' (My translation.) Also consult Khol, n. 1 above. (Khol considers that the Convention does not bind 'third parties' on the international plane, but that it does oblige states to provide for *Drittwirkung* within their domestic legal systems, see *Zwischen Staat und Weltstaat* (1969), 309-22); and T. Öhlinger, 'Cour constitutionnelle autrichienne', 33 *RDIC* (1981), 543-79, esp. 556-7 and 572.

[24] Decision of 22 Feb. 1968, *JT* (1968), 387; *Collection*, art. 8, 17 *bis.*

[25] J. Velu, 'Article 6 of the European Convention on Human Rights in Belgian Law', 18 *AJCL* (1970), 259-92, at 266-7. See also G. Janssen-Pevtschin, J. Velu, and J. Venwelkenhuyzen, 'La Convention de sauvegarde des Droits de l'Homme et des libertés fondamentales et le fonctionnement des juridictions belges', IX *Chronique de Politique Étrangère* (1962), 195-246, at 225.

[26] Decision of 11 Oct. 1973, *JT* (1973), 80-1.

breach of professional secrecy;[27] and in a situation where it was held that clauses in a contract may lead to a permanent and insoluble bond with a private institution, such provisions being, if established, contrary of the right of authors and composers in violation of Article 4 of the Convention.[28] More recently, the *Tribunal Civil* of Brussels declined to enforce a contractual obligation which included a stipulation whereby a private detective was able to use an electronic eavesdropping device in order to obtain proof of an alleged adultery.[29] In so holding, the court accepted the opinion of the *Ministère public* that such a provision was '*contraire à l'ordre public ou aux bonnes mœurs*' and that it violated the right to privacy guaranteed by Article 8 of the Convention. In another case a schoolteacher was dismissed from her post after she had separated from her husband and was found to be cohabiting with another man. The dismissal was held to be unlawful: in a decision dated 24 November 1977 the Brussels *Cour de Travail* saw as a violation of Belgian law a contractual stipulation imposed by a private Catholic school upon the schoolteacher to the effect that the latter could be dismissed were she to be found 'dans une situation personelle ou matrimoniale incompatible avec les lois de la morale chrétienne ou violant gravement les lois de l'Église catholique'. In so holding, the court cited Article 8 of the European Convention on Human Rights, adding that

Il est hors de doute que les droits de l'homme et les libertés fondamentales énumérés par la Convention de sauvegarde appartiennent à l'ordre public, et que toute convention privée qui y porterait atteinte serait entachée de nullité. La Convention de sauvegarde a même primauté sur toute norme nationale, à savoir sur toute loi qui ne constituerait pas [exceptions enumerated in para. 2 of Article 8] .... A cet égard, il faut remarquer que l'interprétation d'une convention internationale ne peut se faire par référence au droit national de l'un des États contractants, et que si le texte appelle interprétation, celle-ci doit se faire sur la base d'éléments propres à la Convention, notamment son objet, son but et son contexte, ainsi que ses travaux préparatoires et sa genèse.[30]

---

[27] *Tribunal de Première Instance de Bruxelles*, 16 Dec. 1972; *Collection*, art. 8, 28. See also R. Senelle, *La constitution belge commentée* (1974), art. 22.

[28] *Rechtbank* of Brussels, 4 Apr. 1973; *Collection*, art. 4, 14. Also consult Ganshof van der Meersch, n. 6 above and 'L'ordre public et les droits de l'homme', *JT* (1968), 658 ff; and F. Perin, *Cour de Droit Constitutionnel* (Liège, 1977), 119.

[29] Decision of 6 Apr. 1976, in *Pas. Bel.* (1976), iii. 51–5.

[30] Reported in *Journal des tribunaux du travail* (1978), 63–4. This judgment affirmed the findings of the *Tribunal du Travail* of Brussels of 26 Nov. 1975, *JT* (1976), 329.

Interestingly enough, the above developments have been noted by the European Court of Human Rights in its recent decision in the case of *Deweer* v. *Belgium*.[31]

Cyprus

In Cyprus, where not only is part of the Constitution more or less modelled on the Convention, but also where this instrument has, as of 1962, a force superior to ordinary laws, it would seem that the constitutional norms (as well as those of the Convention) can be used by the courts to protect individuals' rights not only against state authority but also against interference by private persons.[32] This appears to be the correct understanding of Article 34 of the Constitution which provides that nothing in Part II of the Constitution guaranteeing fundamental rights and liberties 'may be interpreted as implying for any Community, group or person any right to engage in any activity or perform any act aimed . . . at the destruction of any of the rights and liberties set forth in this Part or at their limitation to a greater extent than is provided for therein'.[33]

Denmark

In Denmark, where it appears that the Convention does not possess the status of domestic law, the instrument's direct impact on 'intersubjective' relations would appear to be of little, if any significance.[34]

France

The directly applicable provisions of the Convention probably can be relied upon in relations between individuals in France, and it is interesting to recall that this instrument possesses a hierarchically superior status *vis-à-vis* ordinary laws. It may be

---

[31] Eur. Court HR, judgment of 27 Feb. 1980, ser. A, no. 35, para. 49. (The Court makes reference to some additional case-law.) This judgment is also briefly discussed in sec. C below.

[32] See Z. M. Nedjati, *Human Rights and Fundamental Freedoms* (1972), 25–7.

[33] Ibid., at 27. Art. 34 of the Cypriot Constitution was modelled upon art. 17 of the European Convention on Human Rights.

[34] See O. Espersen, 'Human Rights and Relations between Individuals' in *Cassin*, iii. 177–87; and F. Thygesen, 'Bestand und Bedeutung der Grundrechte: Dänemark', 5 *EGZ* (1978), 438–40.

noted, in this connection, that in the *Baroum* case[35] the Criminal Chamber of the *Cour de Cassation* invoked *ex officio* Articles 6 and 13 of the European Convention when it set aside a judgment of the Court of Appeal of Orleans.[36] What is of particular interest in the context of the present study is the fact that the Convention's provisions were classified by the *Cour de Cassation* as appertaining to *ordre public* in the domestic legal hierarchy.[37]

Federal Republic of Germany

The courts in the FRG have undoubtedly been the most active in this field.[38] For example, the Federal Supreme Court (*Bundesgerichtshof*) declared, in a judgment rendered on 20 May 1958,[39] that Articles 1 and 2 of the Basic Law as well as Article 8 of the Convention were not only binding upon the State and its authorities but must also be respected by individuals in their mutual relations (*Privatrechtsverkehr*). Similarly, the Celle Court of Appeal, in a judgment rendered on 30 September 1964 considered that the constitutional principles enshrined in Articles 1 and 2 of the Basic Law and the principles embodied in Article 8 of the Convention applied in respect of relations between a patient and his doctor.[40] The Federal Constitutional Court (*Bundesverfassungsgericht*), in a decision of 24 July 1968 considered that, although the rights secured by the Convention are probably not directly applicable in respect of relations between private persons, the provisions of the Convention must nevertheless be regarded as objective criteria which must be

---

[35] Mentioned in ch. 3 above, sec. B.

[36] Judgment of 5 Dec. 1978, *Daloz* (1979), Jurisprudence, 50.

[37] For criticism of the court's reference to the Convention see J. Robert, 'Procédure Pénale' (comments on case-law) in *Rev. de science criminelle et droit pénal comparé* (1979), 349–53. But also see comments by C. Nickel-Lanz, in n. 7 above, 13–17; and J. Rivero, 'La protection des Droits de l'Homme dans les rapports entre personnes privées' in *Cassin*, iii. 311–22.

[38] For an analysis of the *Drittwirkung* theory beyond the ambit of the Convention's application, consult Lewan, n. 3 above, and Horan, n. 5 above. See also survey of literature provided in Th. Maunz and G. Dürig, *Grundgesetz, Kommentator*, n. 127 to art. 1, para. 3 of the German Basic Law; W. Morvay, 'Rechtsprechung nationaler Gerichte zur Europäischen Konvention zum Schutze der Menschenrechte und Grundfreiheiten', 21 *ZRV* (1961), 89–112, and 316–47, at 317–21; and A. Bleckmann, *Allgemeine Grundrechtslehren* (1979), at 137–53.

[39] 27 Bgh. (1958), 284–91; *Collection*, art. 8, 3. Also see 9 *NJW* (1956), 384–6.

[40] 18 *NJW* (1965), 362–4; *Collection*, art. 8, 12.

taken into consideration when provisions of private law are considered.[41]

Greece

The Convention has a hierarchically superior status to ordinary laws in Greece, although to date no decisions on its internal application by individuals against third parties have been noted.

Iceland and Ireland

The Convention is not part of domestic law in these countries.[42]

Italy

The Convention does have a status of internal law in Italy, and the courts have made occasional reference to its provisions when determining cases between private persons.[43] One such example can be found in a case decided by the Milan Court of Appeal on 25 January 1972.[44] The Court held that the rules concerning the extinction of a statutory limitation violated not only Articles 2 and 3 of the Constitution but also Article 6(1) of the Convention. The fact that these provisions had been applied in an action opposing a minor to a car owner following a car accident did not constitute a discrimination against the minor since the latter enjoyed the same rights as an adult as provided for by Article 14 of the Convention.

Liechtenstein

Liechtenstein recently ratified the Convention and it is assumed

---

[41] They apparently form part of the FRG's 'value order' (*Wertordnung*). See K. Doehring, 'Non-discrimination and Equal Treatment under the European Human Rights Convention and the West German Constitution with Particular Reference to Discrimination against Aliens', 18 *AJCL* (1970), 305-25, at 317-19.

[42] See ch. 5 above, sec. C, and ch. 7 above, sec. B. Also consult an article by D. M. Clarke, 'The Concept of Common Good in Irish Constitutional Law', 30 *Northern Ireland Legal Quarterly* (1979), 319-42.

[43] See C. Zanghi, n. 5 above. For discussion concerning the application of the *Drittwirkung* effect with regard to Italian constitutional norms consult C. Nickel-Lanz, n. 7 above, at 9-13, G. Lombardi, *Potere privato e diritti fondamentali* (1970), 93-105, and P. Barile, *Il soggetto privato nella costituzione italiana* (1953), *passim*. Note may also be taken of judgments of the *Corte Costituzionale* in case no. 122, XV *Giurisprudenza Costituzionale* (1970), 1529, and case no. 88/1979.

[44] *Collection*, art. 6, 142.

that the Convention's provisions will be interpreted in a manner similar to the Austrian and Swiss courts.

Luxembourg

In Luxembourg there was initially a certain judicial reticence in considering the Convention's norms as self-executing (i.e. directly applicable in domestic law).[45] Thus, unlike in Belgium, case-law in which reference to this instrument is made remains rather sparse and there still appears to be no recorded judgment in which the Convention has been used in interpersonal disputes.

Malta

The Convention does not possess the status of domestic law in Malta.[46] It may, however, be of interest to note that many of the country's constitutional provisions have been modelled on the Convention, and that the human rights sections of the Constitution can be cited in case-law concerning interpersonal disputes.[47]

The Netherlands

The impact of the Convention's substantive provisions in relations between individuals in the Netherlands may be substantial, although to date they have not often been invoked before the domestic courts.[48] However, there is evidence that when adjudicating on matters between private persons, the domestic courts increasingly draw inspiration from human rights principles (embodied in the Dutch Constitution and the European Convention) and take them into account when balancing out interests involved.[49] For example, the so-called horizontal effect of the

---

[45] See ch. 3 above, sec. C.　　　　　　　　[46] See ch. 7 above, sec. C.

[47] Law reports are irregularly published in *The Times* (of Malta), e.g. cases no. 78 (3 Nov. 1969), no. 126 (24 Apr. 1972), and no. 176 (8 Oct. 1973). The Maltese reservation to art. 2, para. 2(a) of the Convention appears to exclude the application of *Drittwirkung* in certain circumstances. See 9 *Yearbook* (1966), 24–7.

[48] See M. H. van Emde Boas, 'The Impact of the European Convention on Human Rights and Fundamental Freedoms on the Legal Order of the Netherlands', 13 *NILR* (1966), 337–73, and 14 *NILR* (1967), 1–13, esp. at 352–7; D. H. M. Meuwissen, *De Europese Conventie en het Nederlandse Recht* (1968), 201–11 and 435–7; and D. Simons, 'Bestand und Bedeutung der Grundrechte: Niederlande', 5 *EGZ* (1978), 450–7.

[49] See M. B. W. Biesheuvel, 'Horizonale werking van grondrechten', 6 *Bulletin of*

Convention was discussed in a case brought against a weekly magazine *NV Televizier* which, it had been alleged, had committed a breach of copyright when it published information and comments on forthcoming radio and television programmes (the case later came before the Commission in Strasbourg). It was argued, on behalf of *Televizier,* that the Dutch Broadcasting Associations were discriminating against the magazine and that such action was contrary to Articles 10 and 14 of the Convention. Although the three courts which dealt with this case — the District Court of The Hague, the Court of Appeal, and the Supreme Court — could have rejected such an argument on the ground that these Articles relate only to the relationship of private individuals with public authorities, it is interesting to note that such an interpretation was not given, and that instead it was found that there had been no contradiction between the Copyright Act and Article 10 of the Convention, in that complex weekly broadcasting programmes did not constitute 'information' in the sense used in Article 10.[50]

It has also been suggested that if a contract between individuals restricting the fundamental freedoms of third persons — such as, for example, a restrictive covenant limiting the sale or lease of real property to third parties on account of race, religion, or nationality — the Dutch courts could strike down such contracts as being contrary to public order and good morals or as being in violation of standards laid down in the Convention.[51] Other interesting cases in the Netherlands include a decision of the Amsterdam Court of Appeal dated 30 October 1980. In this case the *Reclame Code Commissie (RCC)* (created by the private sector to control and evaluate commercial advertisements, the decisions of which bind all contracting parties) considered an advertisement requesting readers not to buy oranges from South Africa to be in breach of its 'Commercial

the *NJCM* (1981), 147–69 and 205–25; and Evans, 'Written Communication', at 169–70. Also consult E. A. Alkema, *Studies over Europese Grondrechten* (1978), esp. at 32–5, 70–5, and 253–9, P. Van Dijk and G. J. H. Van Hoof, *De Europese Conventie in theorie en praktijk* (1979), 12–17, and T. Koopmans, *Vrijheden in Beweging* (1976).

[50] van Emde Boas, n. 48 above, at 355 and 372; *Hoge Raad* 25 July 1965, *NJ* (1966) no. 115.

[51] van Emde Boas, ibid., at 355–6. See, for example, two decisions of the *Hof Arnhem,* 25 Oct. 1948 (*NJ* (1949), no. 331), and 24 June 1959 (*NJ* (1959), no. 473). In this connection it can be noted that the French courts may also accept such an argument: see case decided by *Tribunal Civil de la Seine,* 22 Jan. 1947, *Dalloz* (1947), 126–7. Compare this to developments in the UK, below.

Code'. This decision, in effect, prevented a private group, the *Boycot Outspan Aktie*, from placing the same advertisement in about 90 per cent of Dutch newspapers and periodicals. The Commission's decision was upheld by the district court, but was reversed by the Court of Appeal which ordered that the *RCC* decision be ignored by the press as it infringed the right of free speech which is protected by, among other sources, Article 10 of the European Convention.[52]

A civil law dispute before the Amsterdam Court of Appeal can also be cited. In this case the respondent unsuccessfully invoked Article 6(1) of the Convention when he argued that the settlement of a claim had not been attempted 'within a reasonable time'. In rejecting the respondent's claim, the Court of Appeal appears to have gone out of its way to explain that, despite the outcome of the present case in which Article 6 could not be relied upon, *a priori* it cannot be assumed that the Convention may not have a so-called horizontal operation.[53] In other words, Article 6 imposes a general obligation upon public authorities engaged in the administration of justice, and this includes civil disputes in situations where one party or the court itself — by its action or inaction — may disturb the proper administration of justice in conformity with Article 6 of the Convention.

Portugal and Spain

As yet the courts of these countries (both of which have only recently ratified the Convention) have not had an opportunity to deal with the Convention in interpersonal matters. Nevertheless recent research suggests that in both countries constitutionally

---

[52] *Bulletin of the NJCM* (1980), no. 6, 374, discussed at length by Biesheuvel, n. 49 above.

[53] Cited by L. A. N. M. Barnhoorn, 'Netherlands Judicial Decisions Involving Questions of Public International Law 1976-77', IX *NYIL* (1978), 271-351, at 306-7. (See also the Court of Alkmaar decision of 24 Mar. 1976 referred to at 307.) The *Hoge Raad* judgment of 9 Apr. (in 19 *NJ* (1976), 642; 20 *Yearbook* (1977), 776-9) may also be noted. In the new draft Constitution — forwarded for legislative consideration in 1976 — the Government explicitly affirmed that human rights provisions in both the Constitution as well as in binding international agreements may be relied upon in relations between private persons: see Explanatory Memorandum *MvT* 13.872, *zitting* 1975-6, *Nr.* 3, at 15-16. Also consult *Handelingen Tweede Kamer der Staten-Generaal*, 15 Dec. 1976, 2127; and A. M. Donner, 'Terugtred van de grondwetgever?', *RMT* 1976, 397. (These matters are more fully discussed by Biesheuvel, n. 49 above.)

entrenched human rights norms may be invoked by one private person against another, and it would therefore seem feasible that an evolution of case-law in this direction might well encompass the application of relevant human rights clauses of binding international agreements.[54]

Norway and Sweden

In these countries, the European Convention does not possess the status of domestic law.[55]

Switzerland

The Convention's provisions have been accorded a 'constitutional content' in Switzerland; the *Tribunal Fédéral* equates them with constitutional law, for procedural purposes, in so far as the exhaustion of cantonal remedies is concerned. Legal opinion appears to be favourably inclined to an extension of the Convention's application to relations between private persons; and it will be of considerable interest to see whether the courts will be prepared to give such a horizontal effect to its provisions in domestic law.[56] Although in Switzerland there is no direct *Drittwirkung* in the application of constitutional rights, the various branches of the law are considered as constituting a coherent and integral legal system and as a consequence constitutional rights have a direct influence upon the interpretation of civil rights, particularly in areas where detailed legislation does not exist and where there is a possibility for development on the basis of general principles. The *Tribunal Fédéral* has already made reference to Article 55 of the Federal Constitution

---

[54] See J. J. Abrantes, *L'effet à l'égard des particuliers des droits et libertés fondamentaux: Portugal* (Council of Europe memoir, Sept. 1981), esp. at 30-2 and 36-8; and L. Aguiar de Luque, 'Las garantías constitucionales de los derechos fundamentales en la Constitución Española', **10** *Revista de Derecho Político* (1981), 107-29 at 114-16.

[55] See ch. 5, above, secs. C and D.

[56] See C. Dominicé, 'La Convention européenne des Droits de l'Homme devant le juge national', **XXVIII** *ASDI* (1972), 9-40, at 37-9; and S. Trechsel, *Die Europäische Menschenrechtskonvention, ihr Schutz der persönlichen Freiheit und die schweizerischen Strafprozessrechte* (1974), 82-8; also L. Wildhaber, 'Réflexions sur la discrimination raciale, l'égalité devant la loi et la "Drittwirkung" en droit suisse', **IV** *RDH/HRJ* (1971), 341-9, and G. Müller, 'Die Drittwirkung der Grundrechte. Überblick über den Stand der Diskussion in Lehre und Rechtsprechung' in *Schweizerisches Zentralblatt für Staats- und Gemeindeverwaltung* (1978), 233-44.

(which guarantees freedom of the press) in a case which concerned an alleged attack on an individual's reputation, and to Article 31 (which guarantees freedom of trade and industry) when considering the legality of certain restrictive trade practices.[57] Thus, there is reason to believe that the Swiss courts may also extend the Convention's domestic application in cases concerning disputes between individuals and such powerful instrumentalities as the press and trade unions.[58]

It is certainly interesting to note, in this context, that Article 25 of the proposed new draft Swiss constitution specifically caters for the protection of human rights in interpersonal relations.[59] The French text of this draft Article reads:

1. La législation et la jurisprudence pourvoient à ce que les droits de l'homme s'appliquent par analogie entre personnes privées aussi.
2. Celui qui exerce les droits de l'homme doit considérer aussi les droits de l'homme des autres. Surtout personne n'a le droit de porter atteinte aux droits de l'homme par abus de son pouvoir.

Turkey

Although the European Convention on Human Rights possesses the status of domestic law in Turkey, the courts have generally been rather reluctant to refer to its provisions when determining issues relating to individuals' rights and freedoms;[60] moreover, there appear to be no cases in which the Convention's horizontal effect has been noted.

The United Kingdom

In the United Kingdom, even though the Convention has not been transformed into internal law, the courts are prepared,

---

[57] Evans, 'Written Communication', at 185.

[58] L. Wildhaber considers that those rights from which derogation is not permitted under the European Convention (see art. 15 of the Convention) may even have priority over human rights provisions in the Swiss Constitution: see his 'Erfahrungen mit der Europäischen Menschenrechtskonvention', 98 *Revue de droit suisse* (1979), 230–379, esp. 277–83 and 328–33. Also consult P. Abravanel, 'La protection de l'ordre public dans l'État régi par le droit', 99 *Revue de droit suisse* (1980), 1–145, esp. at 88–94.

[59] See O. K. Kaufmann, 'Bestand und Bedeutung der Grundrechte: Schweiz', 5 *EGZ* (1978), 475–83. Note can also be taken of case-law relating to arts. 27–8 of the Swiss Civil Code. See Nickel-Lanz, n. 7 above.

[60] See Esen, n. 5 above, 163–76.

prima facie, to consider the Convention's norms as an aid to interpretation when faced with a doubtful or uncertain point in domestic law.[61] Unfortunately in so far as the Convention has been invoked in relations between private persons, its impact (legal weight) seems not to have been adequately appreciated; it is sufficient to quote Lord Wilberforce's views on this subject in a case in which the House of Lords refused to make void or invalidate a condition in a will which allegedly discriminated against a potential beneficiary who became a Roman Catholic.

> . . . It was said that the law of England was not set against discrimination on a number of grounds including religious grounds . . . [and after referring to the 1968 Race Relations Act and Article 11 of the Convention, he went on to say] . . . I do not doubt that the conceptions of public policy should move with the times and that widely accepted treaties and statutes may point a direction in which such conceptions, as applied by the courts, ought to move. It may well be that conditions such as this are, or at least are becoming, inconsistent with standards now widely accepted. But acceptance of this does not persuade me that we are justified, particularly in relation to a will which came into effect as long ago as 1936 and which has twice been the subject of judicial consideration, in introducing for the first time a rule of law which would go far beyond the mere avoidance of discrimination on religious grounds. To do so would bring about a substantial reduction of another freedom, firmly rooted in our law, namely that of testamentary disposition. Discrimination is not the same thing as choice: it operates over a larger and less personal area, and neither by express provision nor by implication has private selection yet become a matter of public policy.[62]

It may be added that Lord Wilberforce did recognize that widely accepted treaties can point a direction in which conceptions of public policy ought to move, and the European Convention may well be given a greater weight in a situation where states parties are considered to have positive obligations to ensure that private individuals do not interfere with rights guaranteed under this instrument.[63] Likewise, it may be suggested that reference to the European Convention might be more frequent when the courts elucidate or accommodate a development of the common law. Indications of this may be found in the

---

[61] See ch. 7 above, sec. D.

[62] *Blathwayt* v. *Lord Crawley* [1976] AC 397, at 426; [1975] 3 All ER 625 at 636.

[63] See, for example, Eur. Court HR, *Marckx* case, judgment of 13 June, 1979, ser. A, vol. **31**, para. 31, at 15; and *Airey* case, judgment of 9 Oct. 1979, ser. A, vol. 32, para. 32 at 17; the Commission's report in the *Young & James* case of 14th Dec. 1979, para. 168 at 36; and Eur. Court HR, *Artico* case, judgment of 13 May 1980, ser. A, vol. 36, para. 36.

case of *R. v. Lemon & Gay News* in which Lord Scarman, in holding that the mental element of the common law offence of blasphemy is satisfied by proof of an intention to publish material which a jury may find likely to shock or arouse resentment among believing Christians, considered the issue to be one of 'public policy in the society of today'. He then went on to say:

All this makes legal sense in a plural society which recognises the human rights and fundamental freedoms of the European Convention for the Protection of Human Rights and Fundamental Freedoms (1950) (*Cmd.* 8969). Article 9 provides that every one has the right to freedom of religion, and the right to manifest his religion in worship, teaching, practice and observance. *By necessary implication the Article imposes a duty on all of us to refrain from insulting or outraging the religious feelings of others.* Article 10 provides that every one shall have the right to freedom of expression. *The exercise of this freedom 'carries with it duties and responsibilities'* and may be subject to such restrictions as are presented by law and are necessary 'for the prevention of disorder or crime, for the protection of health or morals, for the protection of the reputation or rights of others . . .' It would be intolerable if by allowing an author or publisher to plead the excellence of his motives and the right of free speech, he could evade the penalties of the law even though his words were blasphemous in the sense of constituting an outrage upon the religious feelings of his fellow citizens. This is no way forward for a successful plural society.[64]

C. The issue in Strasbourg

The domestic developments described above have in turn manifested themselves on the international plane. It can be noted, for instance, that some UN texts contain provisions that appear to grant protection against interference by individuals and groups.[65] Article 2(1)(d) of the 1965 Covenant on the

---

[64] [1979] I All ER 898, at 927; [1979] AC 617, at 665. (Emphasis added.) Cf., the observations of Lord Diplock in *Gleaves* v. *Deakin* [1979] 2 All ER 497, at 498–9, mentioned in ch. 7 above, sec. D. Also consult *Cheall* v. *APEX* [1982] 3 WLR 685.

[65] See Council of Europe doc. H(70)7 of Sept. 1970: 'Problems arising from the co-existence of the UN Covenants on Human Rights and the European Convention on Human Rights', 15. See also UN doc. 2929, reproduced in Official Record of the General Assembly, 10th Session (1955), annexes, agenda item 28 Part III. It is interesting to note that Professor Ganshof van der Meersch – when looking at several of the articles of the Convention – indicated that when the concept of the general interest (*ordre public*) is elevated to the level of a mandatory requirement, it comes near to the concept of *jus cogens* in international law. See his memorandum in *Information of the Court of Justice of the European Communities* (1977), iii, 53–82, at 59. This subject may be linked with the wider concept of the validity *erga omnes* of a certain category of human rights and fundamental freedoms. See De Meyer, n. 1 above, at

Elimination of All Forms of Racial Discrimination (in force since 1969) stipulates that 'Each State Party shall prohibit and bring to an end, by all appropriate means, including legislation as required by circumstances, racial discrimination by any persons, group or organisation.' Similarly, the 1966 Covenant on Economic, Social, and Cultural Rights and the 1966 Covenant on Civil and Political Rights (both in force since 1976) mention in their preambles 'that the individual, having duties to other individuals and to the community to which he belongs, is under the responsibility to strive for the promotion and observance of the rights recognised in the present Covenant.'[66]

The Strasbourg organs have also been confronted with this horizontal development, and emphasis has been placed on two interrelated issues: whether or not the European Convention on Human Rights imposes obligations and duties upon individuals; and to what extent, if at all, a state is responsible before the Strasbourg organs for violations, by a private person within its jurisdiction, of the rights guaranteed in the Convention.[67]

It is probably correct to assume that — in so far as the regional mechanism is concerned — the Convention creates *indirect*

---

271. For a recent survey on this subject consult M. S. McDougal, H. D. Lasswell, and L.-C. Chen, *Human Rights and World Public Order* (1980), 339–50. Reference can also be made in ICJ Reports to the *Barcelona Traction* case 1970, 32, paras. 32–3, the *Namibia* case, advisory opinion, 1971, 45, para. 131, and *US Diplomatic and Consular Staff in Tehran* (merits), 1980, 42, para. 91. Also consult G. S. Goodwin-Gill, *International Law and the Movement of Persons between States* (1978), 58–74, and E.-I. A. Daes, 'Study of the Individual's Duties to the Community and the Limitations on Human Rights and Fundamental Freedoms under Article 29 of the Universal Declaration of Human Rights', UN doc. E/CN.4/Sub.2/432/Rev.1, 1 July 1980 (with seven addenda). Developments in the European Community may also be noted: see A. J. Easson, 'Can Directives Impose Obligations on Individuals?', 4 *EL Rev.* (1979), 67–79.

[66] See *Human Rights, A Compilation of International Instruments* (United Nations, 1978), 3 and 8. Art. 2 of the Covenant on Civil and Political Rights reads: 'Each State Party to the present Covenant undertakes to respect and *to ensure* to *all* individuals within its territory and subject to its jurisdiction the rights recognised in the present Covenant . . .' (Emphasis added.)

[67] The second issue could also be presented in the form of a question which reads as follows: to what extent can a state's *inactivity* with regard to breaches of the Convention by third parties entail its responsibility in Strasbourg? See generally on this subject M.-A. Eissen, 'The European Convention on Human Rights and the Duties of the Individual', 32 *Nordisk Tidsskrift for international Ret* (1962), 230–53, and 'La Convention européenne des Droits de l'Homme et les obligations de l'individu: une mise à jour' in *Cassin*, iii. 151–62; and M.-M. Hahne, *Das Drittwirkung in der Europäischen Konvention zum Schutz der Menschenrecht und Grundfreiheiten* (doctoral dissertation, Heidelberg, 1973). In this context note may also be taken of art. 32 of the 1969 American Convention on Human Rights (in force since July 1978). See *UN Yearbook on Human Rights* (1969), 390–400, at 394–5.

obligations for individuals in that it may oblige the legislature or the courts to protect individuals from one another in such fundamental respects as with regard to everyone's right to life (Article 2 of the Convention), or the right of everyone not to be held in slavery or servitude (Article 4). Similarly, the state may be required to ensure by appropriate means that, for example, the freedoms and rights enumerated in Articles 8, 9, 10, and 11 can in fact be exercised without the risk of physical harm or some form of violent action.[68] Articles 17 and 13 appear to weigh in favour of such an interpretation. Article 17 specifies that the Convention cannot be interpreted 'as implying for any state, *group* or *person* any right to engage in any activity or perform any act aimed at the destruction of any of the rights and freedoms . . . or at their limitation to a greater extent than is provided for in the Convention'.[69] Article 13 can be understood to provide an internationally guaranteed sanction when and if an *'effective* remedy before a *national* authority is *not* secured'.[70]

---

[68] Cf. Oral presentation of the Swedish Government's agent, H. Danelius, in Eur. Court HR, ser. B, no. 18 (1974-5) *Swedish Engine Drivers* case, 151-3. Also consult comments by J. E. S. Fawcett, at 124. In the *Matznetter* case, Eur. Court HR, ser. B no. 7 (1969), the Austrian Government's agent, W. Pahr, was of a more conservative leaning, see 228.

[69] Emphasis added. See also A. M. Williams, 'The European Convention on Human Rights: A New Use?', 12 *Texas Journal of International Law* (1977), 279-92, esp. at 288-91.

[70] Emphasis added. Cf. Raymond, n. 18 above, and Eissen, n. 67 above, at 244. Also see G. Sperduti, 'Nouvelles perspectives des Droits de l'Homme', IX *RDH/HRJ* (1976), 575-6; *Privacy and Human Rights* (ed. A. H. Robertson, 1973), esp. articles by J. Velu, (esp. 20-5), J. De Meyer, 255-75, and K. J. Partsch, 275-82; and P. Mertens, *Le droit de recours effectif devant les instances nationales en cas de violation d'un droit de l'homme* (1973), 103-9. F. Castberg notes on 12-13 of *The European Convention on Human Rights* (1973) that '[T]he argument based on Article 13 of the Convention is somewhat stronger [than that based on Article 17]. Here it is stipulated that anyone whose rights and freedoms under the Convention have been violated, shall have an effective remedy "notwithstanding that the violation has been committed by a person acting in an official capacity" and it seems to be assumed that public officials can violate the Convention even when acting as private persons. Should we not conclude that violations can be committed by any private person, and not only by public officials acting off duty?

'However, the wording of this provision is strange in several ways. For instance, it is peculiar that the right to a remedy is subject to a violation having taken place — thus an allegation of a violation does not suffice. The vague assumption of possible violations of the Convention by private persons seems to be too weak as a basis for reading into the Convention a general and direct obligation for private individuals to comply with it.'

Article 13 of the Convention is also discussed in ch. 2 above, sec. B.

In addition, Article 1 of the Convention considerably broadens the traditional principle of international law which is based upon the rule that a state can only be held responsible for acts committed by its nationals to the prejudice of nationals of other states. This Article may be understood to mean that states must ensure that individuals' rights are respected not only by public authorities but also by *all* other members of society ('the High Contracting Parties *shall ensure* [*reconnaissent*] to *everyone* within their jurisdiction the rights and freedoms . . .').[71] However, the Convention and its Protocols do not appear to establish direct obligations upon individuals *vis-à-vis* others.[72] Certainly, applications directed against private persons are inadmissible as being incompatible *ratione personae* (Article 25).

The extent to which the Convention organs may hold a state party responsible for violations of the Convention's provisions by private persons or organizations is difficult to determine with any accuracy, and the fact that violations of human rights can be made by institutions whose action cannot be controlled or influenced by state authorities illustrates the complexity of this problem.[73] Contributions to case-law on this subject are therefore particularly worthy of note. The Commission, in its report adopted on 27 May 1974 in the *National Union of Belgian Police* case, made the following observations concerning this matter:

It is true that the Convention fundamentally guarantees traditional freedoms in relation to the state as holder of public power. This does not, however, imply that the State may not be obliged to protect individuals through appropriate measures taken against some forms of interference by other individuals, groups or organisations. While they themselves under the Convention may not be held responsible for any such acts which are

---

[71] For an interesting discussion of this subject in a wider context see vol. ii, part 2, *Yearbook of the International Law Commission* (1977), 18–30.

[72] See n. 67 above; also H. Golsong, 'La Convention européenne des Droits de l'Homme et les personnes morales', 15–33, and S. Marcus-Helmons, 'Les personnes morales et le droit international', 35–81, esp. 68–73, in *Les Droits de l'Homme et les personnes morales* (first colloquy of the Human Rights Dept. of the Catholic University of Louvain, 1970.)

[73] See M. Sørensen, 'Do the Rights set forth in the European Convention on Human Rights in 1950 have the same significance in 1975?' in *Proceedings of the Fourth International Colloquy about the European Convention on Human Rights*, Rome, 5–8 Nov. 1975 (Council of Europe, 1976), 83–109, esp. Part III, ('Duties of Individuals') at 104–5. For a recent example consult *Jespers* v. *Belgium*, application no. 8403/78, 22 *D&R*, 100–30.

in breach of the Convention, the State may, *under certain circumstances* be responsible for them.[74]

Similarly, in paragraph 8 of its report dated 6 July 1976 in the case of *De Geillustreerde* v. *the Netherlands*,[75] the Commission expressed its opinion that '. . . the protection of the commercial interests of particular newspapers is not as such contemplated by the terms of Art. 10 of the Convention. These matters *might perhaps* raise an issue under this provision where a State fails in its duty to protect against excessive press-concentrations. . . .'

In comparison, the attitude of the European Court of Human Rights remains more cautious, and it appears from its two judgments on trade union freedom that, for the present, it has intentionally refrained from expressing an opinion on this matter.[76] In these cases, the distinction made by the Swedish Government — differentiating between its action in the capacity of a private employer (*jus gestionis*), as opposed to its *jus imperii* responsibilities — was not, in the eyes of the Court, a distinction which could be found either in Article 11 or in the Convention generally. The Court went on to say:

Article 11 is . . . binding upon the 'State as employer', whether the latter's relations with its employees are governed by public or private law. Consequently, the Court does not feel constrained to take into account the circumstances that in any event certain of the applicant's complaints appear to be directed against both the [Collective Bargaining] Office and the Swedish State as holder of public power. Neither does the Court consider that it has to rule on the applicability, direct or indirect, of Article 11 to relations between individuals *stricto sensu.*[77]

---

[74] Eur. Court HR, ser. B, no. 17 (1974-5), at 48, para. 59. (Emphasis added.) See also Commission's report in the *Swedish Engine Drivers* case, n. 68 above, at 41, para. 62. For earlier case-law see F. G. Jacobs, *The European Convention on Human Rights* (1975), 101 and 227, Eissen, n. 67 above, esp. at 158-9.

[75] Application 5178/71, report of Commission, 6 July 1976, 31; Committee of Ministers Resolution DH(77)1, 20 *Yearbook* (1977), 640-2. (Emphasis added.) See also Commission's comments in the case of the *Association of Parents of Vaccine Damaged Children* v. *UK* application 7154/75 declared inadmissible on 12 July 1978, at 9.

[76] See M.-A. Eissen, (oral intervention) in *Grundrechtsschutz in Europa. Europäische Menschenrechts-Konvention und Europäische Gemeinschaften*, Heidelberg, 28-30 Oct. 1976 (ed. H. Mosler, R. Bernhardt, and M. Hilf, 1977), at 41-42; see also comments of Trechsel, at 41, n. 24.

[77] Eur. Court HR, *Swedish Engine Drivers* case, judgment of 6 Feb. 1976, ser. A, vol. 20, at 14, para. 37, and *Schmidt and Dahlstrom* case, judgment of 6 Feb. 1976, ser. A, vol. 21, at 15, para. 33. See also comments by members of the European Commission of Human Rights in the Commission's report in the *König* case (adopted 14 Dec. 1976), 27-52.

More recent judgments of the Court, it is suggested, appear to clarify the situation somewhat. For example, as there now exists an established *jurisprudence constante* to the effect that the Convention imposes *positive* duties upon states,[78] can it not be argued that, *mutatis mutandis*, states are responsible not *for* but *with respect to* the conduct of public and private persons? Might not inactivity with regard to violations by others entail a state's responsibility on the international plane?[79] An *obiter* in the Court's judgment in the *Deweer* v. *Belgium* case is most revealing:

In an area concerning the public order (*ordre public*) of the member States of the Council of Europe, any measure or decision alleged to be in breach of Article 6 calls for particularly careful review. . . . The Court is not unaware of the firmness with which the Belgian courts have condemned, on the basis of Article 8 of the Convention and Article 6 of the Convention failure to respect the 'right to a court' in private legal relationships. . . . At least the same degree of vigilance would appear indispensable when someone formerly 'charged with a criminal offence' challenges a settlement that has barred criminal proceedings.[80]

Two cases which recently came before the Court are also of significance in this respect. The subject of indirect *Drittwirkung* was brought up in oral proceedings before the Court in the *Van Oosterwijck* v. *Belgium* case,[81] and the Court also briefly alluded to this problem — in the light of the Commission's findings — in the case of *Young, James, and Webster* v. *UK*, in which the Commission explained that:

. . . It is well established by now that apart from protecting the individual against State action, *there are Articles of the Convention which oblige the State to protect individual rights even against the action of others.*

---

[78] See the Strasbourg Court's judgments in the *Marckx, Airey,* and *Artico* cases, n. 63 above.

[79] See n. 71 above. A Soviet expert in this field has explained 'The state is not responsible for the fact that a private person is committing an act contrary to law, but for its own omission.' P. M. Kuris, *Mezhdunarodnyje prawonarushenia i otwetstwennost gosudarstwa* (1973), at 201. In this connection Lord McNair has used the term 'secondary liability' in *International Law Opinions* (1959), ii. at 288. Also consult C. Eagleton, *The Responsibility of States in International Law* (1928), at 214-24.

[80] Eur. Court HR, judgment of 27 Feb. 1980, ser. A, vol. 35, para. 49 at 25-6.

[81] Oral hearings of 24 Apr. 1980, Council of Europe doc. Cour/Misc. (80), 61, 14-18 (comments of Professor De Meyer, the Belgian Government's agent), and Cour/Misc. (80)62, 5-12 (Mr Custers, the Commission's delegate). Also consult the Commission's report, 1 Mar. 1979, esp. 9, 13, 17-20, and 24. In a similar case, application 6699/74, *X* v. *FRG*, a friendly settlement was reached. See report of Commission, 11 Oct. 1979 (and comments on legislative changes in the FRG, doc. Cour/Misc. (80)61, 28 ff.).

(European Court of Human Rights, Marckx Case, Judgment of 13 June 1979, p. 10). The Commission is of the opinion that Art. 11 is such a provision as far as dismissal on the basis of union activity or as a sanction for not joining a specific union is concerned. In the present cases it was the legal system that made it possible that the right to join trade unions was interfered with in the cases of the applicants. After having found that Art. 11 protects against this kind of compulsion, it follows that the State is responsible under the Convention if its legal system makes such dismissal lawful (cf. Application No. 4125/69, X. v. Ireland, Yearbook 14, p. 222). On this basis the responsibility of the United Kingdom is engaged in the present cases. [Paragraph 168.]

. . . In the light of the above findings, the Commission does not find it necessary to establish to which extent, if at all, the Government are responsible for the acts of British Rail, as the employer of the applicants. Having found that the failure to protect the applicants' rights under Art. 11 in their situation entails the responsibility of the Government for their legislation under Art. 11, irrespective of who is the employer, this alternative ground of responsibility would not be decisive in the present cases. [Paragraph 169.][82]

Thus, for the present, it still remains difficult to determine how the case-law of the Strasbourg organs will evolve with regard to the issues here discussed: The Court appears to be more restrained on this subject than does the Commission. If the *Van Oosterwijck* case were to have been dealt with on the merits, the interesting issue of the Belgian Government's responsibility of alleged violation of the rights of a transsexual by other private persons or private institutions might have been brought out.[83] Similarly, if the Court were to have been more explicit in the *Young, James, & Webster* case, by holding that the right to join a trade union under Article 11 of the Convention includes an implied 'inherent right' not to join a trade union,[84] the United Kingdom's policy of neutrality towards closed shop agreements

---

[82] Extract from Commission's report 14 Dec. 1979, p. 36. (Emphasis added.) See Eur. Court HR, judgment of 13 Aug. 1981, ser. A, vol. 44, para. 49. Also consult 6 *HR Rev.* (1981), 133–42.

[83] Eur. Court HR, judgment of 6 Nov. 1980, ser. A, vol. 40. This point was not pursued as the Court held that, by reason of the failure to exhaust domestic remedies, it could not examine the merits of Mr Van Oosterwijck's case.

[84] In his memorial (doc. Cour(78)2, of 27 Jan. 1978), in the *Klass* case before the European Court of Human Rights, Mr Sperduti considered that an ' "inherent right" must be understood as meaning a right which, because it constitutes the logically indispensable premise for, or the inevitable consequence of, the rules laid down, is so necessary in a rule-making context that it does not need to be expressly stated before it can be regarded as part of the system'. See also *X* v. *Belgium*, application 4072/69 in vol. 32, *Coll. of Dec.*, 80–6, at 86 (also reproduced in 13 *Yearbook* (1970), 708–21, at 718).

could have been examined at greater depth in Strasbourg with regard to the State's international responsibility.[85]

D. Assessment and implications

What conclusions can be drawn from the above observations, especially with regard to developments in domestic law of contracting states? Has the Convention's authority been expanded in the domestic forum as a consequence of this horizontal development? And if so, what is the actual value of such an expansion of this instrument's application into interpersonal relations? Adequate answers to these questions are unfortunately difficult to formulate with any precision.

As can be seen from the country-to-country survey above, the use of the norms of the European Convention on Human Rights to impose duties or obligations upon individuals is as yet a developing area of law, very much in embryonic form, in need of cautious and careful definition, and open to much justified criticism. In this context, therefore, certain self-evident points may need emphasis.[86] Most fundamental rights and freedoms protected by the Convention were already guaranteed by the existing domestic legal systems of contracting states prior to the Convention's existence. In addition, private persons have been and are in most instances provided with adequate avenues of redress against third parties under domestic law. The use of the Convention's provisions by the national judicial organs may also cause certain problems. In states where the Convention possesses a status of domestic law, it may appear, for example, that the rights embodied in Article 8 of the Convention — which guarantees the respect for private and family life — are of too global and absolute a character to be applied directly in a law-suit between private persons. In each of the contracting states there are considerable differences in social and legal systems, and national legislation may require constant adjustment and be worked out in detail in order to keep pace with

[85] See n. 82 above. Would it make a difference if the closed shop agreement were entered into by a trade union and a *private* institution? See T. C. Daintith, 'Methods and Scope of Protection of Fundamental Rights against Public and Private Bodies in Great Britain' in *Les Droits de l'Homme et les personnes morales*, n. 72 above, at 123–32.

[86] See in particular, comments of Partsch, n. 70 above, and Alkema, n. 49 above, esp. at 254–6.

various exigencies and evolution of ideas and techniques. For instance, many lawyers might find it difficult to accept as adequate a decision of a domestic court that would provide an individual redress by reference solely to Article 8 of the Convention when and if his honour and reputation have been interfered with by a third party, or if a modern scientific spying or eavesdropping technique had been used against him. Although the Convention obliges states parties to guarantee within their respective national jurisdictions the safeguard of individual rights to privacy against interference by state organs and private persons or institutions, this horizontal effect is most appropriately achieved by legislative measures in the fields of criminal, civil, and administrative law.[87] Thus, only when an individual is unable to sue another in respect of a right guaranteed under the Convention, or if existing domestic law appears not to comply with the international obligation entered into, the state may be held responsible when an application brought against it under either Article 24 or Article 25 is successful. To this extent, therefore, states' obligations under the Convention are of necessity limited in scope in respect of private law relations when these issues are presented before the Strasbourg organs.

It is nevertheless an undisputed fact that the Convention has acquired in some states a specific domestic position in cases between individuals, and this development certainly needs to be monitored closely. It should also be noted that domestic tribunals appear to a growing extent to take the Convention's norms into consideration when and if they provide a greater protection of human rights and fundamental freedoms than does domestic law, and that such reference need not necessarily be limited to those states in which the Convention is considered as a source of internal law. It may in practice be extremely difficult, however, to argue that the courts should take the Convention into consideration in those countries where it has not been incorporated into domestic law; but the possibility of this happening cannot be excluded altogether. What is probably

[87] But see articles by J. Velu (35-138), J. De Meyer (363-86), M. E. Loebenstein (349-58 and 394-9), and M. A. Vanwelkenhuyzen (400-7), in *Vie Privée et Droits de l'Homme* (Centre Universitaire de droit public, 1973). For English translations of the articles by Velu and De Meyer see *Privacy and Human Rights*, n. 70 above. Also see H. Guradze, *Die Europäische Menschenrechtskonvention* (1968), 20-3, and H. Guradze, 'Die Schutzrichtung der Grundrechtsnormen in der Europäischen Menschenrechtskonvention' in *Festschrift für H. C. Nipperdey* (1965), 759-69.

one of the more important aspects of the Convention's domestic applicability between private individuals is the fact that the judiciary may be able, to a limited extent, to control the action of non-governmental institutions and powerful individuals who may otherwise be considered to have acted within the bounds of ordinary law and yet beyond what is considered to be inimical to the fundamental interests and values of the society at large. In this context, the observations of Dr Eissen, the Registrar of the European Court of Human Rights, appear to be particularly instructive:

Que faut-il conclure? Tiendra t on pour évident que la Convention lie l'individu, ou qu'elle ne le lie pas? Ce serait, à coup sûr, pécher par présomption. Hésitations des gouvernements, controverses doctrinales et flottements de la jurisprudence illustrent la complexité d'un problème auquel les artisans de la Convention n'ont sans doute guère réfléchi au cours des travaux préparatoires. Aucun argument décisif ne démontre l'exactitude de la thèse de la 'Drittwirkung' ni de la conception opposée. La première semble pourtant compatible, pour le moins, avec les textes en vigueur; nous avons même la faiblesse de la croire plus solide que la seconde. Elle répond en tout cas beaucoup mieux, nous en avons la ferme conviction, aux besoins profonds du monde moderne. Elle gagne en outre du terrain auprès des juridictions nationales: n'est-ce point la preuve qu'elle offre un intérêt pratique appréciable et qu'elle n'a rien d'artificiel? Si l'on voit dans la Convention une réalité vivante appelée à se développer sans cesse, si l'on préfère aux délices stériles de l'exégèse la recherche de solutions à la fois respectueuses du droit et conformes au bien commun, pourquoi écarter une possibilité de progrès, pourquoi repousser une idée féconde et généreuse?[88]

This novel third-party or 'horizontal' *Drittwirkung* effect provided to the European Convention on Human Rights within the domestic legal structures of the member states may, in due course, be reflected to a greater extent in the jurisprudence of the Strasbourg organs.[89] Alternatively, were the European Court

---

[88] 'La Convention européenne des Droits de l'Homme et les obligations de l'individu: une mise à jour' in *Cassin*, iii. 151–62, at 162.

[89] See H. Mosler, 'L'influence du droit national sur la Convention européenne des Droits de l'Homme' in *Miscellanea W. J. Ganshof van der Meersch* (1972), i. 521–43. See also H. Strebe, 'Einwirkungen nationalen Rechts auf dem Völkerrecht' ['Municipal Law Influences upon International Law'] in 'Völkerrecht als Rechtsordnung — Grundlagen und Quellen', 36 *ZRV* (1976), 168–89; and recent *dicta* in the judgments of the European Court of Human Rights in the cases of *König* (28 June 1978), para. 89, *Engel and others* (8 June/23 Nov. 1976), para. 82, and *Deweer* (27 Feb. 1980), para. 49.

or the Commission of Human Rights to apply the provisions of the Convention in this direction, there is firm evidence to suggest that domestic tribunals may follow suit.

Chapter 9

The Domestic Application of the Convention and European Community Law

A. Preliminary remarks: incorporation and non-incorporation

The developing case-law of the Court of Justice of the European Communities relating to 'general principles of European Community law' — and its increasing reference to the European Convention on Human Rights and other sources of fundamental rights — suggests that the European Convention may have been accommodated into the corpus of European Community law.[1] This 'communitization' of the European Convention may well endow on its substantive provisions special features of Community law in relation to national law, thus radically altering the Convention's status in the domestic law of the ten states parties which are members of the European Community.[2] In the words of the former President of the Luxembourg Court:

Just as Community law has become effectively established thanks to national courts, so the [European] Convention [on Human Rights] can become part of national legislation by means of the combined compulsory force of the decisions of the Court of Justice and national judgments. By interpreting Community law in the light of the Convention, the Court of Justice would place the efficacy of its decisions at the latter's disposal. Direct effect, uniformity, the primacy of Community law could also help the rights safeguarded by the Convention to penetrate both into the Community *and each of the member States.*[3]

---

[1] i.e. integrated into the legal order of the Community. On this subject see the excellent study by W. J. Ganshof van der Meersch 'L'ordre juridique des communautés européennes et le droit international', 148 *R. des C.* (1975), v. 1-433, esp. 144-95, at 161-80; G. Bebr, *The Development of Judicial Control of the European Communities* (1981), 649-61, 701-15; and sec. C below.

[2] D. Evrigenis, 'Reflections on the National Dimension of the European Convention on Human Rights' in *Proceedings of the Colloquy about the European Convention on Human Rights in Relation to other International Instruments for the Protection of Human Rights*, Athens, 21-2 Sept. 1978 (Council of Europe, 1979), 65-80, at 78. (The Court of Justice of the European Communities will hereinafter be cited as 'the Luxembourg Court'.)

[3] R. Lecourt, 'Interferences between the European Convention on Human Rights and the Community Law concerning the Community and National Judicial Control' in Athens colloquy, n. 2 above, 81-107, at 91. (Emphasis added.)

In a similar vein, Dr Toth, in a remarkable study of the Luxembourg Court's case-law, has explained the situation thus:

. . . the Court of Justice [of the European Communities] must regard the standards of protection laid down in the Convention as a yardstick not only in reviewing the legality of the acts of the institutions, *but also in assessing the compatibility with Community law (which now includes the principles enshrined in the Convention) of the conduct of the Member States.* Thus, without impinging upon the jurisdiction of the national courts or of the European Commission and Court of Human Rights, the European Court may (and must) examine, in cases properly brought before it, *any infringement of a fundamental right by a national authority* at least to the extent to which the right alleged to have been infringed may involve a human value of an economic or social nature whose protection falls within the specific objectives and provisions of primary or secondary Community law.[4]

But what is the exact connection between the above citations and the Convention's domestic status? This question requires a reply. The European Convention on Human Rights has been incorporated into the domestic law of the six founding members of the European Communities: Belgium, France, the Federal Republic of Germany, Italy, Luxembourg, and the Netherlands; as well, it has been incorporated by Greece, a member state as of 1 January 1981. It has *not* been incorporated into the legal systems of the three remaining members: Denmark, Ireland, and the United Kingdom.[5] There is a possibility, however, that the instrument's provisions can be cited as persuasive sources of law before domestic courts in all the member states of the European Communities, assuming the European Convention forms part of the corpus of Community law. If this view is accepted, the Convention's provisions will have to be considered by domestic courts in Denmark, Ireland, and the UK as binding norms that must — in certain cases — be applied by them when issues of European Community law are raised, *despite* the fact that this international instrument has not been formally incorporated into internal law.[6] Although this line of reasoning raises a variety of intricate and delicate issues in constitutional, European

---

[4] A. G. Toth, *Legal Protection of Individuals in the European Communities* (1978), i, at 110. (Emphasis added.)

[5] See Part II above, chs. 3 to 7, *passim*. Interestingly enough both potential members of the Communities have secured for the Convention the status of domestic law. These states are Portugal and Spain. Turkey, which has also recently indicated an interest in joining, has likewise incorporated the Convention into domestic law.

[6] See, for example, P. Karpenstein and S. A. Crossick, 'Pleading Human Rights in British Courts — the Impact of EEC Law', 78 *Law Society Gazette* (1981), 90–1.

Community, and international law, it is of sufficient importance to merit at least brief consideration within the more general framework of a study assessing the European Convention's domestic status.

B. The Convention as part of Community law in the domestic forum?

Probably one of the most difficult and complex aspects of European Community law is its relationship with the domestic law of the ten member states, and a study of this relationship is here impossible. It is sufficient for present purposes to note two important decisions of the Luxembourg Court. In one it held that '. . . the Community constitutes a new legal order in international law, for whose benefit the States have limited their sovereign rights, albeit within limited fields, and the subjects of which comprise not only member states but also their nationals'.[7] In another it held that 'By contrast with ordinary international treaties, the EEC Treaty has created its own legal system which, on the entry into force of the Treaty, became an integral part of the legal systems of the member states and which their courts are bound to apply'.[8] It follows that European Community law possesses four specific characteristics: it is an independent legal order or system; it is common to all member states; it must prevail over any domestic law which is incompatible with it; and it can and often does confer rights and impose obligations directly on private persons in the member states.[9]

---

[7] Case 26/62, *Van Gend en Loos* v. *Nederlandse Administratie der Belastingen* [1963] ECR 1, at 12; [1963] CMLR 105, at 129.

[8] Case 6/64, *Costa* v. *ENEL* [1964] ECR 585, at 593; [1964] CMLR 425, at 455. Also consult case 106/77, *Amministrazione delle Finanze dello Stato* v. *Simmenthal* [1978] ECR 629, [1978] 3 CMLR 670, where the court held that 'every national court must, in a case within its jurisdiction, apply Community law in its entirety and protect rights which the latter confers on individuals and must accordingly set aside any provision of national law which may conflict with it, whether prior or subsequent to the Community rule'.

[9] See J.-P. Warner, 'The Relationship between European Community Law and the National Laws of Member States', 93 *LQR* (1977), 348–66, at 349. For further reference consult H. G. Schermers, *Judicial Protection in the European Communities* (1979). See also O. Jacot-Guillarmod, *Droit communautaire et droit international public* (1979), A. G. Toth, *Legal Protection of Individuals in the European Communities*, vol. i (1978), L. Collins, *European Community Law in the United Kingdom* (1980), and D. Lasok and J. W. Bridge, *An Introduction to the Law and Institutions of the European Communities* (1982). It is important to appreciate that the term 'direct effect' in the European Community context means that individuals are

A unique feature of this body of law is that there exists an organic link between the Community Court in Luxembourg and courts and tribunals of member states whereby harmonious application and coherent development of this common system of law can be maintained. The implementation of Community law is primarily carried out by the authorities of member states and applied by their domestic courts, which possess an *exclusive* jurisdiction to apply it in disputes between individuals and between individuals and domestic state authorities.[10] In effect, the European Community legal order has become part of the legal system of member states although it functions independently through an institutional machinery of its own, in order to attain the aims prescribed by the Treaties; it is an autonomous legal order as well as being a body of law which is partially integrated into legal systems of member states, whose domestic courts and tribunals interpret it (although not with a final binding force), apply it, and enforce it.[11] It must therefore be understood, for the purposes of this study, that whereas:

. . . la Convention [européenne des Droits de l'Homme] a permis aux États de maintenir pour les rapports du droit national et de la Convention un système dualiste; dans certains pays un juge national serait donc obligé de maintenir en vigueur une loi nationale et de donner la préférence sur la Convention . . . [This is *not* the case with regard to European Community law.] . . . La seule différence qui existe donc entre les deux régimes *en ce qui concerne la place des juges nationaux* est que le juge national est obligé d'être juge communautaire, tandis que le juge national qui ne se reconnaîtrait pas compétent pour sanctionner la Convention européenne des Droits de l'Homme perd son rôle naturel d'instance préalable au regard des mécanismes de protection européens.[12]

An obvious deduction can be made from the above information: the essential features of European Community law,

bestowed with certain Community rights which are juridically enforceable; it is possible to say that if clear and complete provisions exist, containing absolute duties and in particular leaving no scope for the exercise of a discretionary power, the said provision of Community law possesses direct effect. See Warner, at 354–9, D. Wyatt and A. Dashwood, *The Substantive Law of the EEC* (1980), 25–42; and T. C. Hartley, *The Foundations of European Community Law* (1981), *passim*.

[10] See L. Neville Brown and F. G. Jacobs, *The Court of Justice of the European Communities* (1977), 137.

[11] For more details see n. 9 above and K. Kujath, *Bibliography on European Integration* (1977), esp. 216–31 and 256–69.

[12] P. Reuter, 'Conclusions', 788–94, at 793, made at the *Colloque de Grenoble*, 25–6 Jan. 1973, entitled 'L'efficacité des mécanismes juridictionnels de protection des personnes privées dans le cadre européen', VI *RDH/HRJ* (1973), 603–799. (Emphasis added.)

namely binding force, uniformity, and in particular its primacy
and direct effect in domestic law, clearly indicate that some sort
of common European law is taking shape within specific areas
circumscribed by this evolving body of law. Unfortunately, the
constitutions of the ten member states do not all provide clearly
for the supremacy of Community law over domestic law within
their respective internal legal orders. As a direct result of this,
domestic courts have in many instances found it exceedingly
difficult to accommodate this rather unique body of Community
law into their respective legal systems.[13] Thus, although the
Dutch Constitution specifically provides for the supremacy of
European Community law, including secondary Community law,
over constitutional provisions,[14] no other country's constitution
or legislative enactments appear to be so explicit in this respect.
In Luxembourg and in Belgium case-law has in fact assured the
supremacy of Community law. In Luxembourg a constitutional
revision in 1956 added Article 49 *bis*, whereby certain powers
reserved by the Constitution to the legislature, the executive,
and the judiciary can be devolved upon international institutions.[15] the EEC and Euratom Treaties were ratified on the
basis of this provision. The Belgian Constitution was completely
silent as regards the domestic application of both international
and European Community law up to 1970, when a new provision,
Article 25 *bis* was inserted. The Constitution has now been
interpreted to achieve full supremacy of Community law.[16] In
France Article 26 of the 1946 Constitution was in force when
the country acceded to the Communities. This article provided
that 'diplomatic treaties which have been properly ratified and
published shall have the force of law even where they conflict
with French law without any necessity to adopt legislative
provisions for the purposes of their implementation other than
those necessary to ratify them'. But although Article 55 of the
present Constitution now lays down that treaties have 'authority

---

[13] See generally on this subject P. Pescatore, 'Address on the Application of European Community Law in Each of the Member States' in *Judicial and Academic
Conference*, Luxembourg, 27-8 Sept. 1976 (1979), paper VI, esp. 17-29 (a good
bibliography is provided on 36-45). Also consult vol. i, *Remedies for Breach of
Community Law* (Reports of 9th *FIDE* Conference, London, 25-7 Sept. 1980),
in particular the various national reports; and G. Bebr, *The Development of Judicial
Control of the European Communities* (1981), esp. 613-701.

[14] Arts. 65-7 of the Constitution: see ch. 3 above, sec. D.

[15] See ch. 3 above, sec. C, and case-law cited there.

[16] Consult ch. 3 above, sec. A, in which an extract of the famous *Le Ski* case and
other case-law is cited.

superior to that of laws', Community law has been interpreted by the French courts rather restrictively with the result that this body of law is permitted only a certain measure of supremacy in the internal legal system.[17] The Danish Constitution provides for the 'delegation' of powers vested in the authorities of the realm to international institutions,[18] while Article 29 of the Irish Constitution was amended in 1971, and it now provides that Community law cannot be invalidated by any of the Constitution's provisions.[19] In the UK, as in Denmark and Ireland, the application of Community law by domestic courts appears to raise no major problems;[20] legislative measures invoked in all three new member states provide, in substantively identical terms, that Community law must take effect in the domestic legal system in accordance with the provisions of European Community law itself.[21] Both the German and Italian Constitutions provide for the transfer of sovereign powers to international institutions, but do not clarify the issue of whether law emanating from such institutions enjoys supremacy over domestic constitutional provisions.[22] Lastly it may be added that Greece, the newest and tenth member state, as well as Portugal and Spain (both at present negotiating terms of accession) have, in their new Constitutions, drafted specific provisions in order to accommodate the primacy and direct effect of Community law.[23]

This overview is somewhat inadequate on account of the enormous number of constitutional and legislative factors, but some tentative conclusions concerning the application of Community law by domestic courts can be drawn, and, more

[17] See, for a general survey, G. A. Bermann, 'French Treaties and French Courts: Two Problems of Supremacy', 28 *ICLQ* (1979), 458-90; and F. Weiss, 'Self-Executing Treaties and Directly Applicable EEC Law in French Courts', *LIEI* 1979/1, 51-84. Also consult case-law and references cited in ch. 3 above, sec. B.

[18] Art. 20 of the Constitution. See ch. 5 above, sec. A.

[19] See J. M. Kelly, *The Irish Constitution* (1980), 152-4. Art. 29 of the Constitution is reproduced verbatim in ch. 7 above, sec. B.

[20] Although difficulties do occasionally crop up: see references in n. 9 above. Also consult J. Jaconelli, 'Constitutional Review and Section 2(4) of the European Communities Act 1972', 28 *ICLQ* (1979), 65-71.

[21] See Warner, n. 9 above, esp. 360-6.

[22] Schermers, n. 9 above, at 92-7. Art. 24 of the FRG's Constitution is reproduced in ch. 4 above, sec. B, and art. 11 of the Italian Constitution is reproduced in ch. 6 above, sec. B.

[23] See ch. 6 above, sec. A, C, and D, and references cited there. For a recent article on Greek accession consult A. A. Fatouros, 'Greece Joins the Communities', 6 *EL Rev.* (1981), 495-503.

importantly, it can be shown how the issue of the protection of fundamental human rights has arisen within the context of European Community law. Once this is illustrated, the role (or potential role) of the European Convention on Human Rights as an integral part of this body of law may be more fully appreciated. It is within this constitutionally uncertain, often diversified, and constantly evolving field of judicial 'domestic accommodation' of European Community law — the attribution of whose legal supremacy has found acceptance in the Luxembourg Court's case-law as well as in legal literature — that the issue of fundamental human rights has surfaced. Thus, in both the FRG and in Italy fundamental human rights are constitutionally protected. As a result both the *Bundesverfassungsgericht* and the *Corte Costituzionale*, which exercise constitutional review and examine constitutionality of legislative acts, regard fundamental rights of individuals as an inviolable part of that superior order. Without describing in detail the case-law that has evolved in both these countries in recent years, it is sufficient to note here that whereas the *Bundesverfassungsgericht*, in its famous decision of 29 May 1974, expressly accepted the possibility that it might hold unconstitutional certain provisions of secondary Community law that infringed basic human rights enumerated in the Republic's *Grundgesetz* (Basic Law),[24] the *Corte Costituzionale*, in the *Frontini* case of 18 Dec. 1973, which approached this problem in a rather more indirect manner, rejected any domestic review of secondary Community rules but did not exclude the possibility that it might control the basic Act of Ratification if European Community law infringed constitutionally protected rights of Italian citizens.[25] The *Bundesverfassungsgericht's* attitude was slightly modified in a recent decision in which it held, *obiter*, that 'The Court leaves open whether,

---

[24] 37 *Bverfg.* (1974), 271; [1974] CMLR 540. There is an enormous amount of literature on this case, some of which is referred to in notes to ch. 4 above, sec. B. See in particular W. R. Edeson and F. Wooldridge, 'European Community Law and Fundamental Human Rights: Some Recent Decisions of the European Court and National Courts', *LIEI* 1976/1, 1-54; an article by the author, 'Fundamental Rights and European Communities: Recent Developments', II *HR Rev.* (1977), 69-86; and P. Malanczuk, 'The Supremacy of EEC Law and Human Rights in the Constitution of West Germany', 12 *Bracton Law Journal* (1978/79), 51-62.

[25] In *Foro padana* (1974) iii.10; *Giurisprudenza italiana* (1974), 513; [1974] 2 CMLR 372. Commentaries on this case can be found in Edeson and Wooldridge, n. 24 above, at 48-52; G. Bebr, 'A Critical Review of Recent Case Law of National Courts', 11 *CML Rev.* (1974), 408-31, esp. Part I; and in a case-note by S. Neri, 10 *RTDE* (1974), at 154-9. Also see recent overview of Italian case-law by P. Gori, 6 *EL Rev.* (1981), 222-7.

and if so, to what extent — for instance, in view of political and legal developments in the European sphere occurring in the meantime — the principles contained in its decision of 29 May 1974 can continue to claim validity without limitation in respect of future references of norms of derived Community law'.[26] It may be of interest to note, however, that the basic problem still remains unresolved: should primacy be given to states' constitutional concepts or to directly enforceable European Community law if and when an apparent conflict exists? [27]

Both in the Federal Republic of Germany and in Italy, and possibly in other states,[28] there is an understandable reluctance on the part of the judiciary to curtail the scope and observance of what the courts consider essential guarantees of human rights and freedoms that may be limited (not to say infringed) by the applicability of an outside set of rules and regulations. In effect, there is strong argument to support the reasoning that individuals should not be subjected to a new bureaucratic authority bound neither by constitutionally protected human rights norms (or equivalent domestic guarantees) nor by a discernible catalogue of fundamental human rights within the framework of the Community structure. Whether the Community catalogue takes the form of an extensively enumerated list — as provided in the German and Italian Constitutions — or, alternatively, whether individuals' rights are adequately protected by a relatively loose

[26] *FA Steinike and Weinlig* v. *Bundesamt für Ernährung und Forstwirtschaft*, case 2, BvL 6/77, judgment of 25 July 1979, 6 *EGZ* (1979), 547–51; and [1980] 2 CMLR 531, at 537. The Court considered itself formally bound by interpretative decisions of the Luxembourg Court given in the same case, adding, at 534, that in proceedings under art. 100(1) of the *Grundgesetz* 'an examination of whether norms or principles of the Constitution prevent the application of rules of the EEC Treaty is only proper if, in this respect, it is the German ratification statute to the Treaty which is the object of examination . . . The inapplicability of primary Community law for reasons of contrary federal constitutional law is unthinkable without — if necessary — partial incompatibility of the ratification statute with the Constitution.' In its *obiter dictum*, although the Court does not expressly mention what it means by 'political and legal developments in the European sphere' it would appear that this refers to the recent case-law of the Luxembourg Court, the European Parliamentary elections, and possibly also the Joint Declaration on Fundamental Rights by the Community's political institutions on 5 Apr. 1977 (OJ 103 of 27 Apr. 1977) and the Brussels Commission's memorandum on the accession of the Communities to the European Convention on Human Rights (*Bull. EC Suppl.* 2/79).

[27] This problem may also crop up in Ireland, the third European Community member state in which constitutionality of legislation may be examined, as well as in two potential member states, Portugal and Spain.

[28] See ibid. Also consult M. Sørensen, 'Compétences supranationales et pouvoirs constitutionnels en droit danois', *Miscellanea W. J. Ganshof van der Meersch* (1972), ii. 481–92.

and disjointed list of rights and freedoms, as appears to be emerging at present, is not of crucial importance in this context.[29] It is in the shadow of this general debate relating to the harmonious and uniform development of European Community law and in particular to the way in which it is applied by domestic courts, and to the possible inconsistency of this law — especially secondary Community legislation — with constitutionally entrenched provisions, that the European Convention has come to be considered and 'adopted' by the Luxembourg Court.[30] The organic link existing between the Luxembourg Court's *interpretation* of Community law and the domestic courts' *application* of this law in specific cases provides an avenue for the Convention's provisions to dovetail into the domestic forum as an integral part of European Community law. In short, it can be assumed that the Luxembourg Court's considerable stress on its role as guardian of respect of human rights, and its reference to the Convention's norms to substantiate its holdings to this effect, must be explained in the context of two interrelated developments: the transfer of important national functions to Community organs which were not subject to the same obligations, in respect of fundamental human rights, as had been binding on state organs previously exercising these functions, and the resultant reluctance of certain domestic courts — especially in the Federal Republic of Germany and Italy — to subject domestic constitutional standards to Community law, both of which needed 'accommodation' in order that the unique common system of Community law be maintained.

A study of domestic case-law of the ten member states of the European Communities indicates that to date — with two apparent exceptions in the UK — there have been no reported decisions in which a court has been prepared to grapple with the rather delicate problem of the Convention's status as an integral component of European Community law which must be enforced in the domestic forum. The only reported cases in which this argument has been considered (admittedly in a rather circuitous manner) are those of *Allgemeine Gold- und Silberscheideanstalt* v. *Customs and Excise Commissioners*,[31] and *Kaur* v. *Lord*

---

[29] Further on this subject see the study of Professor R. Bernhardt in *Bull. EC Suppl.* 5/76, *passim*, M. Hilf, 'The Protection of Fundamental Rights in the Community' in *European Law and the Individual* (ed. F. G. Jacobs, 1976) 145–60, and publications referred to in n. 24 above.

[30] An overview of case-law is provided in sec. C below.

[31] [1978] 2 CMLR 291 (at first instance).

Advocate.[32] Interestingly enough, the cases were argued in domestic court proceedings in a country which has *not* incorporated the European Convention's provisions into domestic law! In the former case, the plaintiff, a West German gold and silver refining company, began an action in the UK courts against the Customs and Excise Commissioners claiming that they were the rightful owners of 1,500 gold coins (South African Krugerrands) which had been confiscated by the latter after an unsuccessful attempt had been made by three men to smuggle the coins into the UK. The German company claimed that they had been fraudulently induced by two of the three convicted men to part with the coins, and requested declarations to the effect that they were entitled to the return of the confiscated Krugerrands. Their action was unsuccessful both at first instance and upon appeal.[33] What is of particular interest in the context of the present study is that counsel for the plaintiff suggested to the trial judge that he should ask the Luxembourg Court to give a preliminary ruling — as provided in Article 177 of the EEC Treaty — in order to find out whether Title 1 and in particular Chapter 2 of the Treaty[34] imposes upon member states an obligation not to confiscate property without compensation where that property is of a national of any member state other than the confiscating state. To use the words of the trial judge:

The novelty of this question lies in the fact that [counsel for the plaintiff] does not suggest that any particular Article or Articles of this Treaty has this effect. He paints with a much broader brush. In his submission the Treaty governs all matters concerning inter-state freedom of movement of goods and within that area impliedly guarantees respect for fundamental rights.

The trial judge then went on to say

... [Counsel for the plaintiff] has satisfied me that the fundamental human rights enshrined in the European Convention on Human Rights are relevant to a consideration of the rights and duties of the Community institutions. However, the Commissioners of Customs and Excise are not in this category. He has also satisfied me that they [i.e. the human rights

[32] [1980] 3 CMLR 79.

[33] On appeal, it appears that the Convention was put forward as an *auxiliary* argument to support the view that art. 1 of its First Protocol (see n. 70 below) in itself, or in conjunction with the well established principles of public international law relating to the confiscation of property, obliged the Commissioners of Customs and Excise to have regard to its provisions. Cf. [1980] 2 WLR 555, at 557(D), 558(F), and 561.

[34] Relating to the 'free movement of goods' (Part Two, Title 1, ch. 2, arts. 30–7).

provisions enshrined in the European Convention] may be part of the *background* against which the express provisions of the Treaty *have* to be interpreted. But in this case he has to go much further and satisfy me that they are an unexpressed part of the Treaty. In support of this argument he relies upon the observations of Trabucchi A.-G. in *Watson* v. *Belmann* (118/75).[35] However, I think that these observations have to be considered in the context of an argument on the meaning of specific provisions of the Treaty. They do not in my judgment support a submission that the Treaty contains implied Articles relating to human rights.[36]

It is sufficient to make only two comments in respect of this case. First of all, it appears from the above citation that the trial judge, J. Donaldson, may have accepted implicitly that the Convention's substantive norms are an integral part of European Community law which *must* be taken into consideration by domestic courts in situations where *specific* provisions of the EEC Treaty need elucidation.[37] Secondly, it seems rather unfortunate that the *acte clair* doctrine was applied by the trial judge, in that a ruling on this important point by the Luxembourg Court would certainly have been most instructive.[38]

The second case, that of *Kaur* v. *Lord Advocate*, merits only brief mention because, unlike in the *Allgemeine Gold* case, the substantive issues raised had no relevance to European Community law,[39] Mrs Kaur was an illegal immigrant (overstayer) of

[35] [1976] ECR 1185; [1976] 2 CMLR 552. Extracts from the observations of Trabucchi A.-G. are cited in sec. D, below.

[36] *Per* J. Donaldson, n. 31 above, at 294-5. (Emphasis added.) He then concluded, at 295: '[12] The Solicitor-General submits that the Treaty of Rome takes effect according to its express terms and that there are no implied Articles. He asks, forensically, why so many distinguished people are wasting so much time debating the need for a new Bill of Rights incorporating the provisions of the European Convention on Human Rights, if we already have one in the Treaty of Rome and the relevant British legislation giving effect to that Treaty. It is a good question. In his submission section 44 of the 1952 Act is quite unaffected by the Treaty of Rome. If the plaintiffs think that British domestic legislation infringes the European Convention their remedy lies in a complaint to the European Court of Human Rights.

'[13] I accept the Solicitor-General's submission and do not think that it is necessary to refer any question to the European Court in this case. In the existing state of British law the Krugerrands are, in my judgment, liable to forfeiture under section 44(f) of the Customs and Excise Act 1952, and I have asked counsel on both sides to agree what form of judgment will be most appropriate.'

[37] Such as may be the case, for example, with regard to arts. 7, 48, and 119 of the EEC Treaty. Consult G. Cohen-Jonathan, 'La Cour des Communautés européennes et les Droits de l'Homme', *RMC* (1978), 74-100.

[38] For a critical assessment of the *acte clair* doctrine consult G. Bebr, 'Article 177 of the EEC Treaty in the Practice of National Courts', 26 *ICLQ* (1977), 241-82.

[39] [1980] 3 CMLR 79, commented upon by W. Finnie, 25 *Journal of the Law Society of Scotland* (1980), 434-9. This is apparently the first reported case in which the Convention's domestic status in Scottish law has been argued at length. Mrs

Indian nationality who had three children while in the UK. The three children therefore acquired British nationality as of right. Both Mrs Kaur and her husband (the latter had entered the UK illegally) were deported from the UK pursuant to certain provisions in the 1971 Immigration Act. Although Mrs Kaur did not challenge the legality if her deportation, she considered that her deportation amounted to a breach of Article 8 of the European Human Rights Convention as well as Article 3 of its Fourth Protocol. This argument was rejected outright as the Convention is not part of Scottish law, not to mention the fact that the Fourth Protocol remains unratified by the UK. An additional argument put forward — likewise dismissed — was that the Convention might be part of UK law *via* European Community law. In his judgment Lord Ross accepted 'that for some purposes at least the European Court [in Luxembourg] does enforce the principles contained in the Convention',[40] but, after referring to the pertinent case-law on the subject, he concluded 'that the European Court does not deal with fundamental rights in the abstract; it only deals with them if they arise under Treaties and have a bearing on Community law questions'.[41] And, as the issues raised in this case had no Community law content whatsoever — Mrs Kaur was not even a national of a Community member state — he rejected the suggestion that a request for an interpretation be made in accordance with Article 177.[42]

Developments in the courts of other European Community member states can only be speculated upon. In countries where the Convention already possesses the status of domestic law, intricate (and possibly confusing) issues may have to be considered. Indeed, the Convention's positioning in the domestic hierarchy may differ if its provisions are considered a directly enforceable element of Community law on the one hand, and as directly applicable international treaty norms on the other. Likewise, the establishment of a 'passport-union' within the Community legal structure may require the setting-up of standards in such matters as asylum, the status of refugees,

---

Kaur's application before the European Commission in Strasbourg was unsuccessful: see application 8245/78, admissibility decision of 6 May 1981.

[40] Ibid., at 95.   [41] Ibid., at 96.

[42] Lord Ross did add a rider that if the claimant had made a prima-facie case to the effect that a right under Community law arose within the context of the EEC Treaty, he would have been inclined to use his discretion and make a reference under art. 177.

the granting of residence permits to immigrants and their families, expulsion, etc. These 'Community' standards, duly implemented into domestic law, might conflict with the requirements of Articles 3 and 8 of the European Convention, and also Article 2 of the First Protocol and Article 4 of the Fourth Protocol. Similarly, conflicts might arise in such areas as freedom of association, freedom of movement, and the prohibition of discrimination.[43] Which of the two directly enforceable sets of norms — Community or Convention — would be given priority by domestic courts were differences to emerge? Does the autonomous nature of European Community law secure this body of law a hierarchically superior status in Italy and Germany where the Convention is by and large considered to be a classical treaty which has been 'transformed' and given the rank of ordinary legislation? An auxiliary though important matter — in this context — is the question of precedence granted by domestic courts to conflicting provisions of international agreements. Take for instance Belgium, Luxembourg, and the Netherlands: assuming a conflict were to arise between a ruling or judgment of the Luxembourg Court and a provision of the European Convention, can the courts by virtue of Article 234 of the EEC Treaty uphold the Convention's norms against any judgment or interpretation of the Luxembourg Court which is deemed to be incompatible? Would the same apply in France, which only ratified the Convention in 1974?[44] These and many other issues will need serious consideration in the not too distant future.[45]

In those states which have *not* incorporated the Convention into domestic law, the legislative and executive branches of the states concerned will presumably wish to stem this hybrid development. Would such an attitude be justified? It is unnecessary to answer this question in the present study; suffice it to

---

[43] See *FIDE Conference*, Dutch report, II/11, esp. 34–7, now published in a revised form: E. A. Alkema, 'Fundamental Human Rights and the Legal Order of the Netherlands' in *International Law in the Netherlands* (1980), 109–46. Also see H. Golsong, 'Grundrechtsschutz im Rahmen der Europäischen Gemeinschaften', 5 *EGZ* (1978), 346–52, and references in n. 45 below.

[44] See *FIDE Conference*, ibid., at 37–41. Also consult a case-note by the author in 91 *LQR* (1975), 311–13.

[45] Other examples of potential areas of conflict are referred to by G. Cohen-Jonathan, in a *Rapport* published in V *RDH/HRJ* (1973), 615–49, at 624–7; and by M. Sørensen, 'Meeting Points between the European Convention on Human Rights and the Law of the European Communities' in *Information of the Court of Justice of the European Communities* (1977) iii. 41–52, at 46–51.

say that awareness of this (potential) development has increased in the three countries concerned, namely Denmark,[46] Ireland,[47] and the UK.[48] Likewise, these developments appear to be closely monitored in Greece,[49] the newest member state, as well as in Portugal[50] and Spain.[51]

C. Decisions of the Court of Justice of the European Communities[52]

The problem of basic rights first arose in the case-law of the Luxembourg Court in 1958–9 when, in the *Stork* case[53] it refused to take into consideration the argument that a national of a Community member state should enjoy — within the ambit of

[46] See Sørensen, n. 28 above, and O. Espersen, 'E.F. og de grundlovssikrede menneskerettigheder' (EC and Constitutionally Guaranteed Human Rights), 59 *Juristen* (1977), 487–90. Also J. Færkel, 'The Position of Fundamental Rights in the National Legal System of Denmark; Constitutional Supremacy, General Relationship to International Law and Community Law' unpublished report presented at a human rights seminar at the European University Institute, Florence, May 1977, esp. at 13–16. It is interesting to note that before Norway's abortive attempt to join the European Communities, a Norwegian lawyer appears to have foreseen some of the present problems relating to the protection of human rights when he wrote, 'I have assumed that the commitment may be irrevocable under international law, but must be understood with an "implied reservation" under constitutional law'. (T. Opsahl, 'Limitations of Sovereignty under the Norwegian Constitution', 13 *Scandinavian Studies in Law* (1969), 151–77, at 173; as well as his article in 9 *CML Rev.* (1972), 217–92, esp. at 283–4.)

[47] See Kelly, n. 19 above, and J. Temple Lang, 'Legal and Constitutional implications for Ireland of Adhesion to the EEC Treaty', 9 *CML Rev.* (1972), 167–78; and comments by B. McMahon, 2 *EL Rev.* (1977), 150–4, at 151.

[48] See extract from a Home Office memorandum of Sept. 1978 reproduced in 49 *BYIL* (1978), at 365–6; report of the Standing Advisory Commission on Human Rights, *The Protection of Human Rights by Law in Northern Ireland*, Cmnd. 7009 (1977), 48–50; and Sir L. Scarman, *English Law — the New Dimension* (1974), at 12–13.

[49] See, for example, D. Evrigenis, 'Legal and Constitutional Implications of Greek Accession to the European Communities', 17 *CML Rev.* (1980), 157–69, esp. 162–4.

[50] See I. Jalles, *Implications juridico-constitutionnelles de l'adhésion aux Communautés européennes. Le cas du Portugal* (1981), esp. at 180–214 (problems concerning confiscation of property and Portugal's reservation to art. 1 of the Human Rights Convention's First Protocol are discussed at 187–90); and M. E. Gonçalves, 'Quelques problèmes juridiques que pourra poser l'application du droit communautaire dans l'ordre juridique portugais face à la Constitution de 1976', *RTDE* (1980), 662–93.

[51] See, for example, M. Medina, *La Comunidad Europea y sus principios constitucionales* (1974), esp. at 122–5.

[52] Literature on this subject is extensive. Bibliographies are provided in *Grundrechtsschutz in Europa* (H. Mosler, R. Bernhardt, and M. Hilf, 1977) at 229–39; and in Dr O. Jacot-Guillarmod's *Droit communautaire et droit international public* (1979), at 140–1 and 204.

[53] Case 1/58 [1959] ECR 17.

Community law — protection of certain human rights provisions which were guaranteed by the Constitution of a member state. It explained:

... the Court is only required to ensure that in the interpretation and application of the Treaty, and of rules laid down for implementation thereof, the law is observed. It is not normally required to rule on provisions of national law. Consequently, the High Authority is not empowered to examine a ground of complaint which maintains that, when it adopted its decision, it infringed principles of German constitutional law.[54]

It was not until ten years later that the Court was actually prepared expressly to include fundamental rights of the individual as being part of the general principles of Community law. In the famous *Stauder* case concerning the allocation of vouchers for reduced-price butter,[55] an elderly pensioner in Ulm had complained of having to give his name to obtain such a voucher. He felt that this injured his dignity since he was obliged to make his poverty public, human dignity being protected as a fundamental right in the Federal Republic of Germany. He therefore asked the European Court of Justice to declare the offending EEC regulation null and void.

In its opinion, forwarded to the European Court of Justice, the European Commission took these accusations seriously and drew the Court's attention very emphatically to the fact that all Community institutions — the Commission in its proposals, the Council of Ministers in its decisions, directives, and regulations, and Parliament in its opinions — were under an obligation to maintain fundamental rights based on the *common constitutional traditions* of the member states.[56] This led to the first practical judgment on a question of fundamental rights. The Court summed up the situation as follows: that it could obviously not apply national constitutional law which is outside the sphere of its competence, although it was under an obligation, in the context of its general duties of legislative supervision, to investigate possible infringements of fundamental freedoms, or

[54] Ibid., at 26. Although a similar decision was reached in the '*Geitling*' case, joint cases 36, 37, 38, and 40/59 [1960] ECR 423, an interesting proposal was put forward by A.-G. Legrange in his opinion to the effect that although 'it is not for the Court to apply, *or at least to do so directly*, rules of national law, even constitutional rules, in force in one or another of the Member States ... it may only allow itself to be influenced by such rules in so far as, where appropriate, it may see in them the expression of a general principle of law which may be taken into consideration in applying the Treaty' (at 450).
[55] Case 29/69 [1969] ECR 419; [1970] CMLR 112.
[56] Ibid., at 421–5.

human rights legislation which might for this reason have to be declared invalid. 'Interpreted in this way the provision at issue contains nothing capable of prejudicing the fundamental human rights enshrined in the general principles of Community law and protected by the Court.'[57] The Court showed its sensitivity to the problem in the *Stauder* case and its initially timid approach is justified by concern for the autonomous nature and primacy of Community law. Nevertheless, its earlier decisions were unsatisfactory, in that they rejected the proposition that alleged violations of the norms of a member state are beyond its competence while remaining silent on the question whether or not the Community system contains the means necessary to construct an efficient system for the protection of rights.[58]

Having seized the problem, the Court had occasion to expand on its reasoning in the *Internationale Handelsgesellschaft* case settled by a judgment of 17 December 1970.[59] While denying that a Community measure — which, it was alleged infringed the principle of proportionality derived from Articles 2 and 14 of the German Basic Law — could be subject to conformity with domestic constitutional law, the Luxembourg Court reaffirmed the existence of a Community concept of fundamental rights. It stated: 'Respect for fundamental rights forms an integral part of the general principles of law protected by the Court of Justice. The protection of such rights, whilst inspired by the constitutional traditions common to the Member States, must be ensured within the framework of the structure and objectives of the Community'.[60] It is interesting to observe that on the same day, in the *Einfuhr und Vorratsstelle* case, the Court repeated — without further comments on the subject — that 'respect for fundamental rights forms an integral part of the general principles of law protected by the Court of Justice'.[61]

---

[57] Ibid., at 425. The original French text of this judgment refers to 'les principes généraux du droit communautaire *dont la Cour assume le respect*'. These words repeat the formulation of art. 164 of the EEC Treaty which requires the Court to ensure that in the interpretation and application of the Treaty *the law is observed.*

[58] Reference to other cases can be found in P. Pescatore, 'Fundamental Rights and Freedoms in the System of the European Communities', 18 *AJCL* (1970), 348–51. Also consult J. W. Bridge, 'Fundamental Rights in the European Economic Community' in *Fundamental Rights* (ed. J. W. Bridge, D. Lasok, D. L. Perrott, and R. O. Plender, 1973), 291–305.

[59] Case 11/70 [1970] ECR 1125; [1972] CMLR 255.

[60] Ibid., at 1134. This case had important constitutional repercussions in the FRG: see sec. B above, esp. n. 24.

[61] Case no. 25/70 [1970] ECR 1161, at 1174.

The Court's approach to this subject was more emphatically stated in the *Nold* judgment of 14 May 1974.[62] This was the first case in which it made *indirect* reference to the European Convention on Human Rights. Among the most important points brought out by the judgment was the role of fundamental rights within the Communities. On this point, the judgment reads:

As the Court has already stated, fundamental rights form an integral part of the general principles of law, the observance of which it ensures. In safeguarding these rights, the Court is bound to draw inspiration from constitutional traditions common to the Member States and it cannot therefore uphold measures which are incompatible with fundamental rights recognized and protected by the Constitutions of those States.

Similarly, international treaties for the protection of human rights on which Member States have collaborated or of which they are signatories, can supply guidelines which should be followed within the framework of Community law.[63]

It is worth pointing out at this juncture, that whereas in the *Stauder* case the Luxembourg Court based its decision on 'general principles of Community law', in both the *Internationale Handelsgesellschaft* and *Einfuhr und Vorratsstelle* cases it referred to 'general principles of law'; while in the *Nold* case, 'general principles of law' are coupled with the constitutional traditions common to the member states. This is a reference to general principles of law in the member states. The multiplicity of terms is not surprising: it appears impossible to divide these principles into distinct categories either mechanically or even systematically. In the words of Professor Ganshof van der Meersch: *'Il existe des liens et des chevauchements entre la matière des principes généraux du droit des États membres et*

---

[62] Case no. 4/73 [1974] ECR 291; [1974] 2 CMLR 338.

[63] Ibid., at 507. It is interesting to note that the Court makes reference not only to *ratified* but also to *signed* treaties, as well as to treaties on which the Community's member states have *collaborated*. (France ratified the European Convention a few days before the *Nold* decision was given.) There is also a notable vagueness as to the need of *all* member states necessarily having collaborated, signed or ratified the treaties in question. It will be interesting to see to what extent the Court will in future make reference to the two UN Covenants on Human Rights, the European Social Charter, and certain ILO conventions considered relevant in the context of human rights norms applicable within the Community structure. Many of the Court's judgments already indicate that the provisions of judicial safeguard of basic rights of the individual often surpass much of the work done by the European Commission and the Court of Human Rights, e.g. on the concepts of non-discrimination and *ne bis in idem*, and the principle of proportionality. Thus the Luxembourg Court may well provide a human-rights case-law of a quality superior to that of the Council of Europe's cumbersome and slow machinery established by the European Convention on Human Rights.

*ceux que l'on qualifie comme étant du droit communautaire;
c'est nécessairement le cas dans la matière des droits fondamentaux'.*[64] It thus seems clear from the way in which the Court's
case-law and terminology have evolved that it now considers the
general principles of law of the member states to be embodied
in the 'general principles of Community law' in the broad sense.
This in turn implies that these principles can be divided into
those which are laid down in the texts of the Treaties, such as
non-discrimination and freedom of movement, and those which
are *deduced* from articles in the Treaties or from other sources
which it is for the Luxembourg Court to specify.[65]

The reasoning in the *Nold* case was carried one step further
by the *Rutili* judgment of 28 October 1975.[66] Whereas in the
Nold judgment reference to the European Convention on
Human Rights was vague and generic, in the *Rutili* case the
Court made reference to and used certain articles of the European Convention and the Fourth Protocol in support of its
essential reasoning. Called on to assess the justification for
restrictions on the freedom of movement of workers 'on grounds
of public policy',[67] the Court, to clarify the nature of these
restrictions and their justification, declared that:

Taken as a whole, those limitations placed on the powers of Member
States in respect of control of aliens are a specific manifestation of the
more general principle, enshrined in Articles 8, 9, 10 and 11 of the Convention for the Protection of Human Rights and Fundamental Freedoms,
signed in Rome on 4 November 1950 and ratified by all the Member
States, and in Article 2 of Protocol No. 4 of the same Convention, signed
in Strasbourg on 16 September 1963, which provide, in identical forms,
that no restrictions in the interests of national security or public safety
shall be placed on the rights secured by the above quoted articles other
than such as are necessary for the protection of those interests 'in a
democratic society'.[68]

[64] J. W. Ganshof van der Meersch, 'L'ordre juridique des Communautés européennes
et le droit international', 148 *R. des C.* (1975), v. 1–433, at 167.

[65] Ibid. This distinction was originally made by P. Reuter, in his article 'Le recours
de la Cour de Justice des Communautés européennes à des principes généraux de
droit' in *Mélanges H. Rolin* (1964), 263–83. See also the study by Professor R.
Bernhardt in *Bull. EC* Suppl. 5/76, 17–69, esp. at 66; and T. C. Hartley, *The Foundations of European Community Law* (1981), esp. at 119–44.

[66] Case 36/75 [1975] ECR 1219; [1976] 1 CMLR 140.

[67] Art. 48(3) of the EEC Treaty. This case is more fully discussed by D. Simon,
'Ordre public et libertés publiques dans les Communautés européennes. A propos de
l'arrêt Rutili', 19 *RMC* (1976), 201–23. See also case-note by G. S. Goodwin-Gill,
92 *LQR* (1976), 353–7.

[68] Ibid., at 1232. It may be noted that although the 4th Protocol has been signed
by all member states of the European Communities, Greece and the UK have *not* to
date *ratified* it. (Italy and the Netherlands only ratified it in 1982.)

The importance of the *Rutili* case is twofold: not only did the Court specifically invoke provisions of the European Convention, but it also — and this point needs emphasis — considered this instrument relevant when looking into state action restricting the freedom of movement of workers on grounds of public policy. Thus, before the *Rutili* judgment the Luxembourg Court had invoked 'fundamental Community rights' as a possible ground for review of legality and validity of Community acts, whereas here it *extended* their application to action of member states. This development, to use the words of G. Bebr, 'is certainly a remarkable extension of the protection of fundamental rights of individuals within the Community legal order'.[69]

Since the *Rutili* case, the Luxembourg Court has made express reference to the Convention's provisions on a few occasions. Article 1 of the First Protocol[70] was invoked in two judgments. In the *Hauer* case, decided on 13 December 1979 — a case in which a resident of the German wine-growing district of Bad Dürkheim unsuccessfully argued that the prohibition on planting vines under a Community regulation was illegal — the Court, after referring to its previous *Nold* judgment and the Joint Declaration of 27 April 1977 of the European Parliament, the Council, and the Commission,[71] explained that 'The right to property is guaranteed in the Community legal order in accordance with the ideas common to the constitutions of the Member-States, which are also reflected in the First Protocol to the European Convention for the Protection of Human Rights'.[72] But as the article in question was considered to be too vague, the Luxembourg Court went on to look at relevant constitutional provisions of member states before deciding that

[69] 'Remedies for breach of Community Law: Community report' in vol. 1, *Remedies for Breach of Community Law* (1980, FIDE reports of the 9th Congress, London 25–7 Sept. 1980), report no. 10, at 13.

[70] This article reads: 'Every natural or legal person is entitled to the peaceful enjoyment of his possessions. No one shall be deprived of his possessions except in the public interest and subject to the conditions provided by law and by the general principles of international law. The preceding provisions shall not, however, in any way impair the right of a State to enforce such laws as it deems necessary to control the use of property in accordance with the general interest to secure the payment of taxes or other contributions or penalties.'

[71] OJC no. 103 of 27 Apr. 1977. On this subject see notes by J. Forman, 'The Joint Declaration on Fundamental Rights', 2 *EL Rev.* (1977), 210–15, and by A. Dewaele and P. Lemmens in *Jura Falconis* (1977/78), 307–18.

[72] Case 44/79 [1979] ECR 3727, at 3745; [1980] 3 CMLR 42, at 64. (It then cited art. 1 of the 1st Protocol.)

the restriction imposed on the use of property by the prohibition on the new planting of vines laid down for a limited
period by a regulation was justified by the objectives of general
interest pursued by the Community.[73] In the case of *Valsabbia
and others*, of 18 March 1980,[74] express reference was again
made to Article 1 of the Convention's First Protocol and to the
Nold case when the Court rejected an auxiliary argument put
forward by a number of undertakings when it explained that
property rights guaranteed by Community law cannot be
extended to protect mere commercial interests or opportunities,
the uncertainties of which are part of the very essence of
economic activity.[75] Likewise in its judgment of 5 March 1980
in the *Pecastaing* case the Court considered that it need not
look into the matter of whether the concept of a fair hearing
found in Article 6 of the Convention was guaranteed by Community law as the directive at issue adequately dealt with this
particular point in the case before it.[76] Yet again in the *National
Panasonic* case, decided on 26 June 1980,[77] the Luxembourg
Court appears to have agreed with the views put forward on
behalf of the Commission, as well as the opinion of the Advocate-
General J.-P. Warner,[78] that there existed in Community law
no right to be warned in advance of a duly authorized and lawful
search under express legislative powers for documents required
for the investigation of a serious infringement of public law.
After referring to the above quoted passage in the *Nold* case,[79]
the Court went on to say:

[73] It is interesting to note that A.-G. Capotorti, in his opinion of 8 Nov. 1979, not
only referred to art. 1 of the Convention's First Protocol, but he also cited the case-
law of the European Commission of Human Rights when discussing an issue concerning compensation for expropriation of property: see ibid., 3760-1. He added (at
3759) that 'It is the exclusive task of the Community Court to guarantee such
protection [i.e. the protection of fundamental rights] within the scope of its jurisdiction: the uniform application of Community law and its primacy over the legal
orders of Member-States must not be endangered by the intervention of national
courts, when it is a question of ascertaining whether or not Community provisions
are in conformity with the principles concerning human rights.'

[74] Case 154/79 etc. [1980] ECR 907, at 1010-11.

[75] See also the Commission's view, at 936, that the Convention in itself is not part
of Community law.

[76] Case 98/79, [1980] ECR 691, esp. paras. 21 and 22 at 716. See also the opinion
of A.-G. Capotorti, at 726-7 in which he cites the case-law of both the Strasbourg
Court and Commission.

[77] Case 136/79 [1980] ECR 2033; [1980] 3 CMLR 169.

[78] The Commission's arguments are summarized on 2045. In his opinion of 30
Apr. 1980, A.-G. J.-P. Warner assumed that even if art. 8 of the Convention was
relevant, the Commission's decision was still valid as it fell within the exceptions
listed in para. 2 of the article: ibid., at 2067-8.   [79] See n. 63 above.

[I]t is necessary to point out that Article 8(2) of the European Convention, in so far as it applies to legal persons, whilst stating the principle that public authorities should not interfere with the exercise of the rights referred to in Article 8(1), acknowledges that such interference is permissible to the extent to which it 'is in accordance with the law and is necessary in a democratic society in the interests of national security, public safety or the economic well-being of the country, for the prevention of disorder or crime, for the protection of health or morals, or for the protection of the rights and freedoms of others'.[80]

Lastly, in the *FEDETAB* case, dated 29 October 1980, which concerned an unsuccessful application for the annulment of a competition decision, the Luxembourg Court rejected the suggestion that the Brussels Commission did not comply with Article 6(1) of the European Convention as '[t]he Commission is bound to respect the procedural guarantees provided for by Community law and has done so . . . it cannot, however, be classed as a tribunal within the meaning of the European Convention for the Protection of Human Rights.'[81] Although this case was probably correctly decided, certain reservations must be placed on the Court's reasoning: the Strasbourg organs have clearly indicated in a number of decisions that a classification or non-classification of an organ as a tribunal in itself cannot be the determining factor which brings into or excludes the organ from consideration under Article 6.[82]

The Convention's provisions have also been invoked before the Court on a number of occasions, both by the parties in their submissions and by member states and the Commission in respect of preliminary rulings.[83] In their opinions advocates-general have likewise made reference to the Convention's provisions.

[80] Extract taken from p. 2057 of the Court's judgment. Indirect reference to the Convention has also recently been made by the Luxembourg Court: see the cases of *Testa, Maggio, & Vitale*, joined cases 41/79, 121/79, and 796/79, [1979] ECR, para. 18 at 1996–7; also the opinion of A.-G. Reischl at 2009–11.

[81] Cases nos. 209–15 and 218/78, [1980] ECR 3125, para. 81; [1981] 3 CMLR 134, at 224.

[82] See comments of P. Duffy, 6 *HR Rev.* (1981), at 19–20, and of F. G. Jacobs, *The European Convention on Human Rights* (1975), 76–83.

[83] See esp. *Watson & Belmann*, case 118/75 [1976] ECR 1185 at 1187–95; [1976] 2 CMLR 552. See also *Royer*, case 48/75 [1976] ECR 497, esp. at 507; [1976] 2 CMLR 619 (a note by the author on both these cases can be found in 12 *The Law Teacher* (1978), at 30–7); and *Pescataing*, case 98/79, judgment of 5 Mar. 1980, n. 76 above, esp. paras. 6, 7, 21, and 22. In this case the Belgian Government cited the Strasbourg Court's *Golder* judgment in its submissions. See also the opinion of Capotorti A.-G., 31 Jan. 1980, in which he cites both the case-law of the Commission and the Court of Human Rights. Also see n. 86 below; and *Casati*, case 203/80 [1982] 1 CMLR 365.

Interestingly enough, in most cases this instrument's provisions have been considered as an aid to interpretation or as a reminder of the general principles of which they are an expression,[84] but in one particular instance Capotorti A.-G. — in the *Third Defrenne* case, in which the Luxembourg Court indicated that the protection of fundamental human rights within the Community legal system could not extend beyond the scope of specific provisions of Community legislation — has expressed the opinion that the Convention 'forms part of Community law and must be protected by the Court of Justice'.[85]

Thus, although the European Court of Justice has never expressly stated this to be the case, there exists a general consensus — at least in so far as can be detected from the opinions of the advocates-general and submissions put forward before the Court on behalf of the Brussels Commission[86] — that

---

[84] See the opinion of Mayras A.-G. in the *Royer* case, ibid., esp. at 525; and that of Trabucchi A.-G. in the *Watson & Belmann* case, ibid., esp. at 1206–8. (Already in 1969 Gand A.-G. referred to the Convention in *X* v. *Audit Board of the European Communities*, case 12/68 [1969] ECR 109 at 122; and again in 1972 in the *Boehringer* case the Convention had been cited by Mayras A.-G.: see case 7/72 [1972] ECR 1281, at 1298; [1973] CMLR 864.) In *Henn & Darby*, case 34/79 [1980] ECR 3795, at 3821–2; [1980] 1 CMLR 246 at 255 Warner A.-G. cited art. 10 of the Convention *and* the Strasbourg Court's *Handyside* judgment in his opinion, in order to indicate an approach which might be taken by the Luxembourg Court when it considers the phrase 'justified on grounds of public morality' in art. 36 of the EEC Treaty. See also his comments at 3830.

[85] Opinion of Capotorti A.-G. in *Defrenne* v. *Sabena*, case 149/77 [1978] ECR 1365, at 1385; [1978] 3 CMLR 312. He then cited the case-law of the Luxembourg Court before adding: 'However the significance of the protection of fundamental rights on a Community plane is not the same as on the plane of national law. In the aforementioned judgment in the *Internationale Handelsgesellschaft* case the Court of Justice emphasized that "the protection of such rights, whilst inspired by the constitutional traditions common to the Member States, must be ensured within the framework of the structure of the Community". In my view two conclusions are to be drawn from that statement. First the respect for fundamental rights is a limitation on all Community acts . . . *Secondly* where directly applicable Community measures exist (by the effect of the Treaties of secondary legislation) they *must* be interpreted in a manner which accords with the principle that human rights must be respected. I do not think that it is possible to say more than that. In particular, legal relationships which are left within the powers of the national legislature must be understood to be subject to the constitutional principle that human rights must be respected which applies in the State to which the relationship is subject, *in so far as the internal provisions are not replaced by directly applicable Community provisions.*' (Emphasis added.) The point to note here, of course, is that it is for the Luxembourg Court to determine which Community provisions are to be considered directly effective in domestic law.

[86] In this context particular note may be taken of what P. Leleux, legal adviser of the Commission, said before the Luxembourg Court in the oral procedure in the *Royer* case: see n. 83 above, at 506–7. His observations were summarized thus: 'According to the case-law of the Court of Justice respect for fundamental rights

the Community organs are legally bound by the provisions of
the European Convention on Human Rights in so far as its
provisions form part of the 'general principles of European
Community law'.[87] There does, however, remain a marked
difference of views in respect of another matter, namely, the
extent to which the Convention forms part of the corpus
of European Community law which must be enforced by
domestic courts. This point still remains unresolved.

D. Problems and possible further developments

If one considers the economic and social nature of the context
in which the European Communities pursue their objectives, the
ten member states and the Community institutions are unlikely
prima facie to encroach (directly or indirectly through the
implementation of secondary legislation) on fundamental
rights[88] enumerated either in domestic law or in the European
Convention, if they remain within the confines of the powers
and responsibilities conferred upon them within the ambit of
Community law. And·yet, despite the very rare occasion of
possible conflict, the key question still remains: has the individual
citizen of a member state a judicial remedy *in the domestic
forum* if a member state allegedly violates a provision of the
Convention which may be considered an integral part of European Community law? [89] One can only speculate upon the
answer to this question.

must be ensured within the legal system of the Community; they must, of course,
be protected against infringements caused by the institutions of the Community
but also against the actions of Member States and their authorities ... for the purposes of determining the bounds to be observed by Member States in the matter of an
infringement of the fundamental right of freedom of movement the Court must also
consider the Convention for the Protection of Human Rights and Fundamental
Freedoms of 4 November 1950 which is ratified by *all* the Member States of the EEC
and which is an integral part of Community law.' (Emphasis added.) Compare this
statement to the more cautious approach taken by Mayras A.-G. at 525.

[87] See n. 71 above. Even prior to the Joint Declaration, it can be suggested that the
Council of the European Communities tacitly endorsed this view in *Paris*, case 130/75
[1976] ECR 1589; [1976] 2 CMLR 708. See also *Bull. EC Suppl.* 5/76, para. 28, at 14.

[88] The exact meaning of the term 'fundamental rights' is far from clear: what does
the Luxembourg Court mean by this term? Are fundamental human rights — in the
context of European Community law — ones which possess a status equivalent to
general principles of law or are they a sort of 'higher law', of analogous importance to
fundamental human rights provisions enumerated in the Italian and FRG constitutions?
See J. E. S. Fawcett, 'A Bill of Rights for the United Kingdom?', I *HR Rev.* (1976),
57–64; and *Bull. EC Suppl.* 5/76, *passim*.

[89] On this subject, see in particular M. Waelbroeck, 'La protection des droits

The question was argued at considerable length in 1976 in the *Watson & Belmann* case.[90] In this case the Luxembourg Court held that a penalty imposed on a UK national for failure to comply with immigration formalities must be proportionate to the offence and comparable to the penalties to which Italian nationals were exposed for similar offences.[91] In its written submissions — in accordance with Article 20 of the Protocol to the Statute of the Court of Justice of the EEC — the British Government conceded that within the context of procedure under Article 177 the Luxembourg Court would be able to give rulings on the provisions of the European Convention but only where the Convention was relevant either to the interpretation of the Treaty, of measures adopted by the Community institutions or of the statutes of bodies established by an act of the Council, or to the validity of such acts. In so far as the validity of Community measures was concerned it understood the Court's previous case-law to mean that although the Court will take into account certain fundamental principles common to the member states — a number of which have also been sanctioned by the European Convention — such principles will be regarded by the Court rather as sources of inspiration than as forming part of the actual corpus of Community law. The British Government then went on to explain that there was no justification for treating the principles established by the Convention as part of Community law in the sense of their being directly applicable in the domestic law of member states, except in so far as the rights which they guarantee have been embodied or may be implied in provisions of Community law.[92]

On the other hand, the Commission stressed that following its ratification by all nine (and now ten) member states, the

fondamentaux à l'égard des états membres dans le cadre communautaire', *Mélanges F. Dehousse* (1979), ii. 333-5. (He also discusses the thorny jurisdictional problem posed by art. 1 of the Convention *vis-à-vis* the apparently more restrictive application of European Community law.)

[90] Case 118/75 [1976] ECR 1185; [1976] 1 CMLR 512.

[91] The Court also placed great emphasis on the procedural safeguards provided by Community law in the case of measures based on considerations of public policy or public security. In this judgment the Court did *not* make any reference to the question of whether it considered the European Convention as forming part of the *corpus* of Community law. For a more general survey of EEC immigration law consult T. C. Hartley, *EEC Immigration Law* (1978), *passim*.

[92] Ibid., at 1190-1. Compare this statement to what J. Donaldson had said in the *Allgemeine Gold* case, n. 31 and n. 36 above. See also the written submissions of the Italian Government, summarized at 1191-3.

Convention was legally binding upon the Community as a whole, both in relation to measures adopted by Community institutions *and each time that a provision of Community law is invoked.*[93] The opinion of Advocate-General Trabucchi was rather more circuitous on this particular point. After referring to the *Rutili* case, Trabucchi made a general statement to the effect that:

On the basis of this analogy between rules of Community law and rules of international law accepted by all the Member States, some learned writers have felt justified in concluding that the provisions of the said Convention must be treated as forming an integral part of the Community legal order, whereas it seems clear to me that the spirit of the judgment did not involve any substantive reference to the provisions themselves but merely a reference to the general principles of which, like the Community rules with which the judgment drew an analogy, they are a specific expression.

He then added: '. . . what is really new in the said reference to fundamental rights made in the *Rutili* judgment is the context to which it relates, namely, a situation the essential feature of which was that there existed a right to freedom enshrined in the Community system and a discretionary act by a State severely restricting that right.' Having made these general comments he then went on to say, in what appears to be a carefully phrased passage:

Of course in contrast to what happens in the case of acts of the Community executive, the acts of the States are subject to review by their own national courts which, together with the European Court of Human Rights, already provide effective protection for fundamental rights [*sic!*]. However, without impinging upon the jurisdiction of other courts, *this Court too, can look into an infringement of a fundamental right by a State body, if not to the same extent to which it could do so in reviewing the validity of Community acts, at least to the extent to which the fundamental right alleged to have been infringed may involve the protection of an economic right which is among the specific objects of the Treaty.* In fact, if there were no such connection, State action affecting individuals would be incapable of coming under the Community system, under any available procedure.[94]

As indicated in the text above, this is a fascinating and complex problem the resolution of which can only come about by means of an authoritative finding of the Court of Justice of

[93] Ibid., at 1194. It is a pity that the phrase 'each time that a provision of Community law is invoked' was not explained. But see the comments of P. Leleux in *Royer*, case 48/75 [1976] ECR 497 at 506–7; [1976] 2 CMLR, 619.

[94] Ibid., at 1207–8. (Emphasis added.) He then concluded, at 1208: 'The protection of the rights of man accordingly forms part of the Community system, even against states, in as much as the fundamental right relied upon involves a relationship or a legal situation the regulation of which is among the specific objects of the Treaty.'

the European Communities. In the meantime, one may hazard a guess that until and unless guidance is available from Luxembourg, domestic courts and tribunals will remain extremely reluctant to 'communitize' the Convention in their respective internal legal systems. The use (or possible use) of the European Convention on Human Rights as an integral part of Community law will undoubtedly touch upon politically sensitive as well as extremely complex issues in constitutional, Community, and international law. It is sufficient for the moment to make a few general interim observations in order to highlight real and potential difficulties that can face both the Luxembourg Court and domestic courts of the ten member states:

— Only in three of the ten member states of the European Communities does there exist some form of procedure of constitutional review.[95] In other countries there are considerable variations in enforcing the law in respect of alleged violations of human rights. Thus to what extent is it proper for the Luxembourg Court to 'communitize' fundamental human rights as of its own initiative (i.e. to guarantee their harmonious and uniform evolution) by imposing stringent control over the action of Community institutions *and* possibly also member states' action on a level akin to that which exists only in the minority of member states?[96]

— Despite the diversity of methods used by the ten member states in securing the protection of human rights within their respective jurisdictions a *common* infrastructure exists: the European Convention on Human Rights.[97] But in addition to the European Convention — which since its ratification by France on 3 May 1974 has been ratified by *all* ten member states — there is a variety of other international treaties for the protection of human rights on which member states have collaborated or of which they are signatories,[98] such as the European Social Charter and various ILO agreements which

---

[95] See *Bull. EC Suppl.* 5/76, esp. 33–4 and 38–40.

[96] Here again it may be noted that although the Luxembourg Court has on several occasions used the term 'fundamental rights', it has never explained what this actually means, see n. 88 above.

[97] See ch. 1 above, sec. B.

[98] This rather loose terminology was used by the Luxembourg Court in the *Nold* case. On this subject consult the numerous publications of G. Cohen-Jonathan, e.g. 'Les Droits de l'Homme dans les Communautés européennes' in *Recueil d'études en hommage à Ch. Eisenmann* (1975), 399–418, and his *rapport* at the 'Consultation de Strasbourg' in V *RDH/HRJ* (1972), 615–49. (Greece, a member state since Jan. 1981, ratified the Convention on 28 Nov. 1974.)

likewise make provision for a specific international enforcement procedure.[99] These international agreements all provide *minimum common standards* in their respective areas of specialization. Thus, standards of protecting human rights on the international plane are variable and they may in certain circumstances be considered less favourable to individuals than rights constitutionally or otherwise protected on the domestic plane.[100] Above all, within the context of European Community law, they do not necessarily directly bring about unification or harmonization of the protection of fundamental human rights within the ten member states.[101]

— Although in theory the action of the Community organs is complementary to that of state organs (and vice versa), an area of overlap can certainly exist. As a consequence awkward and difficult problems relating to their respective spheres of responsibility (as well as that of the European Convention's organs!) may need to be clarified.[102] Closely tied to this wider issue is another one: both Community organs and domestic courts applying Community law may be bound to apply human rights norms existing in the Community Treaties themselves or in the 'general principles of Community law'.[103] But when so applied, to which human rights standards must reference be made?[104] Should the Community legal order be subject to limitations analogous to those contained in the member states' constitutions as was suggested by Warner A.-G. in the *IRCA* case?[105]

[99] See, for example, the *3rd Defrenne* case, case 149/77 [1978] ECR 1365, at 1378; [1978] 3 CMLR 312.

[100] See, for example, art. 60 of the European Convention, and art. 5(2) of the UN Covenant on Civil and Political Rights; also P. Pescatore, 'The Protection of Human Rights in the European Communities', 9 *CML Rev.* (1972), 73-99, and the publications of Cohen-Jonathan, n. 98 above.

[101] See ibid., and Duffy, n. 104 below. The possibility of drawing up a Community catalogue of fundamental human rights has been mooted on numerous occasions. See references in sec. B above, n. 29, and D. Nickel, 'Zum Grundrechtsdefizit der Europäischen Gemeinschaften', 7 *Zeitschrift für Rechtspolitik* (1980), 161-8.

[102] See generally on this subject various contributions in *Grundrechtsschutz in Europa* (ed. H. Mosler, R. Bernhardt, and M. Hilf, 1977); J. A. Frowein, 'Die Europäische Menschenrechtskonvention und das Europäisches Gemeinschaftsrecht' in *Die Grundrechte in der Europaischen Gemeinschaft* (1978), 47-59.

[103] See W. J. Ganshof van der Meersch, 'Les Droits de l'Homme dans l'ordre juridique des Communautés européennes' in *Summary of Lectures, 9th Summer Session of the International Institute of Human Rights* (Strasbourg 1978), *passim*.

[104] This issue was discussed by P. J. Duffy in an interesting paper entitled 'The Relationship between Community Law and the European Convention on Human Rights' presented at a colloquium on *The Relationship between Public International Law and Community Law*, London, 21-3 June 1979.

[105] Case no. 7/76 [1976] ECR 1213, at 1237. See Duffy, ibid., esp. 3-7.

Alternatively, must a maximal standard be applied which is derived from national constitutions and/or standards established by the European Convention and other international treaty norms? [106] Or must a distinction be drawn between what P. Duffy terms 'absolute' and 'flexible' maximum standards, whereby the Luxembourg Court 'tries to respect the highest standard, subject to limitations justified by the Communities' situation and their overall objectives and requirements'?[107] A corollary to this is that domestic courts must continue to apply domestic human rights norms (as well as in some cases directly applicable provisions of international agreements) in all other cases. But if the domestic authority's action — taken in compliance with secondary Community legislation which may also be directly effective — is found to contravene domestic constitutional provisions, the Community legislation must in theory ultimately take precedence.[108] Likewise, it could be argued that direct effect must be given to human rights provisions of certain international agreements deemed by the Luxembourg Court to bind the European Communities internally or to which the European Communities have or may possibly accede.[109] Whether this argument would prevail were the Communities formally to accede to the European Convention remains a moot point.[110] An auxiliary point worth noting is

---

[106] See notes 98–100 above and 109 below.

[107] Duffy, n. 104 above, at 6 and 7. He cites, in support of this view, the opinion of Capotorti A.-G. in *Defrenne*, case no. 149/77 [1978] ECR 1365, at 1385; [1978] 3 CMLR 312, at 321: 'The significance of the protection of fundamental rights on a Community plane is not the same as on the plane of national law.'

[108] See case 106/77 [1978] ECR 629, [1978] 3 CMLR 670, and cases cited in section A. Also consult A. G. Toth, *Legal Protection of Individuals in the European Communities* (1978), ii. esp. 186–7; also see i. 107–11.

[109] e.g. certain ILO conventions. See, for instance, *Bresciani*, case 87/75 [1976] ECR 129; [1976] 2 CMLR 62; *Razanatsima*, case 65/77 [1977] ECR 2229; [1978] 1 CMLR 246; and *Chatain*, case no. 65/79 [1980] ECR 1345 (commented upon by P. M. Schneider, 18 *CML Rev.* (1981), 397–405). In so far as this development may have consequences on the domestic plane — in particular in respect of the European Convention — consult the observations of P. Pescatore in *Les recours des individus devant les instances nationales en cas de violation du droit européen* (1978), at 183; and G. Cohen-Jonathan, 'La Convention européenne des Droits de l'Homme et la Communauté européenne' *Mélanges F. Dehousse* (1979), i. 157–68, esp. at 165–6. See also O. Jacot-Guillarmod, *Droit communautaire et droit international public* (1979), esp. at 97–120; K. R. Simmonds, 'The Evolution of the External Relations Law of the European Economic Community', 28 *ICLQ* (1979), 644–68, at 665–6; and H. G. Schermers, *Judicial Protection in the European Communities* (1979), 69–75.

[110] See European Commission memorandum on the accession of the European Communities to the European Convention for the Protection of Human Rights and

that European Community law may — paradoxically — be considered by the Strasbourg organs to entail, in certain circumstances, a state's responsibility under Article 1 of the European Convention.[111]

— On the assumption that domestic courts apply the Convention's substantive norms when determining issues of European Community law, certain technical problems may occur. For example, some states have made reservations in respect of certain of the Convention's articles[112] and others have not ratified the Fourth Protocol,[113] not to mention the most important point — for the purposes of this study — the fact that in Ireland, Denmark, and the UK, where the Convention's provisions have no domestic force, the courts would nevertheless have to apply it were a provision of this instrument relevant in determining an issue within the legal order of the European Community. Even in countries where the Convention does possess the status of domestic law, its provisions may possess a hierarchically superior position when being applied in the context of European Community law, as opposed to a situation where domestic courts consider its provisions directly applicable, or as having been simply transformed into domestic law. An added complication may be the need to determine the legal value, if any, of the decisions of the Convention organs on the domestic plane within

Fundamental Freedoms, 2 May 1979, published in *Bull. EC Suppl.* 2/79. Commentaries on this subject include *L'adhésion des Communautés européennes à la Convention européenne des Droits de l'Homme* (1981, Catholic University of Louvain); F. A. Casadio, and A. Bellando, eds., *Europa e Diritti Umani* (1981); vol. ii *Das Europa der zweiten Generation. Gedächtnisschrift für C. Sasse* (1981); L. Neville Brown and J. McBride, 'Observations on the proposed Accession by the European Community to the European Convention on Human Rights', 29 *AJCL* (1981), 691-705; H. Schermers, 'The Communities under the European Convention on Human Rights', *LIEI* 1978/1, 1-8.

[111] See application 8030/77 *CFDT* v. *European Communities, alternatively, their Member States (a) jointly and (b) severally*, in 13 *D&R*, 231-40; and comments by E. A. Alkema, 'The EC and the European Convention of Human Rights — Immunity and Impunity of the Community?', 16 *CML Rev.* (1979), 498-508. Also consult application 8364/78 *Lindsay* v. *UK*, 15 *D&R*, 247-58; application 8612/79, 15 *D&R*, 259-64; and application 6871/75 *Caprino* v. *UK*, 12 *D&R*, 14-31. For further discussion on this subject see generally *Grundrechtsschutz in Europa* (ed. H. Mosler, R. Bernhardt, and M. Hilf, 1977), esp. paper presented by T. Stein, at 159-80, and oral intervention of M.-A. Eissen, at 183, and of H. Schermers, at 185-6.

[112] See *Collected Texts*, 605-13, *passim*. In addition Greece has not accepted the right of individual petition under art. 25. Art. 15 of the Convention also permits states to derogate from certain of the Convention's provisions in times of emergency, etc.

[113] Namely, Greece and the UK.

the context of Community law.[114] Such a determination may in turn call for a reassessment of the impact that the findings of Convention organs may have in the domestic forum of the ten countries concerned. Similarly, were the European Convention so 'communitized', it would be fascinating to speculate on the extent to which domestic enforcement mechanisms could be applied to it.[115]

Thus, before actually being able to assess the possibility of the European Convention on Human Rights becoming a 'Bill of Rights' within the Community legal order (binding upon both the Community organs *and* domestic courts applying its provisions in the context of Community law), and its subsequent acceptance as, to use the words of Professor Pescatore, *'un droit commun pour l'ensemble des États membres comme pour la Communauté'*,[116] it will be essential to make a more thorough and detailed study of the above noted issues, as well as many others besides.

Finally, reverting to the three countries which have *not* incorporated the European Convention of Human Rights, namely Denmark, Ireland, and the UK: what conclusions, tentative though they be, can be reached on the basis of the above study? If the domestic law-making capacity or freedom to legislate is in some way circumscribed or influenced by European Community law, certain provisions of the European Convention might possibly be deemed relevant in this context by the domestic judge when he attempts to appreciate whether or not there has been an infringement of a fundamental right by a national authority, i.e. an infringement of a general principle of European Community law of which certain provisions of the

[114] What value must be placed, for instance, on the Commission's admissibility decisions or to the Strasbourg Court's judgments by the Court of Justice of the European Communities? See notes 73, 83 and 84 above. Also see Schermers, n. 109 above, and ch. 10 below. Similarly, the *Drittwirkung* problem may arise in respect of the protection of fundamental human rights in general and also possibly with regard to specific provisions of the European Convention when applied as European Community law: see A. Bleckmann, 'L'applicabilité directe du droit communautaire' in *Les recours des individus devant les instances nationales en cas de violation du droit européen* (1978), 85-131, esp. at 119-20. See also sec. C above.

[115] See R. Kovar, 'Voies de droit ouvertes aux individus devant les instances nationales en cas de violation du droit communautaire' in *Les recours des individus devant les instances nationales en cas de violation du droit européen* (ed. J. Velu and M. Waelbroeck, 1978), 245-83. Also consult FIDE 1980 Conference papers in vol. i, *Remedies for Breach of Community Law, passim.*

[116] *FIDE Conference*, 'La protection des droits fondamentaux par le pouvoir judiciaire', report no. II/2, at 32.

Convention appear to form an integral part. What is perhaps clearer it that breaches of the Convention's norms can be argued within the context of challenges to the validity of Community acts which are at the root of the domestic measure that is purportedly violating a human rights provision therein; or alternatively, the domestic court can be persuaded to request an interpretation of the relevant Community act under Article 177 in the light of its compatibility with provisions enumerated in the European Convention.[117] Thus, domestic judges in all three countries must be prepared to take cognisance of arguments alleging violations of the Convention's provisions at least in respect of Community acts, the validity of which must be treated as questions of law. If an interpretation is not sought, the domestic court decides the matter itself!

[117] See S. Ghandi, 'Interaction between the Protection of Fundamental Rights in the European Economic Community and under the European Convention on Human Rights', in *LIEI* 1981/2, 1–33; and M. H. Mendelson, 'The European Court of Justice and Human Rights', in vol. 1 *Yearbook of European Law*, 1981 (ed. F. G. Jacobs, 1982), 125–65.

Chapter 10

The Authority of the Findings of the European Commission, the European Court of Human Rights, and the Committee of Ministers

A. Introductory remarks

There are no provisions in the European Convention on Human Rights which refer to the authority of decisions of the Convention organs in domestic law. And, although member states must certainly 'ensure that their domestic legislation is compatible with the Convention and, if need be, to make any necessary adjustment to this end, since the Convention is binding on all the authorities of the Contracting Parties, including the legislative authority',[1] there appears to be no legal obligation for them to give these decisions any form of binding force in domestic law. It is, nevertheless, of considerable interest to observe the extent to which, if any, these supervisory organs actually do influence national courts, either in domestic proceedings to give effect to their decisions, or as guidelines or indicators which may serve to clarify the extent and nature of the obligations in subsequent domestic case-law.[2] More specifically, domestic courts may use these findings in a variety of different ways. For example, the courts may consider them

[1] *De Becker* v. *Belgium*, European Commission of Human Rights, decision on admissibility of 22 Mar. 1958, 2 *Yearbook* (1958/59), 214–54, at 234.

[2] Among recent studies on this subject are Ch. Schreuer, 'The Impact of International Institutions on the Protection of Human Rights in Domestic Courts', 4 *Israel Yearbook on Human Rights* (1974), 60–88; Th. Buergenthal, 'The Effect of the European Convention on Human Rights on the Internal Law of Member States', *ICLQ*, Supplement no. 11 (1965), 79–106; H. Golsong, 'L'effet direct, ainsi que le rang en droit interne, des normes de la Convention européenne des Droits de l'Homme et des décisions prises par les organes institués par celle-ci', and J. Velu, 'Les voies de droit ouvertes aux individus devant les instances nationales en cas de violation de la Convention européenne des Droits de l'Homme', in *Les recours des individus devant les instances nationales en cas de violation du droit européen (Communautés européennes et Convention européenne des Droits de l'Homme)* (1978), 59–83 and 187–243; R. Higgins, 'The Execution of Decisions of Organs under the European Convention on Human Rights', 31, *RHDI* (1978), 1–30; G. Ress, 'The Legal Effect of

when confronted with an issue in which Convention provisions are invoked directly or in substance; or in situations where issues of a constitutional nature, or perhaps generally recognized rights ('natural rights' etc.) are involved. Likewise, domestic courts may possibly feel themselves bound by certain decisions in Strasbourg, or at least regard decisions as persuasive authority which should not be disregarded unless there is good reason for doing so. Certainly, it is reasonable to assume that at least in those countries in which the Convention possesses the status of domestic law, it would be difficult for the judiciary to disregard developments in Strasbourg. Even in countries which have not incorporated the Convention, the judiciary may be inclined to take judicial notice of the findings of the Strasbourg organs (especially when the latter elaborate or clarify the meaning of the Convention's provisions), since there exists a general presumption

the judgments of the European Court of Human Rights on the Internal Law and before Domestic Courts of the Contracting States' in *Fifth International Colloquy about the European Convention on Human Rights*, Frankfurt, 9-12 Apr. 1980, H/Coll. (80)4; U. Scheuner, 'An Investigation of the Influence of the European Convention on Human Rights and Fundamental Freedoms on National Legislation and Practice', in *International Protection of Human Rights*, Nobel Symposium no. 7 (ed. A. Eide and A. Schou, 1968), 193-215; *Human Rights in National and International Law* (ed. A. H. Robertson, 1968), esp. articles by Scheuner, 214-66, and R. Pinto, 275-82; P. Vegleris, 'Modes de redressement des violations de la Convention européenne des Droits de l'Homme' in *Mélanges Polys Modinos* (1968), 369-88, and 'La Fonction de décision et de sanction', 11 *RDH/HRJ* (1969), 234-51; G. Janssen-Pevtschin, J. Velu, and A. Vanwelkenhuyzen, 'La Convention de sauvegarde des Droits de l'Homme et des libertés fondamentales et le fonctionnement des juridictions belges', XV *Chronique de politique étrangère* (1962), 199-246, at 234-45; A. A. Cançado Trindade, 'Exhaustion of Local Remedies in International Law and the Role of National Courts', 17 *Archiv des Völkerrechts* (1978), 330-70; and J. Velu, *Les Effets des Instruments internationaux en matière des Droits de l'Homme* (1981). For more general works consult C. W. Jenks, *The Prospects of International Adjudication* (1964); Ch. Schreuer, 'The Authority of International Judicial Practice in Domestic Courts', 23 *ICLQ* (1974), 681-708; H. Mosler, 'L'application du droit international public par les tribunaux nationaux', 91 *R. des C.* (1957), 619-709; and three articles bearing the same title, 'La nature juridique des actes des organisations et des juridictions internationales et leurs effets en droit interne': by Ch. Dominicé, in *Recueil de travaux suisses présentés au VIIIe Congrès international de droit comparé* (Pescara, 1970), 249-64; by A.-Ch. Kiss, in *Études de droit contemporain* (1970), 259-71; and by M. Waelbroeck, in *Rapports belges au VIIIe Congrès international de droit comparé* (Pescara, 1970), 503-20; H. G. Schermers, vol. ii *International Institutional Law* (1981); R. B. Lillich, 'The Role of Domestic Courts in Promoting International Human Rights Norms', 24 *NY Law School LR* (1978), 153-78; E. Stein, 'National Procedures giving Effect to Governmental Obligations Undertaken and Agreements Concluded by Governments' in *Rapports généraux au IXe Congrès international de droit comparé*, Tehran, 27 Sept.-4 Oct. 1974 (1977), 581-607; Ch. Schreuer, *Decisions of International Institutions before Domestic Courts* (1981); and H. Mosler, 'Supra-National Judicial Decisions', 4 *Hastings Int. and Comp. L. Rev.* (1981), 425-72.

that the courts should interpret domestic law in such a way as to make it consistent with the state's international obligations.

The Commission and the Court, which were created specifically in order 'to ensure the observance of the engagements of the High Contracting Parties' (Article 19 of the Convention), and the Committee of Ministers of the Council of Europe are the three bodies which supervise the obligations of the contracting states under this instrument,[3] although only the Court and the Committee of Ministers have the ultimate power to decide whether or not a violation of the Convention has occurred.

The Commission

The influence exerted by the Commission generally, and in particular the impact of its decisions on the domestic plane, tend to be greatly underestimated due to this organ's apparent inability to give legally binding decisions. This is not, however, an altogether accurate presentation of its role. In fact the Convention does confer upon the Commission two formal powers of decision. One concerns the admissibility of applications, a power regulated by Articles 26 and 27, which by its nature is not destined as such to have any far-reaching implications for domestic law.[4] The Commission's second power is to choose, once its report has been drawn up and transmitted to the Committee of Ministers, whether or not to refer a case to the European Court of Human Rights within the prescribed period of three months. This second power of decision presupposes, of course, that the state in question has made a declaration under Article 46.[5] In addition, the Commission also possesses what may be termed a power of 'negative final decision'[6] in that

[3] The auxiliary role of the Secretary General under art. 57 should also perhaps be mentioned. See A. H. Robertson, *Human Rights in Europe* (1977), 268-70. See also P. Vegleris, 'Twenty Years' Experience of the Convention and Future Prospects' in *Privacy and Human Rights* (ed. Robertson, 1973), 340-412, esp. 357-9 and 394-404; and Velu, n. 2 above, esp. 210-42.

[4] Although, as will be seen below, these decisions are not necessarily devoid of legal significance in domestic law of states parties.

[5] Arts. 31, 46, and 48 of the Convention.

[6] See Higgins, n. 2 above; i.e. there exists a 'power of decision' as such, but it is limited in so far as the findings remain an 'opinion'. In most cases the Committee of Ministers tends to follow these 'opinions' when making its final decisions under art. 32: see below. An interesting analogy has been made by Professor J. E. S. Fawcett in his book *The Application of the European Convention on Human Rights* (1969) between the functions of the Commission and the Judicial Committee of the Privy Council: see 263-4.

when its endeavours to obtain a 'friendly settlement of the matter on the basis of respect for human rights' have not succeeded, it drafts a report giving its *opinion* as to whether the facts found disclose a breach by the state concerned of its obligations under the Convention (Articles 28 and 31). It may also, when submitting this report, make such proposals to the Committee of Ministers as it thinks fit (Article 31(3)).[7]

Particular note should also be taken of the Commission's conciliatory role when it attempts to secure a so-called friendly settlement. For, although the confidential nature of its work in this field prevents observers from providing many concrete examples of its accomplishments, this lack of information in no way detracts from the positive influence that such settlements may and actually have had upon domestic law generally.[8] This can be seen more clearly when it is appreciated that a very important common feature of friendly settlements is that concessions are actually made by governments which lead in most cases, either directly or indirectly, to administrative or even legislative changes with implications beyond the case in point: '. . . the parties mutually weigh up the risks inherent in the case, relinquish their respective claims, and avoid pressing the dispute to a conclusion; the outcome is mutual concessions, which are never concerned with questions of principle but essentially dictated by practical objectives.'[9]

Moreover, as an international obligation is placed upon a respondent state in such a case, this form of mutually agreed undertaking supervised by the Commission could also have potential repercussions in domestic law, in that a domestic

---

[7] But only in cases where it believes a violation of the Convention has taken place. See Rule 6 of 'Rules Adopted by the Committee of Ministers for the Application of Article 32' in *Collected Texts*, 500-6, at 502.

[8] See J. Raymond, 'Comment s'exerce la fonction de conciliation de la Commission européenne des Droits de l'Homme', II *RDH/HRJ* (1969), 234-51; A. Khol, 'Conciliation and Friendly Settlement of Human Rights Implementation Organs with Particular Emphasis on those of the European Convention on Human Rights' in *Eighth Study Session of the International Institute of Human Rights* (July, 1977); and A. B. McNulty, 'Practice of the European Commission of Human Rights Regarding Friendly Settlement under the European Convention on Human Rights' in *Armagăn T. Balta* (1974), 423-30.

[9] C. Zanghi, 'The Effectiveness and Efficiency of the Guarantees of Human Rights Enshrined in the European Convention on Human Rights' in *Proceedings of the 4th International Colloquy about the European Convention on Human Rights*, Rome 5-8 Nov. 1975 (Council of Europe, 1976), 209-55, at 238-40. Such a friendly settlement must be brought about 'on the basis of respect for Human Rights'. See ch. 1 above, notes 8, 10, and 11, and Fawcett, n. 6 above, at 264-70.

tribunal may regard the friendly settlement as a legally enforceable contract in domestic law in a case where the state organs in question are not prepared to abide by the conditions agreed upon by the settlement.[10]

Consequently, it may be said that the Commission's decisions have an operative impact upon domestic law generally, in that its findings *are liable* to influence domestic courts in their interpretation of Convention law, (especially in countries where this instrument possesses the status of domestic law), although its findings lack any formal legal weight *per se*. And, as the Commission's Secretary has explained:

> The Commission's relationship with a Government is not that of prosecutor-accused, but of a joint effort to examine and, if necessary, satisfy a complaint before it. Wilful or premeditated violations of the Convention do not occur but violations have occurred broadly in three different ways: either through inadvertence, on the part of the Government concerned, in individual cases, or by outmoded legislation or practices sometimes going back to the 19th century, or by an interpretation of the Convention different from that of the complainant, Commission and finally the Court.
> ... The real value of the [Commission's] indirect sanction seems clearly established and may owe its reality in some degree to the collaboration and interdependence of the member States of the Council of Europe ... [and] ... the application of the Convention by the Commission and Court can, in a comparatively limited area, more easily bring about a harmonisation of national legislation and practices.[11]

The Committee of Ministers

Under Article 32 of the Convention, the Committee of Ministers decides, by a majority of two-thirds, whether or not there has been a violation of the Convention in a given case. This decision, although emanating from a political organ, most certainly binds the state or states concerned on the international plane (Article 32(4)).[12] However, it does not necessarily follow that such

---

[10] See J. Frowein, 'The Guarantees Afforded by the Institutional Machinery of the Convention' in *Privacy and Human Rights* (ed. A. H. Robertson, 1973), 284-304, at 288; and Ress, n. 2 above, at 19.

[11] 'Stocktaking', at 220-1. Also consult M. Sørensen, 'Les expériences personnelles de la Convention', VIII *RDH/HRJ* (1975), 329-42, esp. at 334-6.

[12] See further H. Golsong, 'The Control Machinery of the European Convention on Human Rights', *ICLQ*, Supplement no. 11 (1965), 38-69; A. H. Robertson, *Human Rights in Europe* (1977), 237-67; A. H. Robertson, written communication at the 1975 Rome Colloquy, n. 9 above, 257-62; and *Bibliography*, 151. See also A. Morgan, 'European Convention on Human Rights, Article 32: What is Wrong?', I *HR Rev.* (1976), 157-75; and case-note by the author in 41 *MLR* (1978), 337-42.

decisions can or even should be implemented by domestic courts. In this connection it must be borne in mind that although constitutions of member states contain general references to international organizations (Belgium, Article 25 *bis*; Denmark, Article 20(1); Federal Republic of Germany, Article 24; Italy, Article 11; Luxembourg, Article 49 *bis*; Norway, Article 93; Portugal, Article 8; Sweden, Instrument of Government, Chapter 10, Article 5), there are no provisions – with the exception of Article 67 of the Netherlands Constitution[13] – which suggest that domestic courts are to apply *decisions* of international organizations in the same way as they may do with regard to treaties or rules of customary international law. With the particular exception of certain decisions of organs of the European Community,[14] this would appear to be the correct understanding of the present situation pertaining to decisions taken both by political or quasi-judicial international organs[15] as well as those of highly authoritative and fully reasoned findings of international judicial organs.[16] Thus, resolutions of the Committee of Ministers – although possessing undoubted legal authority on the international plane – appear to have little, if any, influence upon domestic case-law. Nevertheless, the role played by the Committee of Ministers may be of considerable importance and its political power should not be underestimated: on a number of occasions governments have been persuaded by it to make legislative and administrative changes. It may also be noted that in addition to this 'declaratory power', paragraph 3 of Article 32 of the Convention gives the Committee of Ministers the authority to decide by a two-thirds majority 'what effect shall be given to its original decision' and obliges it to publish the Commission's report if the contracting

[13] Art. 67 provides for the general application of decisions of international organizations in the same way as treaties by domestic courts. See ch. 3 above, sec. D.

[14] For publications on this subject consult K. Kujath, *Bibliography on European Integration* (1977), 185-283. The judgments of the Court of Justice of the European Communities are directly enforceable in member states (arts. 187 and 192, EEC Treaty). Also see ch. 9 above, *passim*, and see A. Bleckmann, 'L'applicabilité directe du droit communautaire', 85-131, and J.-V. Louis, 'La primauté du droit communautaire', 145-70, in *Les recours des individus* . . . , n. 2 above.

[15] See n. 2 above; Ch. Schreuer, *Die Behandlung internationaler Organakte durch staatliche Gerichte* (1977), and 'The Relevance of United Nations Decisions in Domestic Legislation', 27 *ICLQ* (1978), 1-17; E. Lauterpacht, 'Implementation of Decisions of International Organisations through National Courts' in *The Effectiveness of International Decisions* (ed. S. M. Schwebel, 1971), 57-65.

[16] See n. 2 above; and Ch. Schreuer, 'The Implementation of International Judicial Decisions by Domestic Courts', 24 *ICLQ* (1975), 153-83.

party in question has not taken satisfactory measures to abide by its decision.[17] In this connection, it may be interesting to speculate as to how domestic courts would react if, for example, the Committee of Ministers were to find a violation of the Convention without making a specific order of reparation to a victim of a violation. Presuming, also, that the case concerned an illegal detention contrary to Article 5 of the Convention in a country in which this article is directly applicable in court proceedings, it may be argued that the courts should at least consider the Committee of Ministers finding of a violation as highly authoritative evidence in a claim under Article 5(5), assuming that domestic law relating to this matter were inadequate.[18]

In addition to its function of determining whether or not a violation of the Convention has taken place under Article 32, the Committee of Ministers is also endowed with the responsibility of supervising the judgments of the European Court of Human Rights,[19] a function for which it appears well suited. This is probably so because the European Court of Human Rights, a non-political body, may not perhaps be the most appropriate organ to supervise implementation on a general level; such implementation usually takes place mainly by legislative and administrative methods in order to bring domestic law and measures into harmony with treaty obligations.

The Court

Article 53 of the Convention obliges member states to abide by the decisions of the European Court of Human Rights in cases in which they are parties, and Article 45 extends the Court's jurisdiction 'to all cases concerning the interpretation and application' of the Convention which are referred to it under Article 48. Unlike the Committee of Ministers, the Court is not a political body and its reasoned judgments are considered the

[17] See The *Greek* case, 12 *Yearbook* (1969), 511-15.

[18] The same line of argument could be used with regard to decisions of the Strasbourg Court. See R. Herzog, 'Das Grundrecht auf Freiheit in der Europäischen Menschenrechtskonvention', 86 *Archiv des öffentlichen Rechts* (1961), 194-244, at 235 and 242; and Schreuer, n. 2 above, at 70.

[19] See 'Rules adopted by the Committee of Ministers for the Application of Article 54 of the European Convention on Human Rights' in *Collected Texts*, 507. See also written communications of M.-A. Eissen, 747-52, M. Daubie, 753-67, A. H. Robertson, 768-80, at the *Colloque de Grenoble*, 25-6 Jan. 1973, VI *RDH/ HRJ* (1973); and case-note by the author in 4 *TL* (1982), 71-8, at 76-8.

most authoritative interpretations of the 'law of the Convention'.[20] Thus on the international plane a *jurisprudence constante* may, at least in certain areas, have been created and, for all practical purposes, the Court's decisions appear to be binding authority not only for the states concerned but also for the Commission and possibly also the Committee of Ministers.[21] However, the Court is not a *quatrième instance* nor a *cour de cassation* for it lacks the power either to reverse or to annul judgments of domestic courts which, *vis-à-vis* the Human Rights Court, remain independent rather than hierarchically inferior;[22] although − as will be seen below − the domestic effect of its decisions remains far from negligible in some countries.

Article 50 of the Convention stipulates that if the Court finds that a state has violated the Convention in a particular case at issue it may, 'if necessary, afford just satisfaction to the injured party', provided that 'internal law of the said Party allows only partial reparation to be made for the consequences' of a decision or measure regarded as being contrary to the Convention. This article tends to confirm the view that the Court's decisions are not, *per se*, directly enforceable in internal law and that once the fact of violation has been established, it is for the state party to conclude what it should or should not do in order to abide by the Court's decision.[23] This article can be compared to Articles 63(1) and 68(2) of the 1969 American Convention on Human Rights which stipulate that:

... the [Inter-American] Court [of Human Rights] shall rule that the injured party be ensured the enjoyment of his right or freedom that was

[20] See Robertson, n. 12 above, 193-236; for further references, *Bibliography*, 137-41 and 144-50. The most recent thorough study of the Court's impact in the domestic law of states parties is that of Ress, n. 2 above. Also consult an interesting article by Sir G. Fitzmaurice, 'Strasbourg and the Hague' in *Studi in onore di G. Balladore Pallieri* (1978), ii. 280-305.

[21] Buergenthal, n. 2 above, has pointed out (p. 95) that it can be argued that the Committee of Ministers, in performing its quasi-judicial functions under art. 32 is not hierarchically inferior to the Court but a co-equal and therefore possibly free to disregard the precedental authority of a judgment of the Court.

[22] Buergenthal, ibid.

[23] On this subject consult references in notes 2 and 20 above. And Vegleris, n. 3 above, 400-4; M. Miele, 'L'art. 50 della Convenzione europea sui diritti dell'uomo e le sue prime applicazioni giurisprudenziali', i. 537-50, and R. Luzzatto, 'La Corte europea dei diritti dell'uomo e la riparazione delle violazioni della Convenzione', i. 421-45, *Studi in onore di Manlio Udina* (1975); Velu, n. 2 above, esp. 230-5; R. Higgins, 'Damages for Violation of One's Human Rights' in *Explorations in Ethics and International Relations* (ed. N. A. Sims, 1981); and C. Gray, 'Remedies for Individuals under the European Convention on Human Rights', VI *HR Rev.* (1981), 153-73.

violated . . . [and] . . . if appropriate, that the consequences of the measure or situation that constituted the breach . . . be remedied and that fair compensation be paid to the injured party [Article 63(1)].

That part of a judgment that stipulates compensatory damages may be executed in the country concerned in accordance with the domestic procedure governing the execution of judgments against the state [Article 68(2)].[24]

Accordingly it may be said that the decisions of the Human Rights Court remain potentially a highly authoritative source for domestic courts although, if they are disregarded, no *ipso facto* violation of the Convention is made by the domestic courts, in that, in a strictly technical sense, the Strasbourg Court is not hierarchically superior. It should be pointed out, however, that the Human Rights Court remains in reality the final judicial arbiter of the meaning of the Convention's provisions in states which have recognized its jurisdiction.[25]

It follows that a number of factors should be kept in mind when examining the possible legal authority of this organ's decisions in domestic proceedings. A basic distinction may have to be made between those states in which the Convention possesses the status of internal law and those in which it does not. And, in those in which it does, it may be important to look upon the distinction made by domestic tribunals which consider the Convention to have been 'transformed' into domestic law (e.g. the FRG and Italy), and those in which they consider its substantive norms to have been 'incorporated' upon ratification and to be directly applicable to individuals in court proceedings (e.g. Belgium, Luxembourg, and the Netherlands).[26] Of great significance, in this connection, appears to be the question of whether a state party has accepted the jurisdiction of the Court under Article 46 and/or has made a declaration accepting the right of individual petition under Article 25. Even if it has only accepted the latter, an auxiliary point may need to be studied, namely, whether there exists an indirect domestic impact of the Court's case-law by reason of the fact that the Commission and the Committee of Ministers may or should be bound to follow the Court's decisions. An additional

---

[24] See A. H. Robertson, *Human Rights in the World* (1972), 135 and 268. Also consult Th. Buergenthal, 'The Inter-American Court of Human Rights', 76 *AJIL* (1982), 231-45.   [25] See Buergenthal, n. 2 above, esp. at 94-105.

[26] In the Netherlands it would appear that the executory decisions of the Court as well as the Committee of Ministers can be considered binding upon domestic courts. See Evans, 'Written Communication', at 166.

matter worth monitoring is to study the extent to which the Strasbourg Court's decisions help domestic courts to interpret and elucidate imprecise and perhaps evolving concepts found in the Convention, especially in countries whose constitutions have in part been modelled upon this instrument (Cyprus and Malta). A subsidiary inquiry concerning the possible domestic effect of the Court's judgments may be pursued by an examination of the use of the doctrine of incorporation in respect of international non-treaty norms.[27] In turn, such an inquiry touches upon the more general issues of the reception of the principles of customary international law as sources of law within the domestic framework, and possibly also the relevance or authority of the findings of international judicial organs in this context; for, as the former President of the European Commission of Human Rights has explained — when considering the authority of international decisions in the English courts — although such decisions are not binding precedents they can certainly be of a persuasive authority in so far as they serve to unify generally accepted principles of law.[28]

B. In states in which the Convention has the status of domestic law

Austria

In Austria the European Convention on Human Rights forms an integral part of domestic law. It has the force of constitutional law and direct effect is given to its provisions of a normative character.[29] The provisions of treaties establishing international organizations as well as acts and decisions of such organizations are automatically part of Austrian law *if* these are considered to be self-executing by the courts.[30] By virtue of Articles 32(4)

[27] i.e. international custom *and* general principles of law. See D. P. O'Connell, *International Law* (1970), at i. 56–8; I. Brownlie, *Principles of Public International Law* (1969), 44–59; H. Waldock, 'General Course on Public International Law', 106 *R. des C.* (1962), ii. 1–251, at 96–9 and 133–7.

[28] J. E. S. Fawcett, *The British Commonwealth in International Law* (1963), 55. See also Jenks, n. 2 above, 727–77.

[29] See ch. 4 above, sec. A. The country has also accepted the right of individual petition and the compulsory jurisdiction of the Court.

[30] I. Seidl-Hohenveldern, report on Austria in *Individual Rights and the State in Foreign Affairs: An International Compendium* (ed. E. Lauterpacht and J. G. Collier, 1977), 26–54. See also Ch. Schreuer, 'Beschlüsse internationaler Organe im österreichischen Staatsrecht', 37 *ZRV* (1977), 468–503.

and 53 of the Convention the Austrian authorities will execute
any measure which the country is compelled to take after an
adverse finding by either the Committee of Ministers or the
Court of Human Rights. The reasons given in a judgment of the
Court, however, or to support a decision of the Committee of
Ministers — even in a case in which Austria is a party — are not
considered to be legally binding on the Austrian courts or other
domestic authorities.[31]

The manner in which the Austrian courts appear prepared to
take into account the Convention's interpretation needs special
attention due to the fact that this instrument's substantive
provisions possess the status of constitutional law. It may be
observed, however, that earlier case-law was not particularly
faithful to the interpretations of the Strasbourg organs. For
example, in 1965 the *Verfassungsgerichtshof* (Constitutional
Court) found it unnecessary to analyse the Commission's
practice when interpreting Austria's reservation to Article 5 —
thereby suggesting a conclusion which evidently varied from
that advocated by the Commission.[32] Again, in 1969 when
faced with the task of interpreting the phrase 'civil rights and
obligations' contained in Article 6 of the Convention, the same
Court defined this expression on the basis of the domestic
concept of 'civil law matters' (*Zivilrechtssachen*) rather than
take into account the long-standing practice of the Commission
which has repeatedly continued to interpret 'civil rights and
obligations' as an autonomous concept whose understanding
cannot be based merely upon an interpretation provided to it
by a given state's domestic law.[33] Happily, these cases are
examples of the exception to the rule, and a few relatively
recent cases may be cited to substantiate this contention. In
September 1970 the *Verfassungsgerichtshof* considered that
Article 6 of the Convention was not applicable to disciplinary
proceedings taken by the disciplinary council of the Austrian
Lawyers' Association, and it cited two applications filed before
the Commission in Strasbourg to justify its reasoning.[34] In June

[31] Evans, 'Written Communication', at 122. Also see n. 2 above, *passim*.

[32] See 8 *Yearbook* (1965), 530–6. For more details consult G. Schantl and M.
Welan, 'Betrachtungen über die Judikatur des Verfassungsgerichtshofs zur Menschenrechtskonvention', 25 *Österreichische Juristenzeitung* (1970), 617–47.

[33] See Ch. Schreuer, 'The Impact of International Institutions on the Protection
of Human Rights in Domestic Courts', 4 *Israel Yearbook on Human Rights* (1974),
60–88, at 74–5. For the Austrian authorities the precise scope of this concept still
remains unclear: see Evans, 'Written Communication', at 122–4.

[34] See *Collection*, art. 6, 118.

1973 the same Court annulled a provision of the Tyrol Real Property Sales Act as it considered that the composition of the Tyrol Real Property Sales Commission was not an 'independent and impartial tribunal' within the meaning of Article 6(1) of the Convention.[35] The decision was based in part on that given against Austria by the European Court of Human Rights in the *Ringeisen* case of 16 July 1971.[36] In a case decided on 18 June 1975, the *Oberster Gerichtshof* (Supreme Court) – after holding that compensation for non-material damage may be obtained upon a reading of Article 5 of the Convention – went on to say:

A weighty indication of the correctness of the assumption that the recognition of a right to compensation for non-material damage is contained in the Convention and thus became a part of Austrian law, is provided by the decisions of the European Court of Human Rights of 22.6.1972 and 7.4.1974 in the Ringeisen and Neumeister cases, where it is stated quite clearly that in the event of conduct infringing Article 5 of the Convention pecuniary compensation shall be granted for non-material as well as material damage. It should be added that at the Second International Colloquy on the European Convention on Human Rights held in Vienna in 1965 it was even stated that national authorities were bound, when interpreting the Convention, to follow the decisions of its organs. Mr. Verdross stated for example that although the European Court of Human Rights could not of course set aside a national judgment contrary to its own opinion, a decision of the Court was effective for the future, since the international law principle of good faith bound the Contracting States to ensure that the Convention should be observed as interpreted by its organs.[37]

The Court also went on to refer to the practice of the Commission.[38]

In a more recent case, decided on 15 October 1976, the *Verfassungsgerichtshof* was apparently prepared to deviate from its *jurisprudence constante* according to which Article 6 of the Convention was considered not to be applicable in cases relating to the punishment of civil servants who have failed to observe their personal and professional duties. The Court explained:

According to the judgment of the European Court of Human Rights of 8th June 1976 in Engel and others, this statement is now no longer unqualified. The Court of Human Rights stated that the Convention required

[35] See ibid., 151.

[36] It cited paras. 94 and 95 of the *Ringeisen* judgment, Eur. Court HR, ser. A, vol. 13. See also judgment of 13 Mar. 1973, referred to by Evans, n. 33 above, at 123.

[37] See 19 *Yearbook* (1976), 1105–6; also A. Khol, 'Zur Diskussion um die Europäische Konvention zum Schutze der Menschenrechte und Grundfreiheiten', *Juristische Blätter* (1966), 130–41.

[38] Ibid., at 1107.

the appropriate authorities to allow the accused the benefit of the guarantees of Article 6 CHR in the field of disciplinary proceedings in cases where severe sentences of imprisonment were imposed.

The consequences in domestic law of this judgment of the European Court of Human Rights need not, however, be examined in the instant case since the judgment appealed against does not impose a sentence of imprisonment.[39]

Whether the Austrian courts would consider a decision of the European Court of Human Rights as executory in character in a case in which Austria is obliged to pay compensation (as occured in the *Ringeisen* case), remains a moot point; although in January 1965 the *Oberster Gerichtshof* had this to say about Article 50: 'A decision by the European Court of Human Rights under Article 50 of the Convention to the effect that a judgment by a national court constitutes a breach of the Convention does not quash the said judgment. It is the duty of the national authorities to take steps to implement the decision of the European Court of Human Rights.'[40]

A unique example of how the Austrian authorities have been able to accommodate the Commission's findings in internal law is provided by the Federal Act of 26 March 1963.[41] In a particular set of cases filed with the Commission a certain amount of doubt was cast upon the conformity with the Convention of the 1873 Code of Criminal Procedure — under which appeals proceedings and the hearing of pleas of nullity took place at non-public hearings in the absence of the accused and his counsel but in the presence of the Public Prosecutor or his representative who is heard by the court. In response, the Austrian Government did not contest the Commission's decision declaring the applications admissible, but instead tried to give satisfaction to the complainants and make adequate legislative changes in order that Austrian law might conform to the standards set out in the Convention.[42] Thus, while two of the original four applications were still pending before the Commission (together with some twenty similar cases) the Austrian

[39] **20** *Yearbook* (1977), 686–91, at 689.

[40] *Collection*, art. 50, 1. But see n. 54 below.

[41] **6** *Yearbook* (1963), 804–16 (with an explanatory note of the Federal Ministry of Justice on 808–16).

[42] Applications of *Ofner, Hopfinger, Pataki*, and *Dunshirn* in 6 *Yearbook* (1963), 676–739. Cf. also Schreuer, n. 33 above, at 65–6, and A. H. Robertson, 'Applying the Effective Compliance with Decisions (with Reference to the European Convention on Human Rights)' in *The Effectiveness of International Decisions* (ed. S. M. Schwebel, 1971), 346–50.

authorities passed the Federal Act of 1963 which entitled all those persons whose applications related to an appeals procedure and whose petitions had been declared admissible by the Commission in accordance with Article 28 of the Convention to have these proceedings re-opened. Consequently, in its report, while considering that the earlier procedure was not compatible with the Convention, the Commission requested the Committee of Ministers not to take any action with respect to the outstanding cases, as the legislation of March 1963 apparently gave satisfaction to the applicants. The Committee of Ministers subsequently adopted the Commission's proposals in its resolution of 16 September 1963.[43] Thus, as a direct result of these developments the Austrian courts were able to re-open proceedings in cases where the conditions laid down by the Act of March 1963 had been fulfilled.[44]

The decisions of the Committee of Ministers appear to have much less influence upon domestic courts than those of the Court. This is undoubtedly so because of the political character of the organ itself as well as the fact that its decisions are not fully reasoned, as are those of the Court.[45] Similarly, although Austrian courts tend to take note and sometimes even cite the decisions of the Commission, its views also carry much less weight than do the judgments of the Court in that, apart from its power to decide questions of admissibility, the Commission can only give *opinions* as to whether or not a breach of the Convention has taken place.[46] And, although there is undoubted evidence that friendly settlements (*Simon-Herold* and *Gussenbauer*)[47] as well as a case in which an unofficial arrangement had taken place (*Vampel*)[48] have stimulated legislative and

[43] See ibid.

[44] See *Collection*, art. 26, 1, art. 27, 1, and art. 28, 1. The possibility of a retrial was also referred to by the *Oberster Gerichtshof* in a completely different context: see Ress, n. 2 above, at 18.

[45] For a list of cases in which the Committee of Ministers has made decisions concerning applications brought against Austria consult tableaux of D. Giuliva, VIII *RDH/HRJ* (1975), 475–90; and *Yearbooks* 18–20 (1975–77).

[46] See, for example, case-law cited in 21 *Yearbook* (1978), 669–70, and 673–4; case no. 7063/76 of 3 June 1976 (*Oberster Gerichtshof*) in *Juristische Blätter* (1977), 37–9, at 38 (Commission's case-law *re* art. 1 of 1st Protocol); and 42 *Vfgh* (1977), case no. B248/75 of 26 Mar. 1977, 241–4 (Commission's case-law *re* arts. 9 and 4 of the Convention).

[47] Application 4340/69, *Simon-Herold* v. *Austria*, report of Commission, 19 Dec. 1973, and applications 4897/71 and 5219/71, *Gussenbauer* v. *Austria*, report of Commission 8 Oct. 1974. See 'Stocktaking', 88–9 and 91–2.

[48] Application 4465/70, *Vampel* v. *Austria*, report of Commission, 9 July 1975, 2 *D&R*, 4–10.

administrative changes in the domestic forum, these cases do not, as such, appear to have had any direct impact upon the courts.

Belgium

Since the judgment of the *Cour de Cassation* dated 9 May 1971 in the *SA Fromagerie Franco-Suisse 'le Ski'* case, there appears no doubt that in Belgium the directly applicable provisions of the EEC Treaty have precedence over both prior and subsequent domestic legislation. The same is true of the directly applicable provisions of the European Convention on Human Rights.[49] And, although decisions of international organizations may also have the same domestic effects as decisions of the organs of the European Communities imposing obligations upon the Belgian state (see Article 25 *bis* of the Constitution), the situation is somewhat different with regard to decisions which impose obligations upon individuals. For,

in the European Communities, only regulations and decisions may impose obligations upon individuals. In order to have such an effect, a regulation must be published in the Official Gazette of the European Communities, and a decision must be notified to its addressee. Traditional international organisations generally do not provide for the method of publication of their decisions nor for their notification directly to the individuals affected thereby. Such decisions are generally binding upon the member countries, and it is up to the member countries to take appropriate steps to implement them among the individuals subject to their jurisdictions.[50]

It therefore follows that neither a decision of the Committee of Ministers nor even a reasoned decision of the European Court of Human Rights are as such legally binding as a matter of domestic law. However, this is not to say that in all circumstances domestic courts will not be prepared to take the case-law of the Court (as well as that of the Commission) into consideration: the published opinion of the *Avocat Général* J. Velu in the case of *Pacheco* v. *Minister of Finance* illustrates this point admirably.[51] In a case decided by the *Conseil d'État*

---

[49] See ch. 3 above, sec. A. (It may be recalled that Belgium has made declarations under arts. 25 and 46 of the Convention.)

[50] *Per* M. Waelbroeck, report relating to *Belgium*, in *Individual Rights* . . . , n. 30 above, 55–76, at 68–9. See also Waelbroeck, n. 2 above, esp. 516–17.

[51] *Cour de Cassation*, decision of 23 Sept. 1976, *Pas. Bel.* (1977), i. 83–98, at 85–96. Also consult the *de Giey & Royale Belge* case of 4 Oct. 1978, 147 *Bulletin des Arrêts de la Cour de Cassation* (1979), 153–63, esp. the observations of *Avocat Général* Krings, at 154 and 157–61, *Pas. Bel.* (1979), vol. i.

on 14 November 1974 reference was made to the *Belgian Linguistics* decision of the European Court of Human Rights, of 23 July 1968, when the court rejected an appeal which was in part based upon the Strasbourg Court's judgment.[52]

Similarly, the *Tribunal de Première Instance de Bruxelles* held on 16 January 1976 that it was competent to hear a case brought against the state by a Mr De Wilde, which was based upon Article 5(5) of the Convention;[53] and what is of particular significance here is the fact that in its decision the *Tribunal* took into consideration a judgment of the European Court of Human Rights in a case which had originated with an application brought before the Commission by, among others, the same person who was at that moment seeking redress before the *Tribunal.*[54]

Although in a number of cases the Belgian courts have made reference to the Commission's decisions, the latter most certainly does not have the legal value of '*la chose jugée*' or *res judicata.*[55] This applies not only to the Commission's decisions on admissibility but also its opinions when it draws up its reports in accordance with Article 31(1) of the Convention:

... The decisions of 6th July 1964 and 16th December 1964 of the European Commission of Human Rights are opinions as provided for in Article 31 of the Convention; and it does not follow either from Belgian law or from the Convention itself that such opinions are binding on domestic courts. The accused is therefore not entitled to claim that they should prevail over the previous practice of the Cour de Cassation.[56]

And, although the execution of a judgment of a domestic court

[52] See *18 Yearbook* (1976), 410–12. Similarly in the case of *Kouvas* v. *the State,* the *Conseil d'État* in a judgment dated 7 Aug. 1969, based its decision unequivocally on the *Belgian Linguistics* case: see *7 RBDI* (1971), 740–5. See also *Pas. Bel.* (1978), iii. 4–8, where the *Tribunal Correctionnel* of Verviers cited the Commission's case-law (decision of 21 Dec. 1977).

[53] See *19 Yearbook* (1976), 1118–19. The findings of both the Court and Commission have also been cited by the *Tribunal de Police* of Tubize: see *21 Yearbook* (1978), 696–7 and 702–3.

[54] Eur. Court HR, *De Wilde, Ooms,* and *Versyp* cases ('*Vagrancy*' cases), judgment of 10 Mar. 1972 (art. 50), ser. A, vol. 14. In this case the Court held that the appellants' claim for damages was admissible but not well-founded. Consult in particular the separate opinions of judges Holmback, Ross, and Wold on 13–15. (This case was also cited in a footnote in the case of *Jespers* on 29 Mar. 1977, in *Pas. Bel.* (1977) i. 818–20.) See also Velu, n. 2 above, esp. 202 and 222–3.

[55] See, for example, decisions of the *Cour de Cassation* of 29 Oct. 1971 in *Collection,* art. 6(1), 156, and of 30 June 1975, *18 Yearbook* (1975), 419–20. See also decision of the *Cour d'Appel* of Brussels of 12 Nov. 1976, *20 Yearbook* (1977), 720; and cases cited in notes 52–3 above.

[56] Decision of *Cour d'Appel* of Brussels, 12 Dec. 1967 in *Collection,* art. 6, 88.

may be suspended by the authorities while a case is pending before the Commission in Strasbourg — this actually did happen in the extradition case of *Martinez* v. *Minister of Justice*[57] — the *Cour de Cassation* has explained unequivocally that a 'plainte déposée par le demandeur contre l'État belge auprès de la Commission européenne des Droits de l'Homme et des libertés fondamentales de Strasbourg n'est pas suspensive et qu'une bonne administration de la justice requiert que les décisions disciplinaires et judiciaires produisent leur effet normal'.[58]

The *Martinez* case, cited above, was considered by the *Conseil d'État* in April 1975 and again in January 1978. It merits particular attention. Not only was the Court initially prepared to postpone a decision, relating to the extradition of a Spanish national to his country, until it had studied an admissibility decision of the Strasbourg Commission, but upon receipt of a copy of the decision, it appears to have provided it with some form of 'evidential value'. The relevant passages of the *Conseil d'État*'s judgment read:

Considérant que, par sa décision du 12 décembre 1973, la Commission européenne des droits de l'homme a rejeté comme 'manifestement mal fondée au sens de l'article 27, s.2, de la Convention (de sauvegarde des droits de l'homme et des libertés fondamentales)' la requête que Jésus Rodriguez-Martinez lui avait présentée le 5 janvier 1973 et qui invoquait les mêmes circonstances de fait et le même moyen unique de droit — violation prétendue de l'article 3 de la Convention précitée — que de recours sur lequel il appartient au Conseil d'État de statuer en l'espèce; que ce rejet était notamment fondé sur la constatation que, dans les circonstances de la cause, 'l'affirmation du requérant selon laquelle le Gouvernement espagnol demanderait son extradition pour les motifs d'ordre politique et que, dans ces circonstances, il risquerait d'être soumis à des traitements inhumains ou dégradants, semble dénuée de tout fonde-ment' et que 'l'examen du dossier ne permet donc de déceler, même

---

[57] **164** *Pas. Bel.* (1977) **iv.** 115-18. In this case, 11 Apr. 1975, the *Conseil d'État* decided to reconsider the appeal as it felt that it *'ne peut dès lors statuer sur le moyen unique de la requête sans examiner l'incidence, en espèce, de la décision rendue le 12 décembre 1973 par la Commission européenne des Droits de l'Homme'* (at 118). An extract of this decision is reproduced in **19** *Yearbook* (1976), 1111-13. (A stay of execution of a judgment by the Government and a stay of a judgment by the Court itself are, of course, two quite different matters.)

[58] Decision of 14 Dec. 1976, **20** *Yearbook* (1977), 727-31, at 727. This application, no. 6878/75, was declared admissible: see **6** *D&R*, 79-100. (See subsequent Strasbourg Court judgment of 23 June 1981, *Le Compte, Van Leuven*, and *De Meyer*.) Also consult *Le Compte* case, 24 Oct. 1978, **147** *Bulletin des Arrêts de la Cour de Cassation* (1978), 221-6. But see 'Bringing an Application before the European Commission of Human Rights', *Case-Law Topics*, no. 3 (1972, revised Mar. 1978), 17-18.

d'office, aucune apparence de violation des droits et libertés garantis par la Convention et notamment par l'article 3';
Considérant que cette décision de la Commission européenne des droits de l'homme ne s'impose pas au Conseil d'État en tant que chose jugée;
Considérant toutefois que, dans son dernier mémoire introduit le 13 février 1974, le requérant n'a ni critiqué en droit l'application faite par la Commission de l'article 3 de la Convention, ni allégué de fait précis auquel la Commission n'aurait pas eu — ou n'aurait pas pu avoir — égard; qu'il s'est borné à écrire, en termes généraux, 'que si la Commission européenne des droits de l'homme de Strasbourg avait rendu sa décision en janvier 1974, la publicité donnée aux peines ou traitements inhumains et dégradants infligés en Espagne et révélés fin décembre 1973, cette commission aurait émis un autre avis';
Considérant que, dans ces conditions, la décision de la Commission européenne des droits de l'homme du 12 décembre 1973 apporte *une preuve suffisante* de ce que le moyen unique manque en fait.[59]

The domestic courts appear to have taken little judicial notice of cases in which the Belgian authorities and the Commission have either managed to achieve a friendly settlement or in which some form of unofficial arrangement has taken place, although the *Cour de Cassation* did in fact in one instance consider the *Boeckmans* case when determining *ex officio* that Article 6(1) of the Convention had been violated.[60] And, in cases in which violations have been established by the Commission and the Court, the authorities have either amended legislation which was considered to be contrary to the Convention provisions (*de Becker*,[61] *Belgian Linguistic* cases,[62] and the *Vagrancy* cases),[63] or alternatively, appropriate executive or administrative measures were implemented (*Les Fourons* case).[64] With respect to the Strasbourg Court's judgment of

[59] Decision of 20 Jan. 1978 in *Recueil des Arrêts du Conseil d'État* (1978), 98-9. (Emphasis added.) For a discussion of the above two decisions consult Y. Lejeune, 'Extradition, Conseil d'État et autorité des décisions d'irrecevabilité de la Commission européenne des Droits de l'Homme', *Admin. Publ. trim.* (1978/79), 56 ff.

[60] *Springuel* case, judgment of 31 May 1976, *Pas. Bel.* (1976), i. 1042-3. The case of *Boeckmans* v. *Belgium*, application no. 1727/62, was a friendly settlement: see 15 *Coll. of Dec.*, 66. For other Belgian case-law in Strasbourg consult 'Stocktaking', 50 and 107. But also note the comments of P. Mertens, in *Les recours des individus ...*, n. 2 above, at 288.

[61] Eur. Court HR, judgment of 27 Mar. 1962, ser. A, vol. 4.

[62] Eur. Court HR, judgment of 23 July 1968, ser. A, vol. 6; and resolution of Committee of Ministers, art. 54, 15 *Yearbook* (1972), 62-3.

[63] (i) Eur. Court HR judgment of 18 June 1971, ser. A, vol. 12, and resolution of Committee of Ministers, art. 54, 15 *Yearbook* (1972), 62. (ii) Resolution of Committee of Ministers, art. 32, 15 *Yearbook* (1972), 694-713.

[64] Resolution of the Committee of Ministers, art. 32, 17 *Yearbook* (1974), 542-617. A proposal for legislative reform is pending before the Belgian Parliament concerning the *Marckx* case, and a Government bill is expected shortly concerning

13 June 1979 in the *Marckx* case there is a very interesting judgment of the civil court of Ghent, dated 20 November 1980. In this case the Court held that the distinction between the rights of succession in a 'legal' family and those in a 'natural' family constituted a violation of Articles 8 and 14 of the Convention and of Article 1 of the First Protocol, making express reference to the *Marckx* judgment (even though the Strasbourg Court did not go so far as to declare the above mentioned distinction to be contrary to Article 8 of the Convention read in conjunction with Article 1 of the First Protocol!). The court thereupon decided *not* to apply the still existing statutory rules concerning the 'natural' family, and instead applied the rules concerning the 'legal' family to a 'natural' family situation, thus granting a 'natural' grandchild full protection which the law provides only to a 'legal' grandchild.[65] Similarly, although as yet no legislative action has been taken after the Strasbourg Court's adverse finding in the case of *Le Compte, Van Leuven, & De Meyer* (judgment of 23 June 1981), the French-speaking Appeals Council of the *Ordre des médecins* opened its doors to the public during a disciplinary session held on 6 October 1981, notwithstanding the contrary provisions of the applicable statute. Interestingly enough, the facts of this case bear a striking similarity to the facts of the *Le Compte* case.[66]

Cyprus

The European Convention on Human Rights has the status of domestic law in Cyprus, and by virtue of Article 169 of the

the *Le Compte* case. With respect to the *Marckx* case see F. Rigaux, 'La loi condamnée. A propos de l'arrêt du 13 juin 1979 de la Cour européenne des Droits de l'Homme', 94 *JT* (1979), 513–24, esp. at 521–3; and 'reply' of M. Bossuyt, 'L'arrêt Marckx de la Cour européenne des Droits de l'Homme', *RBDI* (1980), 53–81.

[65] *Rechtskundig Weekblad* (1980–1), cols. 2328–32. See also M. J. Bossuyt, 'The Direct Applicability of International Instruments on Human Rights (with special reference to Belgian and US law)', *RBDI* (1980), 317–54, at 320–5.

[66] The author is indebted to Mr Paul Lemmens for bringing the above two developments to his attention. But also see *Cour de Cassation*, decision of 21 Jan. 1982, *G. v. Ordre des architectes*, 101 *JT* (1982), 438–50 (with comments by J. J. A. Salmon).

For a general survey of changes that have been introduced in Belgian law as a result of findings by the Strasbourg organs consult J. De Meyer, 'Belgie en het Europees Verdrag tot bescherming van de rechten van de mens' in *Belgisch buitenlands beleid in internationale betrekkingen, Liber Amicorum, Prof. O. De Raeymaeker* (1978), 285–93.

Cypriot Constitution it possesses a hierarchically superior force to both prior as well as subsequent conflicting legislation. The country has not, however, accepted the right of individual petition under Article 25 even though it has accepted the compulsory jurisdiction of the Court under Article 46.[67]

Of particular interest is the fact that although Cyprus has not been prepared to supervise its engagements under the instrument, i.e. to assess the practical force of its substantive provisions, at least in so far as the right of individual petition is concerned, the Cypriot courts have on numerous occasions invoked the decisions of the Strasbourg organs as an aid to the interpretation of constitutional or corresponding provisions.[68] It is remarkable how often both the case-law of the European Court of Human Rights and that of the European Commission of Human Rights have been cited.[69] The principal reason for the apparent readiness of domestic courts to invoke not only the Convention's provisions but also the decisions of its organs probably stems from the fact that a part of the Cypriot Constitution of 1960 is, with slight modifications and additions, an actual adaptation of the Convention's substantive provisions.[70]

A recent example may be taken for illustrative purposes: in a judgment of the Supreme Court of Cyprus of 31 October 1977 in the case of *Kouppis* v. *the Republic*, in which the appellant was convicted of homicide, Judge Triantafyllides observed, in his separate judgment, that Articles 30(2) and 12(5) of the Cypriot Constitution resembled closely Article 6(1) of the Convention and that these provisions possessed a 'superior force to any municipal law'.[71] He then went on to refer to over twelve 'decisions' of the European Commission of Human Rights and two decisions of the European Court of Human Rights (namely those of *Neumeister* and *Delcourt*), which in his estimation 'can provide most useful guidance as regards the interpretation and application of the corresponding provisions

---

[67] See ch. 7 above, sec. A.

[68] See Z. Nedjati, *Human Rights and Fundamental Freedoms* (1972), and C. G. Tornaritis, 'The European Convention on Human Rights in the Legal Order of the Republic of Cyprus', 9 *Cyprus Law Tribune* (1976), 1–19.

[69] See, for example, *Collection*, art. 6, 92/1, and 129–31; and 19 *Yearbook* (1976), 1123–4.

[70] See 'The influence of the Convention', 3 *Yearbook* (1960), 675–743, esp. 678–705. (The fact that Judge Triantafyllides is also a member of the European Commission of Human Rights may likewise be of relevance!)

[71] 11 *JSC* (1977), 1860–98, at 1877–9.

of our own Constitution'.[72]

It follows that the decisions of the Convention organs are highly authoritative, especially in cases where they make clear the meaning of certain of this instrument's (as well as the Constitution's) provisions, although they do not appear to have binding domestic force. In so far as the decisions of the Committee of Ministers are concerned, it may be safe to say that they probably possess less authority than those of the Commission when it makes a decision on admissibility. This situation could change, were Cyprus to accept the right of individual petition.

France

In France, as in Cyprus, the European Convention on Human Rights appears to possess a hierarchically superior status to ordinary legislation although unlike Cyprus, where this instrument was actually transformed into domestic law, France 'adopted' the Convention into its legal system upon ratification in 1974. That is to say, in those cases where the courts consider that a given provision of the Convention binds an individual directly, they apply the provision as an international norm directly applicable within the French legal system.[73]

In recent years the French courts have made increasing reference to the Convention's provisions although only in a few recorded cases have they taken into consideration the findings of the Convention's organs. For example, in November 1977 the *Cour d'Appel de Paris*, in the *Croissant* case, referred to an application of the *Baader-Meinhoff Group*[74] which the Commission had held inadmissible in May 1975.[75] More recently, M. Labetoulle, the *commissaire du gouvernement* in his submissions before the *Conseil d'État*[76] — in a case in which it was held that disciplinary hearings against a doctor not held in public did not violate Article 6 of the European Convention — referred to certain judgments of the European Court of Human Rights (*Ringeisen* and *Engel*). He explained that as a consequence of the country's acceptance of the Court's jurisdiction to interpret

[72] Ibid., at 179. See also *Fouri & others* v. *Republic* (1980), 2 *CLR*, 152.
[73] See ch. 3 above, sec. B. The right of individual petition and the Court's compulsory jurisdiction have been accepted by France.
[74] Application 6166/73, 2 *D&R*, 58–67.
[75] Judgment of 16 Nov. 1977, 21 *Yearbook* (1978), 724–9, at 726–7.
[76] *Recueil des décisions du Conseil d'État* (1978), *Debout* case, 27 Oct. 1978, 395–7.

and apply the Convention, '*au moins indirectement et implicite-ment, la jurisprudence de la cour est une donnée dont il faut tenir compte*'.[77] He then added that the court must attempt to reconcile '*deux préoccupations: d'une part éviter toute solution qui serait radicalement incompatible avec la jurisprudence de la cour; d'autre part éviter aussi toute solution qui sur un point marquerait une rupture avec le droit national antérieur*'[78] before expressing his opinion that in this particular case Article 6 of the Convention had not been infringed.

For the present it may be assumed that French courts will adopt an approach similar to that taken by their Belgian counterparts. In the words of Professor A.-Ch. Kiss:

Pour déterminer la nature et les effets des actes émanant d'organisations et de juridictions internationales en droit interne français, il convient avant tout de se demander quelle est la valeur *intrinsèque* de chacun de ces actes. Ceux qui obligent les États auxquels ils s'adressent, sont assimilés aux traités même qui ont donné naissance ou ont conféré les compétences correspondantes à l'organe qui est leur auteur, c'est-à-dire *un caractère obligatoire et même supérieur aux règles de droit interne* est reconnu à ces actes. Par contre, les actes qui dès le départ ne constituaient que des recommandations ou des avis ne seront appliqués que s'ils ont été repris par les organes internes compétents, pour être introduits dans l'ordre juridique interne.[79]

Federal Republic of Germany

In the Federal Republic of Germany the substantive provisions of the Convention possess at least a status equivalent to federal law and, in cases in which the country is a party, the decisions of the Strasbourg Court and of the Committee of Ministers bind the Republic internationally (Articles 53 and 32(4) of the Convention).[80] However, the authority given in domestic law to the decisions of the Court or of the Committee of Ministers remains merely persuasive:

Such decisions have no executory effect in the sense of being directly enforceable in the courts of the Federal Republic. If the decision relates to an administrative act of a public authority, administrative action will

[77] Ibid., 395–406, at 403.
[78] Ibid., at 403–4. The case-law of the Commission was also cited in *Touami Abdeslem, Conseil d'État*, 25 July 1980, in II *Juris-Classeur* (1981), at 19613.
[79] Kiss, n. 2 above, at 271. (Emphasis added.)
[80] See ch. 4 above, sec. B. Declarations have been made under arts. 25 and 46. For more details see H. Guradze, *Die Europäische Menschenrechtskonvention* (1968), 13–37, and K. J. Partsch, *Die Rechte und Freiheiten der Europäischen Menschenrechtskonvention* (1966), 47–51. Also consult Ress, n. 2 above, *passim*.

be taken to correct the situation in so far as possible in accordance with the decision. If the decision relates to legislation, the Government will have an obligation to introduce repealing or amending legislation as required to comply with the decision, but its passage will depend on the will of the legislature. In criminal cases there is at present no procedure for reopening the proceedings before the German courts and the authorities recognise that the possibility of introducing such a procedure may have to be considered. Meanwhile it is not possible to quash a conviction in the light of the decision of the European Court or Committee of Ministers. All that can be done is for the competent Federal or Land authority to grant a pardon or for an award of compensation to be made administratively. The position is the same in the fields of civil and administrative law. Once a final decision has been made by the courts there is no means of overruling or reopening it. It therefore depends on what the administrative authorities can do within their authority to give effect to the decision of the European Court or Committee of Ministers.[81]

To date, the Committee of Ministers has found no violations of the Convention in cases concerning the Federal Republic,[82] while in three cases from the total of six sets of cases brought before the Strasbourg Court the German authorities have taken necessary legislative and administrative measures to make domestic law compatible with the Convention's provisions[83] without directly involving domestic courts in this procedure.

Domestic courts refer very infrequently to the case-law

---

[81] Evans, 'Written Communication', at 151. It is interesting to note that in the recent *Eurocontrol* case 9 *EGZ* (1982), 172-81, the *Bundesverfassungsgericht* has expressed the view that it has the task of controlling the compatibility of German legislation with binding rules of public international law. It is understood that the Court had the European Convention in mind when formulating this sentence, and that this decision may signal the beginning of a case-law that will attempt to take much greater notice of the Convention. In the words of Professor J. A. Frowein, Director of the Max-Planck-Institute for Comparative Public Law and International Law, '[i]t seems very likely on the basis of this development that the Federal Constitutional Court will discuss judgments of the European Court of Human Rights or even decisions of the Commission when this seems important to find out whether or not a right guaranteed by our Constitution has the same meaning as a fundamental right guaranteed by the Convention.' (Letter to the author, 22 Dec. 1981.)

[82] See tableaux of D. Giuliva, n. 45 above, to which may be added the cases of *Levy* and *Hätti*, 19 *Yearbook* (1976), 950-94 and 1024-88, *Brüggeman and Scheuten*, 21 *Yearbook* (1978), 638-40, *Haase*, 11 *D&R*, 78-110, and *Preikhzas*, 16 *D&R*, 5-31.

[83] Eur. Court HR *König* case, judgment of 28 June 1978, ser. A, vol. 27; Eur. Court HR., *Leudicke, Belkacem, and Koç*, judgment of 28 Nov. 1978, ser. A, vol. 29; Eur. Court HR, *Buchholz* case, judgment of 6 May 1981, ser. A, vol. 42. In the *Leudicke* case the European Court of Human Rights held that the decisions of courts in the FRG ordering Messrs Leudicke, Belkacem, and Koç to pay interpretation costs, incurred in criminal proceedings which had led to their conviction, were in breach of art. 6(3) of the Convention. See also *Eckle* case, Eur. Court HR, judgment of 15 July 1982, ser. A, vol. 51.

of the Commission and the Court,[84] and this at first sight appears rather surprising especially when one notes the numerous cases in which reference is made to the Convention's provisions. And, although it is difficult to determine why this is so, this situation may be explained in part by the fact that the members of the bench and the German legal profession have in the past been deprived of adequate translations of these organs' findings, which are usually made available only in French and English, the two official languages of the Council of Europe.[85] This being said, it is of particular interest to note a rather unique judgment of the Cologne *Oberlandesgericht* (Court of Appeal) which actually referred to a decision of the Committee of Ministers.[86] In support of its decision in which the Court rejected an appeal based upon Article 4(1) of the Basic Law, which guarantees freedom of opinion, the Court referred to the decision of the Committee of Ministers in the *Grandrath* case[87] in which it was held that the sentencing of a Jehovah's Witness to imprisonment for refusing to do service in lieu of military service was not in breach of the European Convention on Human Rights.

Another interesting development worth noticing is that concerning the more general area of compatibility of domestic case-law with the obligation of member states to provide those charged with criminal offences with free assistance of an interpreter if they cannot understand or speak the language used in court.[88] While the case of *Luedicke, Belkacem, and Koç* was still pending before the European Court of Human Rights, the German authorities 'arranged for the Länder judicial administrative authorities to suspend the recovery of costs in all individual applications pending on this question until the [Human Rights] Court's decision'.[89]

[84] See, for example, cases cited by Schreuer, n. 33 above, 73 and 75: decision of the *Bundesverfassungsgericht* of 27 Mar. 1974, 17 *Yearbook* (1974), 656-7; of the Stuttgart *Oberlandesgericht* (Court of Appeal), 27 *NJW* (1974), 284-5; and of the Bavarian Supreme Court, 21 *Yearbook* (1978), 739-40.

[85] See W. Bertram, 'Ueberlegungen von Verfahrensbeauftragen der Bundesrepublik Deutschlands', VIII *RDH/HRJ* (1975), 349-60 (with a summary in English).

[86] Decision of 21 July 1967, 20 *NJW* (1967), 2168-70.

[87] Resolution (67) DH 1, of 12 June 1967, 10 *Yearbook* (1967), 626-99.

[88] See *Luedicke, Belkacem, and Koç* v. *FRG*, n. 83 above.

[89] *Per* Mrs Maier, German agent before the Court: doc. Cour/Misc. (78) 53, 25 May 1978, 31 and 32. See also para. 23 of the Court's judgment. An excellent overview of the impact that the Strasbourg proceedings have had within the FRG is provided by Professor G. Ress in his report at the Frankfurt colloquy, n. 2 above, at 32-7.

In addition, in a number of cases where friendly settlements have been achieved under the supervision of the Commission[90] the German Government has, where appropriate, suggested that no general element existed to justify the Commission's continuation of a case in question. In so doing, in the *Mellin* case, the Federal Government's Agent informed the Commission's Secretary by letter that 'In this connection I would refer to the reforms adopted in the Federal Republic in the field of criminal law and procedure ... They include the abolition and the suspension of proceedings when twice the prescription period has elapsed (Article 78(c), para. 2, second sentence, of the Penal Code as amended by the Second Criminal Reform Act).'[91] More recently, in the case of *Liebig*, the Commission was 'informed of the Federal Government's intention, at the forthcoming Conference of Ministers of Justice of the Länder, *to draw attention of the Länder judicial authorities* to the need for the courts to respect the principle of presumption of innocence embodied in Article 6(2) of the Convention when setting out the reasons for decisions relating to expenses under Articles 154 and 467, paragraph 4, of the Code of Criminal Procedure'.[92]

Greece

In accordance with Article 28(1) of the Greek Constitution of June 1975, the European Convention on Human Rights possesses the status of domestic law since its transformation. Those of its substantive provisions which are deemed to be self-executing by the courts would appear to have a hierarchically superior status to both prior as well as subsequent conflicting legislation.[93]

To date there probably exists no case-law in which express reference to the findings of the Convention organs has been made, although it may be assumed that, as in the Federal Republic of Germany or as in Italy, at least the decisions of the European Court of Human Rights will be considered by the

[90] See 'Stocktaking', *passim*.

[91] Report of Commission, 12 Dec. 1973, at 7. This case concerned the length of detention of the applicant. See 'Stocktaking', 89–90.

[92] Report of Commission, 11 May 1978, 17 *D&R*, 5–20, at 20. (Emphasis added.) Also 21 *Yearbook* (1978), 540–54, at 554. In this case the applicant complained to the Commission that to leave him to pay his personal expenses, relating to criminal proceedings which had been discontinued against him, constituted a violation of the presumption of innocence guaranteed by art. 6(2) of the Convention.

[93] See ch. 6 above, sec. A, and Ph. Vegleris, *The European Convention on Human Rights and the Greek Constitution* (in Greek, 1977), esp. 84–111.

Greek courts as being highly authoritative.[94] This being said, it must be borne in mind that Greece has only recently recognized the compulsory jurisdiction of the European Court of Human Rights although no declaration has as yet been made under Article 25. Also, it is not altogether certain to what extent the Greek courts will be prepared to be influenced by outside interpretations of domestic law provisions (in that the Convention has been transformed into Greek law). And it is unclear whether they will regard these findings as 'directly applicable' interpretations of 'generally accepted rules of international law' (Article 28, paragraph 1 of the Constitution).

Regarding the country's joining of the European Communities, the new Constitution specifically provides that:

To serve an important national interest and to promote cooperation with other states, competences under the Constitution may be granted by treaty or agreement to organs of international organisations. A majority of three-fifths of the total number of members of Parliament shall be necessary to vote the law sanctioning the treaty or agreement. [Article 28, paragraph 2.][95]

This provision does not appear to apply to the Convention, as the new Constitution came into force after the Convention's ratification in 1974 and the three-fifths parliamentary majority is lacking.[96] It remains unclear, however, whether a transfer of certain of the constitutional 'competences' has in fact been made and whether the Greek courts would deem this to be the case if the Greek authorities were to be held to have violated certain of the Convention's norms by either the European Court of Human Rights or the Committee of Ministers. Perhaps a more realistic appreciation of the present situation is provided by Professor Ph. Vegleris when he writes:

[94] See N. Patouris, 'Prisoners' Rights in Greece: A Comparative Analysis of the Greek Code of Corrections and the Council of Europe Standards', IV *Journal of Hellenic Diaspora* (1979), 17-64, at 32-3. Also consult C. P. Economides, 'Nature juridique des actes des organisations internationales et leurs effets en droit interne', 23 *RHDI* (1970), 225-38, and shorter commentaries by N. B. Lolis, at 358-62, and by A.-B. Papacostas, at 308-13.

[95] The English translation is from A. Fatouros, 'International Law in the New Greek Constitution', 70 *AJIL* (1976), 492-506, at 494.

[96] 17 *Yearbook* (1974), 2; 28 *RHDI* (1975), 370. For recent studies of this subject see E. Rouconnas, 'Le droit international dans la Constitution Grecque du 9 juin 1975', 29 *RHDI* (1976), 51-73, esp. 61-2; Fatouros, n. 95 above; S. Varouxakis, 'Diritto internazionale, diritto comunitario e diritto costituzionale greco', 17 *Riv. DE* (1977), 318-24; D. Evrigenis, 'Aspects juridiques de l'adhésion de la Grèce aux Communautés européennes' in *La Grèce et la Communauté (Problèmes posés par l'adhésion)*, (1978), 273-86; and Fatouros, 'Greece Joins the Communities', 6 *EL Rev.* (1981), 495-503.

Dans mon esprit, les 'findings', la jurisprudence de Strasbourg, a fort peu d'espoir de pénétrer dans l'interprétation et l'application de la CEDH par les autorités grecques, administratives et judiciaires, tant que la Grèce n'aura pas accepté le 'recours individuel' à l'encontre de ses autorités et que les décisions et arrêts des organes européens — ou leur menace — n'aura pas attiré l'attention de nos tribunaux sur la jurisprudence européenne touchant des questions d'interprétation et d'application d'un droit qui est en même temps un droit domestique, et même un droit 'valorisé'.[97]

Italy

The European Convention on Human Rights was transformed into the Italian legal system by the legislature's 'order of execution' on the 4 August 1955 in accordance with Article 80 of the Italian Constitution, and from that time its substantive provisions form an integral part of domestic law, possessing a status equivalent at least to that of ordinary legislation. Declarations relating to Articles 25 and 46 were made in 1973.[98] It may also be recalled, as a matter of interest, that the *Corte Costituzionale* has accepted the view, at least implicitly, that the Convention's provisions embody the same category of fundamental human rights as those which are constitutionally protected, although the ordinary courts are not prepared to provide this instrument a hierarchically superior position *vis-à-vis* other domestic legislation.[99]

Both Italian case-law and doctrine appear to adhere strictly to the dualist theory, whereby the provisions of international agreements cannot be applied in the domestic legal order unless their contents are transformed into internal law. It follows that, were the Strasbourg organs to find that Italy has violated a provision of the European Convention on Human Rights, internal law would be appropriately adapted.[100] Consequently, the operative provisions of the decisions of the Committee of

---

[97] Letter to the author, 13 Jan. 1982. See also Professor N. E. Devletoglou's letter to *The Times*, 5 Oct. 1981, at 13.

[98] See M. Chiavario, *La Convenzione Europea dei diritti dell'Uomo* (1969), 19-63. See also ch. 6 above, sec. B.

[99] See V. Grementieri and N. Trocker, 'The Protection of Human Rights in Constitutional Law: Italy' in *Italian National Reports to the IXth International Congress of Comparative Law*, Tehran, 1974, 491-504; also case-law cited in ch. 6 above, sec. B.

[100] L. Ferrari-Bravo and A. Giardina, 'Les procédés nationaux de mise en vigueur des obligations souscrites et des accords conclus par les gouvernements' in *Italian National Reports*, ibid., 475-90, esp. 484-6.

Ministers and of the European Court of Human Rights, in cases in which Italy may be a party, would be internationally binding on Italy by virtue of Articles 32(4) and 53 respectively, although the *reasons* given in a judgment by the Strasbourg Court, or to support a decision of the Committee of Ministers, would in all probability have only a persuasive domestic authority. The particular weight given to such decisions — especially that of the Court — would of course depend on their bearing on the matter under consideration; and as in most other countries, the decisions of the Committee of Ministers can be assumed to have less influence than those of the Court both because of the political character of the organ itself and because its findings tend not to be fully reasoned.

Were the Strasbourg Court to decide that Italy should pay compensation in accordance with Article 50 of the Convention, it remains a moot point whether such a finding could constitute a sufficient legal basis for payment of the sum awarded through the domestic courts.[101]

Although Italian courts have in a few cases referred to resolutions of the General Assembly of the United Nations in support of their reasoning — by virtue of Article 10 of the Constitution, which provides for the adaptation of Italian law to the generally recognized principles of international law — they remain extremely cautious in their use of decisions of international organizations and the findings of their organs.[102] And, in so far as the authority of the findings of the European Commission of Human Rights and that of the Court are concerned, to date there appears to be no recorded case in which an Italian court has been prepared to refer to findings of either of these Strasbourg organs in order to substantiate its conclusions in a given matter.[103]

Luxembourg

The European Convention on Human Rights obtained legislative

---

[101] See M. Miele, 'Les organisations internationales et le domaine constitutionnel des états', 131 *R. des C.* (1970), iii. 309-92. See also n. 23 above.

[102] Directly applicable Community law is, of course, an exception to this rule. See case-law quoted by G. Arangio-Ruiz, 'Italy' in Lauterpacht and Collier, n. 30 above, 365-93, at 381-3.

[103] D. Giuliva, of the University of Bari, has a list of over ninety cases in which reference has been made to the Convention's provisions by Italian courts, but *none* in which the case-law of its organs has been used. Also consult V. Starace and C. De Caro, *La Giurisprudenza Costituzionale in materia internazionale* (1977), *passim*.

approval in Luxembourg on 29 August 1953 and became an integral part of the domestic law of the country upon its ratification on 3 September 1953.

As in Belgium and in France those provisions of international agreements deemed by the courts to be directly applicable have priority over both prior and subsequent conflicting legislation, and though the Luxembourg courts have in the past been surprisingly hesitant to regard the substantive provisions of the Convention as directly applicable,[104] this trend has now apparently been halted. Thus, in its decision of 17 January 1972 the *Cour Supérieure de Justice (Chambre correctionnelle)* held that the Convention's *'dispositions doivent prévaloir sur celle de la loi interne, s'opposant à la mise en charge du prévenu acquitté des frais de citations ainsi que des taxes des témoins . . .'*[105]

Although Article 49 *bis* of the Luxembourg Constitution (read in conjunction with Article 37) permits temporary derogation by treaty to institutions of international law — this was in fact done in respect of the EEC — the fact that this Article was introduced *after* the European Convention on Human Rights became an integral part of Luxembourg law would appear to make it inapplicable in so far as the findings of the Convention organs are concerned.[106]

It follows that, in all probability, the findings of the European Court and Commission, as well as the decisions of the Committee of Ministers bearing on the interpretation of this instrument, are not legally binding upon the domestic courts (or other domestic authorities), although they certainly do possess a persuasive authority.

There is, however, an exception to this generally accepted state of affairs. In an Act of 30 April 1981 the legislature has provided for the possibility of a retrial when a person has been convicted in breach of the European Convention. This Act provides for an amendment of the Luxembourg Criminal Code, Article 443(5), to the effect that a person has a right to a retrial if the European Court of Human Rights or the Committee of Ministers decides that his conviction had been obtained in

---

[104] See *Bull. EC Suppl. 5/76*, 41, and ch. 3 above, sec. C.

[105] Taken from **19** *Yearbook* (1976), 1139. See also recent decisions of the same court in **XXII** *Pas. Lux.* (1976-7), 182-9, and in *JT* (1980), 489-92.

[106] See P. Pescatore, *Conclusion et effet des traités internationaux selon le droit constitutionnel, les usages et la jurisprudence du Grand-Duché de Luxembourg* (1964), esp. at 67-73. In addition, such a treaty must be approved like a constitutional amendment, i.e. by a two-thirds majority of the legislature.

contravention of the Convention.[107]

The decision of the *Cour Supérieure de Justice* of 17 January 1972, cited above, appears to be one of the few on record in which a Luxembourg court has made reference to the case-law of the Convention organs.[108]

The Netherlands

Those provisions of the European Convention on Human Rights which are considered by the Dutch courts to be directly applicable have binding force of law in the Netherlands from the date of the instrument's publication in July 1954. Dutch constitutional law in effect recognizes that certain treaty provisions are deemed directly applicable (self-executing) (Article 65 of the Constitution), and that conflicting statutory law, whether prior or subsequent, may be overruled by such treaty provisions (Article 66 of the Constitution). And, although the essence of the basic rights laid down in the European Convention on Human Rights is found in the Dutch *Grondwet*, the special significance of this instrument lies in the fact that Dutch courts are not permitted to examine the conformity of statutes to the Constitution (Article 131(2)), whereas the review of the incompatibility of such legislation with those provisions of the Convention deemed by the courts to be directly binding upon individuals is not only admitted, but even *required*.[109] The Convention is consequently considered the main *international* source of law concerning the guarantee of human rights which protects the individual *within* the Dutch legal system.[110]

The Dutch Constitution not only provides for the precedence

[107] See *Information Bulletin on Legal Activities within the Council of Europe and in member states*, no. 10 (Nov. 1981), 37. The Act also provides for the award of damages to the victim of a miscarriage of justice.

[108] See n. 105 above. This was in fact done *indirectly* when reference was made to the Council of Europe's *Manuel: Convention européenne des Droits de l'Homme* (1963), 38, and to the Commission's case-law cited there. In a more recent case the Strasbourg Court's *Klass* judgment was cited: *Cour de Cassation*, no. 6/80, 20 Nov. 1980 (registry no. 418).

[109] See D. H. M. Meuwissen, *De Europese Conventie en het Nederlandse Recht* (1968); L. J. Brinkhorst and J. G. Lammers, 'The Impact of International Law, including European Community Law on the Netherlands Legal Order' in *Introduction to Dutch Law for Foreign Lawyers* (eds D. C. Fokkema, J. M. Chorns, E. H. Hondius, and E. Ch. Lisser, 1978); and ch. 3 above, sec. D.

[110] It should be added that declarations under arts. 25 and 46 were made in 1960 and have been renewed ever since.

of directly applicable provisions of treaties *vis-à-vis* conflicting domestic legislation, but this precedence is also extended by Article 67(2) to *directly applicable decisions of international organizations* (e.g. regulations of the European Communities) and perhaps also the decisions of international judicial organs. It is appropriate again to cite Articles 63, 65, 66, and 67 of the Dutch Constitution which reads:

Article 63
If the developments of the international legal order require this, the contents of an agreement may deviate from certain provisions of the Constitution.
In such cases only explicit approval can be given; the Chambers of the States-General shall not approve a Bill to that effect except with a two-thirds majority of the votes cast.

Article 65
The provisions of agreements the contents of which may be binding on anyone shall have this binding effect as from the time of publication. Rules with regard to the publication of agreements shall be laid down by law.

Article 66
Legal regulations in force within the Kingdom shall not apply if this application should be incompatible with provisions — binding on anyone — of agreements entered into either before or after the enactment of the regulations.

Article 67
Subject, where necessary, to the provisions of Article 63, certain powers with respect to legislation, administration and jurisdiction may by or in virtue of an agreement be conferred on organizations based on international law.
With regard to decisions made by organizations based on international law, Articles 65 and 66 shall similarly apply.

As an authority on this subject has explained:

Article 67, stipulating that legislative, administrative and judicial powers may be conferred on organisations based on international law, is (therefore) a specific recognition of the fact that written international law is no longer to be found in treaties only, but also in decisions of international organisations. Such decisions need not be submitted for parliamentary approval, as is the case with international agreements. Though the powers conferred may include the power to take decisions directly upon individual persons, they do not include the power to take decisions affecting individual rights if these are specifically guaranteed by the Constitution. In that case the agreement conferring powers which deviate from the Constitution requires *express* approval by Parliament pursuant to Article 63.[111]

---

[111] L. J. Brinkhorst, 'The Effect upon the Traditional Concept of the State of Regional Cooperation' in *Netherlands Report to the VIIIth International Congress of Comparative Law*, Pescara, 1970, 255–66, at 257. See also Brinkhorst and Lammers,

It may therefore be noted that because the European Convention on Human Rights was not enacted into law in accordance with Article 63, as it was not implemented by a two-thirds Parliamentary majority (this is also the case with regard to the EEC and Euratom Treaties), the requirements of Article 63 are irrelevant, and by virtue of Articles 65 and 66 its directly applicable provisions are provided an 'extra-constitutional' status. Likewise, its norms do not conflict with rights guaranteed by the Constitution; the Dutch courts are anyway not competent to judge on the constitutionality of international agreements (Article 60(3) of the Constitution). It follows, curiously enough, that this situation may in reality permit the courts to give decisions of international organizations the force of domestic law on the understanding that such decisions apply, *mutatis mutandis*, in the same way as directly applicable treaty provisions (Article 67(2) read in conjunction with Articles 65 and 66 of the Dutch Constitution). This view was recently reiterated by Professor Alkema who assisted Sir Vincent Evans in a part of his study concerning the authority in internal law of the decisions of the Convention organs. Sir Vincent explained — after quoting paragraph 2 of Article 67: 'This [article] probably gives self-executing decisions of the European Court of Human Rights and Committee of Ministers binding on the Netherlands (including in Mr. Alkema's view parts of such decisions interpreting the Convention) the same precedence over the Netherlands Constitution, Acts of Parliament, subordinate legislation and administrative acts as attaches to the self-executing provisions of the European Convention.'[112]

It will therefore be interesting to monitor developments in the Dutch courts, especially in the light of the judgments of the European Court of Human Rights in the *Engel*[113] and *Winterwerp*[114] cases, and to see whether they will be prepared to consider themselves bound by a decision of the Strasbourg Court. For the present, particular note may be taken of a recent

---

n. 109 above, esp. 574-6; and L. Erades, 'The National Effects of International Agreements' in *Sixième Congrès International de droit comparé* (*contributions néerlandaises*, Hamburg 1963), 111-20.

[112] Evans, 'Written Communications', at 166. Also see E. A. Alkema, *Studies over Europese grondrechten* (1978), at 16. (English summary at 274-5.)

[113] Eur. Court HR, judgment of 8 June/23 Nov. 1976, ser. A, no. 22.

[114] Eur. Court HR, judgment of 24 Oct. 1979, ser. A, no. 33. See, in connection with the case, ministerial circular of 16 Apr. 1980 discussed in ch. 3 above, n. 93.

case decided by the *Hoge Raad*[115] on 18 January 1980, a decision which appears to have extremely far-reaching consequences. The court observed that the legal distinction made between legitimate and natural children has of late undergone strong change, and that this development found expression in the European Court's judgment in the *Marckx* case in an interpretation of Article 8 in conjunction with Article 14 of the Convention. The domestic judge must therefore take cognisance of this important evolution, in the light of the court's findings, when examining matters which come before him on this point. In effect, as one commentator has explained, the *Hoge Raad* may well have assigned the Strasbourg Court's judgment in the *Marckx* case a quasi-legal force in that the said judgment appears to have made a direct impact upon Dutch family law.[116]

Parts of the decisions of the Committee of Ministers under Article 32 of the Convention — especially in cases in which the Netherlands is a party — would appear in principle to be considered directly applicable, although the fact that such decisions emanate from a political organ whose decisions are not motivated in the same way as those of the Strasbourg Court, would probably make domestic courts extremely reluctant to apply them in practice. To date, only one decision taken by the Committee of Ministers has concerned the Netherlands directly, although as no violation of the Convention was found, the courts have apparently taken scant judicial notice of it.[117] This does not, of course, necessarily exclude the possibility of the courts taking into consideration Committee of Ministers resolutions generally, i.e. beyond the context of its specific functions under the Convention. Thus, for example, in a decision dated 1 July 1976 the *Hoge Raad*, when considering an applicant's appeal based partly upon Article 5(1)(c) of the Convention,

[115] Case no. 463, *NJ* (1980); commented upon by E. A. Alkema, in case no. 462 *NJ* (1980).
[116] G. Ress, 'The Legal Effect of the Judgments of the European Court of Human Rights on the Internal Law and before Domestic Courts of the Contracting States' in *Fifth International Colloquy about the European Convention on Human Rights*, Frankfurt, 9–12 Apr. 1980, doc. H/Coll. (80)4, at 39. He adds that such a far-reaching effect of the Strasbourg Court's case-law has not as yet been observed in any other contracting state. Also see p. 14 for an extract from the Court's judgment. See also case no. 588, *NJ* (1979), 1963–5, and case no. 272, *NJ* (1974).
[117] *De Geillustreerde Pers N.V.*, 8 *D&R*, 5–29. (Resolution DH(77)1, at 17.) See Pres. Ab. Amsterdam, no. 90, RvdW/KG (1981). The Court's case-law as well as that of the Commission was also cited by The Hague District Court on 12 July 1979. See overview of Dutch case-law, relating to questions of public international law, by L. A. N. M. Barnhoorn, 11 *NYIL* (1980), 289–313, at 302–5.

took note of Resolution (65)11 which included a recommendation that in cases of remand in custody there should be
'révision d'office à des intervalles réguliers'.[118]

The decisions on admissibility of the European Commission
of Human Rights as well as its opinions have been referred to in
the Dutch courts on a number of occasions. They may be and
certainly are provided some weight in the general interpretation
and elucidation of particular provisions of the Convention even
though they are not legally binding upon the domestic courts.
For example, in an appeal before the *Hoge Raad* dated 16
January 1968 an appellant unsuccessfully invoked Article 6(3)
(a) and (b) of the Convention, as the Court considered that this
Article did not oblige the state to stipulate the exact manner in
which an accused must be informed of the nature and cause of
an accusation brought against him.[119] And, what is of particular
interest in this case is that the acting Attorney-General actually
referred to two decisions of the European Commission of
Human Rights (*Ofner* v. *Austria* and *X* v. *The Netherlands*)[120]
from which he concluded that infringement of Article 6(3)(a)
may not be claimed by an accused if in fact he was fully aware
of the nature and substance of the charge brought against him.
Similarly, in a case dated 10 June 1969, the *Hoge Raad* dismissed an appeal against a conviction under a Road Traffic Act.
In so holding the court took note of the conclusions of the
Attorney-General who made reference to the Strasbourg Commission's decision on admissibility in a case in which it was held
that Article 6(3) of the Convention did not require that an
accused be informed in *writing* of the charge brought against
him.[121] In a more recent case in which an appellant claimed
that his imprisonment for the duration of his whole life was in

---

[118] Case no. 452, *NJ* (1976), 1334-41, at 1337. This resolution, entitled 'Remand
in Custody' was adopted by the Ministers' Deputies on 9 Apr. 1965. Also consult
Hoge Raad judgment of 26 Feb. 1980, *NJ* (1980), no. 246. As to the functions of the
Committee of Ministers *beyond* its ambit of activity circumscribed by the Convention,
see A. H. Robertson, *The Council of Europe* (1961), 24-40.

[119] Case no. 378, *NJ* (1968), 1281-4. An English summary of this case is provided
by V. van der Gaag, 1 *NYIL* (1970), 216-17. See also judgment of 10 Dec. 1965 of
the Rotterdam District Court, 15 *NTIR* (1968), 435.

[120] In the *Ofner* case the Commission provided an 'opinion' (6 *Yearbook* (1963),
678-713) with which the Committee of Ministers subsequently agreed; the case of
X v. *the Netherlands* application 1059/61, was a decision on admissibility (5 *Year-
book* (1962), 262-70). The Commission's case-law was also cited in the case of
Pagel and Brilman, Amsterdam Court of Appeal, 6 Nov. 1975 (noted by L. A. N. M.
Barnhoorn, 9 *NYIL* (1978), 271-351, at 304-5).

[121] See 2 *NYIL* (1971), 240-1.

violation of Article 3 of the Convention, the Hague Court of Appeal held that the deteriorating physical and mental state of the appellant did not in his case constitute inhuman treatment under Article 3. In so finding, the court quoted from a Commission's decision in which it was explained that '[i]nhuman treatment covers at least such treatment as deliberately causes severe suffering, mental or physical, which, in the particular situation, is unjustified. Treatment or punishment of an individual may be said to be degrading if it grossly humiliates him before others or drives him to act against his will or conscience.'[122]

In certain cases courts have been asked to prohibit the Dutch authorities from expelling or extraditing individuals until the European Commission or the Court of Human Rights have reached a definite decision regarding the complaints. In one case, decided by the Hague District Court on 2 September 1980,[123] this argument was accepted: an interlocutory injunction was granted whereby the extradition of the applicant to Belgium was suspended until such time as the Strasbourg Commission had reached an admissibility decision relating to the plaintiff's complaint, which had been lodged on 12 August 1980. In a previous case the same court was initially not prepared to issue an injunction forbidding the expulsion of a Romanian national in anticipation of a decision of the Commission in Strasbourg, which at that time had not yet been seized by the applicant, although an injunction was subsequently issued on the ground that his marriage to a Dutch national in itself constituted a sufficiently urgent humanitarian argument to permit him to apply for a residence permit.[124]

Needless to add, the direct influence of the findings of the Commission (as well as those of the Court and Committee of Ministers) is undeniable when one assesses the Convention's

---

[122] An extract of this case can be found in 20 *Yearbook* (1977), 772-5. Note may also be taken of the *Menten* case (Hague District Court, 4 Dec. 1978, subsequently appealed before the *Hoge Raad*) in which reference was made to the case-law of the Commission. See A. M. M. Orie and E. Myjer, 'Menten en de goede procesorde' in *Delikt en Delinkwent* (1979), 84-95. For more recent case-law see *Bulletin of the NJCM* (1980-2).

[123] *Leenaert* v. *the State of the Netherlands*, no. 80/591, in *Rechtspraak Vreemdelingenrecht* (1980), 113.

[124] See notes on Dutch judicial decisions by L. A. N. M. Barnhoorn, 8 *NYIL* (1977), 269-71. See also 30 *CDE* (1977), 317, 7 *NYIL* (1976), 331-2, and more recent cases cited by Barnhoorn, in 9 *NYIL* (1978), 303-17, at 293-5, esp. n. 57, and in 11 *NYIL* (1980), 300-12, at 302-5.

impact beyond the confines of the courtroom, as the *Wallace*, *Kamma*, *Engel*, and *Winterwerp* cases illustrate.[125]

Portugal

Having become a member state of the Council of Europe in September 1976, Portugal ratified this instrument and its two protocols on 9 November 1978. At the same time the country recognized both the compulsory jurisdiction of the European Court of Human Rights and the competence of the European Commission of Human Rights to receive individual petitions.[126] And, although there appears no doubt that, in accordance with Article 8(2) of the 1976 Constitution, the substantive provisions of this instrument have now secured themselves a status of domestic law, it is too early to assess the extent to which the Portuguese courts will be prepared to refer to it, let alone the findings of its organs. Nevertheless, it may be assumed that as the Constitution emphasizes that 'the rules and principles of general and ordinary international law shall be an integral part of Portuguese law' (Article 8(1)), the courts will be able to adopt an attitude similar to that of their Belgian counterparts.[127]

To date, the author has come across only one case, of 24 July 1979, in which the Constitutional Commission considered an admissibility decision of the Commission. In refusing to accept the petitioner's arguments that a court's judgment against her was unconstitutional because she had been absent from her trial and unable to call a witness in her defence, the Constitutional Council considered that a lower court had abided by all the relevant provisions of both the Portuguese Constitution and the Code of Criminal Procedure. In so holding it cited Article 6(2) of the Convention which guarantees the presumption of innocence in criminal cases. It then referred to an admissibility decision of the Commission in which the Commission considered that a statutory provision which provides that, when certain

---

[125] See E. A. Alkema, 'The Application of Internationally Guaranteed Human Rights in the Municipal Order' in *Essays on the Development of the International Legal Order on Memory of H. F. Van Panhuys* (ed. F. Kalshoven, P. J. Kuyper, and J. G. Lammers, 1980), 181-98, at 184-7.

[126] See ch. 6 above, sec. C.

[127] This subject is further discussed ibid. The existence of an authoritative Portuguese translation of the Convention (which includes reference to Strasbourg case-law) may be of considerable help in this respect: see J.-D. Pinheiro Farinha, *Convenção Europeia dos Direitos do Homen* (1980).

facts are proven by the prosecution, certain other facts shall be presumed — thereby creating a rebuttable presumption of fact which the defence may in turn disprove — does not in itself violate the presumption of innocence which is guaranteed by Article 6(2) of the Convention.[128]

Spain

Upon the ratification of the European Convention on Human Rights by Spain on 4 October 1979 and its subsequent publication in the *Boletín Oficial del Estado* on 10 October 1979, the substantive provisions of this instrument acquired the status of domestic law. Although to date there appears to be no reported case-law in which the Convention's provisions have been invoked by the Spanish courts, it is generally assumed that directly applicable provisions of the Convention will be provided priority — in accordance with Article 10, paragraph 2, of the new Constitution — over both prior and subsequent legislation, should a conflict arise.[129] Thus, whether or not the decisions of the Committee of Ministers (under Article 32), or those of the European Court of Human Rights (under Article 53), or even opinions of the Commission or its decisions on admissibility, will be given judicial notice by the Spanish courts depends on the extent to which such findings will relate to specific problems put before them.[130] This being said, the Spanish acceptance of the Human Rights Court's compulsory jurisdiction as well as the Commission's competence to receive individual applications may lead the domestic courts, or at least lawyers pleading before the courts,[131] to invoke the Strasbourg Court's findings as guidelines which may serve to clarify the extent and nature of obligations assumed by Spain on the international plane.

---

[128] Case no. 14/78, decision of 24 July 1979, in 219 *Boletim do Ministério da Justiça* (Dec. 1979), 341–53, at 351. The case cited was application 5124/71, *X* v. *UK* 42 *Coll. of Dec.*, 135.

[129] See ch. 6 above, sec. D.

[130] It may be added that art. 93 of the Spanish Constitution provides for the 'delegation' of certain powers to organs of international organizations. (This provision was drafted with Spain's eventual accession to the European Communities in mind: see ch. 6 above, n. 57, for the English text.)

[131] See, on this subject, recent developments in France, n. 77 above. Also see unpublished paper of S. Rodríguez Miranda, 'Naturaleza jurídica de los actos de las Organizaciones y jurisdicciones internacionales y sus efectos en derecho interno', (Spanish national report presented at the 1970 Pescara VIIIth International Congress of Comparative Law, 1970).

Switzerland

A Member of the Council of Europe since 1963, the Confederation of Switzerland ratified the Convention in November 1974 and at the same time made declarations under Articles 25 and 46.[132] And, as norms of customary law as well as conventional international agreements are *automatically* incorporated into federal law, the European Convention on Human Rights became an autonomous part of Swiss law at the time of its ratification, with those of its provisions deemed by the courts to be immediately applicable possessing a rank equivalent to at least that of other federal legislation. It may be added that the *Tribunal Fédéral* considers that, as the rights guaranteed in the Convention have *per se* a constitutional content, this instrument must be equated, for procedural purposes, with Swiss written and unwritten constitutional law.[133] Thus, for it to be seized by an appeal based on the Convention's provisions, the *Tribunal Fédéral* requires that the individual can do so only after he has exhausted all available cantonal remedies (with the exception of appeals alleging violation of Article 4 of the Federal Constitution and with respect to Article 87 of the Judicature Act, 1943).

Although Switzerland is internationally bound by both the decisions of the European Court of Human Rights and the Committee of Ministers under Articles 53 and 32 of the Convention respectively, it is not altogether certain that such decisions (specifically concerning Switzerland) are directly applicable in domestic law, i.e. that the reasons given in these cases may be considered binding upon the individual by the Swiss courts. One cannot, however, completely exclude the possibility of a situation occurring in which a court may regard the findings of an organ of an international organization as directly applicable. For, as one informed observer has noted:

La question de *l'application directe* ... se pose à l'égard des actes des organisations internationales dans les mêmes termes, en principe, que pour les traités internationaux ... La juridiction helvétique n'a pas hésité à

---

[132] See ch. 4 above, sec. D.
[133] See case of *Diskont- und Handelsbank AG*, 101 *ATF* (1975), Part I(a), 67-71. (An extract from the judgment can be found in 19 *Yearbook* (1976), 1154-6.) Also see G. Malinverni, 'L'application de la Convention européenne des Droits de l'Homme en Suisse', XV *Journée Juridique* (1975), 1-51, and D. Poncet, *La protection de l'accusé par la Convention européenne des Droits de l'Homme* (1977), 12-14 and 17-26.

envisager l'application, à une situation contentieuse concrète, d'actes d'institutions internationales, sans invoquer d'autres justifications que le caractère obligatoire de ces actes. Il convient de souligner qu'à chaque fois le texte international, de par son objet et sa structure, avait vocation à régir des situations intéressant les particuliers, dans ce sens qu'il fixait notamment les droits ou obligations des individus, et qu'il était suffisamment complet et précis pour se prêter à l'application [directe].[134]

It is therefore not surprising to find that the findings of the European Court of Human Rights and those of the Commission possess substantial persuasive authority; and, as in Austria — where the Convention has 'constitutional status' — the actual weight given to these findings depends essentially on its bearing on the matter under consideration. On the other hand, the fact that the Committee of Ministers does not give fully reasoned decisions and because it is neither a judicial nor a quasi-judicial organ, its decisions appear to carry much less weight.

A few examples in which the case-law of the Convention organs has been cited by the Swiss courts may be referred to for illustrative purposes. In a case brought before the Zürich *Verwaltungsgericht* (Administrative Court) on 29 April 1975, a commercial company *Buchdruckerei Elgg AG* objected to the levying of a church tax by the Reformed Evangelical and the Roman Catholic parishes for the fiscal year of 1974, in that it considered that such a tax violated provisions of the cantonal and federal constitutions as well as Article 9 of the European Convention on Human Rights.[135] In dismissing the company's contentions, the court explained — in so far as Article 9 of the Convention was concerned — that corporate bodies could not invoke this Article unless they were associations of individuals formed for the purpose of religious or philosophical observance

---

[134] Ch. Dominicé, 'La nature juridique des actes des organisations . . .' n. 2 above, at 258. See also report on *Switzerland* by L. Caflisch, in *Individual Rights and State in Foreign Affairs*, n. 30 above, 498–545, esp. at 520–7. But see the views of L. Wildhaber, *Treaty-Making Power and Constitution* (1971), 394–5, expanded upon in 'Erfahrungen mit der Europäischen Menschenrechtskonvention', **98** *Revue de droit suisse* (1979), 230–379, at 328–61; and of Evans in 'Written Communication', at 183–4; also writings referred to in n. 149 below. See also response of *Conseiller* Grobet to a question submitted to the *Conseil Fédéral*, ASDI (1977), 161–2, concerning the Strasbourg Court's decision in the *Engel* case, Eur. Court HR, judgment of 8 June/23 Nov. 1976, ser. A, no. 22. This problem directly concerned Switzerland: see report of Commission, 4 Mar. 1978, in the case of *Eggs* v. *Switzerland*, application 7341/76, and the Committee of Ministers resolution DH(79)7, 19 Oct. 1979. (A new law on military penal procedure was enacted and the Military Penal Code was modified.)

[135] See 32 *ASDI* (1976), 85–90.

and were concerned with the pursuit of this purpose; and, in order to substantiate its reasoning it went on to cite the decision on admissibility of the European Commission of Human Rights in the *Church of Scientology* case in which the Commission considered that the Church (a legal person) was incapable of exercising the rights embodied in Article 9(1) of the Convention.[136] This case subsequently went before the *Tribunal Fédéral* which, on 6 October 1976, confirmed the decision of the Zürich *Verwaltungsgericht*.[137] In so doing it also referred to the *Church of Scientology* case.[138]

In another case which came before the *Chambre d'Accusation* of Geneva in January 1975, the court referred to the case-law of the Commission in order to confirm its finding that applicants were not able to invoke the Convention's provisions prior to the date of its ratification by Switzerland (Article 6(3)).[139] In addition, the court also cited a Committee of Ministers' resolution of 19 January 1973, 'Standard Minimum Rules for the Treatment of Prisoners', and referred to its principle 93 which stipulates that '[a]n untried prisoner shall be entitled . . . to receive visits from his legal adviser with a view to his defence and to prepare and hand to him, and to receive, confidential instructions. At his request he shall be given all necessary facilities for this purpose'.[140]

Similarly, in the *Schiesser* case,[141] the *Tribunal Fédéral* was prepared to cite the Commission's case-law in support of its finding that Article 6(3) of the Convention had not been violated by the authorities of the Canton of Zürich.[142]

---

[136] Extracts of this decision are reproduced in **18** *Yearbook* (1975), 430-2, in English, and in **20** *Yearbook* (1977), 789-93, at greater length in French. The application was brought against the United Kingdom: application 3798/68, **12** *Yearbook* (1969), 306-25, at 314. (The Commission's findings have now changed somewhat on the point raised.)

[137] Case no. 66, **102** *ATF* (1977), i(a), 468-83.

[138] See French *résumé,* **20** *Yearbook* (1977), 798-801, at 800.

[139] See **19** *Yearbook* (1976), 1153-4.

[140] Resolution (73)5. (In effect this was a recommendation: see Robertson, n. 118 above.) The court then added that *'la jurisprudence [suisse] a en effet admis qu'en cette matière, il faut prendre en considération des données relevantes du droit comparé et le cas échéant les principes établis par les organisations internationales'.*

[141] Case no. 28 of 14 July 1976, **102** *ATF* (1976), i(a), 179-85. The case subsequently went before the European Court of Human Rights which held, by five votes to two, that art. 5(3) had not been breached: see Eur. Court HR, judgment of 4 Dec. 1979, ser. A, no. 34.

[142] See English text, **20** *Yearbook* (1977), 793-8. See also decision of *Tribunal Fédéral* of 2 Sept. 1977, case no. 72, **103** *ATF* (1978), i(a), 490-3.

The judgment of the *Tribunal Fédéral* in the *Burger* case,[143] dated 3 November 1976, illustrates well two interesting judicial trends: (i) the constitutional importance that the Convention appears to have secured itself in the eyes of the Swiss judiciary and, (ii) what is more significant for the present study, the willingness of the Swiss courts to refer in some considerable detail to the findings of the European Court of Human Rights. In this case Burger, the appellant, had been accused of embezzlement and was detained on remand. His detention was extended on a number of occasions and, after unsuccessfully applying to the Chief State Counsel of the Basel City Canton, and to the Basel City Committals Board, he entered a constitutional appeal against the Committals Board's decision, alleging that Articles 5(3) and 6(2) of the Convention had been violated in his case. In dismissing his appeal, the *Tribunal Fédéral* reiterated its prior case-law in which it held that 'the Convention takes over and develops further provisions on fundamental freedoms contained in numerous state constitutions or recognised by contracting states as unwritten constitutional principles'.[144] It then went on to hold that the applicant's continued detention in remand was justified as there was a real danger of his absconding. It did so by taking into account 'the unwritten constitutional conventions of the Federation guaranteeing personal freedom in the practical application of which regard must be had to the guarantees conferred by the Convention, which are relied on by the appellant, *and in particular to their interpretation by the decisions of the tribunals set up by the Convention*'.[145] The *Tribunal Fédéral* then made a detailed analysis of the interpretation given to Article 5(3) by the European Court of Human Rights in the *Wemhoff* and *Neumeister* cases,[146] as well as the Commission's decisions which indicated its acceptance of the Strasbourg Court's interpretation after the Commission's own approach to this question had been expressly rejected by the Court in the *Wemhoff* case.[147] The *Tribunal*

[143] Case no. 55, **102** *ATF* (1977) i(a), 379–86; English translation, **20** *Yearbook* (1977), 801–9.
[144] Quotation from **20** *Yearbook* (1977), 801.
[145] Ibid., at 802. (Emphasis added.)
[146] See Eur. Court HR, *Wemhoff* v. *FRG*, judgment of 27 June 1968, ser. A, no. 7, esp. paras. 11 and 12 at 24–5 (also in **11** *Yearbook* (1968), 796–812); and Eur. Court HR, *Neumeister* v. *Austria*, judgment of 27 June 1968, ser. A, no. 3, para. 5, at 37 (also in **11** *Yearbook* (1968), 812–31).
[147] The court referred to case-law cited by F. G. Jacobs in *The European Convention on Human Rights* (1975), 64 ff.

Fédéral also held that the detention was not of an excessive duration, and cited the Strasbourg Court's decision in the *Neumeister* case in support of its findings.[148]

Interesting though these developments may be, it must be admitted that the majority of Swiss writers still tend to view the decisions of the European Court of Human Rights as findings which may bind the Confederation internationally, but which do not *per se* possess executory force on the domestic plane; and as yet no federal procedure has been established whereby a decision of a Swiss court could be reopened if the decision were found to be incompatible with the Convention's provisions.[149] This being said, note can be taken of a development in the canton of Appenzell Rhodes-Extérieur whose new Code of Criminal Procedure offers courts the opportunity to revise their case-law when 'the decision of an international authority so requires'.[150]

---

[148] See n. 143 above, at 804–6 (reference to paras. 4, 13, and 14 of the Strasbourg Court's judgment). Case-law of the Convention's organs has in fact been cited by domestic courts on numerous occasions: see 21 *Yearbook* (1978), 779–82, and the excellent compilations provided by G. Malinverni and L. Wildhaber, 'La pratique suisse relative à la Convention européenne des Droits de l'Homme', 34 *ASDI* (1978), 167–224, and vol. 35 (1979), 181–222. Also see 105 *AFT* (1979), i(a), 98–103. Interestingly enough, in the case of *Minelli* v. *Switzerland* (pending before the Court in Strasbourg), the President of the *Tribunal Fédéral* adjourned the applicant's public law appeal as the European Commission was examining cases which raised similar questions (*Neubecker & Liebig* v. *FRG*; *Geerk* v. *Switzerland*). The proceedings were resumed after the latter cases ended in friendly settlements. See report of Commission, 6 May 1981, para. 17.

[149] According to Sir V. Evans, 'Written Communication', at 183: 'It would therefore be for the appropriate Swiss authorities to find a way of giving effect to the decision in each case on a pragmatic basis. Some jurists think that theoretically an action could be brought in the Swiss courts to enforce an award of compensation made by the European Court or by the Committee of Ministers, but in practice the need for such action is hardly likely to arise.' (Sir Vincent wrote this after consulting three Swiss experts: M. C. Krafft, M. Haller, and H. B. Reimann.) In addition see n. 133 above: Malinverni, 37–47, and Poncet, 240–5; D. Schindler, 'Die innerstaatliche Wirkung der Entscheidungen der europäischen Menschenrechtsorgane' in *Festschrift Max Guldener* (1973), 273–90; and W. Schmid, *Die Wirkungen der Entscheidungen der europäischen Menschenrechtsorgane* (doctoral dissertation, University of Zürich, 1974).

[150] Art. 223, no. 4 of the new code. See Ress, n. 116 above, at 11. Using this canton's new code as an example, a parliamentarian, P. Reiniger, suggested to the *Conseil Fédéral* that a similar procedure be made available for the whole country: proposition 79.497 of 18 Sept. 1979, OJF, LPPF, LPA (information provided to the author by a Swiss lawyer, Dr O. Jacot-Guillarmod). This 'postulate' and the answer of the Federal Council are reproduced in the commentary of G. Malinverni and L. Wildhaber, 36 *ASDI* (1980), 239–72, at 246–8.

Turkey

The European Convention on Human Rights and its First Protocol were transformed into Turkish law in accordance with Article 26 of the former Turkish Constitution, now replaced by Article 65 of the 1961 Constitution. The substantive provisions of this instrument have been secured a status equivalent to other legislation, if not a hierarchically superior internal force, although only on rare occasions have the Turkish courts made reference to them in their judgments.[151]

The operative provisions of decisions of the Convention organs appear to impose no obligations *per se* upon Turkish courts. The decisions of the Committee of Ministers are binding on Turkey on the international plane by virtue of Article 32(4) of the Convention in those instances in which the country is a party, while the decisions of the European Court of Human Rights cannot, for the present, bind Turkey, in that this organ's compulsory jurisdiction under Article 46 has not been accepted. Nevertheless, as the Convention's provisions were given special consideration when the 1961 Constitution was drafted,[152] and because no recourse may be made with regard to this treaty before the *Ana Yasa Mahkemesi* (Constitutional Court),[153] it has recently been explained that

... pour éviter la responsabilité internationale de l'État on a adopté la possibilité d'annulation d'une loi mais refusé l'annulation d'une convention. Or, on en déduit que la Constitution Turque a attribué une valeur supérieure à la Convention à l'égard de la loi ... [and it therefore follows that] ... *l'interprétation* des dispositions de la convention de Sauvegarde des Droits de l'Homme et des Libertés Fondamentales *par la Cour Européenne des Droits de l'Homme peut éclairer le juge turc*; les dispositions elles-mêmes vu l'article 65 de la Constitution peuvent constituer des fondements solides de ses décisions; et en cas de conflit entre les dispositions de la Convention et de la loi, le juge turc peut et doit accorder la priorité d'application aux dispositions de la Convention. Et enfin il est tenu de les appliquer ex-officio.[154]

Whether or not the opinions of the Commission of Human

---

[151] See ch. 6 above, sec. E.

[152] See S. Tanilli, *Anayasalar ve Siyasal belgeler* (1976), *passim.*

[153] See S. Meray, *Devletler Hukukana Giziş* (Public International Law, 1963/4); and E. Çelik, 'La formation des traités en droit international et en droit turc', 20 *Annales de la Faculté de Droit d'Istanbul* (1970), 1-50.

[154] I. Dogan, 'L'influence de la Convention de sauvegarde des Droits de l'Homme et des libertés fondamentales sur l'ordre constitutionnel turc', at 8 and 9. (This paper was presented at a meeting held in Sept. 1978 in Istanbul: see ch. 6 above, n. 77. Emphasis added.)

Rights, or its decisions on admissibility, can be considered to have any authority before domestic courts remains an open question, although the fact that no declaration has been made under Article 25 may be a determining factor. In this connection it is of considerable interest to note a decision of the *Danıştay* (Council of State) rendered on 24 July 1978.[155] In this case a Swedish television company successfully argued before the *Danıştay* that the expulsion of its journalists by the Turkish Minister of the Interior violated Turkish law. And what perhaps merits special attention is that, in annulling the Minister's decision, the *Danıştay* made express reference to the Final Act of the 1975 Conference on Security and Co-operation in Europe which stipulates, *inter alia*, that state signatories made it their aim to improve the conditions under which journalists work, not to render journalists liable to expulsion when they are legitimately pursuing their professional activities, and if expelled to be informed of the reasons for such an act.[156] Thus, as the Final Act was judicially noticed there appears no reason why the Commission's findings (whose legal weight must surely be greater than that of the Helsinki Accord!) cannot likewise be taken into consideration in certain circumstances; it can certainly be argued that the Commission's case-law should be given some weight by the Turkish courts as persuasive authority in matters bearing on the interpretation of the Convention.

It may be added that on 20 January 1979 the Committee of Ministers decided — in accordance with Article 32 — that the Convention had been violated in respect of Turkish activities in Cyprus,[157] although it appears that the Turkish courts have not been provided with the opportunity to take legal cognizance of these developments.

---

[155] Reported in *Le Monde*, 3 Aug. 1978, at 22; case no. 1978/955, discussed by R. Aybay, 'The International Human Rights Instruments and Turkish Law' in *Turkish Yearbook of Human Rights* (1979), 17–25, at 23–5.

[156] See 24 *ILM* (1975), 1292–325, esp. 1315–17. As to the importance of this 'accord' (which is *not* a treaty), see *Human Rights, International Law and the Helsinki Accord* (ed. Th. Buergenthal, 1977), *passim.*

[157] Applications 6780/74 and 6950/75, *Cyprus* v. *Turkey*, resolution DH(79)1. (The documentation was declassified on 31 Aug. 1979.) The Commission has recently declared a third application (no. 8007/77) by Cyprus admissible (10 July 1978): see 13 *D&R*, 85–230.

C. In states in which the Convention does not have the status of domestic law

Denmark

Denmark ratified the European Convention on Human Rights in 1953. As this instrument has not been transformed into domestic law its substantive provisions do not have a status equivalent to other legislation by which domestic courts are bound.[158] This situation may be contrasted to that of Denmark's accession to the European Communities whereby — in applying the procedure set out in Article 20 of the Constitution — the country in effect transferred powers which the Constitution conferred upon Danish authorities to organs of a supranational nature whose decisions may in certain circumstances have immediate and direct effect in domestic law.[159]

Although Denmark is most certainly bound internationally to abide by the decisions of the Committee of Ministers and the European Court of Human Rights in cases in which the country is a party, the findings of the Court as well as the reasons given to support a decision of the Committee of Ministers appear not to possess any legal authority in internal law.[160] This is not to say that such findings will necessarily be ignored. The fact that the Convention is considered to have been 'implemented' by ascertainment of conformity (as explained by the Danish Government in the *Kjeldsen* case),[161] has made necessary the amendment of domestic legislation on a number of occasions.[162] This has occurred 'because the Convention covers vast areas of law in rather laconic language [and] also because the application, and thereby the contents, of the Convention is dynamic and evolves with the development of the case-law of the human rights bodies in Strasbourg'.[163]

[158] See ch. 5 above, sec. A; also A. Ross, *Folkret* (1976), *passim*. (Declarations have been made by Denmark in accordance with arts. 25 and 46.)

[159] See N. Gangsted-Rasmussen, 'Primauté du droit communautaire en cas de conflit avec le droit danois', 11 *RTDE* (1975), 700–7.

[160] The possibility of implementing the Strasbourg Court's decisions in Danish law is discussed by O. Espersen, 2 *Juristen* (1970).

[161] Application 5095/71, 43 *Coll. of Dec.*, 44–56, at 50. (This case later went before the Court. See Eur. Court HR, case of *Kjeldsen, Busk Madsen, and Pedersen*, judgment of 7 Dec. 1976, ser. A, no. 23.)

[162] See J. Færkel, 'The Position of Fundamental Rights in the National Legal System of Denmark; Constitutional Supremacy, General Relationship to International Law and Community Law', report to the Human Rights Seminar of the European University Institute, Florence, May 1977, notes 25, 27, and 28.

[163] Ibid., at 13. It is interesting to observe that a consistory tribunal (of an advisory

The Danish courts have had few occasions (if any) to take note of the case-law in Strasbourg, and this cannot be explained simply by the fact that the Convention possesses no domestic legal status.[164] One of the reasons may be that the Convention organs have rarely been obliged to consider applications lodged against Denmark.[165] In all probability, however, the apathy of the domestic courts may be explained within the wider context of the general relationship between Danish law and international law, and in particular the penetration of the latter into the former:

... Danish law of implementation of international law can be described as a laissez-faire policy of non-incorporation, even in spite of the fact that attitudes have in later years changed to a more receptive perception of international law [see *Acta Scandinavica Juris Gentium* (1971), 65-131]. The main problem however is probably not a problem of law, but a problem of information. It seems (to me) that the knowledge of international law of Danish lawyers (and judges) is quite limited, and the ability and readiness to use international law (which often requires a technique quite different from Danish law) accordingly is not very impressive.[166]

Iceland

The European Convention on Human Rights was not given the status of Icelandic law upon its ratification in 1953, and the substantive provisions of this instrument are rarely referred to by domestic courts.[167] Although it is generally recognized that decisions of the Committee of Ministers under Article 32 of the Convention and the decisions of the European Court of Human Rights under Article 53 would internationally bind Iceland in

character) postponed an examination of a case concerning a given individual pending the decision on admissibility of his application before the European Commission of Human Rights: see application 7374/76, 5 *D&R*, 158-60.

[164] In this connection, see interesting observations made by M. Sørensen, 'Principes de droit international public', 101 *R. des C.* (1960), iii.1-251, at 119-20.

[165] See, for example, *Nielsen* case, application 343/57, 4 *Yearbook* (1961), 490-592; the *Danish Sex Education* cases, n. 161 above; and *Becker*, application 7011/75, 4 *D&R*, 215-56.

[166] Færkel, n. 162 above, at 8. In the eyes of Professor C. A. Nørgaard (letter to the author 30 Dec. 1981) the problem is not really one of lack of information: Strasbourg case-law is not applied by Danish judges, because they consider their law to be in conformity with the Convention, and also because domestic case-law on human-rights topics is rare.

[167] See ch. 5 above, sec. B, and S. Sigurjonsson, 'International Cooperation in the Sphere of Human Rights and the Results thereof', *Icelandic Lawyers' Journal* (1968), 79-97. Declarations have been made under arts. 25 and 48.

cases in which the country were to become a party, these decisions are not in themselves legally binding on the courts and other domestic authorities. It may however be presumed that such decisions — as also possibly the opinions of the Commission and its decisions on admissibility — possess a persuasive authority. It should be noted, in this connection, that '[n]either legal writings nor international law are regarded as sources of Icelandic law, although it is clear that they in fact influence court decisions'.[168] Whether this is true in respect of the findings of the Convention organs is unfortunately difficult to determine.

Ireland

Ireland has not incorporated the substantive provisions of the Convention into domestic law (treaties require specific enactment by the *Oireachtas* under Article 29 of the Constitution) although the right of individual petition under Article 25 as well as the compulsory jurisdiction of the European Court of Human Rights under Article 46 were both accepted when the Convention was ratified in February 1953.

In December 1957, in the famous case of *Ó Laighléis*,[169] the Irish Supreme Court was not prepared to grant an applicant a remedy based upon a provision of the European Convention on Human Rights — as this instrument had not been transformed into domestic law and could therefore not supersede inconsistent Irish law. It may now be correct to assume, however, that Irish courts are prepared to use the Convention's norms at least as persuasive authority when faced with a doubtful or uncertain point of Irish law.[170]

There have been no reported decisions in which findings of the Convention organs have been cited, although there exist no domestic legal impediments which prevent the courts from

[168] Th. Vilhjalmsson, 'Iceland' in *National Reports*, I.1-6, at I.2. The judiciary may become more receptive to Strasbourg case-law since the recent appointment of M. Thoroddsen to the Icelandic Supreme Court (formerly a member of the secretariat of the European Commission of Human Rights).

[169] [1960] IR 93: see ch. 7 above, sec. B; also application of *Woods* [1970] IR 154, applying *Ó Laighléis* in relation to the supremacy of domestic law.

[170] See cases cited in ch. 7 above, notes 20-5. Apparently, in *Shaw* v. *DPP*, an unreported case decided by the Supreme Court on 17 Dec. 1980, the Strasbourg Court's judgment of *Ireland* v. *UK* was referred to by J. Walsh; see J. P. Clarke, *The European Convention on Human Rights and Fundamental Freedoms and Irish Law* (1981), 32-4, at 33.

doing so. Quite the reverse may be true. The *reasons* given in a judgment of the European Court of Human Rights (and perhaps also to support a decision of the Committee of Ministers) may, in a case in which Ireland is a party, be regarded as highly authoritative by the Irish courts, and possibly also as legally binding. This may be so when such decisions reflect general principles of international law.[171] Article 29(3) of the 1937 Irish Constitution stipulates that 'Ireland accepts the generally recognised principles of international law as its rule of conduct in its relations with other states'. And, although these generally recognized principles of international law remain 'a guide' (*ina dtreoir*) and not an absolute restriction on the state's legislative powers[172] it must nevertheless be borne in mind that

a breach by the State or by any organ of the State of a generally recognised principle of international law would not necessarily be justiciable in the domestic courts in all cases. It would, however, be justiciable if the effect of the breach operated within the municipal sphere and more especially if it threatened fundamental personal rights. There is ample judicial authority for the proposition that a person may invoke the intervention of the courts for any breach of the Constitution affecting him. Where the breach is claimed to arise from a breach of the generally recognised principles of international law the courts would have to ascertain the existence of the principles of international law and their effect within the municipal sphere.[173]

And

The effect of this constitutional provision [Article 29(3)] is that at the time when any intervention is called for [by the Irish courts] the state of international law at that particular time is what is to be looked at. The Constitution does not purport to determine what are the general principles of international law but carries on those which are so generally recognised ... Consequently, the impact upon domestic law of this provision of the Constitution would vary with what are currently recognised as the general principles of international law.[174]

As in Denmark and Iceland, decisions of the Commission still

---

[171] See the arguments put forward in n. 27 above. For a similar view in respect of the 1966 UN Covenant, consult N. K. Hevener and S. A. Mosher, 'General Principles of Law and the U.N. Covenant on Civil and Political Rights', 27 *ICLQ* (1978), 596–613.

[172] See *The State (Sumer Jennings) v. Furlong* [1966] IR 183, at 190; also in 53 *ILR*, 9.

[173] View expressed by Judges Walsh, Henchy, Doyle, and Quigley (four members of the eight-member Law Enforcement Commission) in a report of the Law Enforcement Commission to the Secretary of State for Northern Ireland and the Minister for Justice of Ireland, May 1974, Cmnd. 5627, 14–26, at 24.

[174] Walsh, Henchy, Doyle, and Quigley, ibid., at 22–3. (These quotations are taken from the section subtitled, 'The interaction of international law and Irish law'.)

tend not to be considered by the domestic courts, and this is probably due to the simple fact that there are not many cases brought against Ireland which pass the admissibility barrier. The courts may, however, be prepared to consider opinions of the Commission or its decisions on admissibility as persuasive authority in that this case-law can be used as a guideline to clarify uncertain domestic legal issues.

Ireland is, of course, internationally bound under Articles 53 and 32(4) to abide by decisions of the European Court of Human Rights and the Committee of Ministers in cases in which it is a party. On the one hand the case of *Airey* v. *Ireland*,[175] recently decided by the Court, and on the other hand the renewed interest surrounding the possible utility of incorporating this instrument into Irish law[176] may together provide the necessary impetus for the Irish courts to take greater judicial notice of developments in Strasbourg.

Liechtenstein

The Principality of Liechtenstein became the 21st member state of the Council of Europe on 23 November 1978. Upon the deposit of its instrument of accession the country signed the European Convention on Human Rights. This was done shortly after the Parliamentary Assembly had given a favourable opinion to the Committee of Ministers in which it welcomed Liechtenstein's willingness to fulfil the provisions of Article 3 of the Statute of the Council of Europe and the country's intention to sign the Human Rights Convention simultaneously when acceding to the organization.[177]

To date, the European Convention on Human Rights has not been approved by the Diet and promulgated in the National Legal Gazette (*Landesgesetzblatt*), as is required by Article 8 of the Principality's Constitution, and does not as yet possess the status of domestic law. It therefore appears too early to determine with any certainty to what extent the Liechtenstein courts will take the Convention's norms into consideration, let alone the decisions of its organs.

---

[175] Eur. Court HR, judgment of 9 Oct. 1979, ser. A, no. 32.

[176] See *A Bill of Rights* (1976), pamphlet published by the Irish Association of Democratic Lawyers.

[177] See ch. 4 above, sec. C. The Convention *now* has the status of domestic law; Liechtenstein ratified the Convention on 8 September 1982.

Malta

Although the European Convention on Human Rights was ratified by Malta in 1967, this instrument does not possess the status of domestic law (as it was not transformed in accordance with Article 73(4) of the 1964 Constitution, as amended in 1974); and, because no declarations have been made under Articles 25 or 46, the findings of the Convention organs have probably very little — if any — influence upon the Maltese legal system. This is most disappointing in that, as in Cyprus, certain of the provisions of the Maltese Constitution are actually taken verbatim from corresponding Articles in the European Convention on Human Rights to which reference is often made in appeals before the Maltese Constitutional Court.[178] This situation compares even more unfavourably with Cyprus (where the Convention possesses a domestic status superior to ordinary laws), in that the Cypriot courts often refer to decisions of the Convention organs and use these findings as guidelines which serve to clarify the extent and nature of certain legal concepts.[179]

Perhaps if the Maltese legal community were better informed of developments in Strasbourg this unsatisfactory state of affairs could be improved.

Norway

Although the European Convention on Human Rights was not transformed into Norwegian law when the instrument of ratification was deposited in March 1952, there is a presumption that Norwegian courts will conform to its substantive provisions by interpreting domestic law in such a manner that international undertakings are fulfilled; and, in the absence of a domestic legal provision to the contrary, Norwegian law must be assumed to be in harmony with the general principles of law.[180] In this connection it is important to note that this instrument was

[178] See, for example, *The Times* (of Malta), case no. 78 (3 Nov. 1969), no. 126 (24 Apr. 1972), no. 168 (6 Aug. 1973), no. 176 (8 Oct. 1973), no. 302 (21 June 1976), and no. 306 (19 July 1976). Note, however, recent proposals to amend the law: see letter of E. Mizzi, *The Times* (London), 12 Feb. 1981, at 15.

[179] See notes 69, 71, and 72 above; also A. Sceberras Trigona, *Constitutional Change and the Maltese Constitution* (doctorate in Laws, Royal University of Malta, 1972-3).

[180] See C. Smith, 'International Law in Norwegian Courts', 12 *Scandinavian Studies in Law* (1968), 150-201, at 168; also [1950] *Norsk Rettstidende*, 84; and [1933] *Norsk Rettstidende*, 511.

subjected to what may be termed a 'passive transformation' in that a prior detailed study of Norwegian law established the existence of an 'ascertainment of legislative/normative harmony'.[181]

The European Commission of Human Rights has had very few opportunities to consider applications brought against Norway,[182] and as no applications have passed the admissibility stage of proceedings neither the Committee of Ministers nor the European Court of Human Rights have had to take decisions under Articles 32 and 53 in cases in which Norway was a defending party. Similarly, the Norwegian courts seldom refer to the Convention's provisions and its case-law when determining legal issues before them.[183] An apparent exception to this practice is a case decided by the *Høyesterett* (Supreme Court) on 28 March 1966 in which it was held that:

The Provisional Act of 21st June 1956 relating to compulsory public service by dentists is contrary neither to Section 105 of the Constitution, nor to Article 4 of the Convention, which prohibits forced or compulsory labour. In this connection, the Court refers to the grounds on which, on 17th December 1963, a majority of the European Commission of Human Rights declared inadmissible, as manifestly ill-founded, Application No. 1468/62 by *Iversen against Norway*. Since the Acts of 29th June 1962 and 25th June 1965, which are complementary to the Provisional Act of 1956 (relating to compulsory public service for dentists) do not differ from it in this respect, but merely prolong its operation for successive three-year periods, they cannot be regarded as constituting a violation of the aforesaid Article 4 of the Convention.[184]

It is difficult to understand why this form of direct reference to the Commission's findings has not been made more frequently, although lack of Norwegian translations of the Commission's

---

[181] See ch. 5 above, sec. C; the Norwegian Government's report submitted under art. 40 of the 1966 UN Covenant on Civil and Political Rights to the Human Rights Committee: UN doc. CCPR/C/1/Add. 5 of 6 Apr. 1977, esp. 1–2; and J. E. Helgesen, 'Teser om folkerettens anvendelse i norsk rett' (to be published in *Tidsskrift for Rettsvitenskap*, 1982).

[182] Apart from the famous *Iversen* case, application 1468/62 (in 6 *Yearbook* (1966), 278–332), note can be taken of more recent inadmissible applications published in 3 *D&R*, 43–5, and in 9 *D&R*, 37–41. A study of *all* applications brought against Norway has recently been made by M. Spilde, in an unpublished, bi-lingual paper entitled 'Complaints against Norway to the European Commission of Human Rights' (Nov. 1981).

[183] See n. 181 above and Th. Buergenthal, 'The Domestic Status of the European Convention on Human Rights: A Second Look', 7 *Journal of ICJ* (1966), 55–96, at 89.

[184] [1966] *Norsk Rettstidende*, 474–87, at 482–3; English translation from *Collection*, art. 4, 8.

findings or simply an inadequate cognizance of developments in Strasbourg on the part of the Norwegian legal profession may at least in part explain this situation.

The fact that Norway has accepted the right of individual petition and the compulsory jurisdiction of the Human Rights Court may potentially be of great significance in domestic law. This is so because, as pointed out by the Norwegian member of the European Commission of Human Rights, 'There is (however) no reason why they [the Norwegian courts] should not, given relevant cases, apply [the Strasbourg Commission's and Court's] jurisprudence. A statutory amendment of 1969 provides for the reopening of civil and criminal proceedings where the judgment directly or indirectly is based on a point of international law or a treaty which an international tribunal has decided differently and binding for Norway'.[185]

It may be added that in 1962 Article 93 was inserted into the Norwegian Constitution. This Article permits the *Storting* (by a three-fourths majority when at least two-thirds of its members are present at the vote) to delegate to international organizations certain powers which are normally exercised by domestic authorities in accordance with the Norwegian Constitution. Although this article has not yet been applied, it is assumed that a commitment made under it (e.g. to join the European Community) would be irrevocable under international law, but must be understood to include an implied reservation in so far as Norwegian constitutional law is concerned.[186]

---

[185] T. Opsahl, 'Legal Protection for Human Rights in Norway', unpublished paper presented at a symposium organized by the British Institute of Human Rights in England in June 1976. See also comments by T. Wold, in 8 *Svensk Juristtidning* (1964). These statutory provisions give precedence (at least in principle) to general international law, *and to conventions*, over domestic legislation within the area of law covered by them: 'This means', in the eyes of Professor Opsahl, 'that important parts of the Norwegian legal system recognise, *inter alia*, the direct effect of the ECHR'. (Letter to the author, 14 Jan. 1982). The most important examples are para. 5 of the Code of Criminal Procedure, as amended 1962, and para. 1(2) of the Code of Enforcement (respectively '*straffeprosessloven av 1887*' and '*tvangsfullbyrdelsesloven av 1915*', in *Norges Lover* 1685–1979, at 84 and 587). Note must be taken, however, that a new Code on Criminal Procedure was adopted in 1981 and will enter into force in 1982 or 1983. The above points are repeated in the new Code: see para. 4 of the Bill (Ot. prp. Nr. 35, 1978–9).

[186] See T. Opsahl, 'Limitation of Sovereignty under the Norwegian Constitution', 13 *Scandinavian Studies in Law* (1969), 151–77, at 173, and 'Constitutional Implications in Norway of Accession to the European Communities', 9 *CML Rev.* (1972), 271–92; also E. Hambro, 'The New Provision for International Collaboration under the Constitution of Norway' in *Hommage Guggenheim* (1968), 557–72.

Sweden

As in other Scandinavian countries, the European Convention on Human Rights has not been transformed into Swedish law, although on rare occasions reference is made to this instrument's norms by domestic courts.[187]

The new Instrument of Government, which entered into force on 1 January 1975, has in no way fundamentally changed this dualistic approach although an important qualification must be made in respect of a possible limited transfer of power to international organizations or international tribunals.[188] Article 5 of Chapter 10 of the 1974 Instrument of Government stipulates that certain powers which do not relate to the enactment, amendment, or abrogation of a fundamental law 'may to a limited extent be entrusted to an international organisation for peaceful cooperation of which Sweden is or is to become a member or to an International Tribunal . . . Any judicial or administrative function which does not under the present Instrument of Government devolve on the Riksdag, on the Government, or on any other organ referred to in the Instrument, may be entrusted to another state, to an international organisation, or to a foreign or international institution or community'. These transfers of competence require, in both cases, special majority votes of the *Riksdag* members, and have to date not been used.

Sweden is internationally bound to abide by the findings of both the European Court of Human Rights and the Committee of Ministers, and if found to have violated the Convention's provisions in a given case, the authorities will make necessary domestic adjustments to comply with these decisions. Until now, however, the country has not been found to have violated this instrument, and in the few cases that have passed the Commission's admissibility stage, all have eventually been considered unfounded.[189] The case of *Karnell and Hardt*,[190] in which an unofficial arrangement was reached, vividly illustrates how the Swedish authorities cooperate with the European

[187] See, for example, *Collection*, art. 7, 3, and art. 10, 10. Further consult ch. 5 above, sec. D. Declarations under arts. 25 and 46 have been made.

[188] See *Constitutional Documents of Sweden*, The Instrument of Government (published by the Swedish Riksdag, 1975), 26-7 and 55-7.

[189] See Eur. Court HR, *Swedish Engine Drivers* case, judgment of 6 Feb. 1976, ser. A, vol. 20; and *Schmidt & Dahlstrom* case, judgment of 6 Feb. 1976, ser. A, vol. 21. But now see n. 194a.

[190] See report of Commission, 28 May 1973; 'Stocktaking', 112-13.

Commision of Human Rights both at the admissibility stage and afterwards. In this case satisfaction was given to the applicants by a decision of the King-in-Council whereby certain children were exempted from compulsory religious instruction when and if their parents so desired. The case was therefore withdrawn; and did not require any subsequent intervention by domestic organs.

Even in a case which did not pass the admissibility barrier, the Swedish authorities indicated their willingness to change a specific statute which might in certain circumstances be considered to be discriminatory against aliens.[191]

Although the courts are still very reluctant to take judicial notice of provisions of international agreements which have not been incorporated into Swedish law, the Convention's provisions can and should be taken into account as an element in the interpretation of Swedish law, for the simple reason that domestic law should, if possible, be so interpreted as to avoid any conflict with the country's international undertakings.[192] It cannot therefore be altogether excluded that an able counsel — well versed in Convention law — could persuade a court that at least the authoritative decisions of the European Court of Human Rights may provide guidelines to clarify certain aspects of domestic law.[193] This will however be difficult to accomplish in practice, especially in the light of the judgment of 2 October 1972 of the *Högsta Domstolen* (Supreme Court), when the court explained unequivocally that

... Even if Sweden has assented to an international agreement [the European Convention on Human Rights], this would not be applicable for the state within the existing application of the law. To the extent that the agreement gives expression to principles which have not earlier prevailed here in this country, corresponding legislation ('transformation') will be necessary. Such legislation had, however, not been considered necessary when Sweden ratified the agreements referred to by Mr. Sandström. In that respect it should be noticed that these agreements cannot be considered as having the content to which Mr. Sandström refers.[194]

---

[191] See application 7973/77, 17 *D&R*, 74–9.
[192] See ch. 5 above, sec. D.
[193] See Labour Court decision of 18 Feb. 1972, no. 5/72, *Swedish Engine Drivers* case: *Collection*, art. 11, 7.
[194] Case D/T 113/71, *Swedish State* v. *Sandström*, in *Nytt Juridiskt Arkiv* (1973), 423. The extract of this decision was provided to the author by the Registry of the European Court of Human Rights.
[194a] In the *Sporring & Lönnroth* case, Eur. Court HR, judgment of 22 Sept. 1982, ser. A, vol. 52, Sweden was held to have violated art. 6(1) of the Convention and art. 1 of the First Protocol.

United Kingdom

Despite recent attempts to transform the European Convention on Human Rights into domestic law, this instrument still remains an agreement by which the United Kingdom is internationally bound but which does not *per se* possess internal legal authority.[195] This does not, of course, mean that the Convention's provisions are never referred to by the judiciary; for although not a formal source of internal law the Convention is now quite often used as persuasive authority when a clarification of an ambiguity or uncertainty is required.[196]

As the Convention has not been transformed by Parliament into domestic law, and as the courts cannot regard the treaty itself as being a source of internal law which may impose duties and confer rights upon individuals, it follows that the decisions of the Committee of Ministers (as well as the 'opinions' and decisions on admissibility of the Commission) likewise do not *per se* have the force of domestic law. It may nevertheless be noted that 'to the extent that acts of international organisations provide evidence of state practice an English court might take such acts into consideration when it is reviewing the evidence relating to an alleged customary rule of international law'.[197]

However, the fact that the Committee of Ministers is a political organ, which tends to give rather laconic and superficial reasons for its decisions, probably accounts for the fact that its findings possess substantially less influence (if any) before the domestic courts in comparison with the findings of the Commission. Certainly, its 'non-decision' in the *East African Asian* cases,[198] as well as the non-publication of the Commission's findings in the *East African Asian* cases and in

---

[195] See ch. 7 above, sec. D, and paper 176, House of Lords, report of the Select Committee on a Bill of Rights (May 1978). (Declarations under arts. 25 and 46 have been made.)

[196] See P. J. Duffy, 'English Law and the European Convention on Human Rights', 29 *ICLQ* (1980), 585-618, F. A. Mann, 'Britain's Bill of Rights', 94 *LQR* (1978), 512-33, and an article by the author, 'British Courts and the European Human Rights Convention: An Unsatisfactory Situation', *TL* (1979), 38-54.

[197] See J. W. Bridge, 'The Legal Nature of the Acts of International Organisations and International Courts and the Legal Status of such Acts in Municipal Law', UK national report at the 1970 Pescara Congress of the International Academy of Comparative Law (unpublished), pp. 2 and 4. See also n. 28 above.

[198] See case-note by the author in 41 *MLR* (1978), 337-42, and 3 *EHRR*, 76.

those of *Kiss*[199] and *Hilton*[200] does not enhance its authority. The findings of the European Commission have been considered by the English courts on a number of occasions. In the famous case of *R. v. Home Secretary, ex parte B. Singh*, Lord Denning MR stated that,

Clearly a person in prison for a crime does not have a right to leave prison in order to get married. We are referred to a manual (p. 53) which is published by the European Convention on Human Rights [sic]. A man who was detained in a German prison complained that the German prison authorities had refused him permission to marry. He took his complaint before the Commission on Human Rights and they rejected it. They held that article 12 was subject to article 5(i)(c) and (a). Similar considerations apply to an illegal entrant who is detained with a view to his removal . . .[201]

Similarly, in the case of *R. v. Secretary for the Home Department, ex parte Hosenball,*[202] Lord Denning specifically referred to the inadmissible application of *Agee v. UK*. Both Messrs Agee and Hosenball were to be deported by the Home Secretary under the powers conferred upon him by Section 5(1) of the Immigration Act 1971. Under this Act the Secretary of State is permitted to deport non-patrials whose removal is deemed by him to be conducive to the public good 'as being in the interests of national security'. After unsuccessfully appealing before a three-man independent advisory panel Mr Hosenball applied for an order of *certiorari* to quash his deportation order. The Court of Appeal, in dismissing Hosenball's application, considered that the requirement of the public interest to keep certain matters confidential was sometimes greater than the rules of natural justice which were liable to be modified, especially in cases relating to foreigners. In so holding Lord Denning added that

If confirmation is needed, it is to be found in the very recent ruling of the European Commission of Human Rights made in the case of Mr. Agee,

---

[199] See resolution DH(78)3 of 19 Apr. 1978 in 21 *Yearbook* (1978), 642-7; application 6224/73, *Kiss* v. *UK*. (Decision on admissibility in 7 *D&R*, 55-74.)

[200] See resolution DH(79)3 of 24 Apr. 1979, in Council of Europe doc. H(79)7; application 5613/72, *Hilton* v. *UK*. (Decision on admissibility in 4 *D&R*, 177-99.) But see 3 *EHRR*, 104.

[201] [1975] 3 WLR 225, at 231-2. But see the cases of *Hamer* v. *UK*, application 7114/76, and *Draper* v. *UK*, application 8186/78: Committee of Ministers resolution DH(81)1 of 23 Jan. 1981, and DH(81)4 of 2 Apr. 1981. For the Commission's admissibility decision in the *Hamer* case consult 10 *D&R*, 172-204. (Also consult Schedule 3 to the Children Act 1975 — with respect to the above Court of Appeal decision, and *The Times*, 14 Nov. 1980, at 4, article by F. Gibb, 'Rules relaxed on prisoners' right to marry'.)

[202] [1977] 3 All ER 452.

who is running parallel with Mr. Hosenball in these matters. Mr. Agee invoked Article 6(1) of the Convention ... The European Commission held [see application 7729/76, 7 *D&R*, 164-188]:- '... that where the public authorities of a state decide to deport an alien on grounds of security, this constitutes an act of state falling within the public sphere and that it does not constitute a determination of his civil rights or obligations within the meaning of Article 6 ... the state is not required in such cases to grant a hearing'.[203]

An attempt has also as of late been made to suspend the deportation of a married couple pending a final determination by the European Commission of Human Rights of their petition that they should not be separated from their two children who were born in England while both husband and wife lived in the country illegally.[204]

The operative provisions of the decisions of the European Court of Human Rights in cases in which the United Kingdom is a party bind the authorities on the international plane under Article 53 of the Convention. The domestic changes made prior to and after adverse findings by the Court in the cases of *Golder*,[205] *Tyrer*,[206] and *Ireland* v. *UK*[207] bear witness to this. And, although the reasons given in a judgment of the Court do not legally bind the domestic courts, such decisions may undoubtedly possess highly persuasive authority (especially if they reflect the Court's *jurisprudence constante*).[208]   For example, in the *Tyrer* case, the Committee of Ministers in supervising the execution of the Court's judgment under Article 54 of the Convention, took note of the information provided by the United Kingdom representative that the First Deemster (Chief Justice of the Isle of Man) brought the Strasbourg Court's

[203] Ibid., at 457. A curtailment of the principle of natural justice? It is suggested that where UK courts refer to 'admissibility decisions' of the Commission, particular note must be taken of the fact that the procedure entails an examination of *admissibility* issues (basically concerning 'form' and *not* 'substance'), and only when declared admissible, is an application examined on its merits.

[204] *Uppal & Others* v. *Home Office*, reported in *The Times*, 21 Oct. 1978, 21, and 11 Nov. 1978, at 23. Compare this development with case-law in Belgium and the Netherlands, notes 57-9 and 123-4. The application of *Singh, Uppal et al.*, no. 8344/78 ended in a friendly settlement before the Commission: see report of Commission, 9 July 1980, 20 *D&R*, 29-39. Also see *Guilfoyle* v. *Home Office* [1981] 2 WLR 223; commented upon by P. R. Ghandi, 44 *MLR* (1981), 707-10.

[205] Eur. Court HR, judgment of 21 Feb. 1975, ser. A, vol. 18.

[206] Ibid., judgment of 25 Apr. 1978, ser. A, vol. 26.

[207] Ibid., judgment of 18 Jan. 1978, ser. A, vol. 25. The law on contempt of court has also been changed as a result of the Court's ruling in *The Sunday Times* case, judgment of 26 Apr. 1979, ser. A, vol. 30.

[208] For example, the *Golder* case was cited in argument before the Court of Appeal in the *Ex parte Singh* case, n. 201 above, at 228. See also Bridge, n. 197 above, at 6.

judgment to the attention of the island's High Court, the high bailiffs, and the magistrates, i.e. to the attention of all judicial authorities who under existing legislation could pass a sentence of birching. The First Deemster also informed the island's judiciary that judicial corporal punishment must now be held to be in breach of the European Convention.[209]

One case above all others probably merits special attention: *Malone* v. *Commissioner of Police of the Metropolis (no. 2)*.[210] An antique dealer, tried at the Crown Court for various offences of handling stolen property, became aware of the fact that his telephone had been tapped by the Post Office after the police had obtained a warrant for this purpose. He therefore initiated proceedings against the defendant alleging that the recordings made of his private telephone conversations violated his rights to property and privacy and violated Article 8 of the European Convention on Human Rights which guarantees everyone the right to respect of private and family life, home, and correspondence. Without necessarily here attempting to make a detailed study of this case — consisting of an extremely fine and penetrating twenty-eight page judgment of Sir Robert Megarry Vice-Chancellor — particular note can be taken of those sections of the judgment in which reference is made to the Convention. The plaintiff's claim was dismissed, because Sir Robert considered that no right of property (with the exception of copyright) existed in words transmitted along telephone lines; that the right to privacy, including that of holding a telephone conversation without molestation, did not as such exist in English law, and that there existed no duty to respect the confidentiality of such conversations; on the principle that everything is permitted except that which is expressly forbidden, telephone tapping was not unlawful; and that, as the European Convention on Human Rights was not part of the law of the land, Article 8 did not confer any right upon the plaintiff. It therefore followed that whereas the Convention's norms could be used by the English courts as a guide to the interpretation and application of domestic law — in that there exists a presumption that legislation should be construed in order to effectuate this instrument

---

[209] See 21 *Yearbook* (1978), 654–9. See also *The Times*, 22 Nov. 1978, 2. Although the law relating to judicial corporal punishment has *not* been abolished, it has never been applied since the Court's judgment: see Isle of Man Appeal Court judgment of 6 Oct. 1981, discussed below, n. 220.

[210] [1979] 2 All ER 620. For a commentary on this case consult P. J. Duffy, 'Tinkerbell: The European Human Rights Dimension', *TL* (1980), 60–70.

rather than to frustrate it,[211] — the absence of legislation on this subject (desirable though it may be) excluded the use of such a presumption! In his judgment the Vice-Chancellor made extensive reference to the judgment of the European Court of Human Rights in the case of *Klass* v. *Federal Republic of Germany*[212] (in which the Strasbourg Court held that secret surveillance by telephone in itself was a violation of Article 8 of the Convention because the right to private life and private correspondence extended to telephone conversations, although in the specific circumstances of the case the action of the German authorities was justified on the basis of the criteria limitatively enumerated in the second paragraph of Article 8), even though this case had apparently no *legal* significance in English law. It is important to stress, as Sir Robert had done on a number of occasions, the unsatisfactory situation whereby 'it is impossible to read the judgment in the *Klass* case without it becoming abundantly clear that a system which has no legal safeguards whatever has small chance of satisfying the requirements of that court whatever provisions there may be' and that it is 'impossible to see how English law could be said to satisfy the requirements of the Convention, as interpreted in the *Klass* case'.[213]

In the more recent case of *UKAPE* v. *ACAS*,[214] in which the House of Lords allowed an appeal from a decision of the Court of Appeal, Lord Scarman indicated that he was not prepared to adopt the reasoning of Lord Denning MR; he explained that the right to join a trade union (guaranteed by Article 11 of the Convention and by common law) did not necessarily mean that every trade union created in a particular company or industry has automatically the right to recognition for the purposes of collective bargaining, adding 'if it be a possible interpretation of the European Convention, I shall not adopt it unless and until the European Court of Human Rights declares that it is correct'.[215]

[211] 21 *Yearbook* (1978), 648.

[212] Eur. Court HR, judgment of 6 Sept. 1978, ser. A, no. 28.

[213] See n. 210 above, at 648. (Malone has brought an application before the Commission in Strasbourg, application 8691/79.)

[214] [1980] 2 WLR 254.

[215] Ibid., at 266. In the Court of Appeal Lord Denning's reference to art. 11 of the Convention may have to be read in conjunction with his statement that '[w]hen the great majority of workers in a particular group wish to be represented by a union . . .' effect should be given to their wishes: see [1979] 1 WLR 570, at 582-3. But also see the observations of C. Warbrick, 'European Convention of Human

In one case in Northern Ireland it was even accepted that the meaning attributed to a provision of the Convention by the Strasbourg organs may be considered as conclusive: In the case of *R.* v. *McCormick*,[216] McGonigal LJ in dismissing a challenge of one of the accused who had claimed that statements made by him had been obtained in contravention of the Emergency Provisions Act (NI), 1973, Section 6, referred to the case-law of the European Commission of Human Rights in order to establish the exact meaning of the provisions found in the said section of the 1973 Act. He explained that 'Section 6, in effect, incorporates Article 3 of the European Convention on Human Rights and the test of permissible conduct into the test of admissibility of statements. This legislation is, therefore, looking towards Article 3 of the Convention to determine the standard which should be applied and the effect and meaning to be given to those terms — torture or inhuman or degrading treatment.' McGonigal LJ then referred to the report of the Commission in the case of *Ireland* v. *UK* (application 5310/71, adopted on 25 January 1976), and considered that 'the meaning assigned to the terms by the European Commission on Human Rights is, at the least, of *very persuasive effect, if not definite*, in determining the meaning' of the terms. He added that he could not look to 'the decision [of the European Court of Human Rights] for assistance on this point . . . [as] judgment has not yet been delivered'.[217] He then studied certain passages of the Commission's report in some detail and also referred to other case-law mentioned there. This is the first reported case which has come to the attention of the author in which such in-depth consideration was given to developments in Strasbourg, and in this

Rights and English Law', 130 *New Law Journal* (1980), 852-3, at 853. The case-law of the Strasbourg Court has also been cited in *Gold Star* v. *DPP* [1981] 2 All ER 257, at 259 and 265; in *Raymond* v. *Honey* (House of Lords), *The Times*, 5 Mar. 1982; and in *Taylor* v. *Co-Operative Retail Services* (Court of Appeal), *The Times*, 13 July 1982.

[216] [1977] NI 105; [1977] 4 NIJB.

[217] Ibid., at 107; also in 21 *Yearbook* (1978), 789-94 at 792. See further on this subject D. S. Greer, 'The Admissibility of Confessions Under the Northern Ireland (Emergency Provisions) Act', 31 *Northern Ireland Legal Quarterly* (1980), 205-38. The Court's judgment was delivered on 18 Jan. 1978. See Eur. Court HR, ser. A, no. 25, and comments by L. Doswald-Beck, 'What does the prohibition of "torture or inhuman or degrading treatment or punishment" mean? The interpretation of the European Commission and Court of Human Rights', 25 *NILR* (1978), 24-50. In this connection, see the more recent Court of Appeal judgment of *R.* v. *McGrath* [1980] NI 91, at 93, in which certain passages of the Strasbourg Court's judgment in the case of *Ireland* v. *UK* were taken into consideration.

respect it can be considered as a pioneering decision. It may however be pointed out that the 'incorporation' of the said provision of the Convention into the 1973 Act no doubt facilitated the court's decision to refer to the Commission's report, which — and this perhaps needs stressing — remains an *opinion* and not a legally binding decision.

Similarly, in the case of *A.-G.* v. *BBC* both Lords Scarman and Fraser of Tullybelton referred to *The Sunday Times* decision of the European Court of Human Rights.[218] Although this case concerned contempt-of-court proceedings, the House of Lords did not have to take into consideration the Strasbourg Court's ruling in the light of its own 1974 decision in *A.-G.* v. *Sunday Times Newspapers Ltd.*, because it held that the Divisional Court's jurisdiction did not extend to a local valuation court and that the Attorney-General could therefore not pursue his case against the BBC for contempt of court. Nevertheless, an important passage from Lord Scarman's judgment merits citation:

... neither the Convention nor the European Court's decision in *The Sunday Times* case is part of our law. This House's decision, even though the European Court has held the rule it declares to be an infringement of the Convention, is the law. Our courts must continue to look not to the European Court's decision reported as *The Sunday Times* v. *United Kingdom* (1979) 2 E.H.R.R. 245, but to the House of Lords decision reported in *Attorney-General* v. *Times Newspapers Ltd.* [1974] A.C. 273 for the rule of English law. Yet there is a presumption, albeit rebuttable, that our municipal law will be consistent with our international obligations: for an example see *Post Office* v. *Estuary Radio Ltd.* [1968] 2 Q.B. 740, *per* Diplock L.J. at p. 757. Moreover, under the Practice Statement of July 1966 (*Practice Statement (Judicial Precedent)* [1966] 1 W.L.R. 1234) this House has taken to itself the power to refuse to follow a previous decision of its own, if convinced that it is necessary in the interest of justice to depart from it. Though, on its facts, the present case does not provide the House with the opportunity to reconsider its *Sunday Times* decision [1974] A.C. 273 (and we have heard no argument on the point), I do not doubt that, in considering how far we should extend the application of contempt of court, we must bear in mind the impact of whatever decision we may be minded to make upon the international obligations assumed by the United Kingdom under the Convention. If the issue should ultimately be, as I think in this case it is, a question of legal policy, we must have regard to the country's international obligation to observe the Convention as interpreted by the Court of Human Rights.[219]

---

[218] [1980] 3 WLR 109, at 128 (Lord Fraser), and at 130 and 137 (Lord Scarman).
[219] Ibid., at 130. Also consult *Schering Chemicals* v. *Falkman* [1981] 2 WLR 848, esp. observations of Lord Denning at 861-5.

As the United Kingdom is internationally responsible for the Isle of Man, it is of considerable interest to note a recent judgment of the Manx Court of Appeal dated 6 October 1981,[220] especially in the light of the adverse finding in the *Tyrer* case.[221] In this case the appellant was a 16 year old boy who, having pleaded guilty to an offence of unlawful and malicious wounding, was sentenced to four strokes of the birch by lay magistrates in Douglas. This sentence was quashed on appeal and sent back to the magistrates who subsequently sentenced the youth to a period of three months detention.[222] In quashing the original sentence, Judge Hytner QC cited Article 3 of the Convention as well as the *Tyrer* judgment which was considered 'binding on us in respect of the question as to whether or not a particular act is in breach of the Convention'.[223] He noted that although copies of the *Tyrer* judgment had been circulated to all magistrates in the Isle of Man, justices had in fact been given no guidance as to the meaning or effect of this case.[224] Thus, although it was perfectly lawful to sentence a youth in this way under Manx law, as the European Convention had not been incorporated, there existed a presumption that judges should interpret the law in such a way as to try to ensure that the Isle of Man was not in breach of treaty obligations. Relying on persuasive authority of certain English courts, including two recent *dicta* of Lords Scarman and Denning in particular,[225] and bearing in mind that birching was not a mandatory sentence, Judge Hytner ruled that the proper approach to be followed was that of exploring the possible use of all other alternatives as well as any 'contra-indications' as to why a birching sentence should not be passed before the sentence of birching is imposed. What is disturbing in this case — especially in the light of the withdrawal of the right of petition in respect of the Isle of Man — is that the original

... sentence of the magistrates was a perfectly lawful one. It follows that either the United Kingdom and Manx Governments are unconcerned about the possibility of their respective countries being in breach of their

[220] Transcript obtained from the registry of the Court. The case was also reported in *The Times*, 6 Oct. 1981, at 2, and 7 Oct. at 7; and *The Guardian*, 7 Oct. at 3.

[221] Eur. Court HR, judgment of 25 Apr. 1978, ser. A, no. 26.

[222] See *The Times*, 5 Nov. 1981, at 3.

[223] The Court's transcript, at 4; also in 4 EHHR 232 at 236.

[224] Ibid., at 6–7.

[225] i.e., the cases of *BBC* v. *A.-G.*, and *Schering Chemicals* v. *Falkman*, respectively: see n. 219 above.

international treaty obligations, or they are depending on the courts of the Isle of Man always so to exercise discretion (or to vary) perfectly lawful and valid sentences as to extricate them from the consequences of inaction. We regard this as a most unsatisfactory state of affairs . . .[226]

Whether or not a decision taken by the European Court of Human Rights under Article 50 (or by the Committee of Ministers under Article 32(3) or 54), that the United Kingdom should pay compensation to an individual, as had occurred in the Austrian *Ringeisen* case,[227] could result in a legally enforceable right before domestic courts, is difficult to determine.[228]

Certainly, the United Kingdom courts would become more receptive to developments in Strasbourg were the Convention secured the status of domestic law; for, as the Northern Ireland Standing Advisory Commission on Human Rights has pointed out 'incorporation would . . . clarify the present uncertain status of the Convention and *provide our courts with the benefit of the guidance of the case-law of the Convention organs* . . . [and] . . . the anxiety about the manner in which our courts might interpret the Convention would be allayed by the fact that *the courts would be obliged to have regard to the Strasbourg case-law.*'[229]

D. Stock-taking

The European Convention on Human Rights imposes *per se* no legal obligations upon domestic courts to abide by the decisions of its organs: the function of these organs has been and remains basically one of providing a subsidiary collective guarantee of certain common rights governing relations between individuals

---

[226] Extract from p. 8 of the court's transcript. The Committee of Ministers is perhaps also partly to blame for the present situation; after all, its duty of supervising the execution of the Strasbourg Court's judgment (art. 54 of the Convention) appears to have been rather lax in the *Tyrer* case, to say the least. It is improbable that the European Convention will be incorporated into Manx law in the near future: consult *Final Report of the Committee of the House of Keys on the Manx Bill of Rights Bill* (28 Sept. 1981).

[227] See notes 23 and 40 above.

[228] The Strasbourg Court's recent pronouncement in *The Sunday Times* case (art. 50), decided on 6 Nov. 1980, does not clarify this point as the UK Government did not have to pay the applicant's costs in respect of expenses incurred on the domestic plane. But note the out-of-court settlement reached between Mr Golder and the Home Office: *The Guardian*, 6 Feb. 1982, 2. (An indirect impact of the Strasbourg Court's judgment?)

[229] 'The Protection of Human Rights by Law in Northern Ireland', Cmnd. 7009 (Nov. 1977), 56. (Emphasis added.)

and national authorities.[230]

It follows that decisions of the European Court of Human Rights, even in cases in which a given state is a party (with the possible exceptions of Austria, the Netherlands, and Switzerland, where certain operative provisions may be of an executory character), are not binding on domestic courts although they are invariably regarded as highly persuasive authority. Also, to the extent that such decisions of the Court provide evidence of state practice, or when there exists a *jurisprudence constante*, domestic courts are most likely to take these decisions into consideration when reviewing evidence relating to an alleged customary rule of international law. In addition, the Court's judgments may be implemented indirectly under an estoppel theory, assuming that the Convention possesses the status of domestic law in the state concerned.[231] Similarly, an individual may have recourse before his country's courts where the European Court of Human Rights has established that a violation of the Convention has taken place although for some reason has refused to compensate the applicant under Article 50, or alternatively if the state authorities have, in the individual's opinion, inadequately executed the Court's judgment.[232] Such action may, of course, be followed by some form of supervision by the Committee of Ministers in accordance with Article 54 of the Convention.[233]

The possibility of reopening domestic avenues of legal redress after an adverse finding by the Strasbourg Court, particularly in criminal cases relating to complaints under Articles 5 and 6 of the Convention, cannot be excluded, especially in countries such as Austria (where this actually happened in respect of developments before the Commission),[234] the Federal Republic

---

[230] See Eur. Court HR, *Belgian Linguistic* cases, n. 62 above, 34-5, para. 10, *Handyside* case, decision of 29 Apr. 1976, ser. A, no. 24, 22, para. 48, *Swedish Engine Drivers* case, n. 189 above, 18, para. 50, and the case of *Ireland* v. *UK*, n. 207 above, para. 239. See also comments of the Commission in *X & Y* v. *Belgium*, applications 1420/62 and 1477/62, 6 *Yearbook* (1963), 620-9, at 626.

[231] See the observations made by Buergenthal, n. 2 above, at 98.

[232] See comments by Velu, n. 2 above, at 230-1. See also Ch. Schreuer, 'The Impact of International Institutions for the Protection of Human Rights in Domestic Courts', 4 *Israel Yearbook on Human Rights* (1974), 60-88, esp. 66-70, and M. Gerbino, 'Considerazioni sugli effetti della sentenza della Corte Europea dei Diritti dell'Uomo', 3 *Riv. DE* (1963), 14-21.

[233] J. E. S. Fawcett, *The Application of the European Convention on Human Rights* (1969), 229. See also A. H. Robertson, written communication at Rome Colloquy, n. 9 above, 257-62, as well as comments by Daubie, n. 19 above.

[234] See notes 41-4 above.

of Germany, Luxembourg,[235] Norway,[236] and possibly also Switzerland.[237] States are often prepared to take corrective measures while a given matter is pending in Strasbourg rather than await unfavourable findings,[238] and one way of doing so would be to provide individuals with the opportunity to have their cases reviewed before domestic courts on the basis of appropriately amended legislation. Naturally, such innovations are more likely to occur in states in which the Convention has already secured itself the status of domestic law and in those states which have made declarations under Articles 25 and 46.

The findings of the European Commission of Human Rights do not formally bind domestic courts, although one leading authority[239] (now supported, to a certain extent, by developments in Belgium)[240] believes that the Commission's decisions on admissibility may be legally binding within the domestic forum in countries where the Convention possesses the status of internal law. There is also some support for the view that the terms of a friendly settlement secured under the aegis of the Commission may be enforced by an individual in the domestic courts, were a state not to abide by the conditions of the settlement.[241]

The authority in domestic law of the operative provisions of the decisions of the Committee of Ministers remains uncertain. These decisions may be given some weight by domestic courts; and certainly the persuasive value accorded to its findings will in all probability be substantially greater in states directly concerned in a given instance. Nevertheless, they are likely to carry much less weight than the reasoned judgments of the European Court of Human Rights and even possibly the 'opinions' and decisions on admissibility of the Commission. This is so because the Committee of Ministers is a political body and its decisions are not as fully reasoned as are those of the Court.[242]

---

[235] See notes 81 and 107 above.

[236] See n. 185 above.

[237] See notes 149–50 above.

[238] See H. Rolin, 'L'autorité des arrêts et des décisions des organes de la Convention européenne des Droits de l'Homme', VI *RDH/HRJ* (1973), 729–46, esp. 745 and 746. See also A. Khol, 'The Influence of the Human Rights Convention on Austrian Law', 18 *AJCL* (1970), 237–58, at 257; Zanghi, n. 9 above, esp. 230–45; and Scheuner, n. 2 above, esp. 232–4.

[239] See Sørensen, n. 164 above, at 119–20.

[240] See n. 59 above.

[241] See Golsong, n. 2 above, at 82; and Frowein, n. 10 above, at 288.

[242] But see notes 86–7 above. A domestic court may consider more authoritative

Although the Committee of Ministers has not been 'active' in supervising the execution of the Strasbourg Court's judgments — a function which it performs under Article 54 of the Convention — it may be assumed that its work in this field can have a potential domestic legal significance.[243]

this organ's finding under art. 32(3) rather than its initial decision under art. 32(1). See R. Kovar, 'L'autorité des arrêts et des résolutions des organes de protection', **VI** *RDH/HRJ* (1973), 685–706, at 694–7 and 701–2, and Vegleris, n. 2 above, **II** *RDH/ HRJ* (1969), 234–51. Note may also be taken of the possible influence of this body's resolutions *beyond* the context of its functions circumscribed by the European Convention on Human Rights: see notes 118 and 140 above; also Ch. Schreuer, 'Recommendations and the Traditional Sources of International Law', 20 *German Yearbook of International Law* (1977), 103–18.

[243] See n. 19 above; e.g. if the Committee of Ministers keeps postponing its decision under art. 54 on the basis that it may not be satisfied that just satisfaction has been obtained by an individual after the Court's finding under art. 50, a domestic court may well take this postponement into consideration when deciding if an individual can obtain compensation under art. 5(5) of the Convention in a state where this instrument possesses the status of domestic law. Also consult case-note by the author in 4 *TL* (1982), 71–8, at 76–8.

Conclusions to Part III

In Part III of this book emphasis has been placed on selected aspects of the Convention's authority in domestic courts. The three subjects studied are relatively self-contained and unconnected, except for the fact that they all relate to the way in which the courts do or may interpret this growing body of Convention law. It is exactly at this point, that the impact of the Convention's rather unique features is most apparent: although still in embryonic form, there appears to be emerging a sort of European quasi-constitutional or common law, the maintenance of whose uniform minimum standards is considered the responsibility not only of the Convention's organs but also that of the domestic judiciary. This point is important to emphasize for two reasons: Convention law is meant to provide a set of objective international obligations which in substance are owed *to individuals on the domestic plane*. A corollary to this is that the enforcement of this common law must be effectively ensured *on the domestic plane* irrespective of whether or not the Convention's provisions have been incorporated into domestic law, and regardless of their status in the domestic hierarchy if so incorporated.

It is unnecessary to repeat what has been written in Chapters 8, 9, and 10. For present purposes two subjects need to be singled out for particular attention: the extended impact that this instrument has made beyond the confines of the relatively well-functioning mechanism set up in Strasbourg, and the remarkable stature that the judgments of the European Court of Human Rights have acquired before domestic courts.

1. In an important study made by Professor Evrigenis, the Greek judge on the European Court of Human Rights, emphasis was correctly placed on the Convention's role in encouraging harmonization of legal standards on the one hand and the *cristallisation d'un substrat juridique essentiel à la société démocratique des pays européens*' on the other.[1] Two passages

[1] D. J. Evrigenis, 'Le rôle de la Convention européenne des Droits de l'Homme'

from this study are of particular value in the context of what
has been discussed in Part III of this study:

Un . . . aspect de la Convention, qui met en relief l'ampleur de sa fonction
d'harmonisation, est l'extension conceptuelle de la notion même des droits
de l'homme. Les droits et libertés garantis par la Convention se répercutent
sur l'ensemble de l'ordre juridique national. La doctrine contemporaine
des droits fondamentaux contribue continuellement à l'élargissement de
l'emprise de cette matière sur l'ensemble du droit et de la vie sociale avec
des nouvelles constructions, telle que l'effet des droits fondamentaux
sur les rapports privés (Drittwirkung). Ces constructions ne peuvent être
sans influence sur l'interprétation de la Convention.[2]

Likewise:

On se demanderait . . . si l'"insertion' de la Convention dans le droit
communautaire avait pu avoir pour effet, d'attribuer à cet accord les
caractéristiques de droit communautaire et notamment celles de l'applicabilité immédiate et directe et de la primauté sur le droit national. Une
pareille interprétation de l'attitude des Communautés à l'égard de la
Convention pourrait changer profondément la condition de cette dernière
dans les ordres internes de celles des parties contractantes qui sont en
même temps membres de la Communauté européenne, dans le sens même
d'une activation de la fonction harmonisatrice de la Convention.[3]

2. The role played by the European Court of Human Rights,
and the importance of the Court, cannot, unfortunately, be
equated with that of the Luxembourg Court whose directly
enforceable decisions on certain questions of European Community law prevail over all conflicting domestic law, even in
cases of *leges posteriores*.[4] Nevertheless, the reasoned judgments of the Court are the most authoritative interpretations
of 'Convention law' whose findings will undoubtedly in due
course directly influence domestic law in the majority of the
contracting states. The Court itself has recognized, in the
Marckx case, that its decisions have effects extending beyond
the confines of specific cases brought before it.[5] The proposed
extension of the Court's jurisdiction will probably be a vital
step in this direction, and this development may call for close
monitoring by domestic judicial organs. The extension of the

---

in *New Perspectives for a Common Law of Europe* (ed. M. Cappelletti, 1978), 341–
57, at 353.

    [2] Ibid., at 354.   [3] Ibid., at 356.

    [4] See A. G. Toth, *Legal Protection of Individuals in the European Communities*
(1978), esp. vol. ii, and H. G. Schermers, *Judicial Protection in the European Communities* (1981), *passim*.

    [5] Eur. Court HR, judgment of 13 June 1979, ser. A, no. 31, 25, para. 58.

Strasbourg Court's ambit of activity may include, in the not too distant future, an amendment of the ineffective Second Protocol, relating to the Court's capacity to give advisory opinions,[6] and there is also a distinct possibility that the European Community will adhere to the European Convention on Human Rights.[7] The impact of the Court's findings will of course be far greater in those states in which the Convention possesses the status of domestic law (preferably also a superior status to *lex posterior*), and in those states which have accepted the right of individual petition and the Court's compulsory jurisdiction.

An interesting innovation may be noted in this connection. At the oral hearings in the case of *Winterwerp* v. *the Netherlands*,[8] Professor Fawcett, the former President of the European Commission of Human Rights, asked the Court to consider a request made by the United Kingdom Government that it be able to submit — through the Commission — its written observations on the interpretation of Article 5(4) of the Convention. This proposal was accepted by the Court after the President of the Commission had explained that

. . . as the Court is aware, there are other applications before the Commission concerning detention in other European jurisdictions. [Therefore] . . . if the Court should find it necessary in the present case to interpret Article 5(4) in a way that could affect directly or by implication the law and practice on detention in countries other than the Netherlands, it should give careful consideration [to the United Kingdom's request]. We believe that this would be of assistance and we believe that, when the Court is making possibly a wider interpretation — an interpretation of Article 5(4) extending possibly beyond this case — it is important that the counter-arguments be fully presented.[9]

Despite the above-mentioned interesting developments, the more fundamental point needs to be answered: to what extent can and do domestic courts give effect to the findings of the Convention organs generally, and/or use these findings as

[6] Compare art. 64 of the 1969 American Convention on Human Rights (which entered into force in July 1978); A. H. Robertson, *Human Rights in the World* (1972), 269. The idea of empowering the Human Rights Court to provide preliminary rulings at the request of at least the highest judicial instances of member states has been shelved. See General Conclusions below.

[7] Probably in the form of an additional protocol: see *Bull. EC Suppl.* 2/79, and a commentary by K. Economides and J. H. H. Weiler, 42 *MLR* (1979), 683-95.

[8] Eur. Court HR, judgment of 24 Oct. 1979, ser. A, no. 33.

[9] Doc. Cour/Misc. (78) 142, 28 Nov. 1978, 4. Similarly, in the *Young, James & Webster* case, Eur. Court HR, judgment of 13 Aug. 1981, ser. A, no. 44, a TUC memorial was presented before the Court; see doc. Cour/Misc. (81)28 of 4 Mar. 1981. These developments may lead to the institution of *amicus curiae* briefs before the Court.

guidelines in order to clarify the extent and nature of the obligatións imposed by this instrument? The survey in Chapter 10 above has, hopefully, at least partially answered this question. It must, nevertheless, be admitted that when faced with a choice between an international legal norm and an internal text, the natural inclination and professional training of the domestic judiciary more often tend to lead it to rely upon the latter. This is probably so for the simple reason that both the majority of the bar and bench of most member states of the Council of Europe are completely unaware of, or unfamiliar with, the published case-law emanating from Strasbourg. The fact that most publications are made available only in French and English does not alleviate this problem. And, assuming that domestic courts are prepared to construe their internal law in such a way as to ensure that it does not conflict with the interpretation of the Stfasbourg organs, the onus of making the courts aware of such developments remains basically upon the lawyer who represents his client before a domestic court.

Perhaps a Brazilian international lawyer best summarized the existing situation when he observed that:

A survey of national courts' decisions applying [the Convention's] provisions seems to reveal still a certain tendency to look at precedents of the forum-State's courts of last instance rather than at the vast jurisprudence of the Convention organs themselves in interpreting them; it may be hoped that the fewer cases where the highest domestic courts of some member States have openly consulted the case-law of the Convention organs may develop a new awareness amongst municipal judges and influence them to consult not only their statute books and reports of their own supreme court, but also the jurisprudence of the organs of the Convention.[10]

---

[10] A. A. Cançado Trindade, 'Exhaustion of Local Remedies in Internatinal Law and the Role of National Courts', 17 *Archiv des Völkerrechts* (1978), 333–70, at 349–50.

General Conclusions

A. The need for harmonization and uniform application

'Convention law' possesses specific characteristics which make it a unique international instrument setting out a list of international obligations owed by states to individuals within their domestic jurisdiction — a field hitherto traditionally reserved to constitutional law.[1] This does not lessen the possibility that courts in various member states will interpret the Convention's substantive provisions in different ways. If this were to occur, and at present such divergency of case-law is by no means impossible, there could be established a discriminatory guarantee system between member states themselves and/or the Convention organs thereby paving a way for a double system of interpretation of human rights norms where no appeal is made possible to the Court in Strasbourg.[2] The possibility of such divergence could undermine one of the unique features of this international instrument, namely, that of securing a 'common law' in Western Europe, or *ordre public européen*. As Professor Mosler, a former judge on the European Court of Human Rights, has rightly pointed out 'There can be no doubt that it is the aim of the European Convention to arrive at a uniform application of all the agreed fundamental rights in all the Contracting States. This means that in a concrete case the rules of the Convention must be so interpreted that they can be uniformly applied by all the Contracting States.'[3]

---

[1] See ch. 1 above, sec. B, *passim*, and M. Sørensen, 'Do the Rights set forth in the European Convention on Human Rights in 1950 have the Same Significance in 1975?' in *Proceedings of the Fourth International Colloquy about the European Convention on Human Rights*, Rome, 5–8 Nov. 1975 (Strasbourg 1976), 83–109, at 89.

[2] See J. W. Ganshof van der Meersch, 'Aspects de la mise en œuvre d'une sauvegarde collective des Droits de l'Homme en droit international — la Convention européenne' in *Mélanges F. Dehousse* (1979), i.192-208, at 199.

[3] See 'Der "Gemeinschaftliche ordre public" in Europäischen Staatengruppen' in *Instituto 'Francisco de Vitoria' de Derecho Internacional* (1969), at 10. (English translation from an article by H. Golsong, in *Judicial Protection against the Executive* (1971), iii. at 250, n. 15.)

It follows that one of the best methods of maintaining the guarantee system established by the Convention and avoiding discrimination between the beneficiaries of these guarantees lies in the establishment of a preliminary rulings system akin to that existing within the EEC.[4] In addition to the prime objective of ensuring uniform interpretation and at the same time raising common standards, the adoption of a preliminary rulings procedure may help activate the interest of legal experts in the Convention mechanism generally, and encourage genuine cooperation between domestic courts and the European Court of Human Rights as well as between the domestic courts themselves. This subject merits much greater public attention and debate, especially in legal circles, since the institution of such a system would raise complex constitutional problems within the domestic legal systems of member states and could also create the need for fundamental changes or alterations within the framework of the existing regional mechanism.

The idea of conferring on the European Court of Human Rights the competence to give preliminary rulings is based upon Article 177 of the Treaty setting up the European Economic Community.[5] Only sub-paragraph (a) of this Article, which relates to its interpretation, is relevant to the subject under discussion.

---

[4] In Mar. 1979 the Council of Europe's Steering Committee for Human Rights, after a study of this point, forwarded its conclusions to the Committee of Ministers that it was *not* advisable to propose the drafting of a legal instrument which would empower the Court to give preliminary rulings at the request of a national court. See Council of Europe doc. H(79)3, of 1 Mar. 1979. The International Institute of Human Rights (Strasbourg) was commissioned by the Committee, in the capacity of a consultant, to prepare a study on this subject. See doc. DH/Exp. (76)23 of 22 Dec. 1976. For further discussion on this subject see references in n. 16 below; report by Ch. Dominicé, in *Parliamentary Conference on Human Rights*, Vienna, 18-20 Oct. 1971 (Strasbourg 1972), 64-74, at 70-1; and report on the protection of human rights in Europe, by H. Sieglerschmidt, Parliamentary Assembly of the Council of Europe, doc. 3852 of 15 Sept. 1976, esp. 15-16.

[5] This article reads: 'The Court of Justice shall have jurisdiction to give preliminary rulings concerning:

'a. the interpretation of this treaty.

'b. the validity and interpretation of acts of the institutions of the Community;

'c. the interpretation of the statutes of bodies established by an act of the Council, where those statutes so provide.

'When such a question is raised before any court or tribunal of a member State, that court or tribunal may, if it considers that a decision on the question is necessary to enable it to give judgment, request the Court of Justice to give a ruling thereon.

'Where any such question is raised in a case pending before a court or tribunal of a member State, against whose decisions there is no judicial remedy under national law, that court or tribunal shall bring the matter before the Court of Justice.'

The purpose of instituting a system of preliminary rulings is to enable a domestic tribunal to obtain an authoritative interpretation on a point of law when applying the Convention's norms or considering the compatibility of domestic law with the Convention. Such a demand for a preliminary ruling could be made were it to appear, during the proceedings before a domestic court, that a difference of opinion exists as to the exact meaning of a relevant provision or relevant provisions of the Convention. This difference of opinion could exist between the parties themselves or between the parties and the judge. Alternatively, a demand for an interpretation could be made possible if the tribunal in question, or the parties, were not in agreement with a prior interpretation given by the Court in Strasbourg on a similar matter. Under Article 177 of the EEC Treaty, requests for preliminary rulings are merely optional when raised before lower courts and compulsory if the question is raised 'in a case pending before a court or tribunal of a member State, against whose decisions there is no judicial remedy under national law'.[6] Consequently, in the context of 'Convention law' if a request were made optional for lower courts it could also be made *mandatory* in cases where a question of interpretation is raised in a domestic tribunal giving a final ruling.[7]

Arguments favouring such an extension of the Court's functions appear to be convincing. It would seem preferable that the rights and freedoms guaranteed by the Convention

The need for harmonized interpretation of international treaties and domestic documents has become increasingly clear in 'European law' in the wider sense. The technique of preliminary rulings by the Court of Justice of the European Communities has been extended to include the interpretation of The European Convention on the Mutual Recognition of Companies and Legal Persons of 29 Feb. 1968 (Luxembourg, Protocol of 3 June 1971); and the European Convention on Jurisdiction and the Enforcement of Judgments in Civil and Commercial Matters of 27 Sept. 1968 (Luxembourg, Protocol of 3 June 1971). Likewise, provision was made in the *Benelux Treaty of Economic Union* whereby national courts in the three Benelux countries and the Arbitral College can apply to the Benelux Court of Justice for preliminary rulings (Brussels Treaty of 31 Mar. 1965, art. 6, paras. 1-6).

[6] See generally on this subject L. J. Brinkhorst and H. G. Schermers, *Judicial Remedies in the European Communities* (1977), ch. 4. See also G. Bebr, 'Article 177 of the EEC Treaty in the Practice of National Courts', 26 *ICLQ* (1977), 241-82. Particular note should be taken of the misuse of the *acte clair* doctrine.

[7] Such preliminary rulings could, alternatively, be given only at the request of the highest national courts as is provided in The Hague Convention on the Recognition and Enforcement of Foreign Judgments on Civil and Commercial Matters (1964), art. 4(2). But note problems *re* art. 60 of the Convention, discussed below.

and its Protocols should be effectively secured by *domestic* courts and tribunals, since an attempt at vindication through a lengthy process before the Strasbourg organs may well deprive an individual of immediate redress which is associated with domestic law. The institution of such a procedure may thus prevent and/or correct most violations of human rights immediately. There would be fewer violations to establish after the event. This form of ruling may also be politically attractive, in that — as has been accepted to an extent within the context of European Community law — it can be considered part of the domestic judicial system and not an external supervisory machinery which forces a state to wash its dirty laundry publicly. After the provision of a preliminary ruling, it would be for the domestic court to apply the rules provided by the Human Rights Court in the concrete case,[8] although the question whether the ruling would be valid *erga omnes* or only *quoad casum* would need to be answered.[9] The danger arises, however, that certain countries which have accepted the right of individual petition for a fixed period of time (e.g. Austria, Belgium, and the UK) or the Court's compulsory jurisdiction (such as France, Iceland, and Italy) would not renew their declarations.[10] Alternatively other countries may not be prepared to make declarations under Article 25 (e.g. Cyprus, Malta, and Turkey) or Article 46 (Malta and Turkey) on the basis that the acceptance of the preliminary ruling provisions would in effect not only provide the individual greater protection domestically — as it would appear that a precondition of accepting the Court's jurisdiction to give preliminary rulings would be the

[8] See examples of case-law in Luxembourg: cases 28 to 30/62, *Da Costa en Schaake* v. *Dutch Fiscal Administration* [1963] ECR 31; [1963] CMLR 224; case 1/72, *Frilli* v. *Belgium* [1972] ECR 457; [1973] CMLR 286, para. 10 (although the Court cannot pass judgment on domestic law, it is empowered to furnish the national authorities with elements of interpretation under Community law); and case 52/76, *Beneditti* v. *Munari* [1977] ECR 163, at 183: 'the purpose of a preliminary ruling is to decide a question of law and that ruling is binding on the national court as to the interpretation of the Community provisions and acts in question.'

[9] See A. Trabucchi, 'L'effet "erga omnes" des décisions préjudicielles rendues par la Cour de justice des Communautés européennes', 10 *RTDE* (1974), 56–87; and A. Bleckmann, 'L'applicabilité directe du droit Communautaire' in *Les recours des individus devant les instances nationales en cas de violation du droit européen* (1978), 85–131, esp. at 113–15, and discussion at 177–8; also M. Cappelletti, 'The "Mighty Problem" of Judicial Review and the Contribution of Comparative Analysis', *LIEI* 1979/2, 1–29, at 13.

[10] Could such a new procedure be put into effect independently of the existing system?

incorporation of the Convention's norms into domestic law in those States where this has not occurred already — but also that such a short-circuiting of the present procedures could be justified by the provision of rapid, effective, and much less costly legal protection within the domestic legal system.

In addition, the remedies available to individuals in cases where their rights have been held to be violated must be considered in the context of an interest higher than that of the aggrieved party or that of a particular contracting state:[11] in most member states of the Council of Europe there is no check on the constitutionality of legislation. Consequently, if a legislator, be it by mere inadvertence or lack of adequate knowledge or due to the misuse of power for partisan purposes, violates what are considered fundamental rights of individuals, the lack of an adequate form of legal redress can make the national tribunal impotent in so far as it is obliged to apply the law as it stands. The provision of this extra-constitutional form of safeguard could thus guarantee this *common public interest* when a state falls below what is considered the lowest common standard. This form of development should also be seen within the wider context of a developing uniform system of a non-derogable core of human rights law which could be considered as yet another positive step towards the progressive creation of European Constitutional Law.

The competence of the European Court of Human Rights to give preliminary rulings at the request of national tribunals would also have the indisputable advantage of ensuring unity in the interpretation of the Convention's norms. As has been seen in Parts II and III of this book, the case-law of domestic tribunals is in many instances far from impressive. In addition, certain almost self-evident problems of conflicting national decisions are bound to arise. For example, in two very similar cases relating to conscientious objection, judgments given by different French courts (in which Article 9 of the Convention was invoked) ran counter to each other: by means of divergent interpretations of the Convention the two courts came to completely different conclusions, one culminating in release and the other in conviction.[12] Similarly, domestic courts may

[11] See ch. 1 above, sec. B, *passim.*
[12] Case no. 1812, 7 Dec. 1976, *Min. publ.* v. *Lemesle J., Trib. Grande Instance de Béziers*; and case no. 162 14 Feb. 1977, *Lantec P., 3° Gde. Inst. du Havre.* See ch. 3, above, notes 42-3.

make decisions completely at variance with the Convention's provisions. This was strikingly in evidence a few years ago in Greece.[13] Legal ingenuity has also had to play its part: in one particular case, the Austrian Constitutional Court went so far as to send a formal request through the Austrian Ministry of Foreign Affairs to all the contracting states asking for their opinions on the meaning of the term 'civil rights' in Article 6 of the Convention.[14] A well-functioning system of preliminary rulings by the Human Rights Court would not only help to prevent such difficulties and secure harmonious development of Convention law generally, but it would also almost certainly help to raise common standards and speed up the present cumbersome international machinery. The Netherlands Government, in 1971, suggested obtaining the Court's advisory opinion on certain aspects of domestic law in what eventually came before the Court in the case of *Engel and Others* v. *The Netherlands* (judgment rendered on 8 June 1976!), but in view of the restricted nature of the Second Protocol to the Convention, the Committee of Ministers was unable to agree on lodging a request to this end.[15] It may be recalled that under the present advisory machinery instituted by the Second Protocol, an advisory opinion may be requested *only* by the Committee of Ministers and solely in regard to matters other than the rights and freedoms enumerated in Section I of the Convention. Consequently, it can operate only at a later stage in proceedings — if at all — and its scope remains very limited.[16]

[13] See K. Vasak, *La Convention européenne des Droits de l'Homme* (1964), 248-9. Problems of a similar nature have been noted in Austria: see Ch. Schreuer, 'The Impact of International Institutions on the Protection of Human Rights in Domestic Courts', 4 *Israel Yearbook on Human Rights* (1974), 60-88, at 74-5. For a general study of such problems beyond the confines of the Convention mechanism see Schreuer's 'Concurrent Jurisdiction of National and International Tribunals', 13 *Houston Law Review* (1976), 508-26.

[14] See A. Khol, 'The Influence of the Human Rights Convention on Austrian Law', 18 *AJCL* (1970), 237-58, at 257.

[15] See Memorial of the Netherlands Government of 24 Mar. 1975 (CDH(75)17) filed with the Registry of the Human Rights Court in the case of *Engels and Others*, p. 1 (to be published in Eur. Court HR, ser. B, no. 22). Also consult Eissen, n. 16 below, 272.

[16] *Collected Texts*, 120-3. Cf. art. 64 of the American Convention on Human Rights. Recent attempts to amend this protocol have been unsuccessful. See Council of Europe doc. H(80)1, 15 Jan. 1980. See further on this subject A. H. Robertson, 'Advisory Opinions of the Court of Human Rights' in *Cassin*, i.225-40. This article *also* provides an excellent historical account of the origin of the proposal for the Court to give preliminary rulings at the request of national courts (228 ff.), the resurrection of this idea (232-3), and subsequent developments (234-40). Also see

When domestic tribunals are able to choose between an international and internal text in order to motivate their decisions, in the vast majority of cases the natural inclination and professional training of the judiciary lead them to select the latter. This in itself may disappoint an international lawyer, although it is certainly not surprising or unreasonable if one bears in mind that both the judiciary as well as practitioners are seldom aware of, and more often than not completely unfamiliar with, the published case-law emanating from Strasbourg.[17] Consequently, the Convention needs to be recognized as an important element of positive law by domestic courts. Although domestic tribunals often completely disregard the case-law and practice of the Convention organs, this has not to date led to any fundamental discrepancies of interpretation. A system of preliminary rulings — with the pre-condition of domestic incorporation of the Convention — could probably ameliorate the above situation. Systematic reliance on the case-law of the Strasbourg organs by domestic tribunals may also overcome many of the misgivings of domestic courts which are often reluctant to accept the Convention's norms as being directly applicable on the often false assumption that they are vague and that their content is not sufficiently specific to be enforceable domestically.[18] This new procedure could also, perhaps, harmonize the Convention system with that of the 'jurisprudential' protection of fundamental human rights by the Luxembourg Court within the context of European Community law.[19]

Naturally, certain dangers do exist in an attempt to transplant a system of jurisdictional control which must ensure a maximum

---

J. A. Frowein, 'The Guarantee afforded by the Institutional Machinery of the Convention' in *Privacy and Human Rights* (ed. A. H. Robertson, 1973), 284-304, esp. at 296-300. As to circumstances in which the 2nd Protocol could be used, consult E. A. Alkema, 'The EC and the European Convention of Human Rights — Immunity and Impunity for the Community', 16 *CML Rev.* (1979), 498-508 at 507-8; and M.-A. Eissen, 'La France et le Protocole no. 2 à la Convention européenne des Droits de l'Homme' in *Studi in Onore di G. Balladore Pallieri* (1978), ii.249-79, at 273.

[17] See conclusions to Part III above; and Schreuer, n. 13 above, at 73-6.

[18] See G. Schantal and M. Welan, 'Betrachtungen über die Judikatur des Verfassungsgerichtshofs zur Menschenrechtskonvention', 25 *ÖJZ* (1970), 620, 664.

[19] 'I regret the absence from the Convention of any power of this Court, or for national courts, to refer to the European Court of Human Rights for preliminary rulings on questions of interpretation of the Convention that arise in cases before them' *per* Warner, Advocate-General, opinion of 22 Aug. 1976, case 130/75 *Prais v. Council* [1976] ECR 1589, at 1607; [1976] 2 CMLR 708.

common standard to replace national regulations in such matters as the preservation of a regime of equality in matters of production, the free movement of persons, services, and capital, and the right of establishment. The replacement of national regulations and the need for uniform application are a *raison d'être* of the Economic Community. The Convention does not appear to have been designed to replace, as such, national rules, and Article 60 stipulates that 'Nothing in this Convention shall be construed as limiting or derogating from any of the human rights and fundamental freedoms which may be ensured under the laws of any High Contracting Party or under any other agreement to which it is a Party'. Thus, the Court's preliminary rulings could lay down a *minimum* common denominator and no more. It would therefore be imperative to add a proviso to any future instrument setting up this system of preliminary rulings, that domestic tribunals would be *bound* by the Strasbourg Court's rulings although they would not be precluded from providing a higher protection of individuals' rights and freedoms which is secured under domestic law. The inclusion of such a proviso would also go some way in answering the criticisms that the Convention may be unnecessarily referred to before domestic courts when other, more specific, clauses in existing legislation appear to provide the individual more adequate protection.[20] In states in which the use of a particular provision of the Convention (e.g. Articles 8 or 9) would in reality be a mere duplication of legal and/or constitutional provisions, or a repetition of 'jurisprudential' interpretation which is in advance of the concepts and interpretations accepted by the Strasbourg organs and other member states, a formula allowing the courts to accept the interpretation most favourable to the individual must be found without permitting derogation, under any circumstances, from the basic common denominator as interpreted by the Court.

The above problem is tied to a number of other issues. The first concerns the role of the European Commission of Human Rights which might be short-circuited by this new procedure.

---

[20] See comments by Ph. Vegleris, in *Privacy and Human Rights* (ed. A. H. Robertson, 1973), at 366–9. Those arguing in favour of a preliminary-rulings procedure should not underestimate the difficulties in the institution of the proposed system: on such issues as the scope of abortion law, the use of surveillance, or the closed shop, it is already difficult (and virtually impossible, at times) to obtain sound, uniform, or even acceptable judgments by *domestic* courts. A preliminary-rulings procedure could be exposed to similar criticisms.

This objection is not as serious as it looks in that the overriding objective of any human rights mechanism should be the protection of the individual rather than the maintenance of a particular international procedure.[21] Also, if a domestic tribunal were to ask the Human Rights Court for a preliminary ruling, it would appear *imperative* that the Commission be given a *right* to forward its views (e.g. in the form of a legal opinion), and one could envisage that provision could be made for a procedure similar to that prescribed in Article 20 of the Protocol of the Statute of the Court of Justice of the EEC.[22] This form of procedure could also accommodate, if considered desirable, written and oral submissions by other contracting states, either at the invitation of the Court or the state party involved in the procedure, or alternatively as of right.[23] It should be added, that strict time-limits would have to be imposed on all parties concerned in such procedures, as well as upon the Court itself, which would have to be bound — say, within a maximum delay of six months of referral — to give its ruling to the domestic tribunal.

[21] See Robertson, n. 16 above, at 239. The Commission's conciliatory role could diminish, i.e. the friendly-settlement procedure may in future be circumvented, producing, perhaps, a regressive reaction by states which have not as yet accepted the right of individual petition, and which may initially have been encouraged to do so because of the existence of this rather unique form of procedure.

[22] Art. 20 stipulates: 'In the cases governed by Article 177 of this Treaty, the decision of the court or tribunal of a Member State which suspends its proceedings and refers a case to the Court shall be notified to the Court by the court or tribunal concerned. The decision shall then be notified by the registrar of the Court to the parties, to the Member States and to the Commission, and also to the Council if the act, the validity or interpretation of which is in dispute orginates from the Council. Within two months of this notification, the parties, the Member States, the Commission and, where appropriate, the Council, shall be entitled to submit statements of case or written observations to the Court.' For a more general survey of the rights of third parties to intervene in the Luxembourg Court's proceedings, consult G. Vandersanden and A. Barav, *Contentieux Communautaire* (1977), 446–82.

[23] It is suggested that the Commission *must* be given some form of *amicus curiae/* consultative capacity before the Court. The present rules of the Court concerning the Commission's position when an advisory opinion is sought under the 2nd Protocol appears unacceptable: rule 57 stipulates that the Commission *must* be informed of such a request, although it *may* be invited to provide observations. See *Collected Texts*, 418. An interesting development occured in the case of *Winterwerp* v. *the Netherlands* when the Court allowed the Commission to submit a written statement prepared by the UK Government on the interpretation of art. 5(4) of the Convention. See Eur. Court HR, judgment of 24 Oct. 1979, ser. A, vol. 33, 6, para. 7; Conclusions to Part III above, n. 9 (in which a statement of Professor Fawcett is reproduced *verbatim*); and F. Matscher, 'Überlegungen über die Einführung der "Interpretationsintervention" im Verfahren vor dem Europäischen Gerichtshof für Menschenrechte' in *Ius Humanitatis. Festschrift zum 90. Geburtstag von A. Verdross* (1980), 533–56. Also consult the Statute of the International Court of Justice, arts. 62–3 (reproduced in S. Rosenne, *Documents on the International Court of Justice* (1979), at 86–7).

Should the requesting domestic tribunal be legally bound to comply with the preliminary ruling? It would appear that the question should be replied to in the affirmative for the following reasons: (i) the institution of such a procedure would appear to be a *sine qua non* within the context of the basic purpose that this innovation is meant to serve, i.e. the progressive and uniform concretization of a system of European human rights law; (ii) the distinction made between advisory opinions and binding rulings can be somewhat unreal since, for example, the technical status of advisory opinions of the ICJ does not save them from being *felt to be binding* since it could be embarrassing or worse to disregard an advisory opinion;[24] and, (iii) if an advisory opinion were to be disregarded by a domestic court, and the Commission were subsequently to be faced with a similar issue, it would most probably feel itself obliged to follow the Court's reasoning.[25] The acceptance of such compulsory rulings within the domestic legal systems may cause opposition, especially from members of the highest domestic courts, although such structural accommodation would not appear to be an insurmountable problem. Alternatively, if the Court's jurisdiction were to be considered too vast, its competence to provide preliminary rulings could be limited to, for example, issues arising under Articles 5 and 6 of the Convention (the administration of justice) and perhaps also to those rights from which derogation is prohibited.[26] Provision might have to be made to confer special powers upon a supervisory body which could survey situations in which the highest national court may be considered to have misinterpreted the Human Rights Court's ruling.[27] This form of supervision could foreclose the possibility

[24] A view expressed to the author by the Commission's former President, J. E. S. Fawcett. (He believes that it is for this reason largely that the UN specialized agencies have made negligible use of this function of the ICJ.) See also C. W. Jenks, *The Prospects of International Adjudication* (1964), 139-44 and 753-4.

[25] It would appear wrong to legally *bind* the Commision to such rulings. The Court could, however, possibly extend the Convention's applicability by means of a preliminary ruling in a matter in which the Commission's findings appear not to provide redress for the individual (e.g. by extending art. 6 to cover fiscal matters).

[26] Art. 15 of the Convention stipulates that the Convention rights and freedoms may, in time of war or emergency threatening the life of the nation, be derogated from as far as the situation strictly requires (para. 1) excluding from this permitted derogation the right to life (art. 2, save for killings by lawful acts of war), prohibition of torture and inhuman and degrading treatment (art. 3), prohibition of slavery and servitude (art. 4(1)), and prohibition of retroactive penalties or offences (art. 7).

[27] The European Commission of Human Rights may be provided with similar powers of supervision as the Commission of the European Communities possesses (art. 169 of the EEC Treaty).

of an individual lodging a petition before the Commission on the basis that the domestic tribunal had wrongly applied Convention law as interpreted by the Court in Strasbourg.

Other problems are also in need of further study, e.g., should the proposed system allow states to make a declaration that they accept the preliminary-ruling mechanism as being optional or compulsory? Would it be absolutely necessary for states to incorporate the Convention's provisions into domestic law if they would wish to make use of the system? Could this procedure be accepted by states which have not made declarations under Articles 46 and/or 25? Would not such a system require the member states to reassess the Convention's positioning in the domestic legal hierarchy as well as to make the judiciary and other competent domestic organs re-examine which provisions of this instrument were directly applicable and which were not? Specific amendments to the internal rules of procedure of various courts and tribunals would also have to be made. Above all, the obligation of domestic courts to apply Convention law — at least for the purpose of securing conformity with the Strasbourg Court's rulings — will probably create a need for constitutional amendment, especially in states which are not in the EEC. Prima facie it would appear that, by making the Convention an integral part of the legal system — directly applicable and possessing a status superior to that of prior and subsequent conflicting domestic law — the states would have to accept an extension of responsibilities which may have far-reaching constitutional implications. But it should be emphasized that, in effect, the implementation of this system would only entail a more rapid and direct form of enforcement of *already existing* international obligations (see Articles 1, 13, and 57 of the Convention). Articles 32(4), 53, and 54 clearly define the international obligations which require the states parties to secure the rights and freedoms enumerated in the Convention, although at present they have — in the majority of states — only an indirect effect in that, internally, they are not as such necessarily directly enforceable.[28]

An alternative method of extending the reach of the Convention's norms, and at the same time ensuring their relatively uniform application in the domestic legal systems of member states, would be for the Secretary General of the Council of

[28] See ch. 10 above. Note should also be taken of art. 50 of the Convention. Consult *Collection* art. 31, 1, and art. 50, 1.

Europe to make more effective use of the procedure under Article 57 of the Convention on the one hand, and to ensure that all states parties have made declarations under Articles 25 and 46 on the other hand. In addition *all* the states should be persuaded to incorporate the Convention's norms into domestic law. Even though these provisions may in certain respects seem outmoded or may prove to be less liberal than already existing domestic law on a number of points, their application in internal law continues to offer individuals certain extra guarantees. Indeed, it has convincingly been argued that it may at present be more important to make the Convention directly applicable than to secure it uniform interpretation.[29] In this connection, serious thought might be given to the idea that all contracting states should make a declaration of policy in the form of directives for the judiciary, or interpretative declarations to the effect that the Convention's provisions are to be interpreted by domestic courts on the basis of authoritative international interpretations by its Strasbourg organs rather than on the basis of an applicable domestic rule of construction.[30]

It is important not to underestimate the complexity of the issues involved in instituting the proposed system of preliminary rulings. At the same time it is important to make a serious attempt to ameliorate the state of affairs in which 'the Convention continues to lead an independent existence in the individual legal systems of the Contracting States, which is by no means a satisfactory situation'.[31]

---

[29] See U. Scheuner, 'An Investigation of the Influence of the European Convention on Human Rights and Fundamental Freedoms on National Legislation and Practice' in *International Protection of Human Rights* (Nobel Symposium, no. 7, ed. A. Eide and A. Schou, 1968), 193-215, esp. at 204-6.

[30] See C. W. Jenks, n. 24 above, 717. Such 'declarations' or 'interpretative clauses' could be annexed to, or included in, legislation approving or giving effect to the Convention's domestic status, by states which intend to incorporate this instrument.

[31] F. Ermacora, statement made during discussions at a colloquium in Vienna, reproduced in *Human Rights in National and International Law* (ed. A. H. Robertson, 1968), at 44. An alternative approach — not pursued in this study — is the idea of abolishing the European Court of Human Rights and permitting the Court of Justice of the European Communities to take over its responsibilities (or perhaps some form of merger could be arranged); after all, the Luxembourg Court possesses a wealth of experience in the field of ensuring the harmonious and uniform application of European Community law. For more comments on this subject consult H. Lannung, 'Human Rights and the Multiplicity of European Systems for International Protection', V *RDH/HRJ* (1972), 651-61 (and comments of K. Vasak, at 666-7); and M. Sørensen, 'The Enlargement of the European Communities and the Protection of Human Rights', XIX *European Yearbook* (1971), 3-17, esp. at 17.

B. Practice and perspectives

It may be very important to assess the status of the Convention's
provisions in the domestic legal hierarchy as well as the instrument's not insignificant influence upon courts in states which
have not incorporated it, or in the alternative, to analyse the
impact the Strasbourg organs have had in countries which have
accepted the right of individual petition and the Court's compulsory jurisdiction. But these are all, in a way, of a subsidiary
nature to the *fundamental* legal obligation which states have
entered into on the international plane: the guarantee to
individuals or groups of individuals of a certain set of common
rights and freedoms. The uniqueness of this instrument is, above
all, that obligations entered into by contracting states are owed
to *individuals* and not to other states parties on a reciprocal
basis. The Convention is not of a synallagmatic character; it is
rather a specific category of *traité-loi* whose implementation
must be effectively ensured on the domestic plane. The Convention is therefore autonomous in the sense that the standards
it upholds cannot be subjected, on either international or
domestic planes, to any in-built constitutional provision or
similar provisions based on reciprocity. Its autonomy is likewise
ensured by a relatively well functioning collective international
enforcement machinery, i.e. the optional or voluntary acceptance of the supervisory functions of the Convention organs
and the compulsory mechanism of inter-state applications.
Unfortunately, the 'compulsory' mechanism is not working as
well as it might since use of it is sporadic. (Likewise, the supervisory function of the Secretary-General of the Council of
Europe under Article 57 of the Convention also leaves much to
be desired.) It follows that the enforcement mechanism presently
in operation is imperfect; hence the suggestion for reform.

Should the substantive provisions of the European Convention
on Human Rights be incorporated into domestic law by those
states which have not done so? It is submitted that such action
may be deemed desirable, although it is certainly not considered
essential. Of much greater importance is the acceptance of the
right of individual petition and the compulsory jurisdiction of
the European Court of Human Rights. It follows that a comparative study of the Convention's domestic status in the
internal hierarchy, and a survey of the way in which domestic
courts can or do refer to its substantive provisions, appear to be

matters of *secondary* importance to the willingness of states to subject themselves to a relatively effective international machinery in Strasbourg.

Rather than provide a summary of what has been discussed at some considerable length in the book, an attempt can be made here to provide a synthesis in the form of six general observations:

1. The European Convention on Human Rights possesses some unique features which are difficult to classify in terms of traditional international law. It is — in the eyes of its implementing organs — a 'law-making' and 'living instrument' whose primary purpose is to ensure that contracting states adequately comply with their responsibility to serve *l'ordre public de l'Europe*. In so doing the Convention organs not only guarantee and uphold common human rights standards enumerated in the Convention, but they also occasionally 'accelerate' the harmonious evolution of Western European standards. The obligations thereunder are owed by states *to individuals* and *not* to other contracting states.[32]

2. There exists *no* legal obligation on member states to incorporate the Convention's substantive provisions into their domestic legal systems. This is made clear from both the study of the text itself and the practice of states. In addition, it is suggested that the importance of this international instrument stems not so much from the legal niceties of incorporation or non-incorporation, but rather from the *effective* and *practical* implementation of 'minimal common standards'. These and even higher standards may be secured on the domestic plane irrespective of whether individuals are able to invoke the Convention's norms as a source of law in domestic legal proceedings. This being said, incorporation of the Convention does appear desirable.

3. Of the twenty-one member states of the Council of Europe, fourteen have secured the Convention the status of domestic law, while seven have not done so. The exact status of the Convention's provisions in the domestic hierarchy of those states in which its substantive provisions can be used as legal authority is

---

[32] See Conclusions to Part I above.

often uncertain and varies considerably not only from country to country but even from one court to another in the same country. The overview provided in Part II above indicates that in many states the *exact* status of the Convention's norms is difficult and sometimes even impossible to determine with any certainty. While on the one hand it is of considerable interest to note the importance attached to the Convention's provisions by the judiciary in such countries as Austria, Belgium, and the Netherlands, at the same time it is likewise of equal interest to observe the peripheral or subsidiary role that the same set of norms plays *vis-à-vis* constitutional, legislative, or unwritten principles of law in, for example, Italy, the Federal Republic of Germany, and in Spain. The above study tends to suggest (in many instances) that although express reference to the Convention's provisions may be of academic interest to monitor, such citation can often have very little practical significance. In addition it may also be assumed that in many instances the Convention is taken into account even without express reference to its provisions. It follows that the utility of a comparative study of this type is dependent not only upon the more general receptiveness of a particular country's judiciary to accommodate European human rights standards which may occasionally be of a higher level or more beneficial to an individual in a particular case, but also on a given state's willingness to accept some form of an outside or so-called 'objective' means of supervision from Strasbourg which can directly or indirectly ensure better and *effective* protection of human rights on the domestic plane. The crucial role played by the judiciary must not, however, be underestimated. In the words of Professor Cançado Trindade:

Nowadays the role of domestic courts is rendered prominent by the fact that the international legal order remains basically a horizontal rather than a vertical one, in the sense that State behaviour conforming with international duties has been promoted not so much by a vertical hierarchy of international tribunals but rather by a process of interaction with national courts . . . Hence the greater responsibility placed upon national courts, in a way 'exposing' their inadequacies and shortcomings in the course of their administration of justice; when they operate pursuant to, e.g., the European Convention on Human Rights, a certain uniformity of practice can be expected, particularly as those provisions are designed to assist rather than replace them.[33]

___

[33] A. A. Cançado Trindade, 'Exhaustion of Local Remedies in International Law and the Role of National Courts', 17 *Archiv des Völkerrechts* (1978), 333–70, at 364.

4. The Convention's provisions are beginning to be applied in inter-individual relations, at least in a number of states in which the Convention possesses the status of domestic law. It follows that domestic courts (as well as the Convention organs?) may be prepared to assume that certain rights and freedoms guaranteed under the Convention can be invoked by individuals against other private persons or organizations; the subject-matter covered by this international instrument falls within the conceptual framework of the nature and scope of the obligations imposed upon states parties to the Convention, which may necessarily include *all legally regulated activity* within the state's jurisdiction, as defined in Article 1 of the Convention.[34] The use of the Convention's provisions in this way illustrates the growing importance that the Convention's norms have acquired within the domestic law of contracting states. This development appears to have been unforeseen by the drafters of the Convention although it may undoubtedly be beneficial to certain individuals in proceedings before domestic courts. This development is also tied to another matter, namely whether, and if so to what extent, states have a positive duty to act or do something specific in order not to violate provisions of the Convention.

5. Whether the European Convention on Human Rights represents '*un droit commun pour l'ensemble des États membres comme pour la Communauté* [*européenne*]'[35] is as yet uncertain. If this were the case, it would indeed be most interesting to speculate upon the eventuality of the domestic courts of the member state countries of the European Communities making reference to the Convention as an integral part of European Community law. Much will depend on two separate developments: the evolution of case-law of the Court of Justice of the European Communities, and the possible accession of the Community organs to the 'Convention mechanism' with the resultant and as yet unclear effect that such a step can have within the more general framework of European Community law.[36]

---

[34] See ch. 8 above.

[35] *Per* P. Pescatore, 'La protection des droits fondamentaux par le pouvoir judiciaire', *FIDE Conference*, report no. II/2, at 32.

[36] See G. Cohen-Jonathan, 'La Convention européenne des Droits de l'Homme et la Communauté européenne' in *Mélanges F. Dehousse* (1979), i.157-68, at 165-6. Cf., C.-D. Ehlermann, 'Accession of the European Community to the European Convention of Human Rights' in *Do We Need a Bill of Rights?* (ed. C. Campbell, 1980), 114-32, at 128-30.

6. In the words of Dr Vasak:

conçu comme un instrument d'*unification politique* des démocraties européennes, la Convention de Rome s'est transformée, par la suite de la jurisprudence abondante de ses organes, en un instrument d'*unification des régimes juridiques* des droits de l'homme dans les États contractants.[37]

Thus, in their delicate task in interpreting the Convention's 'common law', the Convention organs often place emphasis on the evolutive and progressive elements of this set of common legal norms, taking due account of social, economic, and legal advances made within the domestic legal structures of member states. By so doing they encourage conformity and to a certain extent integration of legal standards as well as — indirectly — their harmonization. These interpretations of 'Convention law' are increasingly being noted by the domestic courts of the contracting states. The comparative study carried out in Chapter 10 above indicates that the findings of the Convention's organs may often be of great assistance to domestic courts. It stands to reason that the domestic judiciary should seek guidelines from Strasbourg in order to clarify the extent and exact nature of obligations which are often very widely and loosely stated in the Convention. In this respect, the judgments of the European Court of Human Rights appear to be of a highly persuasive authority, and possibly they are even legally binding (in certain circumstances) for courts in Austria, the Netherlands, and Switzerland.

A comparative inquiry analysing the domestic status of the European Convention on Human Rights and in particular the interaction between domestic law and this unique multilateral agreement in terms of the latter's impact on domestic legal institutions has led the author to the conclusion that there is a need for the creation of some novel arrangement whereby the harmonious and uniform evolution of Convention law could be better guaranteed, taking into account the special nature of this international instrument. In the words of Professor A. H. Robertson:

While there can be no doubt that its work for human rights is the most important achievement of the Council of Europe, legitimate pride should not degenerate into self-satisfaction. If the European system for the

---

[37] K. Vasak, 'Le droit international des Droits de l'Homme', **140** *R. des C.* (1974), iv.333–415 at 406. (Emphasis original.) See also comments by Mosler, n. 3 above; and F. G. Jacobs, *The European Convention on Human Rights* (1975), 276-7.

protection of human rights is the best yet established by any international organisation, it is by no means perfect and is certainly capable of improvement . . . It is therefore necessary to realise that the task of the Council of Europe in the field of human rights was not finished by the conclusion of the European Convention; indeed, it never will be finished in that or any other way. This is because it is simply not possible in this imperfect world to devise any system which will be perfect and complete. Gaps will be found in any arrangements that have been established; new needs will arise as new developments occur in the organisation of society, particularly in an era of technological and political change; new measures will therefore be necessary from time to time in order to complete and perfect any system that has been instituted.[38]

[38] *Human Rights in Europe* (1977), at 278.

Select Bibliography

Alkema, E. A., *Studies over Europese grondrechten* (1978).

—— 'The European Convention on Human Rights and the Netherlands Legal Order', 23 *NILR* (1976), 314-16.

Andrews, J. A., ed., *Human Rights in Criminal Procedure* (1981).

Aybay, R., 'International Human Rights Instruments and Turkish Law', *Turkish Yearbook of Human Rights* (1979), 17-25.

Balladore Pallieri, G.: *Studi in onore di G. Balladore Pallieri* (2 vols., 1978).

Bari Conference, 17-18 December 1973, proceedings: *Les clauses facultatives de la Convention européenne des Droits de l'Homme* (1974).

Beddard, R., *Human Rights and Europe* (1980).

—— 'The Status of the European Convention on Human Rights in Domestic Law', 16 *ICLQ* (1967), 206-17.

Berchtold, K., 'The European Convention on Human Rights and the Austrian Legal Order: Some Experiences', VIII *RDH/HRJ* (1975), 383-405.

Berka, W., 'Die EMRK und die österreichische Grundrechtstradition', 34 *ÖJZ* (1979), 365-75 and 428-32.

Bernhardt, R., 'The Problems of Drawing up a Catalogue of Fundamental Rights for the European Communities', *Bull. EC* Suppl. 5/76, 19-69.

Bleckmann, A., *Allgeimeine Grundrechtslehren* (1979).

Bossuyt, M. J., 'The Direct Applicability of International Instruments on Human Rights', *RBDI* (1980), 317-43.

Bridge, J. W., 'The Legal Nature of the Acts of International Organisations and International Courts and the Legal Status of such Acts in Municipal Law', UK national report at the 1970 Pescara Congress of the International Academy of Comparative Law (unpublished).

—— 'Fundamental Rights in the European Economic Community' in *Fundamental Rights* (ed. J. W. Bridge, D. Lasok, D. L. Perrott, and R. O. Plender, 1973), 291-305.

Brinkhorst, L. J., and Lammers, J. G., 'The Impact of International Law, including European Community Law, on the Netherlands Legal Order' in *Introduction to Dutch Law for Foreign Lawyers* (ed. D. C. Fokkema, J. M. Chorns, E. H. Hondius, and E. Ch. Lisser, 1978), 561-84.

British Institute of Human Rights, *The European Convention on Human Rights. Two New Directions: EEC; UK* (1980).

Brownlie, I., *Principles of Public International Law* (1979).

—— *Basic Documents on Human Rights* (1981).

Buergenthal, Th., 'The Domestic Status of the European Convention on Human Rights', XIII *Buffalo Law Review* (1963/64), 354-92.

—— 'The Effect of the European Convention on Human Rights on the Internal Law of Member States', *ICLQ* Supplement no. 11 (1965), 76-106.

—— 'The Domestic Status of the European Convention on Human Rights: A Second Look', 7 *Journal of the ICJ* (1966), 55-96.

—— 'The European Convention and its National Application: Interaction of National Law and Modern International Agreements: Some Introductory Observations', 18 *AJCL* (1970), 333-6.

—— 'International and Regional Human Rights Law and Institutions:- Some Examples', 12 *Texas International Law Journal* (1977), 321- 30.

Busuttil, E., *The Frontiers of Human Rights* (1966).

Campbell, C., ed., *Do We Need a Bill of Rights?* (1980).

Cançado Trindade, A. A., 'Exhaustion of Local Remedies in International Law and the Role of National Courts', 17 *Archiv des Völkerrechts* (1978), 333-70.

Cappelletti, M., ed., *New Perspectives for a Common Law of Europe* (1978).

Cassin, René: *René Cassin, Amicorum Discipulorumque Liber, International Institute of Human Rights* (4 vols., 1969-72).

Castberg, F., *The European Convention on Human Rights* (1974).

Centre universitaire de droit public, Brussels, *Vie privée et Droits de l'Homme* (1973).

Chiavario, M., *La Convenzione Europea dei Diritto dell'Uomo nel sistema delle fronti normative in materia penale* (1969).

Clarke, J. P., *The European Convention on Human Rights and Fundamental Freedoms and Irish Law* (1981).

Cohen-Jonathan, G., 'Convention européenne des Droits de l'Homme et droit communautaire: une coordination nécessaire', V *RDH/HRJ*, (1972), 615-49.

—— 'Les Droits de l'Homme dans les Communautés européennes', in *Recueil d'études en hommage à Ch. Eisenman* (1975), 399-418.

Colcatre-Zilgien, A., 'De quelques effets actuels et éventuels de la ratification de la Convention européenne des Droits de l'Homme sur la politique et le droit français', 94 *RDPSP* (1978), 645-78.

Collège d'Europe, Droit communautaire et droit national (Semaine de Bruges, 1965).

Colloque de Besançon, 5-7 November, 1970, 'La France devant la Convention européenne des Droits de l'Homme', III *RDH/HRJ* (1970), 550-738.

Colloque de Grenoble, 25-6 January 1973, 'L'Efficacité des mécanismes juridictionnels de protection des personnes privées dans le cadre européen', VI *RDH/HRJ* (1973), 603-800.

Colloque à l'Université Catholique de Louvain (premier colloque du Département des Droits de l'Homme), Les Droits de l'Homme et les personnes morales (Brussels, 1970).

Compte, P., 'The Application of the European Convention on Human Rights in Municipal Law', IV *Journal of the ICJ* (1962), 94-133.

Conseil Fédéral suisse, Rapport à l'Assemblée Fédérale sur la Convention de sauvegarde des Droits de l'Homme et des libertés fondamentales (1968).

Council of Europe, *Bibliography relating to the European Convention on Human Rights* (Strasbourg, 1978).

Council of Europe, *Case-law Topics*:
  1. 'Human Rights in Prison' (Strasbourg, 1971).
  2. 'Family Life' (Strasbourg, 1972).
  3. 'Bringing an Application before the European Commission on Human Rights' (Strasbourg, 1974, revised in 1978).
  4. 'Human Rights and their Limitations' (Strasbourg, 1973).
—— Chart showing Signatures and Ratifications of Council of Europe Conventions and Agreements (Strasbourg, 15 Dec. 1981).
—— *Collection of Decisions of the European Commission of Human Rights* (volumes 1-46). [Now replaced by *Decisions and Reports.*]
—— *Collection of Decisions of National Courts Referring to the Convention on Human Rights* (1969, with supplements in 1970, 1971, 1973, and 1974).
—— collected editions of the *travaux préparatoires* of the European Convention on Human Rights, volumes 1-8, five volumes published to date (1975-).
—— *Decisions and Reports*, European Commission of Human Rights. (Published from July 1975 to replace *Collection of Decisions*.)
—— doc. H(67)2 of 10 January 1967. *Implementation of Article 57 of the European Convention on Human Rights.*
—— doc H(76)15 of 15 October 1976. *Implementation of Article 57 of the European Convention on Human Rights.*
—— doc. DH/Exp.(76)23 of 22 December 1976. Study prepared by the International Institute of Human Rights: *Competence of the European Court of Human Rights to give Preliminary Rulings at the Request of a National Court.*
—— *European Convention on Human Rights: Collected Texts* (Strasbourg, 1981).
—— *European Convention on Human Rights. National Aspects* (Strasbourg, 1975).
—— *Parliamentary Conference on Human Rights*, Vienna, 18-20 October 1971 (1972).
—— *Proceedings of the Fourth International Colloquy about the European Convention on Human Rights*, Rome 5-8 November, 1975 (Strasbourg, 1976).
—— *Proceedings of the Colloquy about the European Convention on Human Rights in Relation to Other International Instruments for the Protection of Human Rights*, Athens, 21-22 September 1978 (Strasbourg, 1979).
—— 'Stocktaking on the European Convention on Human Rights', a periodic note on the concrete results achieved under the Convention, by H. C. Krüger, Secretary to the European Commission of Human Rights (Strasbourg, 1982).
Council of Europe and the Faculty of Law, University of Strasbourg, *La Protection internationale des Droits de l'Homme dans le cadre européen* (1961).
Court of Justice of the European Communities, 'Visit of the European Court of Human Rights and of the European Commission of Human Rights' in *Information of the Court of Justice of the European Communities* (1977), iii.39-88.

—— *Reports of Cases before the Court*.
Coussirat-Coustère, Y., 'La réserve française à l'article 15 de la Convention européenne des Droits de l'Homme', 102 *Journal de droit international* (1975), 269-93.
Dale, Sir W., 'Human Rights in the United Kingdom — International Standards', 25 *ICLQ* (1976), 292-301.
Danelius, H., *Human Rights in Sweden* (1982).
Daubie, C., 'L'autorité des arrêts et des décisions des organes de la Convention européenne des Droits de l'Homme', IV *RDH/HRJ* (1973), 735-46.
De Figueiro Dias, J., 'La protection des Droits de l'Homme dans la procédure pénale portugaise' in *Boletim do Ministério da Justiça* (1980), 4-34.
Dehousse, F.: Mélanges F. Dehousse (2 vols., 1979).
Del Russo, A. L., *International Protection of Human Rights* (1971).
De Visscher, P., 'Les tendances internationales des constitutions modernes', 80 *R. des C.* (1952), i.511-79.
Dijk, P. van, and Hoof, G. J. H. van, *De Europese conventie in theorie en praktijk* (1979).
Doehring, K., 'Non-discrimination and Equal Treatment under the European Human Rights Convention and the West German Constitution with particular Reference to Discrimination against Aliens', 18 *AJCL* (1970), 305-25.
Dogan, M., 'L'influence de la Convention de sauvegarde des Droits de l'Homme et des libertés fondamentales sur l'ordre constitutionnel turc', presented at an international symposium organized on the occasion of the 100th anniversary of the Istanbul Bar Association in April 1978.
Dominicé, Ch., 'La nature juridique des actes des organisations et des juridictions internationales et leurs effets en droit interne' in *Recueil de travaux suisses présentés au VIIIe Congrès international de droit comparé*, Pescara, 1970 (1970), 249-64.
—— 'La Convention européenne des Droits de l'Homme devant le juge national', 28 *ASDI* (1972), 9-40.
Dowrick, F. E., 'Overlapping European Laws', 27 *ICLQ* (1978), 629-60.
Dronsch, G., *Der Rang der Europäischen Menschenrechtskonvention im deutschen Normensystem* (Dissertation, Göttingen, 1964).
Drzemczewski, A., 'Fundamental Rights and the European Communities: Recent Developments', II *HR Rev.* (1977), 69-86.
—— 'British Courts and the European Human Rights Convention: An Unsatisfactory Situation', *TL* (1979), 38-54.
Duffy, P. J., 'English Law and the European Convention on Human Rights', 29 *ICLQ* (1980), 585-618.
—— 'The Relationship between Community Law and the European Convention on Human Rights', presented at the International Colloquium on Relationships between Public International Law and Community Law, London, 21-3 June 1979 (British Institute of International and Comparative Law).
Edeson, W. R., and Wooldridge, F., 'European Community Law and Fundamental Rights: Some Recent Decisions of the European Court and National Courts', *LIEI* (1976), 1-54.

Eide, A., and Schou, A., eds., *International Protection of Human Rights* (Nobel Symposium no. 7, Uppsala, 1968).

Eissen, M.-A., 'La Convention et les devoirs de l'individu' in *La protection internationale des Droits de l'Homme dans le cadre européen* (1961), 167-94.

—— 'The European Convention on Human Rights and the Duties of the Individual', 32 *Nordisk Tidsskrift for International Ret* (1962), 229-53.

—— 'The Independence of Malta and the European Convention of Human Rights', 41 *BYIL* (1965/66), 401-10.

—— 'La Convention européenne des Droits de l'Homme et les obligations de l'individu: une mise à jour', in *Cassin*, iii.151-62.

Emde Boas, M. J. van, 'The Impact of the European Convention on Human Rights and Fundamental Freedoms on the Legal Order of the Netherlands', 13 *NILR* (1966), 337-73, and 14 *NILR* (1967), 1-32.

Esen, B. N., 'L'État de droit: les Droits de l'Homme, qualité intrinsèque de l'État', in *La Turquie* (1969), 77-119.

—— 'Système turc de protection des Droits de l'Homme dans les rapports entre personnes privées', in *Cassin*, iii.163-76.

Espersen, O., 'Denmark and the European Convention on Human Rights', 18 *AJCL* (1970), 293-304.

—— 'Human Rights and Relations between Individuals. Some Comments on this Complex of Problems in Danish Theory and Legislation with Particular Reference to the Protection of Privacy', in *Cassin*, iii.177-87.

European Court of Human Rights: Series A, *Judgments and Decisions*; Series B, *Pleadings, Oral Arguments, Documents.* (Official publications of the European Court of Human Rights.)

Evans, Sir V., 'The Practice of European Countries where Direct Effect is given to the European Convention on Human Rights in Internal Law', Written Communication in *Proceedings of the Colloquy about the European Convention on Human Rights in Relation to other International Instruments for the Protection of Human Rights*, Athens, 21-2 September 1978 (Council of Europe, 1979), 109-239.

Evrigenis, D. J., 'Le rôle de la Convention européenne des Droits de l'Homme', in *New Perspectives for a Common Law of Europe* (ed. M. Cappelletti, 1978), 341-357.

—— 'Reflections on the National Dimension of the European Convention on Human Rights', in *Proceedings of the Colloquy about the European Convention on Human Rights in Relation to other International Instruments for the Protection of Human Rights*, Athens, 21-2 September 1978 (Council of Europe, 1979), 65-80.

Færkel, J., 'The Position of Fundamental Rights in the National Legal System of Denmark; Constitutional Supremacy, General Relationship to International Law and Community Law', report presented at a human rights seminar at the European University Institute, Florence, May 1977.

Fawcett, J. E. S., 'A Bill of Rights for the United Kingdom?', 1 *HR Rev.* (1976), 57-64.

—— *The Application of the European Convention on Human Rights* (1969).

Fédération internationale de droit européen (FIDE), L'individu et le droit européen. The Individual and European Law. Die Einzelperson und das europäische Recht, FIDE VII, papers of 7th Congress, 2–4 October 1975 (1977).

Fokkema, D. C., Chorus, J. M., Hondius, E. G., and Lisser, E. Ch., eds., *Introduction to Dutch Law for Foreign Lawyers* (1978), vol. i.

Frowein, J. A., 'Die Europäische Menschenrechtskonvention und das Europäischen Gemeinschaftsrecht' in *Die Grundrechte in der Europäischen Gemeinschaft* (1978), 47–59.

Fuss, E. W., *Der Grundrechtsschutz in den Europäischen Gemeinschaften aus deutscher Sicht, mit einer Skisse der Grundrechtsprobleme in Frankreich, Grossbritannien und der Bundesrepublik Deutschland* (1975).

Ganshof van der Meersch, W. J., 'La Convention européenne des Droits de l'Homme a-t-elle, dans le cadre du droit interne, une valeur d'ordre public?', in *Les Droits de l'Homme en droit interne et en droit international* (1968), 151–251.

—— 'L'ordre juridique des Communautés européennes et le droit international', **148** *R. des C.* (1975), v.1–143.

—— 'Aspects de la mise en œuvre d'une sauvegarde collective des Droits de l'Homme en droit international — la Convention européenne', *Mélanges F. Dehousse* (1979), i.192–208.

Golsong, H., *Das Rechtsschutzsystem der Europäischen Menschenrechtskonvention* (1958).

—— 'The European Convention on Human Rights before Domestic Courts', **38** *BYIL* (1962), 445–56.

—— 'Implementation of International Protection of Human Rights', **110** *R. des C.* (1963), 7–151.

—— 'The Control Machinery of the European Convention on Human Rights', *ICLQ* Supplement no. 11 (1965), 38–69.

—— 'L'effet direct, ainsi que le rang en droit interne, des normes de la Convention européenne des Droits de l'Homme et des décisions prises par les organes institués par celle-ci', in *Les recours des individus devant les instances nationales en cas de violation du droit européen (Institut d'Études européennes,* Brussels, 1980), 59–83.

Goy, R., 'La ratification par la France de la Convention européenne des Droits de l'Homme', **22** *NILR* (1975), 32–50.

Grementieri, V., and Trocker, N., 'The Protection of Human Rights in Constitutional Law: Italy', in *Italian National Reports to the IXth International Congress of Comparative Law, Teheran* (1974), 491–503.

Güllü, A. R., *Les Droits de l'Homme et la Turquie* (1958).

Guradze, H., *Die Europäische Menschenrechtskonvention* (1968).

Hambro, E., 'The New Provision for International Collaboration in the Constitution of Norway', in *Études de droit international en hommage à Paul Guggenheim* (1968), 557–72.

Hand, G. J., and Van Den Berghe, eds., *In Memorium C. Sasse. Studies in Human Rights in Europe* (1983).

Harris, D. J., 'Recent Cases on Pre-Trial Detention and Delay in Criminal Proceedings in the European Court of Human Rights', **44** *BYIL* (1970), 87–109.

Herzog, R., *Grundrechtsbeschränkung nach dem Grundgesetz und*

Europäische Menschenrechtskonvention (Dissertation, Munich, 1958).

Higgins, R., 'The Execution of Decisions of Organs under the European Convention on Human Rights', 31 *RHDI* (1978), 1-30.

Hilf, M., Klein, E., and Bleckmann, A., 'Sekundäres Gemeinschaftsrecht und Deutsche Grundrechte, Zum Beschluss des Bundesverfassungsgerichte vom 29 Mai 1974', 35 *ZRV* (1975), 51-107.

Holloway, K., *Modern Trends in Treaty Law* (1967).

Holm, N. E., 'The Protection of Civil and Political Rights in Denmark', VIII *RDH/HRJ* (1975), 167-78.

Home Office, *Legislation on Human Rights, with particular reference to the European Convention: A Discussion Document* (London, 1976).

Horan, M. J., 'Contemporary Constitutionalism and Legal Relationships between Individuals', 25 *ICLQ* (1976), 848-67.

Institut d'Études européennes, Brussels, *Les recours des individus devant les instances nationales en cas de violation du droit européen* (1978).

Irish Association of Democratic Lawyers, *A Bill of Rights* (1976).

Jacobs, F. G., *The European Convention on Human Rights* (1975).

—— ed., *European Law and the Individual* (1976).

—— ed., *Yearbook of European Law* (1982).

Jaconelli, J., 'The European Convention on Human Rights — The Text of a British Bill of Rights?', *Public Law* (1976), 226-55.

—— *Enacting a Bill of Rights* (1980).

Jacot-Guillarmod, O., *Droit communautaire et droit international public* (1979).

Jägerskiöld, S., 'Civil and Political Rights in Sweden', VIII *RDH/HRJ* (1975), 193-200.

Janssen-Pevtschin, G., Velu, J., and Venwelkelhuyzen, A., 'La sauvegarde des Droits de l'Homme et des libertés fondamentales et le fonctionnement des juridictions belges', XV *Chronique de politique étrangère* Brussels, *Institut Royal des Relations Internationales* (1962), 199-246.

Jenks, C. W., *The Prospects of International Adjudication* (1964).

Junod, B. F., *La Suisse et la Convention des Droits de l'Homme* (Doctoral dissertation, Neuchâtel) (1969).

Kägi, W.: Menschenrecht — Foderalismus — Demokratie. Mélanges W. Kägi (1979).

Kellberg, L., 'Sverige och Europarådets Konvention om de mänskliga rättigheterna', *Svensk Juristtidning* (1961), 503-7.

Kelly, J. M., *Fundamental Rights in the Irish Law and Constitution* (1967).

Khol, A., *Zwischen Staat und Weltstaat — Die internationalen Sicherungsverfahren zum Schutze der Menschenrechte* (1969).

—— 'The Protection of Human Rights in Relationships Between Private Individuals: The Austrian Situation', in *Cassin* iii.195-213.

—— 'The Influence of the Human Rights Convention on Austrian Law', 18 *AJCL* (1970), 237-58.

Kiss, A.-Ch., 'La nature juridique des actes des organisations et des juridictions internationales et leurs effets en droit interne', in *Études de droit contemporain* (1970), 259-71.

Kujath, K., *Bibliography on European Integration* (1977).

Lannung, H., 'Human Rights and the Multiplicity of European Systems for International Protection', V *RDH/HRJ* (1973), 651-61.

Lardy, P., *La force obligatoire du droit international en droit interne* (1966).
Lauterpacht, E., and Collier, J. G., eds., *Individual Rights and the State in Foreign Affairs: An International Compendium* (1977).
Lee, L. K., 'European Integration and the Protection of Human Rights, 31 *The George Washington Law Review* (1962/63), 959–76.
Liebscher, V., 'Austria and the European Convention for the Protection of Human Rights and Fundamental Freedoms', IV *Journal of the ICJ* (1961), 282–93.
Liñan Nogueras, D., *El Detenido en el Convencio Europeo de los Derechos Humanos* (1980).
Linde, E., Ortega, L. I., and Sánchez Morón, M., eds., *El sistema europeo de protección de los derechos humanos* (1979).
Linke, R., 'The Influence of the European Convention on Human Rights on National European Criminal Proceedings', XXI *De Paul Law Review* (1971), 397–420.
Louis, J.-V., 'Droits de l'Homme et élargissement des Communautés européennes', V *RDH/HRJ*, (1972), 675–703.
Luard, E., ed., *The International Protection of Human Rights* (1967).
McNair, Lord, 'The European Convention of 1950 for the Protection of Human Rights and Fundamental Freedoms', in *The Expansion of International Law* (1962), 9–28.
Malinverni, G., 'L'application de la Convention européenne des Droits de l'Homme en Suisse', XV *Journée Juridique* (1976), 1–51.
Menzel, E., 'Verfassungsrang für die Normen der Europäischen Menschenrechtskonvention nach dem Recht der Bundesrepublik Deutschlands', in *Recueil d'études de droit international, Festbuch für Guggenheim* (1968), 573–604.
Meriggiola, E., *La Convenzione Europea dei Diritti dell'Uomo* (1968).
Mertens, P., *Droit de recours effectif devant les instances nationales en cas de violation d'un Droit de l'Homme* (1973).
Meuwissen, D. H. M., *De Europese Conventie en het Nederlandse Recht* (1968).
Meuwissen, H. M., and Alkema, E. A., *De Europese Conventie en het Nederlandse Recht* (1976).
Miehsler, H., and Petzold, H., eds., *European Convention on Human Rights. Texts and Documents* (1980, trilingual publication).
Miele, M., 'Les organisations internationales et le domaine constitutionnel des états', 131 *R. des C.* (1970), iii.309–92.
Mitchell, J. D. B., 'Some Aspects of the Protection of Individuals Against Private Power in the United Kingdom', in *Cassin* iii.235–46.
Modinos, Polys: Mélanges Polys Modinos (1968).
Monconduit, F., *La Commission européenne des Droits de l'Homme* (1965).
Morrisson, C., *The Developing European Law of Human Rights* (1967).
—— *The Dynamics of Development in the European Human Rights Convention System* (1981).
Moser, B., *Die Europäische Menschenrechtskonvention und das bürgerliche Recht: Zum Problem der Drittwirkung von Grundrechten* (1972).
Mosler, H., 'L'Influence de droit national sur la Convention européenne des Droits de l'Homme', in *Miscellanea W. J. Ganshof van der Meersch* (1972), i.521–43.

Mosler, H., Bernhardt, R., and Hilf, J., eds., *Grundsrechtsschutz in Europa* (1977).

Müller, J. P., 'Die Anwendung der Europäischen Menschenrechtskonvention in der Schweiz', 94 *Revue de droit suisse* (1975), 373-405.

Nedjati, Z. M., *Human Rights and Fundamental Freedoms* (1972).

—— *Human Rights under the European Convention* (1978).

Nickel-Lanz, C., 'Les effets des droits fondamentaux dans les relations entre personnes privées: étude comparative', submitted at the Colloquium on the Protection of Human Rights in the European Community', held under the auspices of the European University Institute, Florence, 14-17 June 1978.

Opsahl, T., 'The Protection of Civil and Political Rights in Norway', VIII *RDH/HRJ* (1975), 179-91.

—— 'Legal Protection for Human Rights in Norway', unpublished paper presented at a symposium organized by the British Institute of Human Rights in Northampton, June 1976.

—— 'Human Rights Today: International Obligations and National Implementation', 23 *Scandinavian Studies in Law* (1979), 149-76.

Pahr, W., 'Le système autrichien de protection des Droits de l'Homme', I *RDH/HRJ* (1968), 397-406.

Partsch, K. J., *Die Rechte und Freiheiten der Europäischen Menschenrechtskonvention* (1966).

Pellet, A., 'La Ratification par la France de la Convention européenne des Droits de l'Homme', 90 *RDPSP* (1974), 1319-79.

—— 'La reconnaissance par la France du droit de requête individuelle devant la Commission européenne des Droits de l'Homme', 97 *RDPSP* (1981), 69-103.

Peloux, R.: Mélanges R. Peloux (1980).

Pescatore, P., *Conclusion et effet des traités internationaux selon le droit constitutionnel, les usages et la jurisprudence du Grand-Duché de Luxembourg* (1964).

—— 'Les Droits de l'Homme et l'intégration européenne', 4 *CDE* (1968), 629-37.

—— 'Fundamental Rights and Freedoms in the System of the European Communities', 18 *AJCL* (1970), 348-51.

—— 'The Protection of Human Rights in the European Communities', 9 *CML Rev.* (1972), 73-99.

—— 'Address on the Application of Community Law in Each of the Member States', in *Judicial and Academic Conference* 27-8 September 1976 (Luxembourg, 1976), report no. VI.

Poncet, D., *La protection de l'accusé par la Convention européenne des Droits de l'Homme* (1977).

Raymond, J., 'Comment s'exerce la fonction de conciliation de la Commission européenne des Droits de l'Homme', II *RDH/HRJ* (1969), 259-66.

—— 'La Suisse devant les organes de la Convention européenne des Droits de l'Homme', 98 *Revue de droit suisse* (1979), 1-108.

—— 'A Contribution to the Interpretation of Article 13 of the European Convention on Human Rights', V *HR Rev.* (1980), 161-75.

RDH/HRJ — Special Issue, *Twenty-Fifth Anniversary of the European Convention on Human Rights*, in vol. VIII (1975), 323-622.

Reimann, H. B., 'La Convention de sauvegarde des Droits de l'Homme et des libertés fondamentales et la Suisse', **VIII** *RDH/HRJ* (1975), 407-16.

Ress, G., 'The Legal Effect of the Judgments of the European Court of Human Rights on the Internal Law and before Domestic Courts of the Contracting States', in *Fifth International Colloquy about the European Convention on Human Rights*, Frankfurt, 9-12 April 1980, Council of Europe doc. H/Coll(80)4.

Reuter, P.: Mélanges P. Reuter (1981).

Revue de droit suisse, special issue: *La Convention européenne des Droits de l'Homme et son application en droit suisse*, in vol. 94 (1975).

Robertson, A. H., 'The Political Background and Historical Development of the European Convention on Human Rights', *ICLQ* Supplement no. 11 (1965), 24-37.

—— ed., *Human Rights in National and International Law* (1968).

—— 'Advisory Opinions of the Court of Human Rights', in *Cassin* i.225-40.

—— 'The Relationship between the European Convention on Human Rights and Internal Law in General', in *European Criminal Law* (Colloques Européens, Bruxelles, 1970), 3-24.

—— *Human Rights in the World* (1982).

—— (ed.), *Privacy and Human Rights* (1973).

—— *Human Rights in Europe* (1977).

Rolin, H., 'L'autorité des arrêts et des décisions des organes de la Convention européenne des Droits de l'Homme', **VI** *RDH/HRJ* (1973), 729-46.

Rupp, H., 'International Law as Part of the Law of the Land: Some Aspects of the Operation of Article 25 of the Basic Law of the Federal Republic of Germany', 11 *Texas International Law Journal* (1976), 541-7.

Schermers, H. G., *Judicial Protection in the European Communities* (1979).

Scheuner, U., 'An Investigation of the Influence of the European Convention on Human Rights and Fundamental Freedoms on National Legislation and Practice', in *International Protection of Human Rights* (Nobel Symposium no. 7, ed. A. Eide and A. Schou, 1968), 193-217.

—— 'Fundamental Rights in European Community Law and in National Constitutional Law', 12 *CML Rev.* (1975), 171-91.

Schreuer, Ch., 'The Interpretation of Treaties by Domestic Courts', 45 *BYIL* (1971), 255-302.

—— 'The Impact of International Institutions on the Protection of Human Rights in Domestic Courts', 4 *Israel Yearbook on Human Rights* (1974), 60-88.

—— *Die Behandlung internationaler Organakte durch staatliche Gerichte* (1977).

—— *Decisions of International Institutions before Domestic Courts* (1981).

Sohn, L., and Buergenthal, Th., *International Protection of Human Rights* (1973).

Sørensen, M., 'Obligations of a State Party to a Treaty in respect of its Municipal Law', in *Human Rights in National and International Law* (ed. A. H. Robertson, 1968), 11-31.

—— 'The Enlargement of the European Communities and the Protection of Human Rights', **XIX** *European Yearbook* (1971), 3-17.

—— 'Do the Rights set forth in the European Convention on Human Rights in 1950 have the same significance in 1975?', in *Proceedings of the Fourth International Colloquy about the European Convention on Human Rights*, Rome, 5-8 November 1975 (Council of Europe, 1976), 83-109.

Standing Advisory Committee on Human Rights; Northern Ireland, report: *The Protection of Human Rights by Law in Northern Ireland*, Cmnd. 7009 (1977).

Starace, V., 'Italian Acceptance of the Optional Clause of the European Convention on Human Rights', 1 *IYIL* (1975), 42-52.

Starace, V. and De Caro, C., *La Giurisprudenza della Corte Costituzionale in materia internazionale* (1977).

Tehran Congress, 1974 (IXth International Congress of Comparative Law), *Italian National Reports* (1974).

Thornberry, C., 'Some Reflections on the Effectiveness of European Human Rights Techniques, in the light of British Experiences of the Application of the Right of Individual Petition', in Council of Europe and Faculty of Law, University of Bari, *Les Clauses facultatives de la Convention européenne des Droits de l'Homme* (1974), 147-68.

Tornaritis, C. G., 'The European Convention on Human Rights in the Legal Order of the Republic of Cyprus', IX *Cyprus Law Tribune* (1976), 3-19.

Toth, A. G., *Legal Protection of Individuals in the European Communities* (1978). Two volumes.

Trechsel, S., 'Quelques réflexions sur l'importance du droit de recours individuel', in Bari Conference, *Les Clauses facultatives de la Convention européenne des Droits de l'Homme* (1974), 169-76.

—— *Die Europäische Menschenrechtskonvention in Schutz der personlichen Freiheit und die schweizerischen Strafprozessrechte* (1974).

Turku-Åbo Colloquy (June 1974), proceedings published in **VIII** *RDH/ HRJ* (1975), 89-288.

Uppsala Congress 1966 (VIIth International Congress of Comparative Law), *Rapports belges* (1966).

Van Bueren, G., *An Effective Remedy? A Review of the Procedure of the European Convention on Human Rights*, NCCL (1983).

Vasak, K., 'Le contrôle parlementaire des actes de l'exécutif concernant la ratification de la Convention et l'acceptation de ses clauses facultatives', in *La Protection internationale des droits de l'homme dans le cadre européen* (1961), 321-9.

—— *La Convention européenne des Droits de l'Homme* (1964).

—— 'L'Application des droits de l'homme et des libertés fondamentales par les juridictions nationales', in *Droit communautaire et droit national* (Semaine de Bruges, 1965), 335-50.

—— 'Le droit international des Droits de l'Homme', **140** *R. des C.* (1974), iv. 333-415.

—— ed., *Les dimensions internationales des Droits de l'Homme* (1978).

Vatányi, B., 'Some Reflections on Article 25 of the Constitution of the Federal Republic of Germany', 24 *NILR* (1977), 578-88.

Vegleris, Ph., 'Modes de redressement des violations de la Convention européenne des Droits de l'Homme', in *Mélanges Polys Modinos* (1968), 369-88.

—— *The European Convention on Human Rights and the Greek Constitution* (1977). In Greek, with a summary in French.

Velu, J., 'La Convention européenne des Droits de l'Homme et la procédure pénale belge', in *Mélanges Polys Modinos* (Paris, 1968), 389-455.

—— 'L'application et l'interprétation de la Convention européenne des Droits de l'Homme dans la jurisprudence belge', *JT* (1968), 696-703.

—— 'Article 6 of the European Convention on Human Rights in Belgian Law', 18 *AJCL* (1970), 259-92.

—— 'Les voies de droit ouvertes aux individus devant les instances nationales en cas de violation de la Convention européenne des Droits de l'Homme', in *Les recours des individus devant les instances nationales en cas de violation du droit européen* (1978), 187-243.

—— *Les effets directs des instruments internationaux en matière de Droits de l'Homme* (1981).

Verdross, A., 'La place de la Convention européenne des Droits de l'Homme dans la hiérarchie des normes juridiques', XIII *Comunicazioni e studi* (1969), 1-13.

Vilhjalmsson, T., 'The Protection of Human Rights in Iceland', VIII *RDH/HRJ* (1975), 221-33.

Visscher de, P., 'Les positions actuelles de la doctrine et de la jurisprudence belge à l'égard du conflit entre le traité et la loi', in *Etudes de droit international en hommage à Paul Guggenheim* (1968), 605-14.

Waelbroeck, M., 'La Convention européenne des Droits de l'Homme lie-t-elle les Communautés européennes?', in *Droit communautaire et droit national* (Semaine de Bruges, 1965), 305-18.

—— *Traités internationaux et juridictions internes dans les pays du Marché commun* (1969).

—— 'La nature juridique des actes des organisations et des juridictions internationales et leurs effets en droit interne', in *Rapports Belges au VIIIe Congrès international de droit comparé*, Pescara, 1970 (1970), 503-20.

—— 'La protection des droits fondamentaux à l'égard des États membres dans le cadre communautaire', in *Mélanges F. Dehousse* (1979), ii. 333-5.

Waldock, Sir H., 'The European Convention for the Protection of Human Rights and Fundamental Freedoms', 34 *BYIL* (1958), 356-63.

—— 'Human Rights in Contemporary International Law and the Significance of the European Convention', *ICLQ* Supplement no. 11 (1965), 1-23.

—— 'The Legal Protection of Human Rights — National and International', in *An Introduction to the Study of Human Rights* (ed. F. Vallat, 1972), 83-98.

Wiebringhaus, H., 'La Convention européenne des Droits de l'Homme et la Charte Sociale européenne', VIII *RDH/HRJ* (1975), 527-44.

Weil, G. L., *The European Convention on Human Rights* (1963).

Wildhaber, L., *Treaty-Making Power and the Constitution. An International and Comparative Study* (1971).

Wildhaber, L. 'Erfahrungen mit der Europäischen Menschenrechtskonvention', 98 *Revue de droit suisse* (1979), 230-79.

Williams, A. M., 'The European Convention on Human Rights: A New Use?', 12 *Texas International Law Journal* (1977), 279-92.

Wold, T., 'Den europëiske menneskerettskonvensjon og Norge', in *Legal Essays in honour of Frede Castberg* (1963), 353-73 (with a summary in English).

Yearbook of the European Convention on Human Rights (published annually since 1960, with the exception of vol. 1 for the years 1955-9).

Zanghi, C., 'La Protection des Droits de l'Homme dans les rapports entre personnes privées (Italie)', in *Cassin* iii.269-78.

Zuleg, M., 'Fundamental Rights and the Law of the European Communities', 8 *CML Rev.* (1971), 446-61.

Appendix
State of Signatures and Ratifications of the European Convention on Human Rights
(Extract taken from Council of Europe doc. H/Inf (82)1.)

a. *Ratifications*

	Convention	1st Protocol	2nd Protocol	3rd Protocol	4th Protocol	5th Protocol	Agreement relating to persons participating in proceedings before the European Commission and Court of Human Rights
Austria	3.IX.1958	3.IX.1958	29.V.1967	29.V.1967	18.IX.1969	9.X.1969	17.VIII.1981
Belgium	14.VI.1955	14.VI.1955	21.IX.1970	21.IX.1970	21.IX.1970	21.IX.1970	16.III.1971
Cyprus	6.X.1962	6.X.1962	22.I.1969	22.I.1969	–	22.I.1969	23.XI.1970
Denmark	13.IV.1953	13.IV.1953	6.V.1963	6.V.1963	30.IX.1964	20.I.1966	signed
France	3.V.1974	3.V.1974	2.X.1981	3.V.1974	3.V.1974	3.V.1974	signed
Fed. Rep. of Germany	5.XII.1952	13.II.1957	3.I.1969	3.I.1969	1.VI.1968	3.I.1969	3.IV.1978
Greece	28.XI.1974	28.XI.1974	8.I.1975	8.I.1975		8.I.1975	–
Iceland	29.VI.1953	29.VI.1953	16.XI.1967	16.XI.1967	16.XI.1967	16.XI.1967	9.XI.1971
Ireland	25.II.1953	25.II.1953	12.IX.1963	12.IX.1963	29.X.1968	18.II.1966	6.I.1981
Italy	26.X.1955	26.X.1955	3.IV.1967	3.IV.1967	27.V.1982	25.III.1968	signed
Liechtenstein	8.IX.1982	–	8.IX.1982	8.IX.1982		8.IX.1982	10.IX.1970
Luxembourg	3.IX.1953	3.IX.1953	27.X.1965	27.X.1965	2.V.1968	26.VI.1968	30.IV.1971
Malta	23.I.1967	23.I.1967	23.I.1967	23.I.1967		23.I.1967	28.I.1972
Netherlands	31.VIII.1954	31.VIII.1954	11.X.1966	11.X.1966	23.VI.1982	19.V.1971	1.VII.1970
Norway	15.I.1952	18.XII.1952	12.VI.1964	12.VI.1964	12.VI.1964	20.I.1966	23.VII.1981
Portugal	9.XI.1978	9.XI.1978	9.XI.1978	9.XI.1978	9.XI.1978	9.XI.1978	–
Spain	4.X.1979	signed	6.IV.1982	4.X.1979	signed	4.X.1979	
Sweden	4.II.1952	22.VI.1953	13.VI.1964	13.VI.1964	13.VI.1964	27.IX.1966	20.XII.1971
Switzerland	28.XI.1974	signed	28.XI.1974	28.XI.1974		28.XI.1974	28.XI.1974
Turkey	18.V.1954	18.V.1954	25.III.1968	25.III.1968	–	20.XII.1971	
United Kingdom	8.III.1951	3.XI.1952	6.V.1963	6.V.1963	signed	24.X.1967	24.II.1971

Entry into force of the Convention: 3 September 1953
Entry into force of the First Protocol: 18 May 1954
Entry into force of the Second Protocol: 21 September 1970
Entry into force of the Third Protocol: 21 September 1970
Entry into force of the Fourth Protocol: 2 May 1968
Entry into force of the Fifth Protocol: 20 December 1971
Entry into force of the Agreement to persons participating in proceedings: 17 April 1971

b. *Declarations made under Article 25 of the Convention*

The following states have made declarations recognising the competence of the European Commission of Human Rights to receive individual petitions:

Current declaration

	Without interruption since	Date of entry into force	for a period of
Austria	3.IX.1958	3.IX.1982[1]	3 years
Belgium	5.VII.1955	30.VI.1982[1]	5 years
Cyprus	–	–	–
Denmark	13.IV.1953	6.IV.1982	5 years
France	–	2.X.1981[1]	5 years
Fed. Rep. of Germany	5.VII.1955	1.VII.1981[1]	5 years
Greece	–	–	–
Iceland	29.III.1955	25.III.1960[1]	indefinite
Ireland	25.II.1953	25.II.1953[1]	indefinite
Italy	1.VIII.1973	1.VIII.1981	3 years
Liechtenstein	8.IX.1982	8.IX.1982	3 years
Luxembourg	28.IV.1958	28.IV.1981[1]	5 years
Malta	–	–	–
Netherlands	28.VI.1960	1.IX.1979[1,2]	indefinite
Norway	13.XII.1955	29.VI.1982[1]	5 years
Portugal	9.XI.1978	9.XI.1980[1]	2 years[3]
Spain	–	1.VII.1981	2 years
Sweden	4.III.1952	4.III.1952[1]	indefinite
Switzerland	28.XI.1974	28.XI.1980	3 years
Turkey	–	–	–
United Kingdom	14.I.1966	14.I.1981[2]	5 years

[1] This declaration also applies to Articles 1 to 4, Protocol No. 4.
[2] This declaration also applies to certain non-metropolitan territories.
[3] This declaration has been renewed and will be renewed by tacit agreement each time for a further period of two years if an intention to denounce it is not notified prior to the expiry of the period in course.

c. Declarations made under Article 46 of the Convention

The following states have made declarations recognising as compulsory the jurisdiction of the European Court of Human Rights:

	Without interruption since	Current declaration	
		Date of entry into force	for a period of
Austria	3.IX.1958	3.IX.1982[1,3]	3 years
Belgium	5.VII.1955	29.VI.1982[1]	5 years
Cyprus	24.I.1980	24.I.1980[3]	3 years
Denmark	13.IV.1953	6.IV.1982	5 years
France	3.V.1974*	16.VII.1980[1,3]	3 years
Fed. Rep. of Germany	5.VII.1955	1.VII.1976[1,3]	5 years
Greece	27.XII.1978	31.I.1982[3]	3 years
Iceland	3.IX.1958	3.IX.1979[1]	5 years
Ireland	25.II.1953	25.II.1953[1]	indefinite
Italy	1.VIII.1973	1.VIII.1981[3]	3 years
Liechtenstein	8.IX.1982	8.IX.1982	3 years
Luxembourg	28.IV.1958	28.IV.1981[1,3]	5 years
Malta	–	–	–
Netherlands	31.VIII.1954	1.IX.1979[1,2,3]	indefinite
Norway	30.VI.1964	29.VI.1982[1,3]	5 years
Portugal	9.XI.1978	9.XI.1980[1,3]	2 years[4]
Spain	15.X.1979	15.X.1982[3]	3 years
Sweden	15.VI.1966	13.V.1981[1,3]	5 years
Switzerland	28.XI.1974	28.XI.1974[3]	indefinite
Turkey	–	–	–
United Kingdom	14.I.1966	14.I.1981[2]	5 years

[1] This declaration also applies to Articles 1 to 4, Protocol No. 4.
[2] This declaration also applies to certain non-metropolitan territories.
[3] On condition of reciprocity.
[4] This declaration has been renewed and will be renewed by tacit agreement each time for a further period of two years if an intention to denounce it is not notified prior to the expiry of the period in course.
* Interruption from 3.V.1980 to 16.VII.1980.

Index of Authors Cited

368 *Index of Authors Cited*

General Index